# JUDAIC LAW FROM JESUS TO THE MISHNAH

SOUTH FLORIDA STUDIES IN THE HISTORY OF JUDAISM

Edited by
Jacob Neusner
William Scott Green, James Strange
Darrell J. Fasching, Sara Mandell

Number 84
JUDAIC LAW FROM JESUS TO THE MISHNAH
A Systematic Reply to
Professor E. P. Sanders

by
Jacob Neusner

# JUDAIC LAW
# FROM JESUS TO THE MISHNAH

## A Systematic Reply to
## Professor E. P. Sanders

by

Jacob Neusner

Scholars Press
Atlanta, Georgia

# JUDAIC LAW FROM JESUS TO THE MISHNAH

©1993
University of South Florida

Publication of this book was made possible by a grant from the Tisch Family
Foundation, New York City. The University of South Florida acknowledges
with thanks this important support for its scholarly projects.

**Library of Congress Cataloging in Publication Data**
Neusner, Jacob, 1932–
    Judaic law from Jesus to the Mishnah: a systematic reply to
Professor E. P. Sanders/ by Jacob Neusner.
        p. cm. — (South Florida studies in the history of Judaism; no. 84)
    Includes bibliographical references and index.
    ISBN 1–55540–873–7
    1. Judaism—History—Talmudic period, 10–425—Historiography.
2. Sanders, E. P.          I. Title.   II. Series.
BM177.N4735   1993
296'.09'015—dc20
                                             93–15668
                                             CIP

Printed in the United States of America
on acid-free paper

# Table of Contents

Preface ........................................................................................ ix

Introduction ................................................................................. 1

### Part One
### DEFINING JUDAISM:
### THE LAW, LITERATURE, THEOLOGY, AND HISTORY OF
### JUDAISM IN THE FIRST AND SECOND CENTURIES

1.  The Mishnah's Evidence on the Development of Its Judaism's Halakhah ....................................................... 13

2.  Convenantal Nomism: The Piety of Judaism in the First Century .................................................................... 49

3.  Defining the Mishnah ........................................................ 79

4.  Revelation and Reason, Scripture and Mishnah: Their Relationship .................................................................. 117

5.  The Mishnah in the Judaism of Its Time ........................ 165

6.  Accommodating the Mishnah to Scripture in Judaism: The Uneasy Union and Its Offspring ..................................... 187

### Part Two
### DEFENDING JUDAISM?
### FOUR DEBATES WITH E.P. SANDERS

7.  Sanders's Misunderstanding of Purity: Uncleanness as an Ontological, Not a Moral-Eschatological, Category (as He Imagines) Coauthored by Bruce D. Chilton ...................... 205

8.  Sanders's *Paul and Palestinian Judaism* ...................... 231

9.  Sanders's Pharisees and Mine: *Jewish Law from Jesus to the Mishnah* ........................................................................ 247

10. Sanders's *Judaism. Practices and Beliefs. 63 B.C.E. – 66 C.E.* ...... 275

Appendix: Another Harmony of All Judaisms. *From Text to Tradition. A History of Second Temple and Rabbinic Judaism.* By Lawrence H. Schiffman ............................................... 297

Index ........................................................................................ 301

# Preface

In this book I have collected all of my writings relevant to twenty years of the debate on first-century Judaism between Professor E.P. Sanders and me. Contemporaries in age and in parallel, active careers, Sanders and I have argued about the definition and character of "Judaism" in late antiquity, with special reference to the first and second centuries. My reviews of his *Paul and Rabbinic Judaism* and his *Judaism: 63 B.C.E. to 67 C.E.*, separated by fifteen years, read side by side turn out to go over the same ground. What I said he did wrong when he started, he is still doing wrong. And from the same period, he has maintained an equally consistent view. He devoted three-fifths of his *Jewish Law from Jesus to the Mishnah* to critiques of my views of the Pharisees, the myth of the Oral Torah, and the Mishnah, particularly my *Judaism: The Evidence of the Mishnah*.[1] But the debate rests on constructive work on the part of each of us.

The decades-long debate has taken two forms. First, each of us has written books on Judaism. We have, moreover, addressed the same issues, dealt with concentric evidence, and faced the same questions of methods. So an authentic debate – people talking about the same things but taking opposed positions – has taken place, and that has been in entirely constructive settings: what I think about something, what he thinks about the same thing.

Second, each of us has criticized the books and ideas of the other. I have systematically read his three major books on Judaism, and he has read at least the more important books of mine on the chapter in the history of Judaism that concerns him. I have reviewed all of his scholarly books, and he has reviewed at least one of mine, on this area. While neither he nor I should claim that ours has been one of the great scholarly

---

[1](Chicago, 1981: University of Chicago Press). Paperback edition: 1984. Second printing, 1985. Third printing, 1986. Second edition, augmented: (Atlanta, 1987: Scholars Press for Brown Judaic Studies).

debates of the age, it certainly has proved to be an honorable and illuminating one, from which learning ought to have benefited.

But the debate, from my side, has been scattered; those who have followed the argument can find in just two books pretty much everything Sanders wishes to say on the subject under contention, but my articles are widely scattered, and my books are simply too many for anyone to read in the time available for consideration of any one issue, such as this one. Not only so, but I have pursued my own interests, so that my results pertinent to this debate are not always labeled in such a way that colleagues with a special interest in the matters treated here would know to examine them.

That is why, in this book, I have collected in one place the two bodies of discussion of the issues on which Sanders and I have differed, the one constructive, the other critical. In the former, I have set forth the theoretical basis and methodological foundation for my definition of "Judaism" as "Judaic systems," which then would yield "a Judaism," and "Judaisms." The theory is in the introduction, and the issues of method, as to the study of his "Jewish law" and my "Judaic law," are spelled out in Chapter One.

In Chapters Two through Six, I then provide a systematic reprise of my main results pertinent to the ongoing debate with Sanders. I begin in Chapter Two with the most important issue he has raised, and it is one on which we concur: the character of the piety of Judaism. This he classifies, for Protestant theological reasons, as "covenantal nomism," and I find myself in substantial agreement with both the classificatory language he uses and the main points of his characterization of that common piety of ancient Israel in the first century. In Chapter Three, I set forth my view on how the Mishnah is to be described. Since a main point of disagreement between Sanders and myself concerns my view that the Mishnah presents us with philosophy in the form of a law code, I explain in Chapter Four precisely where and how I find philosophy in the Mishnah; in that same context I take up the other source for Mishnaic thought, besides Greco-Roman philosophy, which is Scripture. Covering all of the tractates of the Mishnah one by one, I show which ones I classify as essentially reprises of Scripture, and which as fundamentally recapitulations of familiar philosophical issues. Chapters Five and Six then complete my account of the Mishnah: its place among the Judaisms of its time and place, its position at the head of the history of the Judaism that flowed from it.

In Chapters Seven through Ten, I go over my critique of Sanders's specific positions. I begin with Professor Bruce Chilton's and my account of uncleanness as an ontological, rather than moral-eschatological, category. We maintain that Sanders has completely misunderstood the category into which the Mishnah's treatment of uncleanness falls. In Chapter Eight I reproduce my review of Sanders's first book pertinent to this debate, in Chapter Nine, the second, and in Chapter Ten, the third and last to date.

By bringing together all of the pertinent writings of mine, spread over a long period of time and many places, I mean to advance the argument by laying out, in a systematic way, both my constructive results and also my reasons for rejecting Sanders's definitions, methods, and results, beginning to end. Because these essays all originally stood on their own, there is a measure of overlap among them, but not in considerable measure. To be sure, in the nature of things, the repetition of the same ideas concerning both results and method will not present surprises. That, after all, is what debate best accomplishes: to identify areas of disagreement and also outline the range of concurrence as well.

And that last consideration brings me to point to the numerous specific positions Sanders and I share. Time and again in his *Jewish Law from Jesus to the Mishnah* he says he agrees with me, but for his own reasons, or on the basis of his own, superior, reading of sources and the like. But the range of specific difference, he says, concerns degree, not kind. Not only so, but in all my reviews I have underlined my appreciation of his motivation for his work, which is to undertake a vast apologia for ancient Judaism in the face of centuries-old Christian hostility. To be sure, the character of that apologia, I said in 1978 and I repeat in 1993, is obnoxious because of its condescension. But the intent is wholly pure: to remove one formidable source of anti-Semitism in Christianity, which is, its contempt for Judaism then and now.

I hasten to pay a well-deserved tribute to Sanders's motivation in doing this work. Sanders takes up subjects with a virulent anti-Semitic tradition, and he has devoted his life to presenting Judaism in such a way as to help Christians overcome their ancient heritage of Jew-hatred and contempt for Judaism. This he has done not through apologetics for the Christian tradition of anti-Semitism and anti-Judaism – he never says blatant anti-Semitism is anything other than what it is – but through a positive reading of the Judaism of the time and place of Jesus. Sanders addresses not merely entrenched bigotry, but also bigotry perpetrated and perpetuated by reputable scholars in our own days. For example, as he says, "I have had to argue at length against the prevailing views, which are enshrined in volume II of Schürer's *History of the Jewish People* (now revised and updated by Geza Vermes, Fergus Millar and others)...." The work he has done is for the sake of heaven.

No scholar in our time has done more in his chosen, and important, field, to prevent a future Holocaust involving Christianity's inspiration and, in some countries, institutional complicity – not renegades like

Hitler but priests and bishops, German Christians and their pastors, professors of theology in all the German universities and many of the theological faculties, for instance – as did the one that took place in our own day. Many exemplary Christians, from Pope John XXIII onward, have joined in the task of the rehabilitation of Christianity in the aftermath of the Holocaust, so those words represent a very genuine appreciation of a great labor. Accordingly, Sanders has done more to help Protestant Christianity rid itself of its loathing of Judaism and Jews than any other scholar of our time.

That recognition on my part also explains why, when I have had an opportunity to provide him with an appropriate forum, I offered it to him. I sent him two letters asking him to write the chapter, "Judaism in the Land of Israel in the First Century," in the volume on Judaism of the *Handbuch der Orientalistik* that I have edited for E.J. Brill. The first letter went July 5, 1992, from Cambridge, the second a month later from Tampa; neither was returned, and, alas, neither was answered. In the second, I said that I thought our agreements greater than our differences. The chapter in this book on covenantal nomism should demonstrate that fact. I also pointed out that the entire argument in which we have engaged is solely *leshem shamayyim* – for the sake of heaven. I regret he did not answer my letters of invitation. Since some of his writing is marred by personal animosity toward me, as many reviewers (not to mention the American publishers) of his *Jewish Law from Jesus to the Mishnah* pointed out, it is important to say in so many words that I do not in any measure reciprocate.

To the contrary, I publicly state my admiration for what I believe is his sacred and life-affirming goal, one that embodies in our day the love for the other that Christianity's founder professed. I do say, in so many words, that his is certainly not the way to accomplish so worthy a goal. He defends "Judaism" by making it over in the model of "Christianity." But if a single word in the pages that follow suggests a different attitude from one of appreciation for his life's work and respect, if not very often for his results and methods, then for his motivation and the goals of his scholarly career, I apologize for it. The measure of my respect for his enterprise may be taken by a simple fact: he is one of the few scholars of our time who has set forth a sustained argument with me, one of the few whom I have found an interesting conversation partner. And, I should claim, and I am certain he would concur, both of us have aspired to form a discourse worthy of the transcendent issues that are at stake in the subject at hand.

No work of mine can omit reference to the exceptionally favorable circumstances in which I conduct my research. I wrote this book at the University of South Florida, which has afforded me an ideal situation in which to conduct a scholarly life. I express my thanks for not only the advantage of a Distinguished Research Professorship, which must be the best job in the world for a scholar, but also of a substantial research expense fund, ample research time, and some stimulating and cordial colleagues. In the prior chapters of my career, I never knew a university that prized professors' scholarship and publication and treated with respect the professors who actively pursue research. University of South Florida, and the Florida State University System as a whole, exemplify the high standards of professionalism that prevail in publicly sponsored higher education in the USA and provide the model that privately sponsored universities would do well to emulate. Here there are rules, achievement counts, and presidents, provosts, and deans honor and respect the university's principal mission: scholarship, scholarship alone – both in the classroom and in publication.

JACOB NEUSNER

*Distinguished Research Professor of Religious Studies*
UNIVERSITY OF SOUTH FLORIDA
Tampa, St. Petersburg, Sarasota, Lakeland, Fort Myers

735 Fourteenth Avenue Northeast
St. Petersburg, Florida 33701-1413 USA

# Introduction

Debates concerning first-century Judaism, the Pharisees, Judaic piety, and Judaic law begin in the definition of the term "Judaism." Disagreement concerning details obscures the fundamental points that are at issue. The contrast between the title of this book, *Judaic Law from Jesus to the Mishnah*, and that of E.P. Sanders's book to which it responds, point by point, *Jewish Law from Jesus to the Mishnah* (Philadelphia, 1990: Trinity Press International), shows what is at stake. In common usage, "Jewish" refers to the Jews as an ethnic group and to traits commonly exhibited by that ethnic group, while "Judaic" speaks of a Judaic religious system (in my language) or to (a) Judaism. While, therefore, we may (for the sake of argument) speak of "Jewish food," meaning, food Jews eat (but others, besides Jews, do not eat), we may speak of "Judaic food" only if that food forms a component of a Judaic religious system. "Jewish food" may encompass kosher-style pickles. "Judaic food" speaks of kosher food. In this context, "Jewish law" refers to a law that any Jew, anywhere, observed; Judaic law speaks of a law of (a) Judaism.

How we define (a) Judaism therefore takes precedence over how we debate about the details of a particular Judaism. In my definition, the work of definition commences with what we mean by a religion. Since by "a religion" people may mean an indeterminate number of things (as the definition of religion as a matter of ultimate concern, with the consequent confusion of matters, showed a generation ago), the context of definition takes precedent over a definition. Taking only the public and factual side of religion, we define religion only in its social dimension, and that requires a prior definition as well, one that concerns a theory of the social order.

In the context of the social order, that is, the life of a given group of people, we may speak of an account of the social order as a conception, put forth by a group of people that sees itself as coherent and forming a society, of its way of life, its worldview, and its theory of itself as a social entity; such a conception finds integration in an urgent question that the

1

group finds it necessary to answer in every detail of its social existence, and an answer deemed self-evidently valid by the group. A Judaic religious system, or a Judaism, is a theory of the social order that identifies the social entity formed by the group known as "Israel," and that appeals to the Pentateuch, in particular, for the formation of its worldview and for the formulation of its way of life.

Now, when we speak of "the Jewish people," or "the Jews," we assume that we talk of all the Jews, everywhere. But such a construction in fact fabricates a single, palpable social entity where, in antiquity and today, none existed or now exists, except in ideology, for example, today's Zionism, or theology, for example, Judaic systems through the ages. Nothing is so intangible as a theological entity or an ideological construct: "Israel," God's people, on the one side, or "Israel," the people, one people, on the other. If we invoke any of the ordinary criteria for a social entity of the here and now, we find that none fits the category, "Jewish people," whether in antiquity or today. A social entity in the here and now defines itself by commonalities, whether of territory, or of language and culture, or some other tangible, shared qualities. But of these, the Jews then had and now have none.

Let me speak of antiquity's facts, which everyone acknowledges. In secular terms, there was no single Jewish group, though in various places, there were social entities that met the criteria of forming, in secular terms, well-defined groups. But the conception of "Israel" as a single entity, with shared traits of behavior and belief that we may define and invoke in describing any and all persons called Jews, defies the facts.

Jews lived all over the world; they did not have a single language in common , and by the criteria of economics, on the one side, or politics, on the second, or shared culture, on the third, nothing bound them together. Speaking solely in secular terms, every picture of the Jews as the single entity, "Israel," proves a pious fantasy. No one is so naive as to imagine that all Jews are children of a single couple of remote antiquity, Abraham and Sarah, and no one but a convicted sentimentalist can conceive that all the Jews felt the same way (if they do not think the same thing) about any subject or experience at all. The rich diversity of writings, all of them set forth as authoritative and holy, purporting to speak for what we now call "Judaism," closes off the option of conceiving of a single, encompassing Judaism.

Nor can we be detained by the self-serving notion of a "community of fate," since it is the simple fact that the Jews throughout the world never undertook a single policy on any important matter affecting all of them. When the Jews of the Land of Israel rebelled against Rome, the Jews of the Greek-speaking diaspora kept the peace, though they were of course grieved by the destruction of the Temple. When the Jews of the

Greek-speaking diaspora rebelled, the Jews of the Land of Israel looked the other way. It follows that discourse on the topic, "the Jewish people," itself forms an act of theology (for a Judaism) or ideology (for scholarship, for example, that of Zionism and other formations of a secular Judaic system). When we hear about "Jewish law," therefore, the sounds prove cacophonous. "Judaic" law of course immediately requires the specification: which Judaism's law?

Why do I insist that "the Jewish people" is a construct of imagination, a topic of theological or ideological intellection, a chapter of other-worldly faith – but not something that, in the here and now, we can examine? The reason, as I argued in my *Judaism and Its Social Metaphors. Israel in the History of Jewish Thought* (New York, 1988: Cambridge University Press), is that we do not experience but only imagine "society," because "society" viewed whole is something too abstract and remote from everyday life to afford a concrete encounter. We know individual people. But we generalize and so in our minds conceive, or imagine, that the concrete persons we encounter represent, form part of, that abstraction, society. And that is a natural course of our making sense of the world beyond the here and the now of everyday life. We move from what we know, the concrete and immediate, to what we do not know. And whatever lies beyond our experience, encompassing all modes of abstraction and all conceptions of not merely event but process, demands to be set into relationship with what we already know. Connections that we make, abstractions that we perceive only in their concrete manifestations, processes that we can imagine but not identify in the here and now – not the blow but power, not the caress but love – these form the raw material of mind. Accordingly, when we name and treat as real and concrete what are in fact abstractions and intangible processes, we impose upon ourselves the need to compare the abstract to the concrete. We therefore think in a process of analogy, contrast, comparison, and metaphor about that thing which, to begin with, we ourselves have identified and so made up in our minds.

Take a group for example. When two or more persons perceive themselves to bear traits in common and to constitute a group on account of those indicative traits, they face a range of choices in thinking about the classification and character of that social entity, that group, that they imagine they comprise. It can be immediate, but it does not have to be. A family, a village, a neighborhood, a town – these form part of felt experience; we can walk in the streets, recognize relationship with persons we know and our relationship to whom we can name, and we can trace the outer limits of the settled area. But when people identify with others they have not met and may never meet, the process of the search for appropriate metaphors to take the place of absent experience in the everyday world begins. Then metaphors for the social group present themselves. In thinking about such abstractions as social entities, people appeal to comparisons between the concrete things they know and the abstract things they seek to explain and express for themselves.

That is why, when we speak of such large abstractions as society, or people, or nation, for instance, use the word "family" to mean a social entity or aggregate of persons beyond the one in which we grow up and to which we bear blood relationships, such as, calling a friend or a political ally a "brother," we move onward from the concrete to the abstract. And the notion of "Jewish people" best illustrates that movement, the utterly abstract and general reading of diverse and incongruous concrete facts, for example, of family or a sense of locality (for Israelis) or connection to others of a common family history (for example, immigration from the same general area), genealogy, religion, or gastronomic taste (for the Golah). Let me give one example of Jews that certainly meets the criteria of forming an ethnic group: Jews in the Yiddish-speaking East before World War II. They assuredly did constitute "a people, one people," by any and every criterion, however strictly imposed: territory, language, culture, politics, genealogy, economy, class structure, and marital patterns and child-raising taboos, and the like. All variables pointed to a single conclusion: this really did constitute "a people, one people," and, theologically, the Jews of Eastern Europe could be credibly represented as holy Israel. Jews in antiquity did not meet the same criteria. Anyone who examines the entire literature of religious conviction produced by Jews for their "Israel" will come up with everything and its opposite.

To generalize: The conception of "the Jewish people" itself calls into question whether we deal with this-worldly data subject to analysis. Acts of imagination, whether theological or ideological, are just that: inventions for the moment. That metaphorical mode of thought permits us to speak about things though we cannot point in diurnal encounter to the concrete experience of those things. A principal abstraction and process therefore comprises a social entity that transcends the concrete experience and pragmatic knowledge of two or more people together. How we think about those abstractions that in the most general and indeterminate terms we may call, "social entities," the result of generalization from the here and now to the out-there, the outcome of a process of imagination, fantasy, and reflection, the results of that intellectual process – these lend substance to our perception, through now-real and concrete expectation, of the hitherto unknown and unfelt but merely imagined. In these processes of thought we resort to metaphor so as to treat as a thing what originates out of process or abstraction. That is how reflection and imagination in general terms about the commonalities of specific things form an exercise in metaphorical thought.

Among the many supernatural works of enchantment accomplished by religion, the one treated here is the capacity of religion to transform individuals and families into a corporate body, imputing relationships other than those natural to location or family genealogy. That is the power of religion to name and treat as real the otherwise random confluence, in belief and behavior, of isolated groups of people, to persuade those families that they form part of something larger than their limited congeries, even though no one in those families has ever seen, or can ever encompass in a single vision, the entirety of that something more, that entire nation, mystical body, entity *sui generis*. In simple terms, religions speak of social entities made up of their devotees. These they turn from concrete entity in the here and now into abstractions merely represented, in the here and now, by the present exemplar. The social entity turns into a symbol for something more. So the social group (defined presently) is transformed from what the world sees to what the eye of faith perceives, becoming, in the case of a Judaism, an "Israel."

Why does thinking about the social entity in particular demand metaphorical thinking? It is because a social group that does not rest, for its being, upon constant and palpable interaction exists mainly in the abstract. It is as an abstraction that is (merely) exemplified in the here and now by the group near at hand, the one that does consist of individuals who do interact. When people think about that abstraction, for example, about the Church or the Israel of which they form a part (or "the nation of Islam" for that matter), they invoke a variety of concrete metaphors, for example, family. They may turn to metaphors of another sort altogether than "family," for instance, "people" or "nation." They could just as well call themselves "the wolf pack" or "the clan." But, in all, they are engaged in a transaction of a symbolic character, in which they propose to express their sense not by reference to what they can see and touch, but to what, in the things they can see and touch, corresponds to that entity – that social entity – that is under discussion.

By "social entity," using the most general language I can find, I mean "social group," defined as *two or more persons that exhibit traits of a group.* What are such indicative traits? Traits that characterize a social group by contrast to random individuals emerge when the participants form a common identity, express a feeling of unity concerning common goals and shared norms. The social group involves direct interaction and communication, actions to carry out a system of values. A social group may be a family, a village, or any other entity (two or more persons) in which there is a concrete encounter among persons who perceive themselves to form such a group. It is at this point that the process of abstraction begins.

Specifically, a social group may take shape among persons who do not necessarily interact and communicate with one another, but who do share a common system of values. Then the social group forms an abstraction, rather than a concrete and palpable fact. It may derive from an intangible process, with the result that participants in the group invoke metaphors from the known social world (for example, family) to explain that unknown fact of social life that, in their minds, they now have constituted. That sort of social group differs from the one formed by a family, in which, we may assume, there is interaction; or a village or a neighborhood of like-minded persons, in which there are shared values among persons who see one another and form their sense of constituting a group on the basis of everyday activity. This more abstract social group in the context of a religious system constitutes an entity defined by common goals and shared norms, but – and this explains the metaphorical character of thought about that entity – one in which all its individual members do not interact.

Such social groups may prove formal or informal, but a social group constituted by a religion at its essence is formal, for it is very carefully defined with imposed norms of faith and action. A social group may appeal to extended kinship. By definition religious systems are not made up of genealogical units, though they may identify the social group formed by the religion as a family or an extended family. When they do posit shared ancestry, they engage in a symbolic transaction – once more requiring us to investigate how the *is* becomes the *ought*, which is to say, how the everyday shades into the abstract. Along these same lines, a social group may appeal to the society formed of the encounter among individuals who never, in fact, meet. Here, too, the encounter is one in theory and in the abstract, joining in a single social group persons who imagine that they know and understand one another but who in reality do not intersect.

A further instance of the power of metaphor shows us how a group may in its own mind define its relationship with the outside world. People who share traits with others may determine that they are separate from those others and constitute a minority, as against the majority formed by those others. In its own mind, therefore, a social group may be classified as a minority group, finding definition in contrast with another, more numerous group, defined within the same larger classification. By definition a religious system will create such a minority group, in that the world beyond will be made up of many such groups, of which the one at hand is not likely to form the largest, that is, to constitute a numerical majority. The symbolic transaction commences when the group defines itself by contrast to other groups, when it conceives of itself to constitute a minority-group *type* of group. In all of these ways, it is through metaphors evoked in description of the social group that we see the working of the imagination, hence "imagining society."

Our inquiry carries us deep into symbolic transactions. It is through shared imagination or perception held in common – hence, in the metaphors by which abstractions such as "society" or "nation" reach concrete form in intellect and expectation alike – that these transactions are realized. These metaphors when broadly construed form gossamer threads, yet bond  persons who in fact do not commonly meet at all. The same act of imagination imposes upon persons the consciousness – and concrete character – of community. These symbolic transactions pertinent to the group life posited by a religious system constitute the social theory of that system – the social entity to which and of which the system speaks. And since the symbolic transactions come to concrete expression in metaphors – hence "social metaphors" – we find ourselves sorting out those metaphors that serve, and those that do not, in a given religious system.

In all, we deal with people who come together from time to time – hence, temporarily – but who see themselves as forming a lasting society. They by no means constitute a population, that is, pretty much everyone in a given territory. But they see themselves as a society. They do not have large scale, enduring political organizations or social institutions to draw them together, though, in their conception of the group, they will imagine both and call themselves a nation or a people. They are more than a crowd and far more than a mere category of society, for instance, people of a given age or occupation. But they also are much less in the concrete social facts of their existence than they conceive themselves to be. Hence comes the abstraction with which we deal under the title, "social entity of a religious system," or, in the case of a Judaism, an "Israel."

Now, if we want to ask about the future of a given population, we turn to the social metaphor that that population asks to explain who it is. For a social metaphor tells a group how to identify itself, and this is in two ways. First, the metaphor identifies the type or genus of social group at hand, and, second, it will consequently define the species of, the genus, or type, at hand. These are the pertinent questions: Is the social entity a family? Then how does it compare to other families? Is it a nation? Then in what way does it differ from other nations, and in what context does the category, nation, take on its definitive sense and meaning? Or a social group may declare itself *sui generis*, not like any other social group at all, but a genus unto itself, for example, a third possibility as between two available choices.

A set and sequence of social groups living in different times and places and not continuous with one another, Jews have commonly told themselves tales of how in recorded time they had come into existence as a single social entity, "Israel," in a unitary and harmonious history. In these stories Jews appealed to a variety of social metaphors, of two basic classifications. First of all, some held that the Jews – Israel – were *sui generis*, of a type of social entity lacking all counterpart, and thus not of a type into which all other social groups could be classified. Second, others maintained that Israel formed a distinct species of a common genus, whether family or nation or people. Now what I want to know about these metaphors is simple. Under what conditions or circumstances will one metaphor take priority, and when will a different metaphor appear self-evidently compelling? Along these same lines, if a given metaphor serves, does it carry in its wake a variety of other metaphorical consequences in the way in which the group that invokes the metaphor thinks about itself and explains its collective existence? To state matters simply, if I know the operative metaphor, what else do I know about the group's thinking about itself beyond the metaphor? I should want to be able to form rules of predicting what traits a theory of a social group will carry in the wake of the generative metaphor of the group. These are the sorts of questions that form the centerpiece of interest.

Now these observations bring us back to the question at hand: the matter of defining Judaism. There are, in fact, three approaches to the problem of definition. The first is the extreme nominalist view that every Jew defines Judaism. Judaism is the sum of the attitudes and beliefs of an ethnic group. But each member of the group serves equally well to define Judaism, with the result that questions of the social order – for example, which particular group or social entity of persons held this view, which that – are dismissed. The second is the extreme harmonizing view, which maintains that all Jewish data – writings and other records – together tell us about a single Judaism, which is to be defined by appeal to the lowest common denominator among all the data. That is the view taken by Professor E.P. Sanders, as I show in the final chapter of this book, and by Lawrence H. Schiffman, as I demonstrate in the appendix. The third position is mine: we work our way through the sources, patiently finding those that cohere and distinguishing them from those that do not.

Objective criteria serve to both differentiate and show coherence. One important instance is that of the Dual Torah, Oral and Written. One Judaic system, the paramount one from antiquity to our own day, maintains that at Sinai God revealed to Moses the Torah in two media, oral and written. Presence of the myth of the Dual Torah therefore must be regarded as indicative: a document that exhibits that myth will be differentiated from one that does not. Examples of the former kind will then form one Judaism, the latter, whatever Judaism they form (if any), they are not part of the Judaic system characterized by the myth of the Dual Torah – and therefore do not present us with data relevant in the description of the Judaism of the Dual Torah. On that basis, we speak of a system: its law, its theology, its literature; and we begin, of course, with the sources of that system, rightly identified by a single, factual variable.

In my view, therefore, the correct way to describe "Judaism" is first to recognize that in antiquity, as today, there was no single "Judaism," but several Judaic religious systems, each with its account of the social group that framed that system: its worldview, its way of life, its theory of the social entity constituted by that group; a religious system integrated by its identification of a single, enormous, urgent question, answered in a way self-evidently true to the believers by a single, comprehensive response. Then the description of "Judaism" begins with the differentiation of all the data pertinent to Judaisms, the identification of the data that tell us about a single Judaism, and the analysis of those data and their problems. That is what I have done in the past twenty-five years for the Judaic system adumbrated by the writings that form a continuum from the Mishnah through the Talmud of Babylonia, on the one side, and the counterpart writings of Scripture exegesis produced by the same authorities and characterized by the same mythic structure, on the other.

In replying to Sanders's book on Jewish law, I have framed matters in accord with the theory just now spelled out. That is why, in Chapter One, I discuss the Mishnah's picture of the development of its Judaism's halakhah. The Mishnah speaks for itself, that is, its authors; I think we may find in its pages evidences concerning the formation and history of some elements of the law normative for the group that ultimately produced the Mishnah. I spell out how we may identify those evidences and the history of a particular Judaic legal system set forth therein.

Since Sanders speaks of "covenantal nomism," a conception I find valid but systemically trivial, I define, in Chapter Two, what I think we may mean by that phrase. Since Sanders says what he thinks the Mishnah is, I explain, in Chapter Three, what I think the Mishnah is. Since Sanders rejects my view that the Mishnah forms a statement in the form of law of ideas of a profoundly philosophical character, in Chapter Four I set forth the definition and evidence of the Mishnah as a philosophical law code. Chapters Five and Six then complete my picture:

how I see the Mishnah in the context of its Judaism, and of the Judaic systems of the same general period.

The final four chapters then spell out the consequence of Sanders's profound misunderstanding of the sources of the Judaism of the Dual Torah and the costs of the consequent confusion in his harmonistic reading of all Jews' writings as representative of one Judaism. The first is specific to an issue, the next three, reviews of his three books on Judaism. Seen in chronological order, his theses, and my criticism of them, show two fully worked out and not to be reconciled theories of, not only method and use of evidence, on which we differ profoundly, but conception. If there was one Judaism, which we may harmonize and describe in a coherent way, then I am wrong and he is right. In the end, evidence and argument having been laid forth, considerations of conviction and conscience intervene. Schiffman (as we see in the appendix), for his religious reasons, and Sanders, for his motives of theological apologetic (invariably spelled out in each of his books), come to the evidence with the unshakable conviction of its harmony and unity. To me, what they know as fact is what I should like to find out through testing diverse hypotheses.

Part One

DEFINING JUDAISM:

THE FACTS OF THE LAW, THEOLOGY,
AND HISTORY OF JUDAISM IN THE
FIRST AND SECOND CENTURIES

# 1

## The Mishnah's Evidence
## on the Development of
## Its Judaism's Halakhah

### I. "Jewish Law" or Laws of Jews?

Apart from the scriptural law codes, in antiquity no single system of law governed all Jews everywhere. So we cannot describe "Jewish law" as one encompassing system. The Scripture's several codes of course made their impact on the diverse systems of law that governed various groups of Jews, or Jewish communities in various places. But that impact never proved uniform. In consequence, in no way may we speak of "Jewish law," meaning a single legal code or even a common set of encompassing rules everywhere held authoritative by Jewry. The relationship between the legal system of one distinct group of Jews to that governing some other proves various.[1]

Certain practices to be sure characterized all. But these, too, do not validate the premise that such a thing as "Jewish law" operated, even in the points in common, pretty much everywhere. The fact that Jews ordinarily observed certain taboos, for example, concerning the Sabbath day and forbidden foods, hardly changes the picture. On the basis of the prohibition of pork and the observance of a common calendar one can hardly describe a common law of Jewry, hence "Jewish law." Such evidence as we have of diverse Jews' laws points in the opposite

---

[1]For the contrary view cf. Lawrence H. Schiffman, *Sectarian Law in the Dead Sea Scrolls. Courts, Testimony, and the Penal Code* (Chico, 1983: Scholars Press for Brown Judaic Studies), p. 3: "This system [referring to Judaism and its law] composed of interlocking and re-interlocking parts possessed of an organic connection one to another, is never really divisible." Schiffman does not demonstrate that claim.

direction. What these sets of laws shared in common in part derives
from the Scripture all revered. What turns up in a number of contexts in
further measure proves so general or so fragmentary as to yield no trace
of a single, systematic and comprehensive law common among Jews. An
example of the latter – something too general to make much difference –
is the marriage contract. It is a fact that marriage contracts occur in the
Jewish community records of Elephantine, in the fragments found from
the time of Bar Kokhba, and in the setting of Mishnaic law. But in detail
the contracts that have been found scarcely intersect.[2] The Mishnah's
rules governing the scribal preparation of such contracts hardly dictated
to the authorities of fifth-century B.C. Elephantine[3] or second-century
C.E. Palestine how to do their work. So it is misleading to speak of "the
halakhah," meaning a single system of law operative among all Jews.[4] It
is still more confusing to treat as fragments of a single legal system all of
the bits and pieces of information deriving from various and sundry
communities, scattered throughout the territories of the Near and Middle
East, and dated over a span of hundreds of years.

When, therefore, we wish to investigate the history of halakhah or
Jewish law, in point of fact we must follow the course of distinct bodies
of sources. Each of these several systems of law applying to diverse
Jewish groups or communities emerges from its distinct historical
setting, addresses its own social entity, and tells us, usually only in bits
and pieces of detailed information, about itself alone. Whether whole or
fragmentary, systems of Jewish law do not coalesce into one ideal
system. That is why we may indeed propose to describe any of several
legal systems governing one or more groups of Jews. It is possible to
trace development of systems of halakhah characteristic of communities
of Jews. To begin with, however, an account of the development of such
systems will compare wholes, that is, one system to another system.

True, one might seek the lowest common denominator among all of
the systems of law followed by Jewish groups. That then would be
deemed "the halakhah," or "Jewish law." But details shared among a
variety of Judaisms make sense only in their respective contexts. Each on
its own matters in the system in which it makes its appearance and plays
its role. So if we wish to consider the development of "the halakhah," we

---

[2]Cf. R. Yaron, *The Law of the Aramaic Papyri* (Oxford, 1961: Clarendon).
[3]In addition to Yaron, cf. B. Porten, *Archives from Elephantine. The Life of an
Ancient Jewish Military Colony* (Berkeley and Los Angeles, 1968: University of
California Press); Y. Muffs, *Studies in the Aramaic Legal Papyri from Elephantine*
(Leiden, 1969: E.J. Brill).
[4]Compare the view of E.E. Urbach, *The Law. Its Sources and Development*
(Jerusalem, 1984). (In Hebrew.)

have first to decide whose halakhah, among a variety of candidates, we propose to describe and to analyze. Among a range of choices subject to documentation a choice is to be made. Systematic studies of the halakhah of the Jews in Alexandria,[5] the Jews in Elephantine,[6] the Jews in the Essene community of Qumran,[7] and, of course, the Jews who stand behind the law now presented in the Mishnah and its successor documents[8] all present appropriate foci of inquiry. Among these and other systems of law produced by Jews, the one of greatest importance is that first written down in the Mishnah, ca. 200 C.E.

## II. The Mishnah's Halakhah and Its Importance

The Mishnah is an encompassing law code brought to closure in ca. 200 C.E. under the sponsorship of Judah the Patriarch, ethnic ruler of the Jewish communities of the Land of Israel ("Palestine"). Laid forth in six divisions, the laws of the Mishnah take up the sanctity of the land and its use in accord with God's law ("Seeds" or agriculture), the differentiation and passage of sacred time and its impact upon the cult and the village ("Appointed Times"), the sacred aspects of the relationship between woman and man ("Women" or family law), civil law ("Damages"), the conduct of the cult in appropriate regularity and order ("Holy Things"), and the protection of food prepared under the rules of cultic taboos from contamination ("Purities"). The laws of the document throughout lay stress upon the sanctification of Israel's life in the natural world through conformity to the rules governed by the supernatural world. So the Mishnah's halakhah presents a very particular construction, one proposing to form Israel into a holy community in accord with God's holy law, revealed in the Torah given to Moses at Mount Sinai.

What makes the Mishnah important after its own time in the history of Judaism is a simple fact. The exegesis of the Mishnah became the center, after Scripture, of the articulation of Judaism in law and theology. In the next three hundred years, parts of its system, vastly articulated and reworked, would form the jurisprudential and theological foundations of the practical law, administration, worldview, and way of

---

[5]Erwin R. Goodenough, *The Jurisprudence of the Jewish Courts in Egypt. Legal Administration by the Jews under the Early Roman Empire as Described by Philo Judaeus* (New Haven, 1929).

[6]Porten, Muffs, Yaron, cited above, n. 3.

[7]Lawrence H. Schiffman, *The Halakhah at Qumran* (Leiden, 1975: E.J. Brill); idem., *Sectarian Law*, cited above, n. 1; Joseph M. Baumgarten, *Studies in Qumran Law* (Leiden, 1977: E.J. Brill).

[8]J. Neusner, *Judaism: The Evidence of the Mishnah* (Chicago, 1981: University of Chicago Press).

life of Israel's inner affairs, both in the Holy Land and in the diaspora. Accordingly, the Mishnah contributed some of its tractates to what became the normative Jewish law and theology. That was in the very exact sense that nearly all Jews everywhere, for a long time, would live under a single law code and theological system.

Specifically, once the Mishnah had reached closure, four documents would take up the task of apologia and articulation. The first, tractate Abot, ca. 250, a generation or two beyond the Mishnah, explained the origin and authority of the Mishnah by attributing to its sages positions in the chain of tradition extending from Mount Sinai onward. When, as the text states, "Moses received Torah at Sinai" (Abot 1:1), he thus stood at the head of a chain of sages, which ended among the just deceased authorities of the Mishnah itself. So the new code, in its first and principal apologia, found its place in the setting of the revealed Torah of Moses. The second, third, and fourth dealt with the details of the concrete laws.

The second was the Tosefta, a composite of supplements to the Mishnah's rules, covering nearly the whole of the Mishnah's rules, item by item. That document is generally supposed to have reached closure in the later third or earlier fourth centuries, ca. 300-400.

The third, the Talmud of the Land of Israel, took up thirty-nine of the Mishnah's sixty-two tractates (omitting Abot from the count) and supplied them with paragraph-by-paragraph exegeses. The framers of these exegetical exercises contributed amplifications in one of three classifications. They, first, took up and explained phrases and sentences of the Mishnah paragraph at hand. They, second, brought the Tosefta's supplementary formulations to bear and compared and contrasted them to those of the Mishnah. They, third, composed large-scale theoretical inquiries into the principles of the law, so joining one rule of the Mishnah to several others in a search for the deeper line of order and structure of the law as a whole.

The fourth of the four, the Talmud of Babylonia, ca. 600, contributed the same exegetical exercises to parts of the Mishnah, thirty-seven tractates in all (but not all of the same ones of interest to the compositors of the Talmud of the Land of Israel). While treating the Fifth Division, on Holy Things, the redactors extensively dealt with the three most practical parts of the Mishnah, the Second, Third, and Fourth Divisions, and so they created a complete and encompassing legal system, superimposed on the one of the Mishnah, dealing with everyday religious life, affairs of the individual and the family, and all aspects of civil law.

In one way the authors of the Talmud of Babylonia moved beyond the pattern established by those of the Talmud of the Land of Israel. For the purposes of large-scale organization of discourse, they made use not only of the Mishnah but also of Scripture. The authors of the Talmud of the Land of Israel had relied for order and sequence mainly upon the Mishnah's structure. Those of the other, later Talmud referred also to passages of Scripture. These they would subject to systematic exegesis along exactly those lines that guided their reading of the Mishnah. So the Talmud of Babylonia joined together extensive explanations of the Mishnah's paragraphs with sizable and quite orderly explanations of verses of Scripture. Since the sages by that time regarded the Mishnah as the Oral, or memorized, Torah, and Scripture as the Written Torah, we may define the intent of the framers of the Talmud of Babylonia. It was to join important components of the Torah that had come from Sinai in two media, writing and memorization. So the framers presented as one, whole, and complete Torah this final and encompassing system of law and theology. The importance of the Mishnah in the history of Judaism derives from its position alongside Scripture as one of the two principal structures of organization and legal principles upon which the Talmud of Babylonia created its structure of Jewish law.

## III. The Antiquity of the Mishnah's Halakhah

If we turn to the complementary question of why, looking backward from the Mishnah, the Mishnah constitutes the most important composition in Jewish law up to its own time, a simple answer suggests itself. The fact is that much of the law of the Mishnah derives from the age before its final closure. In the Mishnah we see how a group of jurisprudents drew together a rich heritage of legal and moral traditions and facts and made of them a single system. From Scripture onward, no other composition compares in size, comprehensive treatment of a vast variety of topics, balance, proportion, and cogency. Let us rapidly review the various types of evidence for the antiquity of numerous facts utilized by the Mishnah's framers in the construction of their system.

Some legal facts in the Mishnah, as in other law codes of its place and age, derive from remote antiquity. Categories of law and investment, for instance, prove continuous with Akkadian and even Sumerian ones. To cite a single instance, there are the sorts of investment classified as *nikhse melug* or *nikhse son barzel* (M. Yebamot 7:1-2), investments in which the investor shares in the loss or the profit, on the one side, or in which the investor is guaranteed the return of the capital without regard to the actual course of the investment transaction, on the other. (The former would correspond to common stock, the latter to preferred or even to a government bond, a gilt, in British parlance.) It has been shown that the linguistic and legal datum of Mishnah's rules goes back to Assyrian law.[9] Other important continuities in the common law of the ancient Near East have emerged in a broad diversity of research, on Elephantine law for instance.[10] The issue therefore cannot focus upon whether or not the Mishnah in diverse details draws upon established rules of jurisprudence. It assuredly does.

Yet another mode of demonstrating that facts in the Mishnah's system derive from a period substantially prior to that in which the Mishnah reached closure carries us to the data provided by documents redacted long before the Mishnah. For one example, details of rules in the law codes found in the library of the Essene community of Qumran intersect with details of rules in the Mishnah. More interesting still, accounts of aspects of Israelite life take for granted that issues lively in the Mishnah came under debate long before the closure of the Mishnah. The Gospels' accounts of Jesus' encounter with the Pharisees, among others, encompass rules of law, or topics dealt with, important to the Mishnah.[11] It is, for instance, not merely the datum that a writ of divorce severs the tie between wife and husband. The matter of grounds for divorce proves important to sages whose names occur in the Mishnah, and one position of one of these sages turns out to accord with the position on the same matter imputed to Jesus.[12] It follows that not only isolated facts but critical matters of jurisprudential philosophy came to the surface long before the closure of the Mishnah.

That fact yields one incontrovertible result. The Mishnah's rules have to come into juxtaposition, wherever possible, with the rules that occur in prior law codes, whether Israelite or otherwise. That is the case, even though it presently appears that only a small proportion of all of the rules in the Mishnah fall within the frame of prior documents, remote or proximate. For every rule we can parallel in an earlier composition, the Mishnah gives us dozens of rules that in topic, logic, or even mere detail bear no comparison to anything now known in a prior composition, from Sumerian and Akkadian to Essene and Christian writers alike. (The sole exception, the Hebrew Scripture's law codes, comes under analysis in the next section.) Details of the law, wherever possible, still must stand in comparison with equivalent details in earlier documents, whether

---

[9]Baruch A. Levine, "Mulugu/Melug. The Origins of a Talmudic Legal Institution," *JAOS* 1968, 88:271-85.

[10]Muffs, cited above, n. 3, presents the definitive picture.

[11]J. Neusner, "First Cleanse the Inside," New Testament Studies 1976, 22:486-495, repr. in *Method and Meaning in Ancient Judaism. Third Series* (Chico, 1981: Scholars Press for Brown Judaic Studies).

[12]Cf. M. Git. 9:10 and Mt. 5:31-32, among numerous well-known points of intersection.

narrative or legislative. In that way we gain perspective on what, in the Mishnah, has come into the framers hands from an earlier period. At stake in such perspective is insight into the mind of the Mishnah's framers and the character of their system. We see what they have made out of available materials. What do we learn from the occurrence of facts by the time of the Mishnah more than two millenia old, or of issues important two centuries earlier? We review the resources selected by those who contributed to the traditions brought to closure in the Mishnah.

For the authors of the Mishnah in using available, sometimes very ancient, materials, reshaped whatever came into their hands. The document upon close reading proves systematic and orderly, purposive and well composed.[13] It is no mere scrapbook of legal facts, arranged for purposes of reference. It is a document in which the critical problematic at the center always exercises influence over the peripheral facts, dictating how they are chosen, arranged, utilized. So even though some facts in the document prove very old indeed, on that basis we understand no more than we did before we knew that some facts come from ancient times. True halakhah as the Mishnah presents law derives from diverse sources, from remote antiquity onward. But the halakhah as it emerges whole and complete in the Mishnah, in particular, that is, the system, the structure, the proportions and composition, the topical program and the logical and syllogistic whole – these derive from the imagination and wit of the final two generations, in the second century C.E., of the authors of the Mishnah.

## IV. The Originality of the Mishnah's Halakhah as a System

A simple exercise will show that, whatever the antiquity of rules viewed discretely, the meaning and proportionate importance of rules taken all together derive from the perspective and encompassing theory of the authors of the Mishnah themselves. That is what will show that the history of halakhah as the Mishnah presents the halakhah, can be traced, whole and cogent, only within the data of the Mishnah itself: systemically, not episodically. The desired exercise brings us to the relationship of the Mishnah to Scripture. For, as noted just now, that is the one substantial source to which the authors of the Mishnah did make reference. Accordingly, to demonstrate the antiquity of more than discrete and minor details of law of the Mishnah, we turn to Scripture. There, it is clear, we can find out whether the Mishnah constitutes merely a repository of ancient halakhah.

---

[13]That is the argument of my op. cit., n. 8.

Indeed, proof that there was not merely law characteristic of a given group, but the halakhah, shared by all Israel, should derive solely from the Scripture common to all Israel everywhere. How so? The theory of a single, continuous halakhah rests upon the simple fact that all Israel by definition acknowledged the authority of Scripture, its law and theology. It must follow that, in diverse ways and within discrete exegetical processes, every group now known to us drew its basic legal propositions from Scripture and therefore contributes evidence on the unilinear formation of a single law, based upon a single source, common to all Israel, that is, the halakhah.

In examining the notion of the halakhah, as distinct from the theory, argued here, of diverse systems of halakhah, we turn to the critical issue. It concerns not whether a given rule derives from exegesis of Scripture. That issue, by itself, provides trivial and not probative insight. Rather we want to know how the several systems now known to us define their respective relationships to Scripture. That is to say, we ask about the nature of scriptural authority, the use of Scripture's facts in a code, or system, of law. The answer to the question settles an important issue. If two (or more) systems of law governing groups of Israelites turn out to respond to, to draw upon, Scripture's rules in much the same way, then these discrete systems merge at their roots, in a generative and definitive aspect of their structure. In consequence, we may conclude the two (or more) systems do form part of a single common law, once more, the halakhah. But if two or more systems of law approach Scripture each in its own way and for its own purposes, then we have to analyze each system on its own terms and not as part of, and contributory to, the halakhah.

For the present purpose it will suffice to demonstrate one modest fact. The authors of the Mishnah read Scripture, as they read much else, in terms of the system and structure they proposed to construct. Their goals and conceptions told them what, in Scripture, they would borrow, what they would expand and articulate, what they would acknowledge but neglect and what they would simply ignore. That fact shows that law in the Mishnah, even though shared here and there with other codes, and even though intersecting with still other systems, constitutes a distinct and autonomous system of law, a halakhah on its own. So, to review, the Mishnah then does not absorb and merely portray in its own way established rules of law out of a single, continuous, and cogent legal system, the halakhah. Why not? Because, as we shall now see, the Mishnah's authors turn out to have taken from Scripture what they chose in accord with the criterion of the one thing they wished to accomplish. This was the construction of their system of law with its distinctive traits of topical and logical composition: their halakhah, not the halakhah.

In order to show the preeminence, in the encounter with Scripture's laws, of the perspective and purpose of the authors of the Mishnah, we simply review the Mishnah's tractates and ask how, overall, we may characterize their relationships to Scripture. Were these wholly dependent, wholly autonomous, or somewhere in between? That is, at the foundations in fact and generative problematic of a given tractate, we may discover nothing more than facts and interests of Scripture's law. The tractate's authors may articulate the data of Scripture. Or when we reach the bedrock of a tractate, the point at which the articulation of the structure of the tractate rests, we may find no point of contact with facts, let alone interests, of Scripture's laws. And, third, we may discover facts shared by Scripture but developed in ways distinctive to the purposes of the framers of the Mishnah tractate at hand. These three relationships, in theory, encompass all possibilities. Let us turn to the facts.[14]

First, there are tractates which simply repeat in their own words precisely what Scripture has to say, and at best serve to amplify and complete the basic ideas of Scripture. For example, all of the cultic tractates of the Second Division, the one on Appointed Times, which tell what one is supposed to do in the Temple on the various special days of the year, and the bulk of the cultic tractates of the Fifth Division, which deals with Holy Things, simply restate facts of Scripture. For another example all of those tractates of the Sixth Division, on Purities, which specify sources of uncleanness, depend completely on information supplied by Scripture. Every important statement in Niddah, on menstrual uncleanness, and the most fundamental notions of *Zabim*, on the uncleanness of the person with flux referred to in Lev. 15, as well as every detail in Negaim, on the uncleanness of the person or house suffering the uncleanness described at Lev. 13 and 14 – all of these tractates serve only to restate the basic facts of Scripture and to complement those facts with other important ones.

There are, second, tractates which take up facts of Scripture but work them out in a way in which those scriptural facts could not have led us to predict. A supposition concerning what is important about the facts, utterly remote from the supposition of Scripture, will explain why the Mishnah tractates under discussion say the original things they say in confronting those scripturally provided facts. For one example, Scripture takes for granted that the red cow will be burned in a state of uncleanness, because it is burned outside the camp, meaning the Temple. The priestly writers could not have imagined that a state of cultic cleanness was to be attained outside of the cult. The absolute datum of

---

[14]These are summarized in detail in my *Method and Meaning in Ancient Judaism. Second Series* (Chico, 1981: Scholars Press for Brown Judaic Studies), pp. 101-214.

tractate Parah, by contrast, is that cultic cleanness not only can be attained outside of the "tent of meeting," but that the red cow was to be burned in a state of cleanness exceeding even that cultic cleanness required in the Temple itself. The problematic which generates the intellectual agendum of Parah, therefore, is how to work out the conduct of the rite of burning the cow in relationship to the Temple: Is it to be done in exactly the same way, or in exactly the opposite way? This mode of contrastive and analogical thinking helps us to understand the generative problematic of such tractates as Erubin and Besah, to mention only two.

And third, there are, predictably, many tractates which either take up problems in no way suggested by Scripture, or begin from facts at best merely relevant to facts of Scripture. In the former category are Tohorot, on the cleanness of foods, with its companion, Uqsin; Demai, on doubtfully tithed produce; Tamid, on the conduct of the daily whole-offering; Baba Batra, on rules of real estate transactions and certain other commercial and property relationships, and so on. In the latter category are Ohalot, which spins out its strange problems with the theory that a tent and a utensil are to be compared to one another(!); Kelim, on the susceptibility to uncleanness of various sorts of utensils; Miqvaot, on the sorts of water which effect purification from uncleanness; and many others. These tractates draw on facts of Scripture. But the problems confronted in these tractates in no way respond to problems important to Scripture. What we have here is a prior program of inquiry, which will make ample provision for facts of Scripture in an inquiry to begin with generated essentially outside of the framework of Scripture.

Some tractates merely repeat what we find in Scripture. Some are totally independent of Scripture. Some fall in between. Scripture confronts the framers of the Mishnah as revelation, not merely as a source of facts. But the framers of the Mishnah had their own world with which to deal. They made statements in the framework and fellowship of their own age and generation. They were bound, therefore, to come to Scripture with a set of questions generated elsewhere than in Scripture. They brought their own ideas about what was going to be important in Scripture. This is perfectly natural.

The philosophers of the Mishnah conceded to Scripture the highest authority. At the same time what they chose to hear, within the authoritative statements of Scripture, will in the end form a statement of its own. To state matters simply: All of Scripture is authoritative. But only some of Scripture is relevant. And what happened is that the framers and philosophers of the tradition of the Mishnah came to Scripture when they had reason to. That is to say, they brought to Scripture a program of questions and inquiries framed essentially among themselves. So they were highly selective. Their program itself constituted a statement upon the meaning of Scripture. They and their apologists of one sort hastened to add, their program consisted of a statement of and not only upon the meaning of Scripture.

The authority of Scripture therefore for the Mishnah is simply stated. Scripture provides indisputable facts. It is wholly authoritative – once we have made our choice of which part of Scripture we shall read. Scripture generated important and authoritative structures of the community, including disciplinary and doctrinal statements, decisions, and interpretations – once people had determined which part of Scripture to ask to provide those statements and decisions. Community structures envisaged by the Mishnah were wholly based on Scripture – when Scripture had anything to lay down. But Scripture is not wholly and exhaustively expressed in those structures which the Mishnah does borrow. Scripture has dictated the character of formative structures of the Mishnah. But the Mishnah's system is not the result of the dictation of close exegesis of Scripture, except after the fact.

## V. History of the Mishnah's Halakhah: Methodological Program

The Mishnah's formulation derives from the work of redaction.[15] So we cannot show that sizable components of the Mishnah were written down, pretty much as we have them, long before the closure of the document as a whole. On formal and literary grounds, the opposite is the fact: Most of the Mishnah conforms to a single program of formulation, and that set of rules on formulation derives from encompassing decisions concerning redaction. We can, however, demonstrate that legal issues or principles in the Mishnah, if not the original wording of those ideas, did derive from periods prior to the age of redaction and formulation.

That demonstration rests on two facts. The first is that numerous statements in the Mishnah bear attributions to particular sages, who lived – it is generally assumed – over the period of approximately two centuries prior to the closure of the document. Since we cannot show that the sages to whom sayings are attributed actually said what is assigned to them, on the surface we do not know the historical value of the attributions. But a second fact makes possible a test of falsification and verification. It is that groups of names appear always with one another and never with names found in other distinct groups. Sages A, B, C, D, commonly believed to have lived at one time, occur in dispute with one another. But rarely, if ever, does sage A, B, C, or D, appear with

---

[15]Cf. my *History of the Mishnaic Law of Purities* (Leiden, 1977: E.J. Brill). XXI. *The Redaction and Formulation of the Order of Purities in Mishnah and Tosefta.*

sages W, X, Y, and Z. Those latter sages likewise stay together and rarely intersect with other groups of names. That indicates a simple and obvious fact. The system of attributions works itself out by groups, or generations. To begin with we may collect sayings assigned to sages A, B, C, and D, and treat them as distinct from sayings assigned to W, X, Y, and Z. But what difference does that distinction make?

The answer rests upon the test of falsification or verification. How so? Two or more groups of sayings, each set drawn together on the basis of the appearance of groups of names may intersect in the treatment of a common theme or even problem. In the consideration of that problem we may readily isolate the stages in the argument, identify the components of a theme. We may further show, on grounds of logic, that a given element of a problem or component of a theme takes precedence over some other element or component. The matter is very simple. For example, if we do not know that a woman requires a writ of divorce, we shall not ask about how the writ is supposed to be written. Again, if we do not know that rules dictate the correct composition of the writ of divorce, we are not likely to ask about the consequences of a scribal error in the writing of the document. So we see three stages in the simple problem before us: (1) we must know that if a husband wishes to divorce a wife, he must supply her with written evidence that the marriage is severed, and then (2) we must know that such written evidence conforms to a given formula, before we may ask (3) whether, if the document does not conform, the woman is deemed properly divorced. Yet a further stage in the unfolding of the issue will bring us to the question of how (4) we dispose of the offspring of the woman who, on the basis of a divorce accomplished through an improper document, has remarried and become pregnant.

Now recognizing the obvious stages in the unfolding of an issue, we cannot conclude that these stages in logic correspond to sequences of temporal periods. Why not? Because no one would claim that the logical stages outlined just now mark off fifty-year periods in the history of the law. In a single morning, someone could have thought the whole thing through. But what shall we say if we observe a sequence of correspondences between the order in which groups of sages engage in a discussion of a problem and the logic by which the problem itself unfolds? For example, to revert to the case at hand, we may be able to show that sages A, B, C, and D appear in units of discourse, or pericopes, concerning stage (1) of the issue, sages G, H, I, and J participate in units of discourse on the matter of stage (2), M, N, O, and P at stage (3), and W, X, Y, and Z at stage (4). Then we may propose the thesis that the issue unfolded in the sequence of historical periods in which the groups of sages lived. Why so? Because the order of logical steps not only corresponds to, but also correlates with, the order of the groups of sages to whom pertinent sayings are attributed. Can that thesis undergo a test of falsification? Of course it can, because we may ask whether to a later group of sages, for example, M, N, O, and P, are attributed sayings that concern an issue, principle, or premise already supposedly settled among an earlier group of sages, for example, A, B, C, and D.

Admittedly, the facts at hand do not demand a historical explanation. One may account in other ways for the correlation of logical stages with sequences of groups, or generations, of sages. The method allows the proposed historical results – the picture of the history of the halakhah of the Mishnah's larger system – to undergo tests of falsification and verification. It does not rest on total credulousness in accepting as fact all attributions. But a more critical approach in time to come will improve upon the method outlined here.

I have applied this procedure in a study of the entire Mishnah, each tractate and every unit of discourse of each tractate.[16] The results proved not entirely uniform for two reasons. The first and the more important, the character of the materials did not invariably permit the test of falsification at hand. Some issues arise for the first time in the names of the final group of authorities, the one that would correspond, in my example above, to W, X, Y, and Z. That meant I had no basis other than the attributions on which to assign to the period of those sages the rules attributed to them. But since the sages at hand flourished one generation prior to the closure of the Mishnah, it did not appear an act of mere credulity in assigning what was attributed to that last stage in the formation of the Mishnah's system of halakhah.

The second, the less important matter was that, on rare occasion, it did appear that what was assumed in discourse among an earlier group of sages, for example, A, B, C, and D, in fact produced substantial dispute among a later group, e.g, W, X, Y, and Z. These few exceptions often centered on a critical figure in the attributions, namely, Aqiba, an early second-century authority, who is believed to have flourished prior to the Bar Kokhba War and to have trained the principal authorities of the period after the war. In any event where the test of falsification or verification could be met, an item had to be set aside and not included in an account of the history of the law. To state the upshot of the procedure, we may work out the history of the halakhah of the Mishnah through three principal periods: before 70, from 70 to 130, and from 140 to 170, that is, before the first war with Rome, between the two wars, and after the Bar Kokhba War.

---

[16]Cf. the works cited in the following three notes.

Obviously, we want to know how far before 70 the Mishnah's laws extend their roots. If we rely on the attributions at hand and make use only of those units of discourse in which we can verify or falsify the attributions, the answer is simple. The earliest layers of the laws ultimately joined together in the system of the Mishnah rest upon foundations laid forth somewhat before or at the beginning of the Common Era. No unit of discourse in the entire Mishnah can be shown to contain ideas or facts originating in the Mishnah's system prior to the turn of the first century C.E. To be sure numerous facts and ideas extend back to Scripture; some go back to Sumerian or Akkadian times. But so far as facts or ideas serve a purpose distinctive to the Mishnah's system and so may be called systemic, not merely episodic and routine, all facts and ideas begin at the designated period. To state the matter simply: The system of the Mishnah's halakhah begins at the turn of the first century C.E., though details, commonly routine facts of a common law, may originate as much as two thousand years earlier than that.

## VI. The Mishnah's Halakhah before 70

The halakhah of the Mishnah takes shape in a twofold process. Once a theme is introduced early in the history of law, it will be taken up and refined later on. Also, in the second and third stages in the formation of the Mishnah, many new themes with their problems will emerge. These then are without precedent in the antecedent thematic heritage. The common foundations for the whole always are Scripture, of course, so that I may present a simple architectural simile. The halakhah of the Mishnah is like a completed construction of scaffolding. The foundation is a single plane, the Scriptures. The top platform also is a single plane, the Mishnah itself. But the infrastructure is differentiated. Underneath one part of the upper platform will be several lower platforms, so that the supporting poles and pillars reach down to intervening platforms; only the bottom platform rests upon pillars set in the foundation. Yet another part of the upper platform rests upon pillars and poles stretching straight down to the foundation, without intervening platforms at all. So viewed from above, the uppermost platform of the scaffolding forms a single, uniform, and even plane. That is the Mishnah as we have it, six divisions, sixty-three tractates, five hundred thirty-one chapters. But viewed from the side, that is, from the perspective of analysis, there is much differentiation, so that, from one side, the upper platform rises from a second, intermediate one, and, in places, from even a third, lowest one. And yet some of the pillars reach directly down to the bedrock foundations.

To reveal the result at the outset: What is new in the period beyond the wars is that part of the ultimate plane – the Mishnah as a whole – in fact rests upon the foundations not of antecedent thought but of Scripture alone. What is basic in the period before 70 C.E. is the formation of that part of the Mishnah which sustains yet a second and even a third layer of platform construction. What emerges between the two wars, of course, will both form a plane with what comes before, that platform at the second level, and yet will also lay foundations for a level above itself. But this intermediate platform also will come to an end, yielding that space filled only by the pillars stretching from Scripture on upward to the ultimate plane of the Mishnah's completed and whole system. So let me now describe what I believe to be the state of the law as a whole before 70.

The Mishnah as we know it originated in its Division of Purities. The striking fact is that the Sixth Division is the only one that yields a complete and whole statement of a topic dating from before the wars. Its principal parts are (1) what imparts uncleanness; (2) which kinds of objects and substances may be unclean; and (3) how these objects or substances may regain the status of cleanness. Joined to episodic rulings elsewhere, the principal parts of the Sixth Division speak, in particular, of cleanness of meals, food and drink, pots and pans. It then would appear that the ideas ultimately expressed in the Mishnah began among people who had a special interest in observing cultic cleanness, as dictated by the priestly code. There can be no doubt, moreover, that the context for such cleanness is the home, not solely the Temple, about which Leviticus speaks. The issues of the law leave no doubt on that score. Since priests ate heave-offering at home, and did so in a state of cultic cleanness, it was a small step to apply the same taboos to food which was not a consecrated gift to the priests.

What is said through the keeping of these laws is that the food eaten at home, not deriving from the altar and its provision for the priesthood of meat not burned up in the fire, was as holy as the meal-offerings, meat-offerings, and drink-offerings, consecrated by being set aside for the altar and then, in due course, partly given to the priests and partly tossed on the altar and burned up. If food not consecrated for the altar, not protected in a state of cleanness (in the case of wheat), or carefully inspected for blemishes (in the case of beasts), and not eaten by priests in the Temple was deemed subject to the same purity restrictions as food consecrated for the altar, this carries implications about the character of that food, those who were to eat it, and the conditions in which it was grown and eaten. First, all food, not only that for the altar, was to be protected in a state of levitical cleanness, thus holiness, that is, separateness. Second, the place in the Land, in which the food was grown and kept was to be kept cultically clean, holy, just like the Temple. Third, the people, Israel, who were to eat that food were holy, just like the priesthood, in rank behind the Temple's chief caste. Fourth, the act of eating food anywhere in the Holy Land was analogous to the act of eating food in the Temple, by the altar.

All of these obvious inferences point to a profound conviction about the Land, people, produce, condition, and context of nourishment. The setting was holy. The actors were holy. And what, specifically, they did which had to be protected in holiness was eating. For when they ate their food at home, they ate it the way priests did in the Temple. And the way priests ate their food in the Temple, that is, the cultic rules and conditions observed in that setting, was like the way God ate his food in the Temple. That is to say, God's food and locus of nourishment were to be protected from the same sources of danger and contamination, preserved in the same exalted condition of sanctification. So by acting, that is, eating like God, Israel became like God: a pure and perfect incarnation, on earth in the Land which was holy, of the model of heaven. Eating food was the critical act and occasion, just as the priestly authors of Leviticus and Numbers had maintained when they made laws governing slaughtering beasts and burning up their flesh, baking pancakes and cookies with and without olive oil and burning them on the altar, pressing grapes and making wine and pouring it out onto the altar. The nourishment of the Land – meat, grain, oil, and wine – was set before God and burned ("offered up") in conditions of perfect cultic antisepsis.

In context this antisepsis provided protection against things deemed the opposite of nourishment, the quintessence of death: corpse matter, people who looked like corpses (Lev. 13), dead creeping things, blood when not flowing in the veins of the living, such as menstrual blood (Lev. 15), other sorts of flux (semen in men, nonmenstrual blood in women) which yield not life but then its opposite, so death. What these excrescences have in common, of course, is that they are ambivalent. Why? Because they may be one thing or the other. Blood in the living is the soul; blood not in the living is the soul of contamination. The corpse was once a living person, like God; the person with skin like a corpse's and who looks dead was once a person who looked alive; the flux of the Zab (Lev. 15) comes from the flaccid penis which under the right circumstances, that is, properly erect, produces semen and makes life. What is at the margin between life and death and can go either way is what is the source of uncleanness. But that is insufficient. For the opposite, in the priestly code, of unclean is not only clean, but also holy. The antonym is not to be missed: death or life, unclean or holy.

So the cult is the point of struggle between the forces of life and nourishment and the forces of death and extinction: meat, grain, oil, and wine, against corpse matter, dead creeping things, blood in the wrong setting, semen in the wrong context, and the like. Then, on the occasions when meat was eaten, mainly, at the time of festivals or other moments at which sin-offerings and peace-offerings were made, people who wished to live ate their meat, and at all times ate the staples of wine, oil, and bread, in a state of life and so generated life. They kept their food and themselves away from the state of death as much as possible. And this heightened reality pertained at home, as much as in the Temple, where most rarely went on ordinary days. The Temple was the font of life, the bulwark against death.[17]

Once the meal became a focus of attention, the other two categories of the law which yield principles or laws deriving from the period before the wars present precisely the same sorts of rules. Laws on growing and preparing food will attract attention as soon as people wish to speak, to begin with, about how meals are to be eaten. That accounts for the obviously lively interest in the biblical taboos of agriculture.[18] Since, further, meals are acts of society, they call together a group. Outside of the family, the natural unit, such a group will be special and cultic. If a group is going to get together, it will be on a Sabbath or festival, not on a workday. So laws governing the making of meals on those appointed times will inevitably receive attention.[19] Nor is it surprising that, in so far as there are any rules pertinent to the cult, they will involve those aspects of the cult which apply also outside of the cult, that is, how a beast is slaughtered, rules governing the disposition of animals of a special status (for example, firstborn), and the like.[20]

That the rules for meals pertain not to isolated families but to a larger group is strongly suggested by the other area which evidently was subjected to sustained attention before the wars, laws governing who may marry whom. The context in which the sayings assigned to the authorities before the wars are shaped is the life of a small group of people, defining its life apart from the larger Israelite society while maintaining itself wholly within that society. Three points of ordinary life formed the focus for concrete, social differentiation: food, sex, and

---

[17]Cf. my *History of the Mishnaic Law of Purities* (Leiden, 1974-1977: E.J. Brill). I-XXII.

[18]Cf. Alan J. Avery-Peck, *History of the Mishnaic Law of Agriculture* (Chico, 1985: Scholars Press for Brown Judaic Studies).

[19]Cf. my *History of the Mishnaic Law of Appointed Times* (Leiden, 1981-1983: E.J. Brill). I-V.

[20]Cf. my *History of the Mishnaic Law of Holy Things* (Leiden, 1979: E.J. Brill). I-VI.

marriage. What people ate, how they conducted their sexual lives, and whom they married or to whom they gave their children in marriage would define the social parameters of their group.[21] These facts indicate who was kept within the bounds, and who was excluded and systematically maintained at a distance. For these are the things – the only things – subject to the independent control of the small group. The people behind the laws, after all, could not tell people other than their associates what to eat or whom to marry. But they could make their own decisions on these important, but humble, matters. By making those decisions in one way and not in some other, they moreover could keep outsiders at a distance and those who to begin with adhered to the group within bounds. Without political control, they could not govern the transfer of property or other matters of public interest. But without political power, they could and did govern the transfer of their women. It was in that intimate aspect of life that they firmly established the outer boundary of their collective existence. The very existence of the group and the concrete expression of its life, therefore, comes under discussion in the transfer of women. It therefore seems no accident at all that those strata of Mishnaic law which appear to go back to the period before the wars, well before 70, deal specifically with the special laws of marriage (in Yebamot), distinctive rule on when sexual relations may and may not take place (in Niddah), and the laws covering the definition of sources of uncleanness and the attainment of cleanness, with specific reference to domestic meals (in certain parts of Ohalot, Zabim, Kelim, and Miqvaot). Nor is it surprising that for the conduct of the cult and the sacrificial system, about which the group may have had its own doctrines but over which it neither exercised control nor even aspired to, there appears to be no systemic content or development whatsoever.

Once the group take shape around some distinctive, public issue or doctrine, as in odd taboos about eating, it also must take up the modes of social differentiation which will ensure the group's continued existence. For the group, once it comes into being, has to aspire to define and shape the ordinary lives of its adherents and to form a community expressive of its larger worldview. The foundations of an enduring community will then be laid down through rules governing what food may be eaten, under what circumstances, and with what sort of people; whom one may marry and what families may be joined in marriage; and how sexual relationships are timed. Indeed, to the measure that these rules not only differ from those observed by others but in some aspect or other render the people who keep them unacceptable to those who do not, as much as, to the sect, those who do not keep them are unacceptable to those who

---

[21]Cf. my *History of the Mishnaic Law of Women* (Leiden, 1979-1980: E.J. Brill). I-VI.

do, the lines of difference and distinctive structure will be all the more inviolable.

## VII. The Mishnah's Halakhah between the Wars of 66-70 and 132-135

The period between the wars marks a transition in the unfolding of the Mishnaic law and system. The law moved out of its narrow, sectarian framework. But it did not yet attain the full definition, serviceable for the governance of a whole society and the formation of a government for the nation as a whole, which would be realized in the aftermath of the wars. The marks of the former state remained. But those of the later character of the Mishnaic system began to make their appearance. Still, the systemic fulfillment of the law would be some time in coming. For, as I shall point out in the next section, the system as a whole in its ultimate shape would totally reframe the inherited vision. In the end the Mishnah's final framers would accomplish what was not done before or between the wars: make provision for the ordinary condition of Israelite men and women, living everyday lives under their own government. The laws suitable for a sect would remain, to be joined by others which, in the aggregate, would wholly revise the character of the whole. The shift after the Bar Kokhba War would be from a perspective formed upon the Temple mount to a vision framed within the plane of Israel, from a cultic to a communal conception, and from a center at the locative pivot of the altar, to a system resting upon the utopian character of the nation as a whole.

When we take up the changes in this transitional period, we notice, first of all, continuity with the immediate past. What was taking place after 70 is encapsulated in the expansion, along predictable and familiar lines, of the laws of uncleanness, so to these we turn first.

If the destruction of Jerusalem and the Temple in 70 marks a watershed in the history of Judaism, the development of the system of uncleanness does not indicate it. The destruction of the Temple in no way interrupted the unfolding of those laws, consideration of which is well attested when the Temple was standing and the cult maintained. Development is continuous in a second aspect as well. We find that, in addition to carrying forward antecedent themes and supplying secondary and even tertiary conceptions, the authorities between the wars develop new areas and motifs of legislation. These turn out to be both wholly consonant with the familiar ones, and, while fresh, generated by logical tensions in what had gone before. If, therefore, the destruction of the Temple raised in some minds the question of whether the system of cleanness at home would collapse along with the cult, the rules and system before us in no way suggest so. To be sure, the destruction of the Temple does mark a new phase in the growth of the law. What now happens is an evidently rapid extension of the range of legislation, on the one side, and provision of specific and concrete rules for what matters of purity were apt to have been taken for granted but not given definition before 70, on the other. So the crisis of 70 in the system of uncleanness gives new impetus to movement along lines laid forth long before.

Let us first dwell upon the points of continuity, which are many and impressive. The development of the rules on the uncleanness of menstrual blood, the Zab, and corpse uncleanness is wholly predictable on the basis of what has gone before. The principal conceptual traits carry forward established themes. For example, if we have in hand an interest in resolving matters of doubt, then, in the present age, further types of doubts will be investigated. Once we know that a valid birth is not accompanied by unclean blood, we ask about the definition of valid births. The present thought on the Zab (Lev. 15) depends entirely on the materials assigned to the Houses, which, moreover, appear to be prior to, and independent of, what is attributed to the authorities after 70. The transfer of the Zab's uncleanness through pressure, forming so large and important a part of the tractate of Zabim, begins not with a reference to the Zab at all, but to the menstruating woman. The fresh point in this regard is to be seen as a step beyond Scripture's own rule, a shift based on analogical thinking. Rulings on corpse contamination dwell upon secondary and derivative issues. One new idea is the interest in projections from a house and how they, too, overshadow and so bring corpse uncleanness. It is from this point that an important development begins. Once we treat the tent as in some way functional, it is natural to focus upon the process or function of overshadowing in general. A major innovation in regard to transfer of the contamination of corpse matter through the tent is the notion that the tent takes an active role, combining the diverse bits and pieces and corpse uncleanness into a volume sufficient to impart corpse uncleanness. What is done is to treat the overshadowing as a function, rather than the tent as a thing. Here the mode of thought is both contrastive and analogical.

What is new now requires attention. The comparison of the table in the home to the cult in the Temple is an old theme in the Mishnaic system. What is done at just this time appears to have been the recognition of two complementary sequences, the removes of uncleanness, the degrees of holiness. The former involves several steps of contamination from the original source of uncleanness. The latter speaks of several degrees of sanctification, ordinary food, heave-offering, food deriving from the altar (Holy Things), and things involved in the preparation of purification water. Each of the latter is subject to the effects of contamination produced by each of the former, in an ascending ladder of sensitivity to uncleanness.[22]

An essentially new topic for intense analysis was Holy Things. At issue now is the formation, between the wars, of laws governing the cult. The principal statement of this new system is as follows: The Temple is holy. Its priests therefore are indispensable. But the governance of the Temple now is to be in accord with Torah, and it is the sage who knows Torah and therefore applies it. Since a literal reading of Scripture prevented anyone's maintaining that someone apart from the priest could be like a priest and do the things priests do, it was the next best thing to impose the pretense that priests must obey laymen in the conduct even of the priestly liturgies and services. This is a natural step in the development of the law. A second paramount trait of the version of the system between the wars is its rationalization of those uncontrolled powers inherent in the sacred cult as laid forth by Leviticus. The lessons of Nadab and Abihu and numerous other accounts of the cult's or altar's intrinsic mana (inclusive of the herem) are quietly set aside. The altar sanctifies only what is appropriate to it, not whatever comes into contact with its power. In that principle, the sacred is forced to conform to simple conceptions of logic and sense, its power uncontrollably to strike out dramatically reduced. This same rationality extends to the definition of the effective range of intention. If one intends to do improperly what is not in any event done at all, one's intention is null. Third, attention is paid to defining the sorts of offerings required in various situations of sin or guilt. Here, too, the message is not to be missed. Sin still is to be expiated, when circumstances permit, through the sacrificial system. Nothing has changed. There is no surrogate for sacrifice, an exceedingly important affirmation of the cult's continuing validity among people burdened with sin and aching for a mode of atonement. Finally, we observe that the established habit of thinking about gifts to be paid to the priest accounts for the choices of topics on fees paid to maintain the cult. All pertain to priestly gifts analogous to tithes and heave-offerings. Tithe of cattle is an important subject, and the rules of firstlings and other gifts to the priests are subject to considerable development. The upshot is that the principal concerns of the Division of Holy Things are defined by the end of the age between the wars.

Systematic work on the formation of a Division of Appointed Times did not get under way in the aftermath of the destruction of the Temple. The established interest in rules governing meals, however, was carried forward in laws reliably assigned to the time between the wars. There is some small tendency to develop laws pertinent to the observance of the

---

[22]Cf. M. Tohorot 2:2-7, for instance.

Sabbath; a few of these laws were important and generated later developments. But the age between the wars may be characterized as a period between important developments. Work on legislation for meals on Sabbaths and festivals had begun earlier. The effort systematically and thoroughly to legislate for the generality of festivals, with special attention to conduct in the Temple cult, would begin later on. In the intervening generations only a little work was done, and this was episodic and random.

When fully worked out, the Mishnah's Division of Women would pay close attention to exchanges of property and documents attendant upon the transfer of a woman from her father's to her husband's house. Authorities between the wars provided only a little guidance for such matters. For a very long time before 70 the national, prevailing law must have defined and governed them. What is significant is that broader and nonsectarian matters, surely subject to a long history of accepted procedure, should have been raised at all. It means that, after the destruction, attention turned to matters which sectarians had not regarded as part of their realm of concern. This may have meant that others who had carried responsibility for the administration of public affairs, such as scribes, now made an appearance. And it also may have meant that the vision of the sectarians themselves had begun to broaden and to encompass the administration of the life of ordinary folk, not within the sect. Both meanings are to be imputed to the fact of interest in issues of public administration of property transfers along with the transfer of women to and from the father's home. Concern for definition of personal status devolves upon genealogical questions urgent to the priesthood, and, it follows, in the present stratum are contained matters of deep concern to yet a third constituency. But these matters of interest to scribes and priests do not predominate. It is their appearance, rather than their complete expression and articulation, which is of special interest. Whoever before 70 had settled those disputes about real estate, working conditions, debts and loans, torts and damages, and other sorts of conflicts which naturally came up in a vital and stable society, the group represented in the Mishnah did not.[23]

That is why the Division of Damages, dealing with civil law and government, contains virtually nothing assigned to authorities before the wars. Scribes in Temple times served as judges and courts within the Temple government, holding positions in such system of administration of the Israelite part of Palestine as the Romans left within Jewish control. The Division of Damages is remarkably reticent on what after the destruction they might have contributed out of the heritage of their

---

[23]Cf. my *History of the Mishnaic Law of Damages* (Leiden, 1983-1985: E.J. Brill). I-V.

earlier traditions and established practices. Materials of this period yield little evidence of access to any tradition prior to 70, except (predictably) for Scripture. When people at this time did take up topics relevant to the larger system of Damages, they directed their attention to the exegesis of Scriptures and produced results which clarify what Moses laid down, or which carry forward problems or topics suggested by the Torah. That is not evidence that thinkers of this period had access (or wished to gain access) to any source of information other than that one, long since available to the country as a whole, provided by Moses. It follows that, insofar as any materials at all relevant to the later Mishnaic system of Damages did come forth between the wars, the work appears to have begun from scratch. And not much work could have been done to begin with. There is no evidence of sustained and systematic thought about the topics assembled in the Division of Damages. We find some effort devoted to the exegesis of Scriptures relevant to the division. But whether or not those particular passages were selected because of a large-scale inquiry into the requirements of civil law and government, or because of an overriding interest in a given set of Scriptures provoked by some other set of questions entirely, we cannot say.

The net result of the stage in the law's unfolding demarcated by the two wars is that history – the world-shattering events of the day – is kept at a distance from the center of life. The system of sustaining life shaped essentially within an ahistorical view of reality goes forward in its own path, a way above history. Yet the facts of history are otherwise. The people as a whole can hardly be said to have accepted the ahistorical ontology framed by the sages and in part expressed by the systems of Purities, Agriculture, and Holy Things. The people followed the path of Bar Kokhba and took the road to war once more. When the three generations had passed after the destruction and the historical occasion for restoration through historical – political and military – action came to fulfillment, the great war of 132 to 135 broke forth. A view of being in which people were seen to be moving toward some point within time, the fulfillment and the end of history as it was known, clearly shaped the consciousness of Israel after 70 just as had been the case in the decades before 70. So if to the sages of our legal system, history and the end of history were essentially beside the point and pivot, the construction of a world of cyclical eternities being the purpose and center, and the conduct of humble things like eating and drinking the paramount and decisive focus of the sacred, others saw things differently. To those who hoped and therefore fought, Israel's life had other meanings entirely.

The Second War proved still more calamitous than the First. In 70 the Temple was lost, in 135, even access to the city. In 70 the people, though suffering grievous losses, endured more or less intact. In 135 the land of Judah – surely the holiest part of the Holy Land – evidently lost the bulk of its Jewish population. Temple, Land, people – all were gone in the forms in which they had been known. In the generation following the calamity of Bar Kokhba, what would be the effect upon the formation of the system of halakhah of the Mishnah? It is to that question that we now turn.

## VIII. The Mishnah's Halakhah after the Wars: The System as a Whole

The halakhah reached its full and complete statement, as the Mishnah would present it, after the Bar Kokhba War. Over the next sixty years, from ca. 140 to ca. 200, the system as a whole took shape. To describe the completed halakhah, we survey the six divisions and their tractates and the main points covered in each.

The Division of Agriculture treats two topics, first, producing crops in accord with the scriptural rules on the subject, second, paying the required offerings and tithes to the priests, Levites, and poor. The principal point of the division is that the Land is holy, because God has a claim both on it and upon what it produces. God's claim must be honored by setting aside a portion of the produce for those for whom God has designated it. God's ownership must be acknowledged by observing the rules God has laid down for use of the Land. In sum, the division is divided along these lines: (1) rules for producing crops in a state of holiness – tractates Kilayim, Shebiit, Orlah; (2) rules for disposing of crops in accord with the rules of holiness – tractates Peah, Demai, Terumot, Maaserot, Maaser Sheni, Hallah, Bikkurim, Berakhot.

The Mishnaic Division of Appointed Times forms a system in which the advent of a holy day, like the Sabbath of creation, sanctifies the life of the Israelite village through imposing on the village rules on the model of those of the Temple. The purpose of the system, therefore, is to bring into alignment the moment of sanctification of the village and the life of the home with the moment of sanctification of the Temple on those same occasions of appointed times. The underlying and generative theory of the system is that the village is the mirror image of the Temple. If things are done in one way in the Temple, they will be done in the opposite way in the village. Together the village and the Temple on the occasion of the holy day therefore form a single continuum, a completed creation, thus awaiting sanctification.

The village is made like the Temple in that on appointed times one may not freely cross the lines distinguishing the village from the rest of the world, just as one may not freely cross the lines distinguishing the Temple from the world. But the village is a mirror image of the Temple. The boundary lines prevent free entry into the Temple, so they restrict free egress from the village. On the holy day what one may do in the Temple is precisely what one may not do in the village. So the advent of the holy day affects the village by bringing it into sacred symmetry in such wise as to effect a system of opposites; each is holy, in a way precisely the opposite of the other. Because of the underlying conception of perfection attained through the union of opposites, the village is not represented as conforming to the model of the cult, but of constituting its antithesis.

The world thus regains perfection when on the holy day heaven and earth are united, the whole completed and done: the heaven, the earth, and all their hosts. This moment of perfection renders the events of ordinary time, of "history," essentially irrelevant. For what really matters in time is that moment in which sacred time intervenes and effects the perfection formed of the union of heaven and earth, of Temple, in the model of the former, and Israel, its complement. It is not a return to a perfect time but a recovery of perfect being, a fulfillment of creation, which explains the essentially ahistorical character of the Mishnah's Division on Appointed Times. Sanctification constitutes an ontological category and is effected by the creator.

This explains why the division in its rich detail is composed of two quite distinct sets of materials. First, it addresses what one does in the sacred space of the Temple on the occasion of sacred time, as distinct from what one does in that same sacred space on ordinary, undifferentiated days, which is a subject worked out in Holy Things. Second, the division defines how for the occasion of the holy day one creates a corresponding space in one's own circumstance, and what one does, within that space, during sacred time. The issue of the Temple and cult on the special occasion of festivals is treated in tractates Pesahim, Sheqalim, Yoma, Sukkah, and Hagigah. Three further tractates, Rosh Hashshanah, Taanit, and Megillah, are necessary to complete the discussion. The matter of the rigid definition of the outlines in the village, of a sacred space, delineated by the limits within which one may move on the Sabbath and festival, and of the specification of those things which one may not do within that space in sacred time, is in Shabbat, Erubin, Besah, and Moed Qatan.

While the twelve tractates of the division appear to fall into two distinct groups, joined merely by a common theme, in fact they relate through a shared, generative metaphor. It is, as I said, the comparison, in the context of sacred time, of the spatial life of the Temple to the spatial life of the village, with activities and restrictions to be specified for each, upon the common occasion of the Sabbath or festival. The Mishnah's purpose therefore is to correlate the sanctity of the Temple, as defined by the holy day, with the restrictions of space and of action which make the life of the village different and holy, as defined by the holy day.

The Mishnaic system of Women defines the position of women in the social economy of Israel's supernatural and natural reality. That position acquires definition wholly in relationship to men, who impart form to the Israelite social economy. It is effected through both supernatural and natural, this-worldly action. What man and woman do on earth provokes a response in heaven, and the correspondences are perfect. So the position of women is defined and secured both in heaven and here on earth, and that position is always and invariably relative to men.

The principal interest for the Mishnah is the point at which a woman becomes, and ceases to be, holy to a particular man, that is, enters and leaves the marital union. These transfers of women are the dangerous and disorderly points in the relationship of woman to man, therefore, as I said, to society as well. Five of the seven tractates of the Division of Women are devoted to the formation and dissolution of the marital bond. Of them, three treat what is done by man here on earth, that is, formation of a marital bond through betrothal and marriage contract and dissolution through divorce and its consequences: Qiddushin, Ketubot, and Gittin. One of them is devoted to what is done by woman here on earth: Sotah. And Yebamot, greatest of the seven in size and in formal and substantive brilliance, deals with the corresponding heavenly intervention into the formation and end of a marriage: the effect of death upon both forming the marital bond and dissolving it through death. The other two tractates, Nedarim and Nazir, draw into one the two realms of reality, heaven and earth, as they work out the effects of vows, perhaps because vows taken by women and subject to the confirmation or abrogation of the father or husband make a deep impact upon the marital life of the woman who has taken them. So, in sum, the division and its system delineate the natural and supernatural character of the woman's role in the social economy framed by man: the beginning, end, and middle of the relationship.

The Mishnaic system of Women thus focuses upon the two crucial stages in the transfer of women and of property from one domain to another, the leaving of the father's house in the formation of a marriage, and the return to the father's house at its dissolution through divorce or the husband's death. There is yet a third point of interest, though, as is clear, it is much less important than these first two stages: the duration of the marriage. Finally, included within the division and at a few points relevant to women in particular are rules of vows and of the special vow to be a Nazir. The former is included because, in the scriptural treatment of the theme, the rights of the father or husband to annul the vows of a daughter or wife form the central problematic. The latter is included for no very clear reason except that it is a species of which the vow is the genus.

There is in the Division of Women a clearly defined and neatly conceived system of laws, not about women in general, but concerning what is important about women to the framers of the Mishnah. This is the transfer of woman and property from one domain, the father's, to another, the husband's, and back. The whole constitutes a significant part of the Mishnah's encompassing system of sanctification, for the reason that heaven confirms what men do on earth. A correctly prepared writ of divorce on earth changes the status of the woman to whom it is given, so that in heaven she is available for sanctification to some other man, while, without that same writ, in heaven's view, should she go to some other man, she would be liable to be put to death. The earthly deed and the heavenly perspective correlate. That is indeed very much part of larger system, which says the same thing over and over again.

The formation of the marriage comes under discussion in Qiddushin and Ketubot, as well as in Yebamot. The rules for the duration of the marriage are scattered throughout, but derive especially from parts of Ketubot, Nedarim, and Nazir, on the one side, and the paramount unit of Sotah, on the other. The dissolution of the marriage is dealt with in Gittin, as well as in Yebamot. We see very clearly, therefore, that important overall are issues of the transfer of property, along with women, covered in Ketubot and to some measure in Qiddushin, and the proper documentation of the transfer of women and property, treated in Ketubot and Gittin. The critical issues therefore turn upon legal documents – writs of divorce, for example – and legal recognition of changes in the ownership of property, for example, through the collection of the settlement of a marriage contract by a widow, through the provision of a dowry, or through the disposition of the property of a woman during the period in which she is married. Within this orderly world of documentary and procedural concerns a place is made for the disorderly conception of the marriage not formed by human volition but decreed in heaven, the levirate connection. Yebamot states that supernature sanctifies a woman to a man (under the conditions of the levirate connection). What it says by indirection is that man sanctifies, too: man, like God, can sanctify that relationship between a man and a woman, and can also effect the cessation of the sanctity of that same relationship.

The Division of Damages comprises two subsystems, which fit together in a logical way. One part presents rules for the normal conduct of civil society. These cover commerce, trade, real estate, and other matters of everyday intercourse, as well as mishaps, such as damages by chattels and persons, fraud, overcharge, interest, and the like, in that same context of everyday social life. The other part describes the institutions governing the normal conduct of civil society, that is, courts of administration, and the penalties at the disposal of the government for the enforcement of the law. The two subjects form a single tight and systematic dissertation on the nature of Israelite society and its economic, social, and political relationships, as the Mishnah envisages them.

The main point of the first of the two parts of the division is expressed in the sustained unfolding of the three Babas, Baba Qamma, Baba Mesia, and Baba Batra. It is that the task of society is to maintain perfect stasis, to preserve the prevailing situation, and to secure the stability of all relationships. To this end, in the interchanges of buying and selling, giving and taking, borrowing and lending, it is important that there be an essential equality of interchange. No party in the end should have more than what he had at the outset, and none should be the victim of a sizable shift in fortune and circumstance. All parties' rights to, and in, this stable and unchanging economy of society are to be preserved. When the condition of a person is violated, so far as possible the law will secure the restoration of the antecedent status.

An appropriate appendix to the Babas is at Abodah Zarah, which deals with the orderly governance of transactions and relationships between Israelite society and the outside world, the realm of idolatry, relationships which are subject to certain special considerations. These are generated by the fact that Israelites may not derive benefit (for example, through commercial transactions) from anything which has served in the worship of an idol. Consequently, commercial transactions suffer limitations on account of extrinsic considerations of cultic taboos. While these cover both special occasions, for example, fairs and festivals of idolatry, and general matters, that is, what Israelites may buy and sell, the main practical illustrations of the principles of the matter pertain to wine. The Mishnah supposes that gentiles routinely make use, for a libation, of a drop of any sort of wine to which they have access. It therefore is taken for granted that wine over which gentiles have had control is forbidden for Israelite use, and also that such wine is prohibited for Israelites to buy and sell. This other matter – ordinary everyday relationships with the gentile world, with special reference to trade and commerce – concludes what the Mishnah has to say about all those matters of civil and criminal law which together define everyday relationships within the Israelite nation and between that nation and all others in the world among whom, in Palestine as abroad, they lived side by side.

The other part of the division describes the institutions of Israelite government and politics. This is in two main aspects, first, the description of the institutions and their jurisdiction, with reference to courts, conceived as both judicial and administrative agencies, and, second, the extensive discussion of criminal penalties. The penalties are three: death, banishment, and flogging. There are four ways by which a person convicted of a capital crime may be put to death. The Mishnah organizes a vast amount of information on what sorts of capital crimes are punishable by which of the four modes of execution. That information is alleged to derive from Scripture. But the facts are many, and the relevant verses few. What the Mishnah clearly contributes to this exercise is a first-rate piece of organization and elucidation of available facts. Where the facts come from we do not know. The Mishnah tractate Sanhedrin further describes the way in which trials are conducted in both monetary and capital cases and pays attention to the possibilities of perjury. The matter of banishment brings the Mishnah to a rather routine restatement of punishment by flogging and application of that mode of punishment concludes the discussion.

These matters, worked out at Sanhedrin-Makkot, are supplemented in two tractates, Shebuot and Horayot, both emerging from Scripture. Lev. 5 and 6 refer to various oaths which apply mainly, though not exclusively, in courts. Lev. 4 deals with errors of judgment inadvertently made and carried out by the high priest, the ruler, and the people; the Mishnah knows that these considerations apply to Israelite courts, too. What for Leviticus draws the chapters together is their common interest in the guilt-offering, which is owing for violation of the rather diverse matters under discussion. Now in tractates Shebuot and Horayot the materials of Lev. 5-6 and 4, respectively, are worked out. But here is it from the viewpoint of the oath or erroneous instruction, rather than the cultic penalty. In Shebuot the discussion is intellectually imaginative and thorough, in Horayot, routine. The relevance of both to the issues of Sanhedrin and Makkot is obvious. For the matter of oaths in the main enriches the discussion of the conduct of the courts. The possibility of error is principally in the courts and other political institutions. So the four tractates on institutions and their functioning form a remarkable unified and cogent set.

The goal of the system of civil law is the recovery of the prevailing order and balance, the preservation of the established wholeness of the social economy. This idea is powerfully expressed in the organization of the three Babas, which treat first abnormal and then normal transactions. The framers deal with damages done by chattels and by human beings, thefts, and other sorts of malfeasance against the property of others. The Babas in both aspects pay closest attention to how the property and person of the injured party so far as possible are restored to their prior condition, that is, a state of normality. So attention to torts focuses upon penalties paid by the malefactor to the victim, rather than upon penalties inflicted by the court on the malefactor for what he has done. When speaking of damages, the Mishnah thus takes as its principal concern the restoration of the fortune of victims of assault or robbery. Then the framers take up the complementary and corresponding set of topics, the regulation of normal transactions. When we rapidly survey the kinds of transactions of special interest, we see from the topics selected for discussion what we have already uncovered in the deepest structure of organization and articulation of the basic theme.

The other half of this same unit of three tractates presents laws governing normal and routine transactions, many of them of the same sort as those dealt with in the first half. Bailments, for example, occur in both wings of the triple tractate, first, bailments subjected to misappropriation, or accusation thereof, by the bailiff, then, bailments transacted under normal circumstances. Under the rubric of routine transactions are those of workers and householders, that is, the purchase and sale of labor; rentals and bailments; real estate transactions; and inheritances and estates. Of the lot, the one involving real estate transactions is the most fully articulated and covers the widest range of problems and topics. The Babas all together thus provide a complete account of the orderly governance of balanced transactions and unchanging civil relationships within Israelite society under ordinary conditions.

The character and interests of the Division of Damages present probative evidence of the larger program of the philosophers of the Mishnah. Their intention is to create nothing less than a full-scale Israelite government, subject to the administration of sages. This government is fully supplied with a constitution and bylaws (Sanhedrin, Makkot). It makes provision for a court system and procedures (Shebuot, Sanhedrin, Makkot), as well as a full set of laws governing civil society (Baba Qamma, Baba Mesia, Baba Batra) and criminal justice (Sanhedrin, Makkot). This government, moreover, mediates between its own community and the outside ("pagan") world. Through its system of laws it expresses its judgment of the others and at the same time defines, protects, and defends its own society and social frontiers (Abodah Zarah). It even makes provision for procedures of remission, to expiate its own errors (Horayot).

The (then nonexistent) Israelite government imagined by the second-century philosophers centers upon the (then nonexistent) Temple, and the (then forbidden) city, Jerusalem. For the Temple is one principal focus. There the highest court is in session; there the high priest reigns. The penalties for law infringement are of three kinds, one of which involves sacrifice in the Temple. (The others are compensation, physical punishment, and death.) The basic conception of punishment, moreover, is that unintentional infringement of the rules of society, whether "religious" or otherwise, is not penalized but rather expiated through an offering in the Temple. If a member of the people of Israel intentionally infringes against the law, to be sure, that one must be removed from society and is put to death. And if there is a claim of one member of the people against another, that must be righted, so that the prior, prevailing status may be restored. So offerings in the Temple are given up to appease heaven and restore a whole bond between heaven and Israel, specifically on those occasions on which without malice or ill will an Israelite has disturbed the relationship. Israelite civil society without a Temple is not stable or normal, and not to be imagined. And the Mishnah is above all an act of imagination in defiance of reality.

The plan for the government involves a clear-cut philosophy of society, a philosophy which defines the purpose of the government and ensures that its task is not merely to perpetuate its own power. What the Israelite government, within the Mishnaic fantasy, is supposed to do is to preserve that state of perfection which, within the same fantasy, the society to begin with everywhere attains and expresses. This is in at least five aspects. First of all, one of the ongoing principles of the law, expressed in one tractate after another, is that people are to follow and maintain the prevailing practice of their locale. Second, the purpose of civil penalties, as we have noted, is to restore the injured party to his prior condition, so far as this is possible, rather than merely to penalize the aggressor. Third, there is the conception of true value, meaning that a given object has an intrinsic worth, which, in the course of a transaction, must be paid. In this way the seller does not leave the transaction any richer than when he entered it, or the buyer any poorer (parallel to penalties for damages). Fourth, there can be no usury, a biblical prohibition adopted and vastly enriched in the Mishnaic thought, for money ("coins") is what it is. Any pretense that it has become more than what it was violates, in its way, the conception of true value. Fifth, when real estate is divided, it must be done with full attention to the rights of all concerned, so that, once more, one party does not gain at the expense of the other. In these and many other aspects the law expresses its obsession with the perfect stasis of Israelite society. Its paramount purpose is in preserving and ensuring that that perfection of the division of this world is kept inviolate or restored to its true status when violated.

The Division of Holy Things presents a system of sacrifice and sanctuary: matters concerning the praxis of the altar and maintenance of the sanctuary. The praxis of the altar, specifically, involves sacrifice and things set aside for sacrifice and so deemed consecrated. The topic covers these among the eleven tractates of the present division: Zebahim and part of Hullin, Menahot, Temurah, Keritot, part of Meilah, Tamid, and Qinnim. The maintenance of the sanctuary (inclusive of the personnel) in dealt with in Bekhorot, Arakhin, part of Meilah, Middot, and part of Hullin.

Viewed from a distance, therefore, the Mishnah's tractates divide themselves up into the following groups (in parentheses are tractates containing relevant materials): (1) rules for the altar and the praxis of the cult – Zebahim Menahot, Hullin, Keritot, Tamid, Qinnim (Bekhorot, Meilah); (2) rules for the altar and the animals set aside for the cult – Arakhin, Temurah, Meilah (Bekhorot); and (3) rules for the altar and support of the Temple staff and buildings – Bekhorot, Middot (Hullin, Arakhin, Meilah, Tamid). In a word, this division speaks of the sacrificial cult and the sanctuary in which the cult is conducted. The law pays special attention to the matter of the status of the property of the altar and of the sanctuary, both materials to be utilized in the actual sacrificial rites, and property the value of which supports the cult and sanctuary in general. Both are deemed to be sanctified, that is: qodoshim, "Holy Things."

The system of Holy Things centers upon the everyday and rules always applicable to the cult: the daily whole-offering, the sin-offering and guilt-offering which one may bring any time under ordinary circumstances; the right sequence of diverse offerings; the way in which the rites of the whole-, sin-, and guilt-offerings are carried out; what sorts of animals are acceptable; the accompanying cereal-offerings; the support and provision of animals for the cult and of meat for the priesthood; the support and material maintenance of the cult and its building. We have a system before us: the system of the cult of the Jerusalem Temple, seen as an ordinary and everyday affair, a continuing and routine operation. That is why special rules for the cult, both in respect to the altar and in regard to the maintenance of the buildings, personnel, and even the hold city, will be elsewhere – in Appointed Times and Agriculture. But from the perspective of Holy Things, those divisions intersect by supplying special rules and raising extraordinary (Agriculture: land-bound; Appointed Times: time-bound) considerations for that theme which Holy Things claims to set forth in its most general and unexceptional way: the cult as something permanent and everyday.

The order of Holy Things thus in a concrete way maps out the cosmology of the sanctuary and its sacrificial system, that is, the world of the Temple, which had been the cosmic center of Israelite life. A later saying states matters as follows: "Just as the navel is found at the center of a human being, so the Land of Israel is found at the center of the world …and it is the foundation of the world. Jerusalem is at the center of the Land of Israel, the Temple is at the center of Jerusalem, the Holy of Holies is at the center of the Temple, the Ark is at the center of the Holy of Holies, and the Foundation Stone is in front of the Ark, which spot is the foundation of the world." (Tanhuma Qedoshim 10).

The Division of Purities presents a very simple system of three principal parts: sources of uncleanness, objects and substances susceptible to uncleanness, and modes of purification from uncleanness. So it tells the story of what makes a given sort of object unclean and what makes it clean. The tractates on these several topics are as follows: (1) sources of uncleanness – Ohalot, Negaim, Niddah, Makhshirin, Zabim, Tebul Yom; (2) objects and substances susceptible to uncleanness – Kelim, Tohorot, Uqsin; and (3) modes of purification – Parah, Miqvaot, Yadayim.

Viewed as a whole, the Division of Purities treats the interplay of persons, food, and liquids. Dry inanimate objects or food are not susceptible to uncleanness. What is wet is susceptible. So liquids activate the system. What is unclean, moreover, emerges from uncleanness through the operation of liquids, specifically, through immersion in fit water of requisite volume and in natural condition. Liquids thus deactivate the system. Thus, water in its natural condition is what concludes the process by removing uncleanness. Water in its unnatural condition, that is, deliberately affected by human agency, is what imparts susceptibility to uncleanness to begin with. The uncleanness of persons, furthermore, is signified by body liquids or flux in the case of the menstruating woman (Niddah) and the Zab (Zabim). Corpse uncleanness is conceived to be a kind of effluent, a viscous gas, which flows like liquid. Utensils for their part receive uncleanness when they form receptacles able to contain liquid. In sum, we have a system in which the invisible flow of fluidlike substances or powers serve to put food, drink, and receptacles into the status of uncleanness and to remove those things from that status. Whether or not we call the system "metaphysical," it certainly has no material base but is conditioned upon highly abstract notions. Thus in material terms, the effect of liquid is upon food, drink, utensils, and man. The consequence has to do with who may eat and drink what food and liquid, and what food and drink may be consumed in which pots and pans. These loci are specified by tractates on utensils (Kelim) and on food and drink (Tohorot and Uqsin).

The human being is ambivalent. Persons fall in the middle, between sources and loci of uncleanness, because they are both. They serve as sources of uncleanness. They also become unclean. The Zab, the menstruating woman, the woman after childbirth, the Tebul Yom, and the person afflicted with nega – all are sources of uncleanness. But being unclean, they fall within the system's loci, its program of consequences. So they make other things unclean and are subject to penalties because they are unclean. Unambiguous sources of uncleanness never also constitute loci affected by uncleanness. They always are unclean and never can become clean: the corpse, the dead creeping thing, and things like them. Inanimate sources of uncleanness and inanimate objects are affected by uncleanness. Systemically unique, man and liquids have the capacity to inaugurate the processes of uncleanness (as sources) and also are subject to those same processes (as objects of uncleanness). The Division of Purities, which presents the basically simple system just now described, is not only the oldest in the Mishnah, it also is the largest and contains by far the most complex laws and ideas.

### IX. The Outcome of the Development of the Halakhah Down to the Mishnah: Statement of the Whole

The critical issue in economic life, which means, in farming, is in two parts. First, Israel, as tenant on God's Holy Land, maintains the property in the ways God requires, keeping the rules which mark the Land and its crops as holy. Next, the hour at which the sanctification of the Land comes to form a critical mass, namely, in the ripened crops, is the moment ponderous with danger and heightened holiness. Israel's will so affects the crops as to mark a part of them as holy, the rest of them as available for common use. The human will is determinative in the process of sanctification. Second, what happens in the Land at certain times, at "appointed times," marks off spaces of the Land as holy in yet another way. The center of the Land and the focus of its sanctification is the Temple. There the produce of the Land is received and given back to God, the one who created and sanctified the Land. At these unusual moments of sanctification, the inhabitants of the Land in their social being in villages enter a state of spatial sanctification. That is to say, the village boundaries mark off holy space. This is expressed in two ways. First, the Temple itself observes and expresses the special, recurring holy time. Second, the villages of the Land are brought into alignment with the Temple, forming a complement and completion to the Temple's sacred being. The advent of the appointed times precipitates a spatial reordering of the Land, so that the boundaries of the sacred are matched and mirrored in village and in Temple. At the heightened holiness marked by these moments of appointed times, therefore, the occasion for an effective sanctification is worked out. Like the harvest, the advent of an appointed time such as a pilgrim festival is also a sacred season and is made to express that regular, orderly, and predictable sort of sanctification for Israel which the system as a whole seeks.

The counterpart of the Divisions of Agriculture and Appointed Times are Holy Things and Purities, dealing with the everyday and the ordinary, as against the special moments of harvest, on the one side, and special time or season, on the other. The Temple, the locus of sanctification, is conducted in a wholly routine and trustworthy, punctilious manner (Holy Things). The one thing which may unsettle matters is the intention and will of the human actor. This is subjected to carefully prescribed limitations and remedies. The Division of Holy Things generates its companion, the one on cultic cleanness, Purities. A system of cleanness, taking into account what imparts uncleanness and how this is done, what is subject to uncleanness, and how that state is overcome – that system is fully expressed, once more, in response to the participation of the human will. Without the wish and act of a human being, the system does not function. It is inert. Sources of uncleanness, which come naturally and not by volition, and modes of purification, which work naturally and not by human intervention, remain inert until human will has imparted susceptibility to uncleanness, that is, introduced into the system food and drink, bed, pot, chair, and pan, which to begin with form the focus of the system. The movement from sanctification to uncleanness takes place when human will and work precipitate it.

The middle divisions, the third and fourth, on Women and Damages, finally, take their place in the structure of the whole by showing the congruence, within the larger framework of regularity and order, of human concerns of family and farm, politics and workaday transactions among ordinary people. For without attending to these matters, the Mishnah's system does not encompass what, at its foundations, it is meant to comprehend and order. So what is at issue is fully cogent with the rest. In the case of Women, attention focuses upon the point of disorder marked by the transfer of that disordering anomaly, woman, from the regular status provided by one man, to the equally trustworthy status provided by another. That is the point at which the Mishnah's interests are aroused: once more, predictably, the moment of disorder. In the case of Damages, there are two important concerns. First, there is the paramount interest in preventing, so far as possible, the disorderly rise of one person and fall of another, and in sustaining the status quo of the economy of Israel, the holy society in stasis. Second, there is the necessary concomitant in the provision of a system of political institutions to carry out the laws which preserve the balance and steady state of persons.

The halakhic system presented by the Mishnah consists of a coherent logic and topic, a cogent worldview and comprehensive way of living. It is a worldview which speaks of transcendent things, a way of life in response to the supernatural meaning of what is done, a heightened and deepened perception of the sanctification of Israel in deed and in deliberation. Sanctification means two things, first, distinguishing Israel in all its dimensions from the world in all its ways; second, establishing the stability, order, regularity, predictability, and reliability of Israel at moments and in contexts of danger. Danger means instability, disorder, irregularity, uncertainty, and betrayal. Each topic of the system as a whole takes up a critical and indispensable moment or context of social being. Through what is said in regard to each of the Mishnah's principal topics, what the halakhic system as a whole wishes to declare is fully expressed. Yet if the parts severally and jointly give the message of the whole, the whole cannot exist without all of the parts, so well joined and carefully crafted are they all.

# 2

## Convenantal Nomism:
## The Piety of Judaism in the
## First Century

### I. The Limits of Our Knowledge

When we invoke the word "Judaism" in the study of the religion of first-century Jews in the Land of Israel, we introduce a category that no one at that time would have grasped. The "-ism" of Judaism defines this category. Through this classification we seek to describe that order, system, and encompassing doctrine which, all together, characterized Israel's common faith and holy way of life in the Land of Israel. But the evidence that would make possible such a description of a common worldview and way of life characteristic of the people, Israel, in its Land, does not come to hand.

To list the range of our ignorance: We do not know what the people as a whole thought, or how they felt, or what they did, because of faith in God and in the Torah. On the basis of contemporary evidence we cannot describe, from beginning to end, the course of a single individual's life. We do not have access either to the shared convictions of the people as a whole or to the singular manner in which an individual mediated, into a private mode of living, the people's religion and culture. We lack descriptions by external observers in communication with, and subject to the correction of, insiders. We have no records, letters, diaries, and the like, of participants in the religious culture. By contrast from the second century onward, we can take up the life and thought of important figures of Christianity. In sheer volume we have more knowledge of Augustine, for example, than we do of all individual Jews of the Land of Israel in the first century. Later on, moreover, for the mode of Judaism that became dominant, the way of life and worldview laid forth by the sages ("rabbis") of the Mishnah and its successor documents down to the Talmud of Babylonia, (ca. A.D. 200-600), we do have an official record for guidance. Through these documents we can know how an important group of people saw things and how they instructed the people to live. Even though we know little about what people actually did, the literary record, augmented by the archaeological testimonies, permits description of a world through the artifacts of people whose views we claim to portray.

For first-century Israel, by contrast, none of this is possible, since there is scarcely an individual portrayed through his or her own documents, and little evidence deriving from representative authors of the time and place. It follows that we cannot describe either the common theology or the shared piety, of the Jewish population of the country as a whole. There are no direct sources for this.

A second formidable difficulty derives from our intent on ordering what, in the time of which we speak, exhibited no such proportion and balance. The problem is not only that our knowledge of the facts exhibits flaws. It is also that, when we speak of an -ism such as "Judaism," we conceive of a systematic and orderly composition. But each of the documents in hand bears its own witness to its own system, and none permit us to imagine a single system that encompasses them all. Or, if we can identify such a single Judaism that will accommodate every kind of evidence, the system and order prove rather vacuous, too abstract and general to bear much heuristic sense. The upshot is that the concept, "Judaism," turns out to tell us rather less than, in resorting to it, we might wish.

## II. The Nature of the Sources

What, then, is the kind of evidence for the piety of Judaism that we do have? It consists, on the one side, of writings emerging from small groups ("sects"), and, on the other, of parts of libraries preserved by groups that later enjoyed a dominance they could not have at first imagined possible. Into the former category fall those parts of the Gospels that not only refer to, but derive from, the Land of Israel and its Jews, as well as those components of the Essene library at Qumran that were written down in the first century. In the latter category we find the canon of Judaism from the Mishnah through the Talmud of Babylonia, which presents convictions about ideas held in the first century, or portrays events that then took place. These, it is claimed, were handed on through time. But they were given authoritative status in writing only much later, as in the Mishnah and its associated documents. Out of the Land of Israel in the first century, we have only the pseudepigraphic writings that appeal to the authority of earlier holy men, such as Ezra or Baruch, and the works of Josephus. There is practically nothing else deriving from the Land of Israel in the first century.

What "Judaism" did or did not teach must, in the end, therefore be garnered from evidence not for a single homogeneous and monolithic "Judaism," as a national way of life and commonly held worldview. Rather, we know about "Judaisms," ways of life and worldviews framed by distinct and not necessarily representative groups. In no way did such groups claim to speak about, or for, or even to, all Israel. However, the absence of a recognized and well-documented orthodoxy, such as did emerge in the Judaism defined by the later authoritative canon of the ancient sages, that is, the orthodoxy system summarized in the Talmud of Babylonia and associated writings, does not present insuperable obstacles. Any sketch of the piety of the nation-religion to invoke the two appropriate, if anachronistic, categories, will appeal to two distinct approaches to the available evidence.[1] First, we may ask about common denominators. Second, we may sort out the points of special emphasis, that is differences, characteristic of various groups ("sects"), whose writings we do have. In this way we may gain some perspective on the common denominators.

The principal common denominator must in social terms derive from the ordinary people called *am haares*.[2] The piety of Judaism comes to expression – speaking descriptively – when we know, or can credibly surmise, what the ordinary folk had in mind. Access to their wit and imagination, to the givens of their everyday lives as individuals and as a large and, in important aspects, homogeneous group, will permit us entry into the piety of Judaism. How so? As we stated, comparison between the generality of the people, on the one side, and the points of emphasis of particular groups, on the other, allows us to sort out differences and gain perspective on the totality. If we could have a grasp of the points of special interest of such groups, we might then hope to

---

[1] "Nation" is anachronistic for the period at hand, and "religion" also imposes a distinction between secular and sacred that at this time few in Israel would have grasped. Israel was a people of a shared Scripture and collective consciousness – hence, we should invoke the term "nation." Israel assuredly framed its way of life and worldview in ways we should regard as religious, believing that God wanted things as they were. But, as is clear, we have to take note of the imposition, by us, of a category at that time not available.

[2] The *am haares* – people of the Land – would correspond in general to the Roman *paganus*. In the rabbinic writings they defined the category of "outsider," as distinct from the insider, who engaged in certain approved practices. Later on the term acquired the still more negative sense of "total ignoramus," ordinarily applied to anyone with whom a learned man does not agree.

know what Israelites generally understood to be, and practiced as, the way of life of Judaism. Alongside, what people commonly perceived that way of life to have meant, the ethos of the religion, the people as a whole, will emerge.

## III. The Four Pillars of Second Temple Judaism

That is not to suggest we may identify no common and unifying core, even though the conception that we speak of a well-composed system of ideas, that is, Judaism, seems not entirely justified. James D.G. Dunn has set forth a sound account:

> We can still speak of a common and unifying core for second Temple Judaism, a fourfold foundation on which all these more diverse forms of Judaism built, a common heritage which they all interpreted in their own ways. We cannot say that the four common elements were Judaism, since each group or "sect" differed in emphasis and understanding and in the way it brought the common core to expression. Even when Ioudaismos ("Judaism") is used in texts of the time, it may well have included something at least of a sectarian understanding of the term. Nevertheless, the fact remains that the word could be used; there was something recognizable as "Judaism," something common to these various diverse expressions of second Temple Judaism(s).[3]

Dunn's four pillars are [1] monotheism; [2] the conviction that Israel was chosen by God, "that the one God had bound himself to Israel and Israel to himself by a special contract or covenant"; [3] the centrality of the Torah in Israel's self-consciousness of being God's chosen people; and [4] the role of the Temple at the center of Israel's national and religious life at that time. Corollaries of the basic axiom of covenantal nomism identified by Dunn are [a] Israel's distinctiveness as the people specifically chosen by the one God to be his people; [b] the sense of privilege in being the nation specially chosen by the one God and favored by gift of covenant and law. This was expressed in concrete terms in circumcision, the Sabbath, and the dietary laws. Dunn concludes:

> These then can be fairly described as the four pillars on which the Judaism(s) of Jesus' time was built: the axiomatic convictions around which the more diverse interpretations and practices of the different groups within Judaism revolved.

---

[3]*The Partings of the Ways between Christianity and Judaism and Their Significance for the Character of Christianity* (London: SCM Press, and Philadelphia: Trinity Press International, 1991), pp. 18-36.

No one familiar with the Old Testament will call into question Dunn's judgment of the covenantal foundations for the nomism of Judaism, as herein defined. But while outlining the givens of all Judaic systems, Dunn's account may not prove entirely congruent to the character of any given documentary statement of a concrete Judaism, for example, the Mishnah, or the Manual of Discipline; setting specific statements side by side for comparison, we may well wonder how profound the weight of any one of them is borne by these (and other possible) "pillars." In these four points, we identify what we must call the lowest common denominator that characterizes all Judaic systems equally. But we should understand none of them by appeal only to these four fundamental traits of mind and faith. For what each Judaic system had in common with others proves, as we shall see, systemically inert, hardly active, let alone definitive, in setting forth what to any given Judaism proved its critical point: its self-evidently valid answer to the question it identified as urgent and immediate. But it is that urgent question that leads us to the center of any given Judaic system; what was a given to all systems gave life and power to none of them. So much for the four pillars that, admittedly, sustained every Judaism – but, as we shall see, tell us what is important about no one of them.

## IV. From the Particular to the General

Where are we to begin? In seeking definitions, we do best to start with the negative. The piety of Judaism is not a "philosophy" nor the outcome of a philosophy. We must be guided by the excellent observations of Morton Smith, who states:

> It must be remembered that Judaism to the ancient world was a philosophy. That world had no general term for religion. It could speak of a particular system of rites or a particular set of beliefs or a legal code or a body of national customs or traditions; but for the peculiar synthesis of all these which we call a "religion," the one Hellenistic word which came closest was "philosophy."[4]

What we want to know, however, is not the "philosophy" of Judaism in the Greco-Roman sense. Ours is a different question. We ask about the religious experience in the formation of culture, in the bonding of society, and in the conduct of everyday life, which was afforded by that cogent system, way of life, and worldview, addressed to that single social group, Israel, we today evoke when we use the word "Judaism." For this quest the data of the Greco-Roman philosophical vocabulary prove irrelevant. We may simply assume that, in the Land of Israel in the first century C.E.

---

[4]"Palestinian Judaism in the First Century," in M. Davis, ed., *Israel: Its Role in Civilization* (New York, 1956: Harper), p. 79.

as through much of human history, nearly everywhere, such a religious system, such an "-ism," bearing doctrines about the supernatural, did serve to define culture, frame society, and impart order and meaning to the personal and common life.

Our second negative, yielding a more concrete and positive approach to piety, brings us to those distinctive points of emphasis that separated each group from others. We know not about the people at large but only about sects. I refer to the distinctive groups, separate from the commonality of Israel, about which we do have information. For if we do not know what the people as a whole believed, we have ample access to small groups, for example, records deriving from the Essenes and Pharisees, and disciples of Jesus, contemporary stories concerning the activities of coherent political and social groups, and other data about distinctive and hardly representative elements of the nation as a whole. Our task in utilizing the data concerning, and even coming from, such special groups is simple. First, we must describe the emphases of small components of the larger social construct. Second, we have to ask how what we know about the particular groups may inform us about what was held in common.

To investigate the piety of Judaism as the common faith of the people, I shall describe three sects' religions, representing three "Judaisms," seen as ideal types and then ask what, to the shared or common religious life, is contributed by each ideal type. By spelling out what characterized these ideal types and interpreting their definitive traits or points of emphasis in the context of ordinary life, we may thus move from the special to the general.

Since we are seeking to describe and interpret modes of piety within the Israel of late antiquity, we seek to imagine from what people said and did, how things appeared to groups of people whom we now know only at a considerable distance. In doing this we have to treat the mixed as pure. To begin with, we have to sort out the different strands of these groups' faith and to characterize each one. The principal strands that are discernible emerge in the distinct types of holy men we know as priests, scribes, and messiahs, and in the definitive activities of cult, school and government offices, and (ordinarily) the battlefield. Ancient Israel's heritage yielded the cult with its priests, the Torah with its scribes and teachers, and the prophetic and apocalyptic hope for meaning in history and an eschaton mediated by messiahs and generals. From these derive the three elements indicated: Temple, school, and (in the apocalyptic expectation) battlefield on earth and in heaven.

## V. Three Types of Israelite Piety

In positing these three ideal types of Israelite piety – the priestly, the scribal, the messianic[5] – we must suspend for the moment our disbelief that things could have ever been so simple. Indeed, we recognize the contrary, their complexity. The troops of a messianic army also observed Scripture's sacred calendar. Their goal was not only to enthrone the King-Messiah, their general, but also to rebuild the Temple, reestablish the priesthood, and restore the sacrificial cult. Moreover, that the Messiah's army valued the scribal heritage is readily apparent in the writings which Bar Kokhba's troops preserved.[6] These include women's carefully wrapped up documents covering divorces and marriage settlements, land titles, and other scribal deeds. The Essene community at Qumran also united the themes we treat as separate: priesthood, Messiah, Torah study. Among the earliest writers in Jewish Christianity, Jesus finds ample representation not only as King-Messiah, but as Prophet, perfect priest, and sacrificial victim, and always as sage or rabbi (which is why most of the sublime ethical sayings ascribed to him in fact are commonplaces in other versions of Judaism). Accordingly, none of the symbolic systems at hand, with their associated modes of piety, faith, and religious imagination, ever existed pure and unalloyed, ideal types awaiting singular description and interpretation as we treat them here.

To seek a typology of the modes of Israelite piety, we must look for the generative symbol of each mode: an altar for the priestly ideal, a scroll of Scripture for the scribal ideal of wisdom, a coin marked "Israel's freedom: year one" for the messianic modality. In each of these visual symbols we perceive things we cannot touch, hearts and minds we can only hope to evoke. We seek to enter into people's imagination, long ago and far away. Our effort is to understand the way in which they framed the world, and encapsulated everything in some one thing: the sheep for the sacrifice, the memorized aphorism for the disciple, the stout heart for the soldier of light. Priest, sage, soldier – each figure stands for the whole of Israel. When all would meld into one, there would emerge a

---

[5]There now seems a somewhat curious disjuncture between Dunn's four pillars and the three ideal types of Israelite piety dealt with here. Land, Torah, chosenness, monotheism – all presumably bore deep meaning to all three types; but what was important to the several types in these categories is not to be gainsaid. For the scribe, for instance, while Torah stood at the center, monotheism although a given hardly formed a generative category of thought, and God in the Mishnah is part of the scarcely articulated background.

[6]See Yigael Yadin, *Bar Kokhba* (New York, 1971: Random House), and Peter Schaefer, "The Causes of the Bar Kokhba Revolt," in *Studies in Aggadah, Targum, and Jewish Liturgy in Memory of Joseph Heinemann* (Jerusalem, 1981), pp. 74-94. Schaefer provides an up-to-date bibliography on the topic.

fresh and unprecedented Judaism, whether among the heirs of scribes and Pharisees or among the disciples of Christ.

The issues of the symbols under discussion – Temple altar, sacred scroll, victory wreath for the head of the King-Messiah – largely covered Jewish society.   We need not reduce them to their merely social dimensions to recognize that in them we deal with the foundations of the organization of Israelite society and its interpretation of its history.   Let us rapidly review the social groups envisaged and addressed by the framers of these symbols.

First, the priest viewed society as organized along lines of structure emanating from the Temple.  His caste stood at the top of a social scale in which all things were properly organized, each with its correct name and proper place.  The inherent sanctity of the people of Israel, through the priest's genealogy, came to its richest embodiment in the high priest. Food set aside for the priests' rations, at God's command, possessed that same sanctity; so, too, did the table at which priests ate their rations.  To the priest, for the sacred society of Israel, history was an account of what happened in, and (alas) on occasion to, the Temple.[7]

Secondly, to the sage, the life of society demanded wise regulation. Relationships among people required guidance by the laws enshrined in the Torah and best interpreted by scribes.   The task of Israel was to construct a way of life in accordance with the revealed rules of the Torah. The sage, master of the rules, stood at the head.

Thirdly, as for prophecy's insistence that the fate of the nation depended upon the faith and moral condition of society, history testified both to events outside its borders and to the inner condition of Israel, viewed as a whole.  While both sage and priest saw Israel from the aspect of eternity, the nation had to live out its life in this world, among other peoples coveting the very same land, and within the context of Roman imperial policies and politics.  The Messiah's kingship would resolve the issue of Israel's subordinate relationship to other nations and empires, establishing once and for all the desirable, correct context for priest and sage alike.

Implicit, therefore, in the messianic framework was a perspective on the world beyond Israel for which priest and sage cared not at all.  The priest perceived the receding distances of the world beyond the Temple as, at first, less holy, then, unholy, then, unclean, as at M. Kelim 1:1-4.  All lands outside the Land of Israel were unclean with corpse uncleanness; all other peoples were unclean just as corpses were unclean. Accordingly, life abided within Israel, and, in Israel, within the Temple.

---

[7]This viewpoint finds expression in the priestly narratives, e.g., in Leviticus and Chronicles.

Outside, in the far distance, were vacant lands and dead peoples, comprising an undifferentiated wilderness of death – a world of uncleanness. From such a perspective on the world, no doctrine about Israel among the nations, no interest in the history of Israel and its meaning, was apt to emerge.

The sagacity of the sage, in general, pertained to the streets, marketplaces, and domestic establishments (the household units) of Israel. What the sage said was wisdom, indeed, as much for gentiles as for Israel. This universal wisdom in the nature of things proved international, moving easily across the boundaries of culture and language, from eastern to southern to western Asia. It focused, by definition, upon human experience common to all and undifferentiated by nation, essentially unaffected by the large movements of history. Wisdom spoke about fathers and sons, masters and disciples, families and villages, not about nations, armies, and destiny.

Because of their very diversity these three principal modes of Israelite existence might readily cohere. Each focused on a particular aspect of the national life, and none essentially contradicted any other. One could worship at the Temple, study the Torah, and fight in the army of the Messiah – and some did all three. Yet we must see these modes of being, and their consequent forms of piety, as separate, each with its own potentiality of full realization without reference to the others.

The three modes of human existence expressed in the symbolic systems of cult, Torah, and Messiah demanded choices. If one thing was more important, then the others must have been less important. Either history matters, or it happens, without significance, "out there." The proper conduct of the cult determines the course of the seasons and the prosperity of the Land, or it is merely ritual. The Messiah will save Israel, or he will ruin everything. Accordingly, while we take for granted that people could have lived within the multiple visions of priest, sage, and Messiah, we also recognize such a life was vertiginous, inducing a blurred perception. Narratives of the war of 66-73 emphasize that priests warned messianists not to endanger their Temple. Later sages –Talmudic rabbis – paid slight regard to the messianic struggle led by Bar Kokhba, and after 70 claimed the right to tell priests what to do.[8]

It must follow that the way in which symbols were arranged and rearranged was crucial. Symbol change is social change. A mere amalgam of all three symbols by itself hardly serves as a mirror for the

---

[8]On the later rabbis' views of Bar Kokhba, note Y. Ta. 4:5 as a representative case. Bar Kokhba was held to have sinned through his arrogance, and, by the way, also to have mistreated and murdered sages. On rabbis telling priests what to do, see J. Neusner, *Life of Yohanan ben Zakkai* (Leiden, 1970: E.J. Brill), pp. 196-227.

mind of Israel. The particular way the three were bonded in a given system reflects an underlying human and social reality. That is how it should be, since, as we saw, the three symbols with their associated myths, the worldviews they projected, and the ways of life they defined, stood for different views of what really matters. In investigating the existential foundations of the several symbolic systems available to Jews in antiquity, we penetrate to the bedrock of Israel's reality, to the basis of the life of the nation and of each Israelite, to the ground of being – even to the existential core that we the living share with them.

## VI. Responses to Time and Eternity

Let us unpack the two foci of existence, public history and private establishment of home and hearth. We may call the first focus "time." Its interest is in *events* that happen day by day in the here and now of continuing history. The other focus we may call "eternity." Its interest is in the recurrent *patterns* of life, birth and death, planting and harvest, the regular movement of the sun, moon, stars in heaven, night and day, Sabbaths, festivals, and regular seasons on earth. The shared existential issue is this: How do we respond to the ups and downs of life? Every group that survives experiences the noteworthy events we call "history." The events of the individual life – birth, maturing, marriage, death – do not make history, except for individuals. But the events of group life, the formation of groups, the development of social norms and patterns, depression and prosperity, war and peace – these do make history. When a small people coalesces and begins its course though history in the face of adversity, two things can happen. Either the group may disintegrate in the face of disaster and lose its hold on its individual members, or the group may fuse, being strengthened by trial, and so turn adversity into renewal.

The modes around which human and national existence were interpreted – those of priests, sages, and messianists (including Prophets and apocalyptists) – emerge, we must remember, from the national and social consciousness of ancient Israel. The heritage of the Written Torah (*Tanakh*, the Hebrew Scriptures or "Old Testament") was carried forward in all three approaches to Judaism. The Jewish people knew the mystery of how to endure through history. In ancient Israel adversity elicited self-conscious response. Things did not merely *happen* to Israelites. They shaped, reformulated, and interpreted them, and so treated events as raw material for renewing the life of the group. Israelites regarded their history as important, teaching significant lessons. History was not merely "one damn thing after another." It had a purpose and was moving somewhere. The writers of Leviticus and Deuteronomy, of the historical books from Joshua through Kings, and of the prophetic literature, agreed that, when Israel did God's will, it enjoyed times of peace, security, and prosperity; when it did not, it was punished at the hands of mighty kingdoms raised up as instruments of God's wrath. This conception of the meaning of Israel's life produced another question: How long? When would the great events of time come to their climax and conclusion? And as one answer to that question, there arose the hope for the Messiah, the anointed of God, who would redeem the people and set them on the right path forever, thus ending the vicissitudes of history.

Now when we reach the first century A.D., we come to a turning point in the messianic hope. No one who knows the Gospels will be surprised to learn of the intense, vivid, prevailing expectation among some groups that the Messiah was coming soon. And that anticipation is hardly astonishing. People who fix their attention on contemporary events of world-shaking dimensions naturally look to a better future. That represents one context for the messianic myth.

More surprising is the development among the people of Israel of a second, quite different response to history. It is the response of those prepared once and for all to transcend historical events and to take their leave of wars and rumors of wars, of politics and public life. These persons undertook to construct a new reality beyond history, one that focused on the meaning of humdrum everyday life. After 70 there was no mere craven or exhausted passivity in the face of world-shaking events. We witness, in particular among the sages after 70 ultimately represented in the Mishnah, the beginnings of an active construction of a new mode of being. Their decision was to exercise freedom uncontrolled by history, to reconstruct the meaning and ultimate significance of events. That is to seek a world not outside this one formed by ordinary history, but a different and better world. This second approach was a quest for eternity in the here and now, an effort to form a society capable of abiding amid change and stress. Indeed, it was a fresh reading of the meaning of history. The nations of the world suppose that they make "history" and think that their actions matter. But these sages in Israel knew that it is God who makes history, and that it is the reality formed in response to God's will that counts as history: God is the King of kings of kings.

This conception of time and change, in fact, formed the focus of the earlier priestly tradition, which was continued later in the Judaism called rabbinic or Talmudic. This sort of Judaism offered essentially a meta-historical approach to life. It lived above history and its problems. It expressed an intense inwardness. The Judaism attested in the rabbis' canon of writings emphasized the ultimate meaning contained within small and humble affairs. Rabbinic Judaism came in time to set itself up as the alternative to all forms of messianic Judaism – whether in the form of Christianity or militaristic zealotry and nationalism – which claimed to know the secret of history, the time of salvation and way to redemption. But paradoxically the canonical writings of rabbis also disclosed the answers to these questions. The Messiah myth was absorbed into the rabbis' system and made to strengthen it. The rabbinical canon defined in a new way the uses and purposes of all else that had gone before.[9]

This approach to the life of Israel, stressing continuity and pattern and promising change only at the very end, when all would be in order at the last, represents the union of two trends. The one was symbolized by the altar, the other by the Torah scroll, the priest and the sage. In actual fact, the union was effected by a special kind of priest manqué, and a special kind of sage. The former was the Pharisee, the latter the scribe.

The Pharisees were a particular sect of people who pretended, in their homes, that they were priests in the Temple. The scribes, on the other hand, were members not of a sect but of a profession. The scribes knew and taught Torah. They took their interpretation of Torah very seriously, and the act of study for them had special importance. The Pharisees had developed, for their part, a peculiar perception of how to live and interpret life. We may call this an "as if" perception. In very specific ways the Pharisees claimed to live "as if" they were priests, "as if" they had to obey at home the laws that applied to the Temple. When the Temple was destroyed in 70, the Pharisees were prepared for that tremendous event. They continued to live "as if" the Temple stood, and "as if" there were a new Temple composed of the Jewish people.

These, then, represent the different ways in which great events were experienced and understood by special groups. One was the historical messianic way, stressing the intrinsic importance of events and concentrating upon their weight and meaning. The other was the meta-historical, scribal-priestly-rabbinic way, which emphasized Israel's power of transcendence and the construction of an eternal, changeless mode of being in this world, capable of riding out the waves of history.

---

[9]That is to say, the established categories, e.g., Torah, Messiah, priest, sacrifice, and the like, all were taken over by the rabbis of the two Talmuds and given new meaning. The study of Torah, for one instance, was held to be equivalent to making a Temple sacrifice; the Messiah was represented as a learned rabbi; the Torah was no longer a single, written Scripture but encompassed all of the writings of sages themselves, beginning with the Mishnah. So while the categories remained fixed, the meaning imputed to them vastly changed. As is clear, the Christians did the same thing, e.g., in Hebrews with the priest, sacrifice, and Temple.

Once we have identified the principal strands of Judaic consciousness, we must deal with this pressing question. What made one particular focus – the priestly and the sagacious, or the messianic, trend – appear more compelling than the other? The answer becomes obvious when we realize that each kind of piety addressed its distinctive concern, speaking about different things to different people. We may sort out the types of piety from one another if we return to our earlier observations. Priests and sages turned inward, toward the concrete everyday life of the community. They addressed the *sanctification* of Israel. Messianists and their prophetic and apocalyptic teachers turned outward, toward the affairs of states and nations. They spoke of the *salvation* of Israel. Priests saw the world of life in Israel, and death beyond. They knew what happened to Israel without concerning themselves with a theory about the place of Israel among the nations. For priests, the nations formed an undifferentiated realm of death. Sages, all the more, spoke of home and hearth, fathers and sons, husbands and wives, the village and enduring patterns of life. What place was there in this domestic scheme for the realities of history – wars and threats of war, the rise and fall of empires? It rather expressed the consciousness of a singular society amidst other societies. At issue for the priest was "being," for the Prophet and Messiah, "becoming."

In the light of these distinctive and partial formulations of a worldview and way of life, how shall we gain access to a general picture of the whole? For, as we have emphasized, we realize that what we know comes to us from distinct and special groups, each with its own emphasis, whether embodied in the Messiah or the scribe or the priest – or in all of them all together. Let me state with appropriate emphasis: *To learn about Judaism, in particular the inner piety in the first-century Jews, we have to place in perspective what we know, which concerns the special, and then proceed to extrapolate from the known to the unknown, which involves the general.*

Specifically, let us ask how what is uncommon and sectarian testifies to what was shared, the common piety of the people in its land. Once more, for a definitive summary of what is known about first-century Judaism on the basis of the distinctive and special evidence in hand, we turn to Morton Smith, who states:

> In sum, then, the discoveries and research of the past twenty-five years have left us with a picture of Palestinian Judaism in the first century far different from that conceived by earlier students of the period. We now see a Judaism which had behind it a long period of thoroughgoing Hellenization – Hellenization modified, but not thrown off, by the revival of nationalism and nationalistic and antiquarian interest in native tradition and classic language (an interest itself typically

Hellenistic). As the Greek language had permeated the whole country, so Greek thought, in one way or another, had affected the court and the commons, the Temple and the tavern, the school and the synagogue. If there was any such thing, then, as an "orthodox Judaism," it must have been that which is now almost unknown to us, the religion of the average "people of the land." But the different parts of the country were so different, such gulfs of feeling and practice separated Idumea, Judea, Caesarea, and Galilee, that even on this level there was probably no more agreement between them than between any one of them and a similar area in the Diaspora. And in addition to the local differences, the country swarmed with special sects, each devoted to its own tradition. Some of these, the followings of particular Prophets, may have been spontaneous revivals of Israelite religion as simple as anything in Judges. But even what little we know of these Prophets suggests that some of them, at least, taught a complex theology. As for the major philosophic sects – the Pharisees, Sadducees, and Essenes – the largest and ultimately the most influential of them, the Pharisees, numbered only about 6000, had no real hold either on the government or on the masses of the people, and was, as were the others, profoundly Hellenized.... This period of Palestinian Jewish history, then, is the successor to one marked by great receptivity to outside influences. It is itself characterized by original developments of those influences. These developments, by their variety, vigor, and eventual significance, made this small country during this brief period the seedbed of the subsequent religious history of the Western world.

Smith's picture leads us to the critical question. As stated, we must move from the particular to the general, from the evidence cherished by small groups to the larger totality taken for granted in that evidence but not attested in a particular by any of it. In the light of Smith's correct stress on the disagreements and differences characteristic of the country, its sects, and divided people, we have now to address the points they shared in common, we seek the bridges across diverse experiences and practices that characterized distinct regions, social groups, and layers and levels of society, however differentiated, and characterized by special traditions.

## VII. "Orthodox" Judaism

Using the word in the loosest sense, we ask, therefore, how we may describe "orthodox" "Judaism," which intersects with what Dunn has described as "four pillars." The use of "Judaism" has already been explained. What of "orthodox"? By "orthodox" we here understand simply the commonly practiced way of life, the generally shared worldview, characteristic – as a matter of fact – of the Jewish population in the Land of Israel. If we wish to choose the three critical elements in the common piety of a "religion-people," they should surely include mode of address to God, hence, prayer; mode of revelation from God, hence, the encounter with revelation; and mode of workaday expression of what is revealed, hence, those aspects of everyday life that imparted meaning to the whole. In the case of Israel in its land, we wish to know:

1.   the prayers people generally said;
2.   the revelation they commonly recognized and how they made it their own;
3.   the cycle of the natural year and of history and how, at specified points, its turnings uniformly turned people to the divine.

Here our interest is in piety, not in the -ism called "Judaism," and hence we part company from Dunn's definition, at the same time readily acknowledging the correctness of his conception of "covenantal nomism." In these three aspects, however, we gain some access to not rather generalized verbal affirmations ("monotheism" or "chosenness") but rather definitive traits of the worldview and way of life and piety of the social group at hand. But how, in the light of what we know about special and particular groups and their Judaisms, do we justify the selection of the specified categories as the valid ones for the description of that piety? If we revert to the three foci of piety designated as distinctive or particular to special groups, represented by priest, sage, and Messiah, we may see in the categories at hand a statement in general terms of the emphasis of a singular ideal type. How so?

1.   The address to God in prayer for the generality of Israel corresponds to the special case of the priests' service in the cult.

2.   The inquiry into revelation and the hearing of God's message form the counterpart to the scribes' distinctive focus on learning.

3.   The quest, in everyday life, for what imparted meaning to history brought Israelites to the Messiah aspect. For the Messiah theme was one mode by which small groups of people imparted meaning to the historical life of the nation as a whole. So here, in each case, we find the bridge from the particular to the general.

## VIII. The Definitive Role of Scripture:
### The Old Testament and the Definition of the
### Common Faith of Judaism

Clearly, Scripture – *Tanakh* or the Written Torah in Judaism, the Old Testament in Christianity – formed the principal source of information on what could have been held in common among all Israel in its land. Scripture, of course, provided not only what united, but also what divided, the community. Meanings imputed to verses served as indicators of what was defined as special to a group that was otherwise quite undifferentiated within the people as a whole. Each special group read the Scriptures in its own way. So, too, the Temple and its cult, the focus of national institutions and politics, united most Israelites into a single community. At the same time, the group's definition of its relationship to the Temple indicated what was special about that small group. For example, imitating the Temple cult, by eating ordinary meals, in accord with the levitical regulations that dictated conduct of priests at the altar and in the holy place, in part defined what was particular about Pharisees and Essenes. Widely held convictions about the character of the people as especially loved by God found general acceptance in a shared view of the sanctified character of the people and the Land, as well as of the heightened meaning of what happened to the one and in the other.

So when distinct groups took up positions of their own on questions of history and salvation, on procedures of the cult and sanctification, they stood on a single continuum. They adopted singular and special positions within categories characteristic of the people and shared by them as a whole. In turning to the general categories at hand – prayer, the encounter with revelation, the common way of life followed throughout the year – what do we find as a bridge from sect to nation-religion? We take up precisely those divisions in the classification of the worldview and way of life of the nation-religion that differentiated and characterized distinct groups ("sects") about which we indeed are well-informed. That is how we work backward from the known, the special, to the besought, the general. We find that, in the distinctive, in fact we deal with extreme and special statements of what was shared and commonplace. These commonalities then defined the foci of special concern to distinct groups. So we turn to the components of the common piety of first-century Judaism.

## IX. Prayer

The worship of God encompassed sacrifice in the Temple and prayer outside. The priestly code, Leviticus 1-15, lays out the requirements of the former, as these were defined by the time of Ezra and Nehemiah. The substance of the prayers outside the Temple presents a puzzle, because we do not have direct evidence of how people ordinarily prayed beyond the walls of the holy place. On the basis of the statement, "Simeon Happaqoli arranged the Eighteen Benedictions in their proper order under the authority of Rabban Gamaliel in Jamnia" (Bavli Berakhot 28b), the acknowledged expert on the subject, Joseph Heinemann, states:

> We may safely conclude...that the evolution of the fixed prayers began hundreds of years before the destruction of the Second Temple and reached the period of consolidation and editing...in the generation following the destruction of the Temple, at that time the details of the principal obligatory prayers and the laws which govern them were fixed.... The basic structures and content of the prayers determined at that time have never since been altered, and to this very day constitute the essential components of the Jewish liturgy.[10]

Sayings attributed to authorities after 70 deal with the formalization of details of practices assumed to be familiar and defined by that time. The authenticity of these attributions to authorities between 70 and 130 cannot be proved. But secondary opinions on the same matters make their appearance in the names of authorities a generation later, after 135. It therefore does not appear unreasonable to assume that the first two generations of authorities after 70, and assuredly the latter of the two, did legislate concerning the regularization of well-established practices. The intent of the legislation proves clearer than the final date of its literary formulation. That intent was to establish some sort of common order and practice from among diverse traditions.

If we turn to the particular prayers which people generally used, our evidence derives from the Mishnah, which attained closure only about a century and a quarter after the destruction. Recognizing the uncertainty involved, we note the prayers that the framers of the Mishnah, in the name of earlier authorities, catalogued. In its account of the Temple rites, the authorship of Mishnah-tractate Tamid provides the following:

A. The superintendent said to them, "Say one blessing."

B. They [the priests] said a blessing, pronounced the Ten Commandments, the *Shema* [*Hear O Israel* (Deut. 6:4-9)], *And it shall come to pass if you shall hearken* (Deut. 11:13-21), and *And the Lord spoke to Moses* (Num. 15:37-41).

C. They said three blessings over the people: "True and sure," "*Abodah*," and the blessing of priests ["May the Lord bless you and keep you"].

M. Tamid 5:1A-C

---

[10]Joseph Heinemann, *Prayer in the Period of the Tannaim and the Amoraim*, English translation by Richard S. Sarason (Jerusalem, 1976), p. 13.

There is no reason to doubt the existence of a formal liturgy in the Temple. Quite discrete discourse on the disposition of Temple rites after the destruction in 70, moreover, underlines the probability that prior to 70, a formal liturgy, though in diverse forms, did govern synagogue prayer.

To review the principal elements of the formal liturgy, we turn to the exposition supplied in Schuerer-Vermes-Millar (pp. 454-459), which follows.

I. The *Shema<sup>c</sup>* consists of three texts, Deut. 6:4-9, Deut. 11:13-21 and Num. 15:37-41: those Torah passages, therefore, which proclaim mainly that YHWH alone is the God of Israel and ordain certain memorials for the constant remembrance of him. The opening and closing benedictions (*berakhoth*) are arranged around this nucleus; the Mishnah lays down that the morning *Shema<sup>c</sup>* is to be preceded by two benedictions and followed by one, and that the evening *Shema<sup>c</sup>* is to be preceded by two and followed by two. The first words of the closing benediction are cited in the Mishnah exactly as they are used today. Accordingly, although the wording of the blessings was later considerably expanded, they nevertheless belong basically to the Mishnaic period.

This prayer, or more correctly, confession of faith, is required to be uttered twice a day, morning and evening, by every adult male Israelite. Women, slaves and children are exempt. It need not be said in Hebrew, but can be recited in any language.

The antiquity of the custom of reciting the *Shema<sup>c</sup>* is already apparent from the fact that such detailed directions are given in the Mishnah. But the Mishnah also mentions that the prayer is said by the priests in the Temple, which presupposes that it was in use at least before A.D. 70. In fact, Josephus regards its origin as so remote that he sees it as having been laid down by Moses himself.

II. The *Shemoneh <sup>c</sup>Esreh*, though somewhat more recent than the *Shema<sup>c</sup>*, is fundamentally still very old. The chief prayer of Judaism, every Israelite, including women, slaves and children, is required to recite it three times a day, in the morning, the afternoon (at the time of the minhah-offering) and the evening. So much is it the prayer of prayers that it is known simply as "the Prayer." In its later form in the Babylonian recension, it consists not of eighteen *berakhoth*, as its name suggests, but nineteen:

1. Blessed art thou, Lord our God and God of our fathers, God of Abraham, God of Isaac and God of Jacob, great, mighty and fearful God, most high God, who bestowest abundant grace and createst all things and rememberest the promises of grace to the fathers and bringest a Redeemer to their children's children for thy Name's sake out of love. O King, who bringest help and salvation and who art a shield. *Blessed art thou, Lord, shield of Abraham.*

2. Lord, thou art almighty for ever, who makest the dead alive. Thou art mighty to help, thou who sustainest the living out of grace, makest

the dead alive out of great mercy, supportest those who fall, healest the sick, freest the captive, and keepest thy word faithfully to them who sleep in the dust. And who is like thee, Lord of mighty deeds, and who is comparable to thee, King, who makest dead and alive and causest help to spring forth. And thou art faithful to make the dead alive. *Blessed art thou, Lord, who makest the dead alive.*

3.    Thou art holy and thy Name is holy and the holy praise thee every day. *Blessed art thou, Lord, holy God.*

4.    Thou grantest knowledge to mankind and teachest men understanding.    Grant us the knowledge, understanding and discernment (which come) from thee. *Blessed art thou, Lord, who grantest knowledge.*

5.    Lead us back, our Father, to thy Torah; and bring us, our King, to thy service, and cause us to return in perfect repentance to thy presence. *Blessed art thou, Lord, who delightest in repentance.*

6.    Forgive us, our Father, for we have sinned; pardon us, our King, for we have transgressed. For thou forgivest and pardonest. *Blessed art thou, Lord, gracious, rich in forgiveness.*

7.    Look on our affliction and plead our cause, and redeem us speedily for thy Name's sake; for thou at a mighty redeemer. *Blessed art thou, Lord, redeemer of Israel.*

8.    Heal us, O Lord, and we shall be healed, save us and we shall be saved; for thou art our praise. And bring perfect healing to all our wounds. For thou art a God and King who heals, faithful and merciful. *Blessed art thou, Lord, who healest the sick of thy people Israel.*

9.    Bless this year for us, Lord our God, and cause all its produce to prosper; and bless the land; and satisfy us with goodness; and bless our year as the good years. *Blessed art thou, Lord, who blessest the years.*

10. Proclaim our liberation with the great trumpet, and raise a banner to gather together our dispersed, and assemble us from the four corners of the earth. *Blessed art thou, Lord, who gatherest the banished of thy people Israel.*

11. Restore our judges as in former times and our counsellors as in the beginning; and take from us sorrow and sighing; and reign over us, thou Lord alone, in grace and mercy; and justify us in judgment. *Blessed art thou, Lord, who lovest justice and judgment.*

12. And for informers let there be no hope; and let all who do wickedness quickly perish; and let them all be speedily destroyed; and uproot and crush and hurl down and humble the insolent, speedily in our days. *Blessed art thou, Lord, who crushest enemies and humblest the insolent.*

13. Over the righteous and over the pious; and over the elders of thy people of the house of Israel; and over the remnant of their Torah scholars; and over the righteous proselytes; and over us, may thy mercy shower down, Lord our God. And give a rich reward to all who faithfully trust in thy Name. And cause our portion to be with them for ever, that we may be put to shame. For we have trusted in thee. *Blessed art thou, Lord, support and trust of the righteous.*

14. And to Jerusalem, thy city, return with mercy and dwell in its midst as thou hast spoken; and build it soon in our days to be an everlasting building; and raise up quickly in its midst the throne of David. *Blessed art thou, Lord, who buildest Jerusalem.*

15. Cause the shoot of David to shoot forth quickly, and raise up his horn by thy salvation. For we wait on thy salvation all the day. *Blessed art thou, Lord, who causest the horn of salvation to shoot forth.*

16. Hear our voice, Lord our God; spare us and have mercy on us, and accept our prayer with mercy and pleasure. For thou art a God who hearest prayers and supplications; and let us not return empty, our King, from before thy Face. For thou hearest the prayer of thy people Israel with mercy. *Blessed art thou, Lord, who hearest prayer.*

17. Be pleased, Lord our God, with thy people Israel and with their prayer. Bring back the worship into the Holy of Holies of thy house and accept in love and pleasure the sacrifices of Israel and her prayer. And may the worship offered by Israel thy people be pleasing to thee always. O that our eyes might see thy return with mercy to Zion. *Blessed art thou, Lord, who causest thy presence to return to Zion.*

18. We praise thee, for thou art the Lord our God and the God of our fathers for ever and ever, the rock of our life, the shield of our salvation from generation to generation. We praise thee and recount thy praise, for our life that is given into thy hand and for our souls which are in thy charge; and for thy wonders to us everyday; and for thy marvels; and for thy deeds of goodness at every time, at evening and morning and midday. All-Good, of whose mercy there is no end, Merciful One, whose grace increases, we wait on thee forever. And for all this be praised and thy Name be exalted, our King, forever in all eternity. And may all that lives praise thee, *selah*, and praise thy Name in truth, thou God, our salvation and our help, *selah*. *Blessed art thou, Lord, All-Good is thy Name, and it is fitting to praise thee.*

19. Bring peace, goodness and blessing, grace and favour and mercy over us and over all Israel, thy people. Bless us our Father, all of us together, with the light of thy Face. For by the light of thy Face thou hast given us Lord our God, the Torah of life and loving kindness and righteousness and blessing and mercy and life and peace. And may it be good in thine eyes to bless thy people Israel at all times and in every hour with thy peace. *Blessed art thou, Lord, who blessest thy people Israel with peace. Amen.*

Of these nineteen *berakhoth*, the first three praise God's omnipotence and grace, and the last two (18 and 19) thank him for his goodness and beg his blessing in general. In between are supplications proper: nos. 4-9 ask for knowledge, repentance, forgiveness, deliverance from evil, health and a fruitful land; nos. 10-17 pray for the reunion of the dispersed, the restoration of national supremacy, the destruction of the godless, the reward of the just, the rebuilding of Jerusalem, the sending of the Messiah, the hearing of prayer and the reinstitution of sacrificial worship.

From its content it is evident that the Prayer did not reach its final form until after the destruction of Jerusalem in A.D. 70, for nos. 14 and 17 presuppose the fall of the city and the cessation of sacrifice. Accordingly, it must have been given the form of eighteen benedictions in around A.D. 70-100, but the underlying foundation of the Prayer is certainly much older.

Form analysis makes possible the identification, within the Mishnah, of a handbook on prayer, handed on probably in written form and deriving from the period before 70. If we turn to the opening statements of a number of paragraphs in Mishnah-tractate Berakhot, we find a set of formalized rules governing the recitation of prayers required, in the Mishnah's authors' conception, of all Israelites, and not only of priests or of those sages who formulated the law. The tractate opens with the following:

> From what time do they read (*qorin*) the *Shema*<sup>c</sup> in the evening? From the time that the priests go in to eat their heave-offering.
>
> M. Ber. 1:1A

Then follows the time at which one no longer may read the *Shema*<sup>c</sup>:

B.   "Until the end of the first watch" – the word of R. Eliezer.

C.   Sages say, "Until midnight."

D.   Rabban Gamaliel says, "Until the morning star rises."

> M. Ber. 1:1B-D

The three sayings in M. Ber 1:1.B-D have been formulated in the same way, <sup>c</sup>*ad* (until) plus the specified time. They take for granted that the time from which the *Shema*<sup>c</sup> may be recited requires no comment. That language is singularly inappropriate to ordinary folk. How so? Not everyone was a priest waiting the permissible time for eating heave-offering. Most were not. The language of the opening clause is important, because it establishes as a pattern the use of the present participle in the plural: *qorin* in M. Ber 1:1A. This usage provides a key to how later passages continue the opening one, as we shall now see.

M. Berakhot 1:2 proceeds in the same formula, "From what time do they read the *Shema*<sup>c</sup> in the morning?" Eliezer provides an answer different from that given anonymously. Then follows, "And he completes it before (<sup>c</sup>*ad*) sunrise." Joshua gives a different opinion, which is glossed. M. Berakhot 1:3 now introduces a completed Houses pericope, and M. Berakhot 1:4 tells us about the blessings said before and after reciting the *Shema*<sup>c</sup>, with allusions to various customs. The present participle in the plural next occurs in M. Berakhot 1:5, "They make mention of the going forth from Egypt at night." This then is glossed by a saying of Eleazar b. <sup>c</sup>Azariah. So the whole of M. Berakhot Chapter One, when attributed at all, is assigned to early figures, just beyond A.D. 70, and the attested passages all use the same verbal construction.

The next available passage following the earlier participial construction, tells us that women, slaves, and children are free of the obligation of saying the *Shema^C* and putting on phylacteries (*Tefillin*), but they are liable to say the Prayer. That is to say, they are required to recite the Eighteen Benedictions of the Prayer, just now reviewed by us, but they are not required to put on phylacteries and to recite the *Shema^C*. This is unattested. (M. Ber. 3:4, 5, and 6 deal with unclean people in connection with the *Shema^C*. Chapter Four does not contain the important participial construction.) This brings us to M. Ber. 5:1, "They do not stand to say the Prayer (the Eighteen Benedictions) except reverentially.... They make mention of the Power of Rains in the [prayer for] the resurrection of the dead and ask for rains in the blessing of the years [this is the ninth benediction] and *Havdalah* [at the end of the Sabbath, marking the division of holy and ordinary time] in 'Who graciously grants knowledge.'"[11] This is attested by Aqiba and Eliezer, who hold different opinions. M. Ber. 5:3-5 deal with other matters and do not use the present participle in the plural, which next occurs in M. Ber. 6:1: "How do they bless fruit?" This is answered with *^Comer*, "one blesses," and is attested by Judah b. Ilai. M. Ber. 7:2 has, "Women, slaves and children are not invited to participate in the blessing of food after meals." Then M. Ber. 7:3, "How do they invite to participate in the blessing of food after meals?" This is answered, at some length, by *^C*Aqiba, Ishmael, and Yosé the Galilean. Chapter Eight deals with the purity rules of the Houses of Hillel and Shammai and how they affect meals. Only one is relevant to a catalogue of participial constructions. M. Ber. 8:6 reads, "They do not bless the light, spices of gentiles, nor the light or spices prepared for the dead." Chapter Nine is not relevant, for it does not exhibit the specified response verbal construction.

What is the upshot? Placed side by side, the passages which use the present participle in the plural, produce the following little enchiridion:

### I. *The Shema*

    1.   Reciting the *Shema^C*, evening and morning.

    2.   Referring to the Exodus in the evening *Shema^C*.

    3.   Women, slaves, and children are not obligated to recite the *Shema^C* (etc.).

### II. *The Prayer*

    4.   When they say the Prayer, they must do so with reverence.

---

[11]Heinemann, *Prayer*, p. 13.

5.   They include Powers of Rain in the paragraph of the Prayer dealing with resurrection, rains in the Blessing of the Years, and *Habdalah* in "Who graciously favors man with knowledge."

## III. *Saying Blessings*

6.   How do they say a blessing over fruit? [This shifts to "he says" [singular participle] and is attested only by Judah b. Ilai. The rest of the chapter ignores the present plural participle form, even where it might be used, for example, 6:6.]

7.   How do they invite [people] to say the Blessing of Food?

8.   They bless the light and spices not of gentiles or of the dead, etc. [in connection with *Habdalah*].

The foundations of tractate Berakhot as suggested by the specified verbal form, that is, the present participle in the plural, deals with the most fundamental matters of prayer: (1) the *Shema$^c$*, (2) the Prayer, (3) saying blessings over food and other substances of enjoyment and particularly the Grace after Meals.

We cannot now know what other items were included in the list. But that we have, in the passages indicated, an enchiridion for the liturgical life seems likely. We deal with the three things people evidently were expected to know: *Shema$^c$*, the Prayer, and Grace after Meals. We have already observed that the more important items in the handbook, when attested at all, are attested by the earliest strata of authorities after A.D. 70. It would carry us too far afield to show how this list has been broken up and augmented, glossed, filled with interpolations, and otherwise expanded by later generations, beginning with the authorities who in the first place witness to its original elements. But that the Mishnah-tractate Berakhot starts here seems beyond serious question. The substance as well as the form of the later strata build upon foundational items that we have isolated. We do not know who was responsible for the original handbook (if that is what it was), why it was formulated in so consistent a way as seems (if our hypothesis is sound) to have been the case, or when it was originally composed. But it is very likely that it was composed before A.D. 70-80, that is, the time of Eliezer and Gamaliel, and this leads us to a period before A.D. 70, as Heinemann has persuasively maintained.

What of the piety expressed generated in and by the recitation of the prayers at hand? We turn again to Heinemann:

If each individual is required to pray daily at fixed times and in a set
fashion, his prayer must in time become more than a mere device for
giving expression to personal emotions and thoughts. It becomes, over
and above this, a means for actually stimulating and arousing such
emotions and thoughts. It is doubtful whether the average man,
absorbed as he is in the monotonous routine of daily life, would ever
turn his thoughts spontaneously to God, except perhaps in times of
extreme joy or distress. It is, then, the aim of fixed prayer to provide
man with a stimulus to turn his thoughts to God; to remove the
individual from the realm of the mundane and the routine, and to
elevate his thoughts and feelings to the level of the Divine and the
Absolute. This objective of self-education is manifest not only in the
obligation to say the Eighteen Benedictions *three times daily*, but even
more explicitly in the manifold benedictions which the Sages instituted
for the individual to recite during the performance of his everyday
functions, and which permeate his daily routine. A man is obliged to
recite a benediction upon beholding any overwhelming or fearsome
aspect of nature; before and after enjoying food or drink; on particularly
joyous occasions. The benediction which is to be recited before eating,
for example, is certainly intended to lift that mundane daily activity
from its biological level of significance, and to transform it into an act of
divine worship. The benediction to be recited upon performing a ritual
commandment is likewise geared to deepen the devotion and
concentration of the individual, and to prevent him from performing the
commandment mechanically. If the Sages saw fit to multiply the
number of benedictions to the point where they said: "A man is obliged
to recite one hundred benedictions each day" (*B. Menahot* 43b), their
pedagogical intent would seem to be obvious: the benediction aims to
sanctify man's daily activities by constantly infusing their performance
with a sense of holiness and with the consciousness of the Divine
Presence.[12]

Heinemann is fully justified in turning to the act and substance of the
liturgy in the description of the religious life of Judaism in the period at
hand.

We come to the description of the other two foci of piety. The second
focus is the study of the Torah which, in general, reached the people at
large and, in particular, formed the point of scribal emphasis. The third
focus of piety, the Temple, concerned the meaning of the life of the
people as a whole, in natural and historical terms. The quest in the
Temple for the significance of the collective life of Israel constituted a
common concern. This also found particular expression in the messianic
movements of the day. These two matters require less detailed
exposition than did the liturgical life.

---

[12]Heinemann, *op. cit.*, pp. 17-18.

## IX. The Reading of the Scriptures

The piety of Israel in the Land of Israel encompassed not only prayer but the public recitation and exposition of the Scriptures. Scholars concur that, by the first century, people observed the rite of the reading of the Torah, that is the Pentateuch, as well as of prophetic lections in the synagogue. No one now can identify with certainty the lections in the Prophets that accompanied various passages in the Pentateuch, nor do we know how long it took for the recitation of the whole Pentateuch, whether one year or three years. We do not know who took charge of the public reading of Scripture. Scribes, required in the preparation of governmental and other legal documents, and teachers of the law, could not have found positions in every synagogue. We cannot know who would have taken their place and role in places where well-educated scribes did not exist.

On the work of the scribes in relationship to the life of the country we are better informed. On this matter, Schuerer-Vermes-Millar state (p. 330):

> In regard to the theoretical formation of the law itself, its basic principles were of course thought to be fixed, implicitly or explicitly, in the Written Torah. But no legal code is so detailed that it requires no further interpretation. In any case, the directions provided by the law of Moses are in part very general. There was, therefore, wide scope for the work of the Torah scholars. They had to develop, with the help of careful casuistry, the general precepts given in the Torah in such a way as to guarantee that their bias was really understood in accordance with the precepts' full significance and extent. Where the Written Torah advances no direct ruling, this had to be made good, either by determining the common law, or by reasoning from other legal regulations already valid. Owing to the assiduity with which this whole operation was carried on in the last centuries B.C., biblical law gradually became a complex and intricate branch of knowledge. And as this law was not fixed in writing but was mainly handed down by word of mouth, continuous study was necessary even to become familiar with it. But knowledge of legal obligations was never more than the basis and prerequisite of the Torah scholars' professional activity. Their real business was to go on developing what was already lawful by continuous methodical work, in ever finer casuistical detail.

It is difficult to see how these special scribal interests bore much relationship to the general piety of the community. But the symbolism of the Torah, joined to the concrete lessons learned from it, assuredly did speak to everyone, not only specialists.

The interpretation of the contemporary meaning and requirements of the Torah and of the Prophets not only occupies a principal place in accounts of such special groups as the disciples of Jesus and the Essenes. It also formed the background of public life in a world that constantly and ubiquitously invoked the authority of the Torah as validation for the policies and practices of everyday life. The contribution of the Torah to the common piety derived, in the end, from the conviction that "God revealed Torah to Moses at Sinai" (M. Abot 1:1f). That meant that, when people acted rightly and in conformity to the Torah, they carried out the requirements of the covenant that Israel had made with God. Life under the Torah was a life of sanctification in the here and now and salvation in age to come, because all life found meaning under the aspect of the covenant.

Clearly, the conception that the national life found definition in Scripture rests on the premise that education, formal and informal, constituted a broad opportunity for the population at large. Certainly people learned Scriptures, which formed the center of synagogue worship and defined the nation's sense of itself in the world. We have slight evidence deriving from the period under discussion on the basis of which to describe an institution so formal as a school system. We cannot say what, beyond Scripture and aspects of piety such as formal prayer, people would have learned in such schools. The absence of concrete information on schooling, however, should not obscure the fact that the population at large, in *every* available account, is represented as informed about the Scripture and traditions of the nation. It must follow that these literary works found their way, through some institutional means, into the lives of the people. It is hardly farfetched to call "a school system" whatever media brought learning to the people at large. But beyond that simple surmise, nothing can presently be said.

Certainly one mode of popular education lay in the translation of Scripture into the vernacular, which was Aramaic in the countryside and Greek and Aramaic in the towns, such as Jerusalem. The Scriptures, read in Aramaic, gained access to the people that public recitation in a language no one spoke would have denied them. We do not now have the Aramaic translations, or Targumim, exactly as these would have been read in the synagogue in the first century. Nonetheless, successful, if limited, efforts at recovering the contents of such translations have produced solid results. Bruce Chilton's account of the version of Isaiah, in Aramaic, that underlies certain sayings ascribed to Jesus, for example, makes it clear that, with future progress, we may hope to gain a clearer picture than we now have of exactly how Scripture reached first-century Israelite synagogues.

To state matters simply, the life of Israel in its land in the first century found structure and meaning in the covenant between God and Israel as contained in the Torah revealed by God to Moses at Mount Sinai. The piety of Israel, defined by the Torah, in concrete ways served to carry out the requirements of the covenant. This holy life under the

Torah has been properly called by Dunn and Sanders, "covenantal nomism."[13] Life under the Torah was so lived as to fulfill Israel's covenant with God.

## X. The Temple and Pilgrimages

The third aspect of the piety of Israel in its land entailed pilgrimages to the Temple on festivals in celebration of nature and in commemoration of historical events. Specifically, the encounter with God and the yearning for salvation at the end of time came to a climax in the coincidence of those turnings in the natural year, spring and fall, identified as the natural year's beginning and end, and explained in all forms of Judaism as celebrations of great events in the life of historical Israel. At these intense moments of heightened reality during the natural year, Scripture required a pilgrimage to the Temple. Accordingly, in theory at least, "all Israel," or as many as could make it, assembled in the holy place, the Temple in Jerusalem. They then together celebrated the passage of the natural year, on the one hand, and the past and future of the people, on the other.

In the dimension of the future, of course, messianic hopes were associated with the pilgrim festivals, both Tabernacles and Passover, in particular. The pilgrim festivals, joined not only in sectarian doctrine to the moment at which the Messiah would come (as did Christ at Passover, and, as, in the sages' later writings, would the Messiah at Tabernacles), drew the nation to the Temple in Jerusalem. These festivals found their first definition in Scripture. Passover came in the spring. Tabernacles came in the fall. The festal season inaugurated at Passover, on the 15th of Nisan (corresponding to April). That marks the first full moon after the vernal equinox. The festival continued through seven days, with a further festival coming fifty days after the beginning of the first on the 15th of Nisan. This second festival was Pentecost, in Hebrew, *Shabuot*.

The corresponding high point of the year in the autumn, Tabernacles, *Sukkot*, came to its climax on the first full moon after the autumnal equinox. It was on the 15th of Tishré, that is, the first full moon after September 21. However, the holy season began two weeks earlier, on the eve of the 1st of Tishré, and ended a week later, on the 21st of Tishré. The opening of the holy season of autumn, the 1st of Tishré, with the celebration of the New Year, then the Day of Atonement on the 10th of Tishré, marked (as is still the case) a penitential season of repentance, fasting, and charity.

---

[13]Note also the usage by E.P. Sanders, *Paul and Palestinian Judaism. A Comparison of Patterns of Religion* (Philadelphia, 1977: Fortress Press).

Both pilgrim festivals thus celebrated in particular the sun's movement around the earth relative to that of the moon (and so the seasons of the Land). Especially important were dramatic shifts in the pattern of the rains in the Holy Land itself. The fall festival marked the beginning of the autumnal and winter rains, on which the life of the Land depended. The spring festival marked the end of the same rainy season. Scripture identified the Passover with the liberation of Israel from Egypt and the beginning of the life of the people. As indicated, the autumnal season focused upon the moral condition of individuals and of the people as a whole. In the pilgrim festivals the affairs of the individual, the people, the natural and supernatural world, all reached a climax in a massive and impressive celebration in the cult.

The Temple, therefore, marked the point of the convergence of lines of historical, social, and political order and God as ruler on earth, corresponding to the rules of nature and of God as creator in heaven. Assembling within its walls, the priesthood, Levites, and Israelites, men, women, and children, as well as lower castes, embodied in one place and at one time the people as a whole. Symbolizing the social order, honoring the political structure, celebrating the regularity of nature, the people, corporate Israel drawn together as pilgrims, offered up to God what the Torah defined as appropriate service, in the smoke of burning meat and grain and the other offerings. Looking backward, the pilgrim people, the assembly of Israel before God, celebrated its very formation in the exodus from Egypt. Looking forward, the nation prayed for the prosperity brought by rain in the autumnal season and for safe passage through the dry season to come. Clearly, in its pilgrim festivals, the people corporately brought to expression a piety encompassing all reality. In the pilgrim rites in the Temple, Israel corporately fulfilled what, as noted, Sanders properly calls "covenantal nomism." But obedience to the covenant also expressed itself in fulfillment of the law, which promised sanctification in nature, salvation in history, and piety also reached expression in individual prayer and synagogue study of Torah.

## XII. Conclusion

All the radical claims of holiness sects, such as Pharisees and Essenes, of professions such as the scribes, and of followers of Messiahs, each in its particular manner, gave expression to an aspect or emphasis of the common piety of the nation. Priest, scribe, Messiah – all stood upon the same continuum of faith and culture with the rest of Israel, the Jewish people. Each expressed in a particular and intense way a mode of piety all in common understood and shared. That is why we can move from the particular to the general in our description of the common faith of Israel in the first century in its land. That that common faith also distinguished Israel from all other peoples of the age, whatever the measure of "Hellenization" of the country's life, hardly requires argument. There was no "common theology of the ancient Near East," so far as Israel was concerned, not then, not before, and not afterward.

No wonder then that the two new modes of the definition of Judaic piety to emerge from the period before 70 and to thrive long after that date, the Judaism framed by sages from before the first to the seventh century, and Christianity, both redefined the inherited categories while remaining true to emphases of these same categories. What happened was that the established classifications – priest, scribe, and Messiah – were taken over and infused with new meaning, so that, while in categories nothing changed, in substance nothing remained what it had been. That is why both Christian and Judaic thinkers reread the received Scriptures – "the Old Testament" to the one, "the Written Torah" to the other – and produced, respectively, "the New Testament" and "the Oral Torah." The common piety of the people Israel in its land defined the program of religious life for the Judaism and the Christianity to emerge beyond the caesura of the destruction of the Temple. The bridge to Sinai – worship, revelation, national and social eschatology – was open in both directions.

Thus Christ as perfect sacrifice, teacher, Prophet, and King-Messiah in the mind of the Church brought together but radically recast the three foci of what had been the common piety of Israel in Temple times. Still later on, the figure of the Talmudic sage would encompass but redefine all three categories as well. How so? After 70, study of Torah and obedience to it came to be a substitute, for the time being, for the Temple and its sacrifice. The government of the sages in accord with "the one whole Torah of Moses, our rabbi," revealed by God at Sinai, carried forward the scribes' conception of Israel's proper government. The Messiah would come when all Israel, through mastery of the Torah and obedience to it, had formed that holy community which, to begin with, the Torah prescribed in the model of heaven revealed to Moses at Sinai. Jesus as perfect priest, rabbi, Messiah, was a protean figure. The Talmudic rabbi as Torah incarnate, priest manqué, and, in the model of (Rabbi) David, progenitor and paradigm of the Messiah, was also such. In both cases we find an unprecedented rereading of established symbols in new and striking ways.

The history of the piety of Judaism therefore is the story of successive rearrangements and revisioning of symbols. From ancient Israelite times onward, there would be no classification beyond the three established taxa. But no category in content would long be left intact. When Jesus asked people who they thought he was, the enigmatic answer proved less interesting than the question posed. For the task he set himself was to reframe everything people knew in the encounter with what they did not know: a taxonomic enterprise. When the rabbis of late antiquity rewrote in their own image and likeness the entire Scripture and history of Israel, dropping whole eras as though they had never been, ignoring vast bodies of old Jewish writing, inventing whole new books for the canon of Judaism, they did the same thing. They reworked what they had received in light of what they proposed to give. No mode of piety could be left untouched, for all proved promising. But, in Judaism from the first century to the seventh, every mode of piety would be refashioned in the light of the vast public events represented by the religious revolutionaries at hand, rabbi-clerk, rabbi-priest, rabbi-Messiah. Accordingly, the piety of Israel in the first century ultimately defined the structure of the two great religions of Western civilization: Christianity, through its Messiah, for the gentile, Judaism, through its definition in the two Torahs of Sinai and in its embodiment in the figure of the sage, for Israel.

# 3

## Defining the Mishnah

Falling into the hands of someone who has never seen this document before, the Mishnah must cause puzzlement. From the first line to the last, discourse takes up questions internal to a system which is never introduced. The Mishnah provides information without establishing context. It presents disputes about facts hardly urgent outside of a circle of faceless disputants. Consequently, we start with the impression that we join a conversation already long under way about topics we can never grasp anyhow. Even though the language is our own, the substance is not. We shall feel as if we are in a transit lounge at a distant airport. We understand the words people say, but are baffled by their meanings and concerns, above all, by the urgency in their voices: What are you telling me? Why must I know it? Who cares if I do not?

No one can take for granted that what is before us makes sense in any context but the Mishnah's own, inaccessible world. Each step in the inquiry into the meaning and importance of the document must be laid forth with ample preparation, taken with adequate care. For before us is a remarkable statement of concerns for matters not only wholly remote from our own world, but, in the main, alien to the world of the people who made the Mishnah itself. It is as if people set down to write letters about things they had never seen, to people they did not know – letters from an unknown city to an undefined and unimagined world: the Mishnah is from no one special in utopia, to whom it may concern.

To state matters more directly: The Mishnah does not identify its authors. It permits only slight variations, if any, in its authorities' patterns of language and speech, so there is no place for individual characteristics of expression. It nowhere tells us when it speaks. It does not address a particular place or time and rarely speaks of events in its own day. It never identifies its prospective audience. There is scarcely a "you" in the entire mass of sayings and rules. The Mishnah begins nowhere. It ends abruptly. There is no predicting where it will commence or explaining why it is done. Where, when, why the document is laid out and set forth are questions not deemed urgent and not answered.

Indeed, the Mishnah contains not a hint about what its authors conceive their work to be. Is it a law code? Is it a schoolbook? Since it makes statements describing what people should and should not do, or rather, do and do not do, we might suppose it is a law code. Since, as we shall see in a moment, it covers topics of both practical and theoretical interest, we might suppose it is a schoolbook. But the Mishnah never expresses a hint about its authors' intent. The reason is that the authors do what they must to efface all traces not only of individuality but even of their own participation in the formation of the document. So it is not only a letter from utopia to whom it may concern. It also is a letter written by no one person – but not by a committee, either. Nor should we fail to notice, even at the outset, that while the Mishnah clearly addresses Israel, the Jewish people, it is remarkably indifferent to the Hebrew Scriptures. The Mishnah makes no effort at imitating the Hebrew of the Hebrew Bible, as do the writers of the Dead Sea Scrolls. The Mishnah does not attribute its sayings to biblical heroes, prophets, or holy men, as do the writings of the pseudepigraphs of the Hebrew Scriptures. The Mishnah does not claim to emerge from a fresh encounter with God through revelation, as is not uncommon in Israelite writings of the preceding four hundred years; the Holy Spirit is not alleged to speak here. So all the devices by which other Israelite writers gain credence for their messages are ignored. (We return to this puzzle in the next chapter.) Perhaps the authority of the Mishnah was self-evident to its authors. But, self-evident or not, they in no way take the trouble to explain to their document's audience why people should conform to the descriptive statements contained in their holy book.

If then we turn to the contents of the document, we are helped not at all in determining the place of the Mishnah's origination, the purpose of its formation, the reasons for its anonymous and collective plane of discourse and monotonous tone of voice. For the Mishnah covers a carefully defined program of topics, as I shall explain presently. But the Mishnah never tells us why one topic is introduced and another is omitted, or what the agglutination of these particular topics is meant to accomplish in the formation of a system or imaginative construction. Nor is there any predicting how a given topic will be treated, why a given set of issues will be explored in close detail, and another set of possible issues ignored. Discourse on a theme begins and ends as if all things are self-evident – including, as I said, the reason for beginning at one point and ending at some other.

In all one might readily imagine, upon first glance at this strange and curious book, that what we have is a rule book. It appears on the surface to be a book lacking all traces of eloquence and style, revealing no evidence of system and reflection, serving no important purpose. First glance indicates in hand is yet another sherd from remote antiquity – no different from the king lists inscribed on the ancient sherds, the random catalogue of (to us) useless, meaningless facts: a cookbook, a placard of posted tariffs, detritus of random information, accidentally thrown up on the currents of historical time. Who would want to have made such a thing? Who would now want to refer to it?

The answer to that question is deceptively straight forward: The Mishnah is important because it is a principal component of the canon of Judaism. Indeed, that answer begs the question: Why should some of the ancient Jews of the Holy Land have brought together these particular facts and rules into a book and set them forth for the Israelite people? Why should the Mishnah have been received, as much later on it certainly was received, as a half of the "whole Torah of Moses at Sinai"? The Mishnah was represented, after it was compiled, as the part of the "whole Torah of Moses, our rabbi," which had been formulated and transmitted orally, so it bore the status of divine revelation right alongside the Pentateuch. Yet it is already entirely obvious that little in the actual contents of the document evoked the character or the moral authority of the Written Torah of Moses. Indeed, since most of the authorities named in the Mishnah lived in the century and a half prior to the promulgation of the document, the claim that things said by men known to the very framers of the document in fact derived from Moses at Sinai through a long chain of oral tradition contradicted the well-known facts of the matter. So this claim presents a paradox even on the surface: How can the Mishnah be deemed a book of religion, a program for consecration, a mode of sanctification? Why should Jews from the end of the second century to our own day have deemed the study of the Mishnah to be a holy act, a deed of service to God through the study of an important constituent of God's Torah, God's will for Israel, the Jewish people?

In fact, the Mishnah is precisely that, a principal holy book of Judaism. The Mishnah has been and now is memorized in the circle of all those who participate in the religion, Judaism. Of still greater weight, the two great documents formed around the Mishnah and so shaped as to serve, in part, as commentaries to the Mishnah, namely, the Babylonian Talmud and the Palestinian Talmud, form the center of the curriculum of Judaism as a living religion. Consequently, the Mishnah is necessary to the understanding of Judaism. It hardly needs saying that people interested in the study of religions surely will have to reflect upon the same questions I have formulated within the context of Judaism, namely, how such a curious compilation of materials may be deemed a holy book. And, self-evidently, scholars of the formative centuries of Christianity, down to the recognition of Christianity as a legal religion in the fourth century, will be glad to have access to a central document of the kind of Judaism taking shape at precisely the same time as the Christianity studied by them was coming into being. In all, we need not apologize for our interest in this sizable monument to the search for a holy way of life for Israel represented, full and whole, in this massive thing, the Mishnah.

Let me now briefly describe the Mishnah. It is a six-part code of descriptive rules formed toward the end of the second century A.D. by a small number of Jewish sages and put forth as the constitution of Judaism under the sponsorship of Judah the Patriarch, the head of the Jewish community of the Land of Israel at the end of that century. The reason the document is important is that the Mishnah forms the foundation for the Babylonian and Palestinian Talmuds. It therefore stands alongside the Hebrew Bible as the holy book upon which the Judaism of the past nineteen hundred years is constructed. The six divisions are: (1) agricultural rules; (2) laws governing appointed seasons, for example, Sabbaths and festivals; (3) laws on the transfer of women and property along with women from one man (father) to another (husband); (4) the system of civil and criminal law (corresponding to what we today should regard as "the legal system"); (5) laws for the conduct of the cult and the Temple; and (6) laws on the preservation of cultic purity both in the Temple and under certain domestic circumstances, with special reference to the table and bed. These divisions define the range and realm of reality.

## I. The Mishnah in Context: Israelite History in the Later First and Second Centuries

The world addressed by the Mishnah is hardly congruent to the worldview presented within the Mishnah. Let us now consider the time and context in which the document took shape. The Mishnah is made up of sayings bearing the names of authorities who lived, as I just said, in the later first and second centuries. (The book contains very little in the names of people who lived before the destruction of the Temple of Jerusalem in A.D. 70.) These authorities generally fall into two groups, namely, two distinct sets of names, each set of names randomly appearing together, but rarely, if ever, with names of the other set. The former set of names is generally supposed to represent authorities who lived between the destruction of the Temple in 70 and the advent of the

second war against Rome, led by Simeon Bar Kokhba, in 132. The latter
set of names belongs to authorities who flourished between the end of
that war, ca. 135, and the end of the second century. The Mishnah itself
is generally supposed to have come to closure at the end of the second
century, and its date, for conventional purposes only, is ca. A.D. 200.
Now, of these two groups – sages from 70-130, and from 135-200 – the
latter is represented far more abundantly than the former.
Approximately two-thirds of the named sayings belong to mid-second-
century authorities. This is not surprising, since these are the named
authorities whose (mainly unnamed) students collected, organized, and
laid out the document as we now have it. So, in all, the Mishnah
represents the thinking of Jewish sages who flourished in the middle of
the second century. It is that group which took over whatever they had
in hand from the preceding century – and from the whole legacy of
Israelite literature even before that time – and revised and reshaped the
whole into the Mishnah. Let us briefly consider their world.

In the aftermath of the war against Rome in 132-135, the Temple was
declared permanently prohibited to Jews, and Jerusalem was closed off
to them as well. So there was no cult, no Temple, no holy city, to which,
at this time, the description of the Mishnaic laws applied. We observe at
the very outset, therefore, that a sizable proportion of the Mishnah deals
with matters to which the sages had no material access or practical
knowledge at the time of their work. For we have seen that the Mishnah
contains a division on the conduct of the cult, namely, the fifth, as well as
one on the conduct of matters so as to preserve the cultic purity of the
sacrificial system along the lines laid out in the book of Leviticus, the
Sixth Division. In fact, a fair part of the Second Division, on appointed
times, takes up the conduct of the cult on special days, for example, the
sacrifices offered on the Day of Atonement, Passover, and the like.
Indeed, what the Mishnah wants to know about appointed seasons
concerns the cult far more than it does the synagogue. The Fourth
Division, on civil law, for its part, presents an elaborate account of a
political structure and system of Israelite self-government, in tractates
Sanhedrin and Makkot, not to mention Shebuot and Horayot. This
system speaks of king, priest, Temple, and court. But it was not the Jews,
their kings, priests, and judges, but the Romans, who conducted the
government of Israel in the Land of Israel in the time in which the
second-century authorities did their work. So it would appear that well
over half of the document before us speaks of cult, Temple, government,
priesthood. As we shall see, moreover, the Mishnah takes up a
profoundly priestly and Levitical conception of sanctification. When we
consider that, in the very time in which the authorities before us did their
work, the Temple lay in ruins, the city of Jersalem was prohibited to all

Israelites, and the Jewish government and administration which had centered on the Temple and based its authority on the holy life lived there were in ruins, the fantastic character of the Mishnah's address to its own catastrophic day becomes clear. Much of the Mishnah speaks of matters not in being in the time in which the Mishnah was created, because the Mishnah wishes to make its statement on what really matters.

In the age beyond catastrophe, the problem is to reorder a world off course and adrift, to gain reorientation for an age in which the sun has come out after the night and the fog. The Mishnah is a document of imagination and fantasy, describing how things "are" out of the sherds and remnants of reality, but, in larger measure, building social being out of beams of hope. The Mishnah tells us something about how things were, but everything about how a small group of men wanted things to be. The document is orderly, repetitious, careful in both language and message. It is small-minded, picayune, obvious, dull, routine – everything its age was not. The Mishnah stands in contrast with the world to which it speaks. Its message is one of small achievements and modest hope. It means to defy a world of large disorders and immodest demands. The heirs of heroes build an unheroic folk in the new and ordinary age. The Mishnah's message is that what a person wants matters in important ways. It states that message to an Israelite world which can shape affairs in no important ways and speaks to people who by no means will the way things now are. The Mishnah therefore lays down a practical judgment upon, and in favor of, the imagination and will to reshape reality, regain a system, reestablish that order upon which trustworthy existence is to be built.

If we now ask ourselves why people in our own age should take an interest in that long-ago time, the answer is not difficult to find. And it is not a claim for mere antiquarianism, let alone knowledge "for its own sake" – whatever that might mean. The sages of the Mishnah addressed Israel at the very end of its thousand-year life of sanctification through God's service in the Temple, of anointed kings and holy priests organizing (at least in theory) time and space of the Land in accord with the model of the sacred Temple and along lines of structure emanating therefrom. The Mishnah, we notice, is the work of men who had survived the second war against Rome. Now when we realize that that war was fought roughly three generations after the destruction of the Temple, we notice yet another point of importance. When the Temple had been destroyed earlier, in 586 B.C., the prophetic promises of divine forgiveness had been kept. So the Temple was restored: Israel regained its homeland. Now, half a millennium later, the Temple had lain in ruins for another three generations. A great and noble war had been fought to regain Jerusalem, rebuild the Temple, and restore the cult. But what had happened was incomprehensible. The pattern established in the first destruction and restoration now proved no longer to hold. Indeed, nothing stood firm. This time around, not only was the Temple not rebuilt, the cult not restored. Jerusalem itself was declared off-limits to Israelites. The very center was made inaccessible.

In this context, it is not difficult to look for points of commonality between one age of uncertainty and another, also cut loose from ancient moorings. What the second-century sages of the Mishnah have to teach the generations of the last decades of the twentieth century and the first of the twenty-first, is how to make use of imagination and fantasy to confront, defy, and overcome chaos and disorder. Behind the Mishnah lay the ruins of half a millennium of continuous, orderly, and systematic Israelite life, which had been centered on the regular and reliable offering of the produce of the field and flock upon the altar of the Temple in Jerusalem, the ordering of society around that Temple, the rhythmic division of time in response to that cult, and the placing of people and things into their proper station in relationship to that center. One disastrous war had ended in the destruction of the Temple. The second, three generations later, had made certain it would not be rebuilt in the foreseeable future – nor, as it now appears, ever. In the aftermath of these two terrible wars the Israelite nation entered upon an existence far more precarious in mind than in material reality. Within a century the social and agricultural effects of the wars had worn off. Galilean synagogues of the third and fourth century testify to an age of material surplus and good comfort. But it would be a very long time before the psychological effects of dislocation and disorientation would pass. In some ways, for the Jewish people, they never have. Our age, which looks back upon the destruction of enduring political and social arrangements in the aftermath of two terrible wars (with numerous skirmishes in between and since), has the power to confront the second century's world of ancient Judaism, because, it seems, there is a measure of existential congruence between the two ages and their common problems. For both are the kind which challenge the imagination and the will.

Now it is one thing to point out why, in general, a person in a wholly alien world might want to open the pages of the Mishnah. It is quite another to explain what one should look for and actually seek in reading what these people say. For those questions I asked at the outset, about why people then should have talked about an imaginary world and even today may want to listen to this incomprehensible chatter about what then was not and what today lies even beyond ordinary comprehension – those questions have to be answered in all the specificity of the hundreds of chapters, set forth in the dozens of tractates, of which the Mishnah is composed. This brings me to the three concrete matters worth protracted attention (as mere history is not): (1) the specific modes of discourse attained by the Mishnah; (2) the system of world building laid forth in the Mishnah; and (3) the interplay between that system and the massive heritage of Scripture which lay behind the Mishnah. These three things – language, system, heritage – have now to be explained.

Before proceeding, I want to point out to the reader the obvious fact that, for the period in which the Mishnah was taking shape, the Mishnah is hardly the only, or the most important, historical source. While up to now I have insisted on dealing with this particular document alone and have emphasized what is to be learned about the people behind it, we must now remind ourselves of two things.

First, the people who produced the Mishnah may well have produced other documents, or, more important, materials now incorporated in other, later documents, materials which surfaced only after the Mishnah was completed in 200. So we cannot suppose that all we know about the framers of the Mishnah derives from the Mishnah.

Second, in the same period as that in which the Mishnah's sages flourished, other Jews developed their own ideas. Many of these ideas may be shown to have entered into documents, also accepted by the Talmudic rabbis, which came to formation and completion after the Mishnah, even long afterward. Consequently, we have to see the Mishnah as only one important document of its day and of its group. We have, further, to understand that, in the formation of Judaism on the foundations of the Mishnah, much done in the Mishnah's own day would find its place only later on.

We have sound reason to believe that, in the later first and second century, there were important Jewish institutions of politics, culture, and religion (in those times, they were not so easy to differentiate), such as a court system, a patriarch (or ruler of the Jewish community of the Holy Land), academies, synagogues, and the like. To treat as if they did not exist ideas and institutions not attested in the book before us may well carry us deep into the worldview of the people whose creative imagination is richly, if tediously, revealed in the pages of the Mishnah. But it would not provide us with an exhaustive and reliable account of the world actually viewed by those people, I mean, the world of the Jewish people of the first and second centuries in the Land of Israel. There is more to be learned about the Mishnah's context than the Mishnah tells us. That is all the more reason to receive the Mishnah as a powerful judgment upon its times, not merely a report about them. It is all the more necessary to see the Mishnah as an effort to respond in a systematic and encompassing way to a whole and total encounter with the world, not merely as a set of rules and regulations.

Through regulating a world constructed mainly in mind, the sages of the Mishnah built a world that would endure from their time to ours. In exercising the power of the mind and the heart to find order in chaos and reframe a reliable and predictable mode of being in an age of successive calamities, these sages erected a vast construction of philosophy and theology, law and hermeneutics, social policy and metaphysical theory. To ask them to tell us, in addition, what – in general – happens to have happened in their day and age is to ask a master chef to boil a hot dog. So now let us return to the matter before us, not what we do not find but what we do.

## II. Language: The Mishnah's Patterned Language and Its Forms

Let us start our study of the language of the Mishnah with the simple question of how the document is organized. The answer is that the preferred mode of layout is through themes, spelled out along the lines of the logic imbedded in those themes. The Mishnah is divided up – as we already know – into six principal divisions, each expounding a single, immense topic. The tractates of each division take up subtopics of the principal theme. The chapters then unfold along the lines of the (to the framers) logic of the necessary dissection of the division. While that mode of organization may appear to be necessary or "self-evident" (it is how we should have written a law code, is it not?), we should notice that there are three others found within the document, but not utilized extensively or systematically. These therefore represent rejected options. One way is to collect diverse sayings around the name of a given authority. (The whole of tractate Eduyyot is organized in that way.) A second way is to express a given basic principle through diverse topics, for example, a fundamental rule cutting across many areas of law, stated in one place through all of the diverse types of law through which the rule or principle may be expressed. A third way is to take a striking language pattern and collect sayings on diverse topics which conform to the given language pattern. (There also is the possibility of joining the second and the third ways.) But faced with these possible ways of organizing materials, the framers of the Mishnah chose to adhere to a highly disciplined, thematic, logical principle of organization.

In antiquity paragraphing and punctuation were not commonly used. Long columns of words would contain a text – as in the Torah today – and the student of the text had the task of breaking up those columns into tractates, chapters, sentences, large and small sense units. Now if we had the entire Mishnah in a single immense scroll and spread the scroll out on the ground – perhaps the length of a football field! – we should have no difficulty at all discovering the point, on the five yard line, at which the first tractate ends and the second begins, and so on down the field to the opposite goal. For from Berakhot at the beginning to Uqsin at the end, the breaking points practically jump up from the ground like white lines of lime: change of principal topic. So, the criterion of division, internal to the document and not merely imposed by copyists and printers, is thematic. That is, the tractates are readily distinguishable from one another since each treats a distinct topic. So if, as I said, the Mishnah were to be copied out in a long scroll without the significance of lines of demarcation among the several tractates, the opening pericope of each tractate would leave no doubt that one topic had been completed and a new one undertaken.

The same is so within the tractates. Intermediate divisions of these same principal divisions are to be discerned on the basis of internal evidence, through the confluence of theme and form. That is to say, a given intermediate division of a principal one (a chapter of a tractate) will be marked by a particular, recurrent, formal pattern in accord with which sentences are constructed, and also by a particular and distinct theme, to which these sentences are addressed. When a new theme commences, a fresh formal pattern will be used. Within the intermediate divisions, we are able to recognize the components, or smallest whole units of thought (hereinafter, cognitive units), because there will be a recurrent pattern of sentence structure repeated time and again within the unit and a shifting at the commencement of the next theme. Each point at which the recurrent pattern commences marks the beginning of a new cognitive unit. In general, an intermediate division will contain a carefully enumerated sequence of exempla of cognitive units, in the established formal pattern, commonly in groups of three or five or multiples of three or five (pairs for the first division).

The cognitive units resort to a remarkably limited repertoire of formulary patterns. The Mishnah manages to say whatever it wants in one of the following ways:

1. the simple declarative sentence, in which the subject, verb, and predicate are syntactically tightly joined to one another, for example, he who does so-and-so is such-and-such;

2. the duplicated subject, in which the subject of the sentence is stated twice, for example, he who does so-and-so, lo, he is such-and-such;

3. mild apocopation, in which the subject of the sentence is cut off from the verb, which refers to its own subject, and not the

one with which the sentence commences, for example, he who does so-and-so..., it [the thing he has done] is such-and-such;

4. extreme apocopation, in which a series of clauses is presented, none of them tightly joined to what precedes or follows, and all of them cut off from the predicate of the sentence, for example, he who does so-and-so..., it [the thing he has done] is such-and-such..., it is a matter of doubt whether...or whether...lo, it [referring to nothing in the antecedent, apocopated clauses of the subject of the sentence] is so-and-so...;

5. in addition to these formulary patterns, in which the distinctive formulary traits are effected through variations in the relationship between the subject and the predicate of the sentence, or in which the subject itself is given a distinctive development, there is yet a fifth. In this last one we have a contrastive complex predicate, in which case we may have two sentences, independent of one another, yet clearly formulated so as to stand in acute balance with one another in the predicate, thus, he who does...is unclean, and he who does not...is clean.

It naturally will be objected: Is it possible that a simple declarative sentence may be asked to serve as a formulary pattern, alongside the rather distinctive and unusual constructions which follow? True, by itself, a tightly constructed sentence consisting of subject, verb, and complement, in which the verb refers to the subject, and the complement to the verb, hardly exhibits traits of particular formal interest. Yet a sequence of such sentences, built along the same gross grammatical lines, may well exhibit a clear-cut and distinctive pattern. When we see that three or five "simple declarative sentences" take up one principle or problem, and then, when the principle or problem shifts, a quite distinctive formal pattern will be utilized, we realize that the "simple declarative sentence" has served the formulator of the unit of thought as aptly as did apocopation, a dispute, or another more obviously distinctive form or formal pattern. The contrastive predicate is one example; the Mishnah contains many more.

The important point of differentiation, particularly for the simple declarative sentence, therefore appears in the intermediate unit, as I just said, thus in the interplay between theme and form. It is there that we see a single pattern recurring in a long sequence of sentences, for example, the X which has lost its Y is unclean because of its Z. The Z which has lost its Y is unclean because of its X. Another example will be a long sequence of highly developed sentences, laden with relative clauses and other explanatory matter, in which a single syntactical pattern will govern the articulation of three or six or nine exempla. That sequence will be followed by one repeated terse sentence pattern, for example, X is so-and-so, Y is such-and-such, Z is thus-and-so. The former group will treat one principle or theme, the latter some other. There can be no doubt, therefore, that the declarative sentence in recurrent patterns is, in its way, just as carefully formalized as a sequence of severely apocopated sentences or of contrastive predicates or duplicated subjects.

In order to appreciate the highly formal character of the Mishnah, we rapidly turn to its correlative document, Tosefta, a corpus of supplementary materials serving to augment, amplify, and expand the Mishnah in various ways, brought to redaction between ca. A.D. 200 and 400. Tosefta's tractates follow those of the Mishnah. This is hardly surprising, since Tosefta is a supplement to the Mishnah. When, however, we examine the ways in which Tosefta's tractates are subdivided, we do not see the slightest effort to group materials in accord with a confluence of common theme and form, or to redact intermediate divisions in accord with a single fixed number of exempla, for example, threes or fives. Furthermore, Tosefta's units of thought are not highly patterned and exhibit none of the traits of carefully stylized formulation which we find in the Mishnah – except in those pericopae in which the Mishnah itself is cited and glossed (and they are very many). Accordingly, Tosefta, a document dependent on the Mishnah, in no way exhibits careful traits of structured redaction, formal correspondence between formulary patterns and distinctive themes, for the internal demarcation of an intermediate division, or highly formalized formulation of individual units of thought. The Mishnah's traits emerge most clearly in the contrast established by its supplementary document. The mode of grouping cognitive units in Tosefta is in accord with one of three fixed relationships to the Mishnah. Pericopae which cite the Mishnah verbatim will stand together. There commonly will follow units which do not cite the Mishnah but which clearly complement the principal document, augmenting its materials in some obvious ways. And, at the end will be grouped together still other groups which supplement the Mishnah but which in no clear way depend upon the Mishnah for full and exhaustive exegesis. Accordingly, Tosefta's arrangement of its materials clearly relates to the Mishnah; and the contrast in the ways in which the Mishnah's own groups of cognitive units are set forth could not be more blatant.

This brief survey of the literary traits of the Mishnah permits us to turn to the question: What is to be learned about the authorities who bear responsibility for the peculiar way in which the Mishnah is formulated and redacted from the way in which they express their ideas? We speak, in particular, of the final generation represented in the Mishnah itself, the authorities of the period ca. A.D. 200 who gave the document its present literary character.

The dominant stylistic trait of the Mishnah as they formulated it is the acute formalization of its syntactical structure, and its carefully framed sequences of formalized language, specifically, its intermediate divisions, so organized that the limits of a theme correspond to those of a formulary pattern. The balance and order of the Mishnah are particular to the Mishnah. So the document itself now must be asked to testify to the intentions of the people who made it so. About whom does it speak? And why, in particular, have its authorities distinctively shaped language in rhymes and balanced, matched, declarative sentences, imposing upon the conceptual, factual prose of the law a peculiar kind of poetry? Why do they create rhythmic order, grammatically balanced sentences containing discrete law, laid out in what seem to be carefully enumerated sequences, and the like? Language not only contains culture, which could not exist without it. Language, in our case, linguistic and syntactical style and stylization, expresses a worldview and ethos. Whose worldview is contained and expressed in the Mishnah's formalized rhetoric?

There is no reason to doubt that if we asked the authorities behind the Mishnah the immediate purpose of their systematic use of formalized language, their answer would be to facilitate memorization. For that is the proximate effect of the acute formalization of their document. Much in its character can be seen as mnemonic.

So the Mishnah's is language for an occasion. The occasion is particular: formation and transmission of special sorts of conceptions in a special way. The predominant, referential function of language, giving verbal structure to the message itself, is secondary in our document. The expressive function, conveying the speaker's attitude toward what he is talking about, the conative function, focusing upon who is being addressed, and other ritualized functions of language come to the fore. The Mishnah's language, therefore, as I said, is special, meant as an expression of a nonreferential function. So far as the Mishnah was meant to be memorized by a distinctive group of people for an extraordinary purpose, it is language which includes few and excludes many, unites those who use it, and sets them apart from others who do not.

The formal aspects of Mishnaic rhetoric are empty of content. This is proved by the fact that pretty much all themes and conceptions can be reduced to the same few formal patterns. These patterns are established by syntactical recurrences, as distinct from recurrence of sounds. The same words do not recur. Long sequences of patterned and disciplined sentences fail to repeat the same words – that is, syllabic balance, rhythm, or sound – yet they do establish a powerful claim to order and formulary sophistication and perfection. That is why we could name a pattern, he who...it is...-apocopation: the arrangement of the words as a grammatical pattern, not their substance, is indicative of pattern. Accordingly, while we have a document composed along what clearly are mnemonic lines, the Mishnah's susceptibility to memorization rests principally upon the utter abstraction of recurrent syntactical patterns, rather than on the concrete repetition of particular words, rhythms, syllabic counts, or sounds.

A sense for the deep, inner logic of word patterns, of grammar and syntax, rather than for their external similarities, governs the Mishnaic mnemonic. And that yields the fundamental point of this analysis: Even though the Mishnah is to be memorized and handed on orally, it expresses a mode of thought attuned to abstract relationships, rather than concrete and substantive forms. The formulaic, not the formal, character of the Mishnaic rhetoric yields a picture of a subculture – the sages who made up the book – which speaks of immaterial, and not material, things. In this subculture the relationship, rather than the thing or person which is related, is primary, constitutes the principle of reality. The thing in itself is less than the thing in cathexis with other things, so, too, the person. It is self-evident that the repetition of form creates form. But what is repeated, as I have explained, is not external or superficial form. Rather we find formulary patterns of deep syntax, patterns effected through persistent grammatical or syntactical relationships and affecting an infinite range of diverse objects and topics. Form and structure emerge not from concrete, formal things but from abstract and unstated, yet ubiquitous and powerful relationships.

This fact – the creation of pattern through grammatical relationship of syntactical elements, more than through concrete sounds – tells us that the people who memorized conceptions reduced to these particular forms were capable of extraordinarily abstract cognition and perception. Hearing peculiarities of word order in diverse cognitive contexts, their ears and minds perceived regularities of grammatical arrangement, repeated functional variations of utilization of diverse words. They grasped from such subtleties syntactical patterns not expressed by recurrent external phenomena such as sounds, rhythms, or key words, and autonomous of particular meanings. What they heard, it is clear, were not only abstract relationships but also principles conveyed along with and through these relationships. For, I repeat, what was memorized was a recurrent and fundamental notion, expressed in diverse examples but in recurrent rhetorical syntactical patterns. Accordingly, what the memorizing student of a sage could and did hear was what lay far beneath the surface of the rule: the unstated principle, the unsounded pattern. This means that the prevalent mode of thought was attuned to what lay beneath the surface; minds and ears perceived what was not said behind what was said and how it was said. They besought that ineffable and metaphysical reality concealed within, but conveyed through, spoken and palpable, material reality.

Social interrelationships within the community of Israel are left behind in the ritual speech of the Mishnah, just as, within the laws, natural realities are made to give form and expression to supernatural or metaphysical regularities. The Mishnah speaks of Israel, but the speakers are a group apart. The Mishnah talks of this-worldly things, but the things stand for and speak of another world entirely. The language of the Mishnah and its formalized grammatical rhetoric create a world of discourse quite separate from the concrete realities of a given time, place, or society. The exceedingly limited repertoire of grammatical patterns by which all things on all matters are said gives symbolic expression to the notion that beneath the accidents of life are a few comprehensive relationships. Unchanging and enduring patterns lie deep in the inner structure of reality and impose structure upon the accidents of the world. This means, as I have implied, that reality for Mishnaic rhetoric consists in the grammar and syntax of language: consistent and enduring patterns of relationship among diverse and changing concrete things or persons. What lasts is not the concrete thing but the abstract interplay governing any and all sorts of concrete things.

There is, therefore, a congruence between rhetorical patterns of speech, on the one side, and the substantive framework of discourse established by these same patterns, on the other. Just as we accomplish memorization by perceiving not what is said but how it is said and is persistently arranged, so we undertake to address and describe a world in which what is concrete and material is secondary. How things are said about what is concrete and material in diverse ways and contexts is principal. The Mishnah is silent about the context of its speech – place and time and circumstance – because context is trivial. Principle, beginning in syntactical principles by which all words are arranged in a severely limited repertoire of grammatical sentences ubiquitously pertinent but rarely made explicit, is at the center.

The skill of the formulators of the Mishnah is to manipulate the raw materials of everyday speech. What they have done is so to structure language as to make it strange, to impose a fresh perception upon what to others (and what in Tosefta) are merely unpatterned and ordinary ways of saying things. What is said in the Mishnah is simple. How it is said is arcane. Ordinary folk could not have had much difficulty understanding the words which refer to routine actions and objects. How long it must have taken to grasp the meaning of the patterns into which the words are arranged! How hard it was and is to do so is suggested (at the very least) by the necessity for the creation of the Tosefta, the Talmuds, and the commentaries in the long centuries since the Mishnah came into being. In this sense the Mishnah speaks openly about public matters, yet its deep structure of syntax and grammatical forms shapes what is said into an essentially secret and private language. It takes many years to master the difficult argot, though only a few minutes to memorize the simple patterns. That constitutes a paradox reflective of the situation of the creators of the Mishnah.

Up to now I have said only a little about tense structure. The reason is that the Mishnah exhibits remarkable indifference to the potentialities of meaning inherent therein. Its persistent preference for the present participle, thus the descriptive present tense – "they do...," "one does..." – is matched by its capacity to accept the mixture of past, present, and future tenses. These can be found jumbled together in a single sentence and, even more commonly, in a single pericope. It follows that the Mishnah is remarkably uninterested in differentiation of time sequences. This fact is most clearly shown by the Gemisch of the extremely apocopated sentence with its capacity to support something like the following: "He who does so-and-so... the rain came and wet it down... if he was happy... it [is] under the law, if water be put." Clearly, the matter of tense, past, present, future, is conventional. Highly patterned syntax is meant to preserve what is said without change (even though we know changes in the wording of traditions were effected for many centuries thereafter). The language is meant to be unshakable. Its strict rules of rhetoric are meant not only to convey, but also to preserve, equally strict rules of logic, equally permanent patterns of relationship. What was at stake in this formation of language in the service of permanence? Clearly, how things were said was intended to secure eternal preservation of what was said. Change affects the accidents and details. It cannot reshape enduring principles. Language will be used to effect and protect their endurance. What is said, moreover, is not to be subjected to pragmatic experimentation. Unstated, but carefully considered, principles shape reality. They are not shaped and tested by and against reality. Use of pat phrases and syntactical clichés, divorced from different thoughts to be said and different ways of thinking, testifies to the prevailing notion of unstated, but secure and unchanging, reality behind and beneath the accidents of context and circumstance:

God is one, God's world is in order, each line carefully drawn, all structures fully coherent.

Two facts have been established. First, the formalization of the Mishnaic thought units is separate from the utilization of sound, rhythm, and extrinsic characteristics of word choice. It depends, rather, upon recurrent grammatical patterns independent of the choices of words set forth in strings. The listener or reader has to grasp relations of words in a given sequence of sentences quite separate from the substantive character of the words themselves.

Accordingly, second, the natural language of Middle Hebrew, as the Mishnah's kind of Hebrew is called, is not apt to be represented by the highly formal language of Mishnah. Mishnaic language constitutes something more than a random sequence of words used routinely to say things. It is meant as a highly formulaic way of expressing a particular set of distinctive conceptions. It is, therefore, erroneous to refer to Mishnaic language. Rather, we deal with the Mishnaic revision of the natural language of Middle Hebrew. And, it is clear, what Mishnah does to revise that natural language is ultimately settled in the character of the grammar, inclusive of syntax, of the language. Middle Hebrew has a great many more grammatical sequences than does Mishnaic Hebrew. It follows, Mishnaic Hebrew declares ungrammatical – that is, refuses to make use of – constructions which Middle Hebrew will regard as wholly grammatical and entirely acceptable. The single striking trait of the formalization of Mishnaic language, therefore, is that it depends upon grammar. And just as Chomsky says, "Grammar is autonomous and independent of meaning," so in the Mishnah, the formalization of thought into recurrent patterns is beneath the surface and independent of discrete meanings. Yet Mishnah imposes its own discipline, therefore its own deeper level of unitary meaning, upon everything and anything which actually is said.

There are these two striking traits of mind reflected within Mishnaic rhetoric: first, the perception of order and balance; second, the perception of the mind's centrality in the construction of order and balance. I refer to the imposition of wholeness upon discrete cases in the case of the routine declarative sentence and upon discrete phrases in the case of the apocopated one. Both order and balance are contained from within and are imposed from without. The relationships revealed by grammatical consistencies internal to a sentence and the implicit regularities revealed by the congruence and cogency of cases rarely are stated. But they always are to be discerned. Accordingly, the one thing which Mishnah invariably does not make explicit but which always is necessary to know is, I stress, the presence of the active intellect, the participant who is the hearer. It is the hearer who ultimately makes sense of, perceives the sense in, the Mishnah. Once more we are impressed by the Mishnah's expectation of high sophistication and profound sensitivity to order and to form on the part of its impalpable audience. Again we note that, to the Mishnah, the human mind imposes meaning and sense upon the world of sense perceptions. In this sense the Mishnah serves both as a book of laws and as a book for learners, a law code and a schoolbook. But it is in this sense alone.

If the Mishnah is a law code, it is remarkably reticent about punishments for infractions of its rules. It rarely says what one must do or must not do, if he or she becomes unclean. The Mishnah hardly even alludes to punishments or rewards consequent upon disobedience or obedience to its laws. Clean and unclean rhetorically are the end of the story and generate little beyond themselves.

If the Mishnah serves as a schoolbook, it never informs us about its institutional setting, speaks of its teachers, sets clear-cut, perceptible, educational goals for its students, nor, above all, attempts to stand in relationship to some larger curriculum or educational and social structure. Its lack of context and unself-conscious framework of discourse hardly support the view that, in a this-worldly and ordinary sense, we have in our hands of a law code or a schoolbook.

Nor is the Mishnah a corpus of "traditions," that is, true teachings which lay claim to authority or to meaning by virtue of the authorities cited therein. That is why the name of an authority rarely serves as a redactional fulcrum. It is also why the tense structure is ahistorical and antihistorical. Sequences of actions generally are stated other than in the descriptive present tense. Rules attain authority not because of who says them but because (it would seem) no specific party, at a specific time, stands behind them. The Mishnah, as I have emphasized, is descriptive of how things are. It is indifferent to who has said so, uninterested in the cumulative past behind what it has to say. These are not the traits of a corpus of "traditions." I am inclined to think that law code, schoolbook, and corpus of traditions all are not quite to the point of the accurate characterization of the Mishnah.

Yet, if not quite to the point, all nonetheless preserve a measure of proximate relevance to the definition of the Mishnah. The Mishnah does contain descriptive laws. These laws require the active participation of the mind of the hearer, thus are meant to be learned through reason, not merely obeyed as ritual, and self-evidently are so shaped as to impart lessons, not merely rules to be kept. The task of the hearer is not solely or primarily to obey, though I think obedience is taken for granted. The Mishnah calls one to participate in the process of discovering principles and uncovering patterns of meaning. The very form of the Mishnaic rhetoric, its formalization and function of that form – all testify to the role of the learner and hearer, that is, the student, in the process of definitive and indicative description (not communication) of what is, and of what is real.

Self-evidently, the Mishnah's persistent citation of authorities makes explicit the claim that some men, now dead, have made their contribution and, therefore, have given shape and substance to tradition, that tradition which is shaped by one and handed onward by another. Choices were made; authorities made them. So the Mishnah indeed is, and therefore is meant as, a law code, a schoolbook, and a corpus of tradition. It follows that the purpose for which the Mishnah was edited into final form was to create such a multipurpose document, a tripartite goal attained in a single corpus of formed and formal sayings. And yet it is obvious that the Mishnah is something other than these three things in one. It transcends the three and accomplishes more than the triple goals which on the surface form the constitutive components of its purpose.

To describe that transcendent purpose and conclude this part of the discussion, we turn to Wittgenstein's saying, "The limits of my language mean the limits of my world." On the one side, the Mishnah's formulaic rhetoric imposes limits, boundaries, upon the world. What fits into that rhetoric and can be said by it constitutes world, world given shape and boundary by the Mishnah. The Mishnah implicitly maintains, therefore, that a wide range of things fall within the territory mapped out by a limited number of linguistic conventions, grammatical sentences. What is grammatical can be said and, therefore, constitutes part of the reality created by the Mishnaic word. What cannot be contained within the grammar of the sentence cannot be said and therefore falls outside the realm of the Mishnaic reality. The Mishnaic reality consists in those things which can attain order, balance, and principle. Chaos lies without.

On the other side, if we may extrapolate from the capacity of the impoverished repertoire of grammar before us to serve for all sorts of things, then we must concede that all things can be said by formal revision. Everything can be reformed, reduced to the order and balance and exquisite sense for the just match, characteristic of the Mishnaic pericope. Anything of which we wish to speak is susceptible to the ordering and patterning of the Mishnaic grammar and syntax. That is a fact which is implicit throughout the Mishnah. Accordingly, the territory mapped out by the Mishnaic language encompasses the whole of the pertinent world under discussion. There are no thematic limitations of the Mishnaic formalized speech.

Clearly, the Mishnah is formulated in a disciplined and systematic way. We therefore must now ask how the language of the Mishnah adumbrates the character and concerns of the Mishnah's substantive ideas, its religious worldview and the way of life formulated to express that worldview. For I maintain that the document before us constitutes much more than an ancient rule book, of no special interest or humanistic value, which happens to have survived. The Mishnah is, rather, a book deliberately formed for the very group, Israel, and purpose which, for nearly nineteen centuries, it indeed has served. So the language just now described, as much as the system awaiting description, has to be asked to testify to the meaning and purpose of the whole.

The "Judaism" expressed by the Mishnah not only speaks about values. Its mode of speech – the way it speaks, not only what it says – is testimony to its highest and most enduring, distinctive value. Now let us take note. This language does not speak of sacred symbols but of pots and pans, of menstruation and dead creeping things, of ordinary water which, because of the circumstance of its collection and location, possesses extraordinary power; of the commonplace corpse and ubiquitous diseased person; of genitalia and excrement, toilet seats and the flux of penises, of stems of pomegranates and stalks of leeks; of rain and earth and wood, metal, glass and hide. This language is filled with words for neutral things of humble existence. It does not speak of holy things and is not symbolic in its substance. This language speaks of ordinary things, of things which everyone must have known. But because of the peculiar and particular way in which it is formed and formalized, this same language not only adheres to an aesthetic theory but expresses a deeply embedded ontology and methodology of the sacred, specifically of the sacred within the secular, and of the capacity for regulation, therefore for sanctification, within the ordinary: All things in order, all things then hallowed by God who orders all things, so said the priests' creation tale.

Worldview and ethos are synthesized in language. The synthesis is expressed in grammatical and syntactical regularities. What is woven into some sort of ordered whole is not a cluster of sacred symbols. The religious system is not discerned with such symbols at all. Knowledge of the conditions of life is imparted principally through description of the commonplace facts of life, which symbolize, stand for, nothing beyond themselves and their consequences, for example, for the clean and the unclean or liability and exemption from liability. That description is effected through the construction of units of meaning, intermediate divisions composed of cognitive elements. All is balanced, explicit in detail, but reticent about the whole; balanced in detail but dumb about the character of the balance. What is not said is what is eloquent and compelling, as much as what is said. Accordingly, that simple and fundamental congruence between ethos and worldview is to begin with, for the Mishnah, the very language by which the one is given cognitive expression in the other. The medium of patterned speech conveys the meaning of what is said.

## III. System: The Mishnah's Principal Topics.
## The Mishnah as a Statement of a Worldview

By "Judaism" I mean a worldview and way of life formed by a group of people who regard themselves, and are properly regarded by others, as Israelites, in which the life of the group is both defined and explained within the framework of Israel's holiness. By this definition, there have been diverse forms or kinds of Judaism. But from the time of the Mishnah onward, most of these kinds have referred not only to Scripture but also to the Mishnah and its companions, the two Talmuds and cognate writings. So these diverse kinds have formed exemplifications of a single, fundamental kind of Judaism. If, therefore, we wish to make sense of nearly all religious expressions of "being Jewish" and nearly all types of Judaism from the second century to the twentieth, we must begin with the Mishnah (though, obviously, we must not end there).

Now the Judaism shaped by the Mishnah consists of a coherent worldview and comprehensive way of living. It is a worldview which speaks of transcendent things, a way of life in response to the supernatural meaning of what is done, a heightened and deepened perception of the sanctification of Israel in deed and in deliberation. Sanctification means two things, first, distinguishing Israel in all its dimensions from the world in all its ways; second, establishing the stability, order, regularity, predictability, and reliability of Israel at moments and in contexts of danger. Danger means instability, disorder, irregularity, uncertainty, and betrayal. Each topic of the system as a whole takes up a critical and indispensable moment or context of social being. Each orders what is disorderly and dangerous. Through what is said in regard to each of the Mishnah's principal topics, what the system as a whole wishes to declare is fully expressed. Yet if the parts severally and jointly give the message of the whole, the whole cannot exist without all of the parts, so well joined and carefully crafted are they all.

Let me now describe and briefly interpret the six components of the Mishnah's system. The critical issue in the economic life, which means, in farming, is in two parts, revealed in the first division. First, Israel, as tenant on God's Holy Land, maintains the property in the ways God requires, keeping the rules which mark the Land and its crops as holy. Next, the hour at which the sanctification of the Land comes to form a critical mass, namely, in the ripened crops, is the moment ponderous with danger and heightened holiness. Israel's will so affects the crops as to mark a part of them as holy, the rest of them as available for common use. The human will is determinative in the process of sanctification.

Second, in the Second Division, what happens in the Land at certain times, at appointed times, marks off spaces of the Land as holy in yet another way. The center of the Land and the focus of its sanctification is the Temple. There the produce of the Land is received and given back to God, the one who created and sanctified the Land. At these unusual moments of sanctification, the inhabitants of the Land in their social being in villages enter a state of spatial sanctification. That is to say, the village boundaries mark off holy space, within which one must remain during the holy time. This is expressed in two ways. First, the Temple itself observes and expresses the special, recurring holy time. Second, the villages of the Land are brought into alignment with the Temple, forming a complement and completion to the Temple's sacred being. The advent of the appointed times precipitates a spatial reordering of the Land, so that the boundaries of the sacred are matched and mirrored in village and in Temple. At the heightened holiness marked by these moments of appointed times, therefore, the occasion for an affective sanctification is worked out. Like the harvest, the advent of an appointed time, a pilgrim festival, also a sacred season, is made to express that regular, orderly, and predictable sort of sanctification for Israel which the system as a whole seeks.

If for a moment we now leap over the next two divisions, the third and fourth, we come to the counterpart of the Divisions of Agriculture and Appointed Times. These are the Fifth and Sixth Divisions, namely Holy Things and Purities, those which deal with the everyday and the ordinary, as against the special moments of harvest, on the one side, and special time or season, on the other.

The Fifth Division is about the Temple on ordinary days. The Temple, the locus of sanctification, is conducted in a wholly routine and trustworthy, punctilious manner. The one thing which may unsettle matters is the intention and will of the human actor. This is subjected to carefully prescribed limitations and remedies. The Division of Holy Things generates its companion, the Sixth Division, the one on cultic cleanness, Purities. The relationship between the two is like that between Agriculture and Appointed Times, the former locative, the latter utopian, the former dealing with the fields, the latter with the interplay between fields and altar.

Here, too, in the Sixth Division, once we speak of the one place of the Temple, we address, too, the cleanness which pertains to every place. A system of cleanness, taking into account what imparts uncleanness and how this is done, what is subject to uncleanness, and how that state is overcome – that system is fully expressed, once more, in response to the participation of the human will. Without the wish and act of a human being, the system does not function. It is inert. Sources of uncleanness, which come naturally and not by volition, and modes of purification, which work naturally, and not by human intervention, remain inert until human will has imparted susceptibility to uncleanness, that is, introduced into the system, that food and drink, bed, pot, chair, and pan, which to begin with form the focus of the system. The movement from sanctification to uncleanness takes place when human will and work precipitate it.

This now brings us back to the middle divisions, the third and fourth, on Women and Damages. They take their place in the structure of the whole by showing the congruence, within the larger framework of regularity and order, of human concerns of family and farm, politics and workaday transactions among ordinary people. For without attending to these matters, the Mishnah's system does not encompass what, at its foundations, it is meant to comprehend and order. So what is at issue is fully cogent with the rest.

In the case of Women, the Third Division, attention focuses upon the point of disorder marked by the transfer of that disordering anomaly, woman, from the regular status provided by one man, to the equally trustworthy status provided by another. That is the point at which the Mishnah's interests are aroused: once more, predictably, the moment of disorder.

In the case of Damages, the Fourth Division, there are two important concerns. First, there is the paramount interest in preventing, so far as possible, the disorderly rise of one person and fall of another, and in sustaining the status quo of the economy, the house and household, of Israel, the holy society in eternal stasis. Second, there is the necessary concomitant in the provision of a system of political institutions to carry out the laws which preserve the balance and steady state of persons.

The two divisions which take up topics of concrete and material concern, the formation and dissolution of families and the transfer of property in that connection, the transactions, both through torts and through commerce, which lead to exchanges of property and the potential dislocation of the state of families in society, are both locative and utopian. They deal with the concrete locations in which people make their lives, household and street and field, the sexual and commercial exchanges of a given village. But they pertain to the life of all Israel, both in the Land and otherwise. These two divisions, together with the household ones of Appointed Times, constitute the sole opening outward toward the life of utopian Israel, that diaspora in the far reaches of the ancient world, in the endless span of time. This community from the Mishnah's perspective is not only in exile but unaccounted for, outside the system, for the Mishnah declines to recognize and take it into account. Israelites who dwell in the land of (unclean) death instead of in the Holy Land simply fall outside of the range of (holy) life. Priests, who must remain cultically clean, may not leave the Land – and neither may most of the Mishnah.

Now if we ask ourselves about the sponsorship and source of special interest in the topics just now reviewed, we shall come up with obvious answers. So far as the Mishnah is a document about the holiness of Israel in its land, it expresses that conception of sanctification and theory of its modes which will have been shaped among those to whom the Temple and its technology of joining heaven and Holy Land through the sacred place defined the core of being, I mean, the caste of the priests.

So far as the Mishnah takes up the way in which transactions are conducted among ordinary folk and takes the position that it is through documents that transactions are embodied and expressed (surely the position of the relevant tractates on both Women and Damages), the Mishnah expresses what is self-evident to scribes. Just as, to the priest, there is a correspondence between the table of the Lord in the Temple and the locus of the divinity in the heavens, so, to the scribe, there is a correspondence between the documentary expression of the human will on earth, in writs of all sorts, in the orderly provision of courts for the predictable and just disposition of exchanges of persons and property, and heaven's judgment of these same matters. When a woman becomes sanctified to a particular man on earth, through the appropriate document governing the transfer of her person and property, in heaven as well, the woman is deemed truly sanctified to that man. A violation of the writ therefore is not merely a crime. It is a sin. That is why the Temple rite involving the wife accused of adultery is integral to the system of the division of Women. So there are scribal divisions, the third and fourth, and priestly divisions, the first, fifth, and sixth; the second is then shared between the two groups.

These two social groups are not categorically symmetrical with one another, the priestly caste and the scribal profession. But for both groups the Mishnah makes self-evident statements. We know, moreover, that in time to come, the scribal profession would become a focus of sanctification. The scribe would be transformed into the "rabbi," honored man par excellence, locus of the holy through what he knew, just as the priest had been and would remain locus of the holy through what he could claim for genealogy. The divisions of special interest to scribes-become-rabbis and to their governance of Israelite society, those of Women and Damages, together with certain others particularly relevant to utopian Israel beyond the system of the Land – those tractates would grow and grow. Many, though not all, of the others would remain essentially as they were with the closure of the Mishnah. So we must notice that the Mishnah, for its part, speaks for the program of topics important to the priests. It takes up the persona of the scribes, speaking through their voice and in their manner.

At this point much has been said about priests in general. The reader familiar with the New Testament will wonder about a particular type of priest or lay person pretending to be a priest, namely, the Pharisee. Two matters require some attention. First, we want to ask what we learn about the Pharisees from the Mishnah. Second, we inquire about the relationship of the Pharisees to the Mishnah. As to the Pharisees as a group in the various groups of pietists in Judaism before 70, there are diverse references, difficult to square with one another. As I pointed out in Chapter Six, the one set of references pertinent to the materials before us is those in the Gospels, in which the Pharisees are represented as a group which emphasized certain ("external") religious practices, involving distinctive views on the resurrection of the dead, on strict observance of the Sabbath, and on careful tithing of agricultural produce and eating food in a state of purity generally associated only with the Temple cult. Now so far as the Mishnah takes for granted that Jews must strictly observe the Sabbath in a certain way, carefully tithe the agricultural produce they eat, and preserve a state of cultic or Levitical cleanness (that is, observe the curious taboos of Lev. 11-15 when eating their food at home, not merely meat deriving from animals barbecued in the Temple), it certainly accords with views attributed to Pharisees. On the other hand, the Mishnah rarely refers to the Pharisees. When it does, it does not represent them as its definitive authorities. Sages, not Pharisees, are the Mishnah's authorities. A few of the Mishnah's authorities, particularly Gamaliel and Simeon b. Gamaliel, are known from independent sources to have been Pharisees; Paul tells us about Gamaliel, and Josephus about Simeon b. Gamaliel. But that is the sum and substance of it. Consequently, to assign the whole of the Mishnah to the Pharisees who flourished before 70 and who are known to us from diverse sources, all of them composed in the form in which we know them after 70, is hardly justified. We learn little about the Pharisees from the Mishnah, except in the handful of sayings referring to them (M. Hag. 2:4-7; M. Sot. 3:4; M. Toh. 4:12; and M. Yad. 4:6-8), or assigned to people who we have good reason to believe were Pharisees.

As to the relationship of the Pharisees to the Mishnah, we learn somewhat more. For the Mishnah contains a great many principles and propositions which can be shown to go back to the period before 70. Some of the most striking and important of these principles, those in the Divisions on Agriculture and Purities in particular, but also a few in the

Divisions on Appointed Times and Women, may be shown to serve sectarian, and not general or societal, interests. It would carry us far afield to specify what these propositions are and why they evidently speak out of a sectarian context. (The chapters on Hillel have offered some observations on this matter.) The main point should not be missed. When we speak about the Pharisees, we speak about Jews who thought that when they ate their meals at home, they should do so in the way, in general, in which the priests eat their meals of meat, meal, and wine, supplied from the leftovers of God's meal on the altar of the Temple in Jerusalem. So some of them were priests who pretended that their homes were little Temples. And, it seems reasonable to suppose, others of them were lay people pretending to be priests and engaged in the same fantasy. When in these pages we speak of "priests," these are the particular priests whose viewpoint will be expressed in those parts of the document which lay stress upon eating at home as if one is in the Temple.

But this, too, requires qualification. First, Pharisees were not the only Jews who had a special interest in the cultic cleanness of their food. The Essene community at Qumran also maintained that its food was in a state of cultic cleanness, as if it were prepared on the altar of God in the holy Temple. Consequently, we cannot take for granted that when a saying indicates the conviction that ordinary food must be kept pure as if it were the Lord's food in the Temple, that saying must derive from a Pharisee and from no other sect, group, or source. That simply is not so.

Second, there are many other parts of the document in which interests of all priests are at hand. For instance, there is the whole of the Fifth Division, Holy Things. In vast stretches of the First Division, Agriculture, in which the separation of tithes and heave-offering as the priestly ration is described, all priests are equally represented. No one had to be a Pharisee in particular to take up these matters. Any priest who cared about his income (either at the present time or in the time in which the Mishnah's law would everywhere prevail) would take these same matters to heart. So the Mishnah is very much a priestly document. It may also be a document reflecting in some measure the partisan interests of a certain kind of priests (and associated lay people). But it cannot be called a document only or mainly of this second group. Its social constituency, as I said, included a large cohort of priests interested in their income and emoluments. Some of these may have regarded as important those special matters stressed in parts of the Sixth Division, but all of them would have cared about the laws of the First, Second, Fifth, and the bulk of the Sixth Divisions as well.

This brief statement of the substance of the Mishnah's system and the evident caste and professional sponsorship of the Mishnah once more brings us to the question of how people in our own time may profitably consult the contents of this document from long ago and far away. The sages of the late first and second centuries produced a document to contain the most important things they could specify. They chose as their subjects six matters, of which, I am inclined to think, for the same purpose we should have rejected at least four, and probably all six. That is, four of the divisions of the Mishnah are devoted to purity law, tithing, laws for the conduct of sacrifice in the Temple cult, and the way in which the sacrifices are carried on at festivals – four areas of reality which, I suspect, would not have found a high place on a list of our own most fundamental concerns. The other two divisions, which deal with the transfer of women from one man to another and with matters of civil law – including the organization of the government, civil claims, torts, and damages, real estate and the like – complete the list. When we attempt to interpret the sort of world the rabbis of the Mishnah proposed to create, therefore, at the very outset we realize that that world in no way conforms, in its most profound and definitive categories of organization, to our own. It follows that the critical work of making sense and use of the Mishnah is to learn how to hear what the Mishnah wishes to say in its own setting and to the people addressed by those who made it up. For that purpose it is altogether too easy to bring our questions and take for granted that, when the sages seem to say something relevant to our questions, they therefore propose to speak to us. Anachronism takes many forms. The most dangerous comes when an ancient text seems readily accessible and immediately clear.

For the Mishnah is separated from us by the whole of Western history, philosophy, and science. Its wise sayings, its law, and its theology may lie in the background of the law and lore of contemporary Judaism. But they have been mediated to us by many centuries of exegesis, not to mention experience. They come to us now in the form which much later theologians and scholars have imposed upon them. It follows that the critical problem is to recognize the distance between us and the Mishnah. Our task is the work of allowing strange people to speak in a strange language about things quite alien to us, and yet of learning how to hear what they are saying. That is, we have to learn how to understand them in their language and in their terms. Once we recognize that they are fundamentally different from us, we have also to lay claim to them, or, rather, acknowledge their claim upon us.

As I shall argue at the end, what makes the Mishnah important is that it supplies us with another, particularly full and well-organized, corpus of "for examples," that is, examples of how people did one thing and not some other, problems for interpretation, by one theory or another, of why people did one thing and not some other. The Mishnah captures a whole vision of a complete world. It describes the house and household of Israel, an architect's plan in tedious detail, as useful plans must be. Because the Mishnah does not generalize, it allows us to look for what is general in all of its particularities. Because of its tiresome babble about details, the Mishnah permits us to try and test our theories of the whole. But in saying so, I have moved beyond my story. Let us now turn to another side of context, not the one of synchronic history, nor the one of language and culture, but the Mishnah's diachronic setting in Israelite revelation: the Mishnah and God's word in the revelation of the Torah to Moses at Mount Sinai.

## IV. Heritage: Mishnah and Scripture. The Open Canon of Judaism

To this point in the discussion, the reader must imagine that the Mishnah falls into the category of documents found in a desert cave, produced by a nascent group with no past at all, a document like the Pentateuch, addressed to a mixed multitude of a no-people. For up to now I have proceeded to introduce the Mishnah as if it stood only at the head of a long line of Israelite religion and law, but not at the end of one. That, of course, is not so. Every significant creation in ancient Israel from the formation of the Hebrew Scriptures and conclusion of the canon onward necessarily forms a response to the Torah. This Torah is the revelation of God to Moses at Mount Sinai, contained in the Pentateuch, as well as the other biblical books, known to Israel all together as Tanakh (for Torah, Nebiim, Ketubim, that is, Torah, prophets, writings), and to Christendom as the Old Testament. For each such fresh creation is inevitably a reworking of available materials of revelation. Each therefore either claims for itself a place within the canon defined by the Israelite Scriptures, or it deliberately excludes itself and seeks a place outside of, but in relationship to, that same canon. Consequently, at the end of this account of the Mishnah, we have to ask about the relationship between the Mishnah and the Holy Scriptures which define and frame the Israelite world – worldview, way of life – to which the framers of the Mishnah addressed themselves and within which they, too, took shape.

On the surface, Scripture plays little role in the Mishnaic system. The Mishnah rarely cites a verse of Scripture, refers to Scripture as an entity, links its own ideas to those of Scripture, or lays claim to originate in what Scripture has said, even by indirect or remote allusion to a scriptural verse of teaching. So, superficially, the Mishnah is totally indifferent to Scripture. That impression, moreover, is reinforced by the traits of the language of the Mishnah. The framers of Mishnaic discourse, amazingly, never attempt to imitate the language of Scripture, as do those of the Essene writings at Qumran. The very redactional structure of Scripture, found so serviceable to the writer of the Temple scroll, remarkably, is of no interest whatever to the organizers of the Mishnah and its tractates, except in a very few cases (Leviticus 16, Yoma; Exodus 12; Pesahim).

I wish now to dwell on these facts. Formally, redactionally, and linguistically the Mishnah stands in splendid isolation from Scripture. It is not possible to point to many parallels, that is, cases of anonymous books, received as holy, in which the forms and formulations (specific verses) of Scripture play so slight a role. People who wrote holy books commonly imitated the Scripture's language. They cited concrete verses. They claimed at the very least that direct revelation had come to them, as in the angelic discourses of IV Erza and Baruch, so that what they say stands on an equal plane with Scripture. The internal evidence of the Mishnah's sixty-two usable tractates (excluding Abot), by contrast, in no way suggests that anyone pretended to talk like Moses and write like Moses, claimed to cite and correctly interpret things that Moses had said, or even alleged to have had a revelation like that of Moses and so to stand on the mountain with Moses. There is none of this. So the claim of scriptural authority for the Mishnah's doctrines and institutions is difficult to locate within the internal evidence of the Mishnah itself. (We shall return to this matter in Chapter Ten.)

We cannot be surprised that, in consequence of this amazing position of autonomous, autocephalic authority implicit in the character of Mishnaic discourse, the Mishnah should forthwith have demanded in its own behalf some sort of apologetic. Nor are we surprised that the Mishnah attracted its share of quite hostile criticism. The issue, in the third century, would be this: Why should we listen to this mostly anonymous document, which makes statements on the nature of institutions and social conduct, statements we obviously are expected to keep? Who are Meir, Yosé, Judah, Simeon, and Eleazar – people who from the perspective of the third-century recipients of the document, lived fifty or a hundred years ago – that we should listen to what they have to say? God revealed the Torah. Is this Mishnah, too, part of the Torah? If so, how? What, in other words, is the relationship of the Mishnah to Scripture, and how does the Mishnah claim authority over us such as we accord to the revelation to Moses by God at Mount Sinai?

There are two important responses to the question of the place of Scripture in the Mishnaic tradition. First and the more radical: the Mishnah constitutes torah. It, too, is a statement of revelation: "Torah revealed to Moses at Sinai." But this part of revelation has come down in a form different from the well-known, written part, the Scripture. This tradition truly deserves the name "tradition," because for a long time it was handed down orally, not in writing, until given the written formulation now before us in the Mishnah. This sort of apologetic for the

Mishnah appears, to begin with, in Abot, with its stunning opening chapter, linking Moses on Sinai through the ages to the earliest named authorities of the Mishnah itself, the five pairs, on down to Shammai and Hillel. Since some of the named authorities in the chain of tradition appear throughout the materials of the Mishnah, the claim is that what these people say comes to them from Sinai through the processes of *qabbalah* and *massoret* – handing down, "traditioning."

So the reason (from the perspective of the Torah myth of the Mishnah) that the Mishnah does not cite Scripture is that it does not have to. It stands on the same plane as Scripture. It enjoys the same authority as Scripture. This radical position is still more extreme than that taken by pseudepigraphic writers, who imitate the style of Scripture, or who claim to speak within that same gift of revelation as Moses. It is one thing to say one's holy book is Scripture because it is like Scripture, or to claim that the author of the holy book has a revelation independent of that of Moses. These two positions concede to the Torah of Moses priority over their own holy books. The Mishnah's apologists make no such concession, when they allege that the Mishnah is part of the Torah of Moses. They appeal to the highest possible authority to the Israelite framework, claiming the most one can claim in behalf of the book which, in fact, bears the names of men who lived fifty years before the apologists themselves. That seems to me remarkable courage.

Then there is this matter of the Mishnah's not citing Scripture. When we consider the rich corpus of allusions to Scripture in other holy books, both those bearing the names of authors and those presented anonymously, we realize that the Mishnah claims its authority to be co-equal with that of Scripture. Many other holy books are made to lay claim to authority only because they depend upon the authority of Scripture and state the true meaning of Scripture. That fact brings us to the other answer to the question of the place of Scripture in the Mishnaic tradition.

Second, the earliest exegetical strata of the two Talmuds and the legal exegetical writings produced in the two hundred years after the closure of the Mishnah take the position that the Mishnah is wholly dependent upon Scripture. Whatever is of worth in the Mishnah can be shown to derive directly from Scripture. So the Mishnah – "tradition" – is deemed distinct from, and subordinate to, Scripture. This position is expressed in an obvious way. Once the Talmuds cite a Mishnah pericope, they commonly ask, "What is the source of these words?" And the answer invariably is, "As it is said in Scripture." This constitutes not only a powerful defense for the revealed truth of the Mishnah. For when the exegetes find themselves constrained to add prooftexts, they admit the need to improve and correct an existing flaw.

That the search for the scriptural bases for the Mishnah's laws constitutes both an apologetic and a criticism is shown in the character of a correlative response to the Mishnah, namely, the Sifra and its exegesis of Leviticus. The Sifra is a commentary on the Book of Leviticus, citing the same authorities as appear in the Mishnah itself. But the fundamental structure of the Sifra derives from the period after the Mishnah had taken shape, since the Sifra is a polemical document. The polemic is against the failure of the Mishnah to cite Scripture very much or systematically to link its ideas to Scripture through the medium of formal demonstration by exegesis. This polemic is expressed over and over again. The Sifra's rhetorical exegesis follows a standard redactional form. Scripture will be cited. Then a statement will be made about its meaning, or a statement of law correlative to that Scripture will be given. That statement sometimes cites the Mishnah, often verbatim. Finally, the author of Sifra invariably states, "Now is that not (merely) logical?" And the point of that statement will be, Can this position not be gained through the working of mere logic, based upon facts supplied (to be sure) by Scripture? The polemical power of Sifra lies in its repetitive demonstration that the stated position, citation of a Mishnah pericope, is not only not the product of logic, but is, and only can be, the product of exegesis of Scripture.

What is still more to the point, exegesis in Sifra's and the Talmud's view is formal in character. That is, it is based upon some established mode of exegesis of the formal traits of scriptural grammar and syntax, assigned to the remote antiquity represented by the names of Ishmael or Aqiba. So the polemic of Sifra and the Talmuds is against the positions that, first, what the Mishnah says (in the Mishnah's own words) is merely logical; and that, second, the position taken by the Mishnah can have been reached in any way other than through grammatical syntactical exegesis of Scripture. That other way, the way of reading the Scripture through philosophical logic or practical reason, is explicitly rejected time and again. Philosophical logic and applied reason are inadequate. Formal exegesis is shown to be not only adequate, but necessary, indeed inexorable. It follows that Sifra undertakes to demonstrate precisely what the framers of the opening pericopes of the Talmud's treatment of the Mishnah's successive units of thought also wish to show. The Mishnah is not autonomous. It is not independent. It is not correlative, that is, separate but equal. It is contingent, secondary, derivative, resting wholly on the foundations of the (written) revelation of God to Moses at Mount Sinai. Therein, too, lies the authority of the Mishnah as tradition.

So, there are two positions which would rapidly take shape when the Mishnah was published. First, tradition in the form of the Mishnah is deemed autonomous of Scripture and enjoys the same authority as that of Scripture. The reason is that Scripture and ("oral") tradition are merely two media for conveying a single corpus of revealed law and doctrine. Second, tradition in the form of the Mishnah is true because it is not autonomous of Scripture. Tradition is secondary and dependent upon Scripture.

The authority of the Mishnah is the authority of Moses. That authority comes to the Mishnah directly and in an unmediated way, because the Mishnah's words were said by God to Moses at Mount Sinai and faithfully transmitted through a process of oral formulation and oral transmission from that time until those words were written down by Judah the Patriarch at the end of the second century. Or, that authority comes to the Mishnah indirectly, in a way mediated through the written Scriptures.

What the Mishnah says is what the Scripture says, rightly interpreted. The authority of tradition lies in its correct interpretation of the Scripture. Tradition bears no autonomous authority, is not an independent entity, correlative with Scripture. A very elaborate (and insufferably dull) technology of exegesis of grammar and syntax is needed to build the bridge between tradition as contained in the Mishnah and Scripture, the original utensil shaped by God and revealed to Moses to convey the truth of revelation to the community of Israel. Or matters are otherwise. I hardly need to make them explicit.

Let me now state the facts of the relationship of the Mishnah to Scripture, beyond the picture of the third-century apologist critics of the Mishnah. First, there are tractates which simply repeat in their own words precisely what Scripture has to say, and at best serve to amplify and complete the basic ideas of Scripture. For example, all of the cultic tractates of the Second Division, the one on Appointed Times, which tell what one is supposed to do in the Temple on the various special days of the year, and the bulk of the cultic tractates of the Fifth Division, which deals with Holy Things, simply restate facts of Scripture. For another example, all of those tractates of the Sixth Division, on Purities, which specify sources of uncleanness, depend completely on information supplied by Scripture. I have demonstrated in detail that every important statement in Niddah, on menstrual uncleanness, and the most fundamental notions of Zabim, on the uncleanness of the person with flux referred to in Leviticus Chapter Fifteen, as well as every detail in Negaim, on the uncleanness of the person or house suffering the uncleanness described at Leviticus Chapters Thirteen and Fourteen – all of these tractates serve only to restate the basic facts of Scripture and to complement those facts with other important ones.

There are, second, tractates which take up facts of Scripture but work them out in a way in which those scriptural facts cannot have led us to predict. A supposition concerning what is important about the facts, utterly remote from the supposition of Scripture, will explain why the Mishnah tractates under discussion say the original things they say in confronting those Scripturally provided facts. For one example, Scripture takes for granted that the red cow will be burned in a state of uncleanness, because it is burned outside the camp – Temple. The priestly writers cannot have imagined that a state of cultic cleanness was to be attained outside of the cult. The absolute datum of tractate Parah, by contrast, is that cultic cleanness not only can be attained outside of the "tent of meeting." The red cow was to be burned in a state of cleanness even exceeding that cultic cleanness required in the Temple itself. The problematic which generates the intellectual agendum of Parah, therefore, is how to work out the conduct of the rite of burning the cow in relationship to the Temple: Is it to be done in exactly the same way, or in exactly the opposite way? This mode of contrastive and analogical thinking helps us to understand the generative problematic of such tractates as Erubin and Besah, to mention only two.

Third, there are, predictably, many tractates which either take up problems in no way suggested by Scripture, or begin from facts at best merely relevant to facts of Scripture. In the former category are Tohorot, on the cleanness of foods, with its companion, Uqsin; Demai, on doubtfully tithed produce; Tamid, on the conduct of the daily whole-offering; Baba Batra, on rules of real estate transactions and certain other commercial and property relationships, and so on. In the latter category are Ohalot, which spins out its strange problems within the theory that a tent and a utensil are to be compared to one another (!); Kelim, on the susceptibility to uncleanness of various sorts of utensils; Miqvaot, on the sorts of water which effect purification from uncleanness; Ketubot and Gittin, on the documents of marriage and divorce; and many others. These tractates draw on facts of Scripture. But the problem confronted in these tractates in no way responds to problems important to Scripture. What we have here is a prior program of inquiry, which will make ample provision for facts of Scripture in an inquiry to begin with generated essentially outside of the framework of Scripture. First comes the problem or topic, then – if possible – comes attention to Scripture.

So there we have it: Some tractates merely repeat what we find in Scripture. Some are totally independent of Scripture. And some fall in between. Clearly, we are no closer to a definitive answer to the question of the relationship of Scripture to the Mishnah than we were when we described the state of thought on the very same questions in the third and fourth centuries. We find everything and its opposite. But to offer a final answer to the question of Scripture-Mishnah relationships, we have to take that fact seriously. The Mishnah in no way is so remote from Scripture as its formal omission of citations of verses of Scripture suggests. In no way can it be described as contingent upon, and secondary to Scripture, as many of its third-century apologists claimed. But the right answer is not that it is somewhere in between. Scripture confronts the framers of the Mishnah as revelation, not merely as a source of facts. But the framers of the Mishnah had their own world with which to deal. They made statements in the framework and fellowship of their own age and generation. They were bound, therefore, to come to Scripture with a set of questions generated other than in Scripture. They brought their own ideas about what was going to be important in Scripture. This is perfectly natural.

The philosophers of the Mishnah conceded to Scripture the highest authority. At the same time what they chose to hear, within the authoritative statements of Scripture, will in the end form a statement of its own. To state matters simply: All of Scripture is authoritative. But only some of Scripture is relevant. And what happened is that the framers and philosophers of the tradition of the Mishnah came to Scripture when they had reason to. That is to say, they brought to Scripture a program of questions and inquiries framed essentially among themselves. So they were highly selective. That is why their program itself constituted a statement upon the meaning of Scripture. They and their apologists of one sort hastened to add their program consisted of a statement of the meaning of Scripture.

In part, we must affirm the truth of that claim. When the framers of the Mishnah speak about the priestly passages of the Mosaic law codes, with deep insight they perceive profound layers of meaning embedded ("to begin with") in those codes. What they have done with the priestly code, moreover, they also have done, though I think less coherently, with the bulk of the deuteronomic laws and with some of those of the covenant code. But their exegetical triumph – exegetical, not merely eisegetical – lies in their handling of the complex corpus of materials of the priestly code.

True, others will have selected totally different passages of Scripture, not in the Mosaic codes to begin with. Prophecy makes its impact on the holy books of other Israelites of the same ancient times, as, for instance, Q, Matthew, and Mark. Surely we must concede that, in reading those passages, other writers, interested in history and salvation, displayed that same perspicacity as did the framers of the Mishnaic tradition who interpreted the priestly code as they did and so formed a theory of Israel's sanctification. It is in the nature of Scripture itself that such should be the case. The same Scripture which gives us the prophets gives us the Pentateuch as well – and gives priority to the pentateuchal codes as the revelation of God to Moses.

## V. Conclusion

In introducing the reader to the Mishnah, I wish to make possible a protracted acquaintance, a long friendship, even though, as I have stressed, it is between people essentially and profoundly alien to one another. What joins the ages is not only our interest in their world. First, it also is our interest in any encompassing and important statement of how humankind might in imagination create a world. The Mishnah is a specimen of Utopia. That is why what we find in the Mishnah is more than insight into the world created within one kind of Judaism in the formative centuries of Western civilization.

In the Mishnah contemporary humanists may gain a more ample account of a tiny part of the potentialities of humanity: that part expressed within the Judaic tradition in its rabbinical formulation. When we find out what it is that the Mishnaic system contains within itself, we discover yet another mode for the measure of humankind. The human potentialities and available choices within one ecological frame of humanity, the ancient Jewish one, are defined and explored by the sages. The same question – the possibilities contained within the culture of ancient Judaism – is to be addressed to the diverse formations and structures, at other times in its history besides that of late antiquity. But we have to learn how to do the work in some one place, and only then shall we have a call to attempt it elsewhere. What we must do is first describe, then interpret.

But what do we wish to describe? I am inclined to think the task is to encompass everything deemed important by some one group, to include within, and to exclude from, its holy book, its definitive text. We wish to make sense of a system and its exclusions, its stance in a taxonomy of systems. For, on the surface, what sages put in they think essential, and what they omit they do not think important. If that is self-evident, then the affirmative choices are the ones requiring description and then interpretation. But what standpoint will permit us to fasten onto the whole and where is the fulcrum on which to place our lever? For, given the size of the evidence, the work of description may leave us with an immense, and essentially pointless, task of repetition: saying in our own words what the sources say, perfectly clearly, in theirs.

So when I say that a large part of work is to describe the worldview of the sages of the Mishnah, at best I acquire a license to hunt for insight. What defines the work as well as I am able, is what has run through this introduction to the Mishnah: the idea of a system. That is a whole set of interrelated concerns and conceptions which, all together, both express a worldview and define a way of living for a particular group of people in a particular economic and political setting. The Mishnah brings to the surface the integrated conception of the world and of the way in which the people should live in that world. All in all, that system both defines and forms reality for Jews responsive to the sages of the Mishnah.

Now, self-evidently all worth knowing about the sages and the Jews around them is not contained within their system, that is, the Mishnah as they lay it out. There is, after all, the hard fact that the Jews did not have power fully to shape the world within which they lived out their lives and formed their social group. No one else did either. There were, indeed, certain persistent and immutable facts which form the natural environment, the material ecology for their system. These facts do not change and do have to be confronted. There are, for instance, the twin facts of Jewish powerlessness and minority status. Any system produced by Judaism for nearly the whole of its history will have to take account of the fact that the group is of no account in the world, a pariah people. Another definitive fact is the antecedent heritage of Scripture and associated tradition, which define for the Jews a considerably more important role in the supernatural world than the natural world affords them. Israel is God's first love, not Rome's last victim. These two facts, the Jews' numerical insignificance and political unimportance and the Jews' inherited pretensions and fantasies about their own centrality in the history and destiny of the human race, created (and still create) a certain dissonance between any given Jewish worldview, on the one side, and the world to be viewed by the Jews, on the other. And so is the case for the Mishnah.

But we cannot take for granted that what we think should define the central tension of a given system in fact is what concerned the people who created and expressed that system. If we have no way of showing that our surmise may be wrong, then we also have no basis on which to verify our thesis as to the core and meaning of the system before us. The result can be at best good guesses. A mode for interpreting the issues of a system has therefore to be proposed.

One route to the interpretation of a system is to specify the sorts of issues it chooses to regard as problems, the matters it chooses for its close and continuing exegesis, our exegesis of the canon of topics. When we know the things about which people worry, we have some insight into the way in which they see the world. So, when we approach the Mishnah, we ask about its critical tensions, the recurring issues which occupy its great minds. It is out of concern with this range of issues, and not some other, that the Mishnah defines its principal areas for discussion. Here is the point at which the great exercises of law and theology will be generated – here and not somewhere else. This is a way in which we specify the choices people have made, the selections a system has effected. When we know what people have chosen, we also may speculate about the things they have rejected, the issues they regard as uninteresting or as closed. We then may describe the realm of thought and everyday life which they do not deem subject to tension and speculation. It is these two sides to this vast document – the things people conceive to be dangerous and important, the things they set into the background as unimportant and uninteresting – which provide us with a key to the culture of community or, as I prefer to put it, to the system constructed and expressed by a given social group.

# 4

## Revelation and Reason, Scripture and Mishnah: Their Relationship

When we formulate the question of the relationship of the Mishnah to Scripture, we adopt the language and categories that the authorship of the Mishnah wanted us to use. For (to personify that authorship in the name of Judah the Patriarch) what the patriarch accomplished through remarkably adroit imposition of uniform rhetoric and logic upon the discussion of discrete topical materials was precisely that: to treat everything as one thing. Hence we rightly identify "the Mishnah" as a single work. We see it as uniform because whatever topic it discusses among its sixty-one relevant tractates (I omit reference to Pirqe Abot as outside of the entire rhetorical, logical, and topical program of the document, and to Eduyot as a mere reprise), the authorship of the Mishnah does what appears to be the same thing. That is to say, that authorship formulates its ideas within a strikingly limited formal repertoire. It appeals for cogency to a narrow range of logical possibilities, generally limited to what we know as *Listenwissenschaft*, that is, the making of lists that in detail register a single general rule (about which I shall have more to say), and, throughout, preserves a remarkably cogency of style.

But what if we introduce analytical variables of our own making? Then the unity and uniformity of the Mishnah prove to conceal considerable diversity. The sixty-one tractates of the Mishnah, each analyzed on its own, turn out to yield as much diversity in structure – for example, relationship to other writings – as they do in topic. And we must not be deceived by the authorship's genius in its uniform formalization of the whole to assume that the topical differentiation that that same authorship has adopted for its organizing principle effects difference merely at the surface of things. For while the Mishnah's authorship has made things appear as though all that differs, in the vast cogent writing, is subject matter, subject matter matters. That is to say, differences on topic from one tractate to another (and one division to another) prove very real and contradict uniformity in rhetorica and even in prevailing logic.

And if that is the case, it must follow, the relationships between the document and other writings also have to be characterized with nuance and full recognition of the differentiated components of the whole. That is especially the case when, as I shall explain, our analytical variables appeal, in part, to the quite varied relationships between components of the Mishnah and Scripture. It becomes impossible to make a single statement of the relationship of the Mishnah to Scripture that serves to characterize all tractates. But it becomes quite possible to form groups of tractates, each set of which bears its own distinctive relationship to Scripture.

Since our interest lies in how tractates relate to Scripture, we shall adopt that criterion as our point of analytical differentiation. Simple logic dictates that, when we ask about relationships, there can be only three classes of relationship: total, none at all, and something in the middle. Here, too, we can postulate as a matter of theory that a Mishnah tractate may stand in a totally dependent relationship with Scripture, may have no relationship at all to Scripture, or may fall somewhere in-between. That is a matter of theory. Now let me spell out the theory in terms of concrete facts. There are three possibilities in a relationship between a Mishnah tractate and a passage of Scripture. First of all, Scripture supplies the topic and also provides the analytical program of the authorship of a Mishnah tractate, chapter, or pericope. Therefore nothing within the Mishnah's treatment of the topic goes beyond the logical program of the theme Scripture provides within the details that Scripture sets forth. Second, Scripture sets forth a topic but does not then dictate the inner logic by which the topic will be worked out in a series of illustrative cases, as is the fact in the first relationship. Therefore the subject matter is scriptural, but the treatment of the subject entirely autonomous of Scripture. Third, even the subject matter is unknown to Scripture or is so casually and elliptically treated in Scripture that the Mishnah tractate, theme and logic all together, is wholly autonomous of Scripture.

First let us consider how a Mishnah tractate may stand in total dependence upon Scripture. Precisely what I mean by that classification requires definition, since it is not a subjective judgment. Let me give a single example of the first of the three relationships, since, from the viewpoint of the analysis of the Mishnah tractates' agenda, that is the single operative classification. For that purpose I present first the relevant passages of Scripture, then the Mishnah's treatment of those passages. I believe it will be self-evident to readers that nothing in the Mishnah's discussion moves beyond the requirements of the exposition of the scriptural topic within the lines of analysis defined by Scripture. Here is the relevant scriptural passage, Deut. 23:25-26:

> When you go into your neighbor's vineyard, you may eat your fill of grapes, as many as you wish, but you shall not put any in your vessel. When you go into your neighbor's standing grain, you may pluck the ears with your hand, but you shall not put a sickle to your neighbor's standing grain.

This is further read in light of the statement, Deut. 25:4

> You shall not muzzle an ox while it is threshing.

On that basis, the rule is that workers are permitted to nibble on grain or grapes on which they are working. What follows is the Mishnah's treatment of this same topic.

7:1    A.    He who hires [day] workers and told them to start work early or to stay late –

B.    in a place in which they are accustomed not to start work early or not to stay late –

C.    he has no right to force them to do so.

D.    In a place in which they are accustomed to provide a meal, he must provide a meal.

E.    [In a place in which they are accustomed] to make do with a sweet,

F.    he provides it.

G.    Everything accords with the practice of the province.

H.    M'SH B: R. Yohanan b. Matya said to his son, "Go, hire workers for us."

I.    He went and made an agreement with them for food [without further specification].

J.    Now when he came to his father, [the father] said to him, "My son, even if you should make for them a meal like one of Solomon in his day, you will not have carried out your obligation to them.

K.    "For they are children of Abraham, Isaac, and Jacob.

L.    "But before they begin work, go and tell them, '[Work for us] on condition that you have a claim on me [as to food] only for a piece of bread and pulse alone.'"

M.    Rabban Simeon b. Gamaliel says, "He had no need to specify that in so many words.

N.    "Everything [in any case] accords with the practice of the province."

7:2    A.    And these [have the right to] eat [the produce on which they work] by [right accorded to them in] the Torah:

B.    he who works on what is as yet unplucked [may eat from the produce] at the end of the time of processing;

C.    [and he who works] on plucked produce [may eat from the produce] before processing is done;

D. [in both instances solely] in regard to what grows from the ground.
E. But these do not [have the right to] eat [the produce on which they labor] by [right accorded to them in] the Torah:
F. he who works on what is as yet unplucked, before the end of the time of processing;
G. [and he who works] on plucked produce after the processing is done;
H. [in both instances solely] in regard to what does not grow from the ground.

7:3 A. [If] one was working with his hands but not with his feet,
B. with his feet but not with his hands,
C. even [carrying] with his shoulder,
D. lo, he [has the right to] eat [the produce on which he is working].
E. R. Yosé b. R. Judah says, "[He may eat the produce on which he is working] only if he works with both his hands and his feet."

7:4 A. [If the laborer] was working on figs, he [has] not [got the right to] eat grapes.
B. [If he was working] on grapes, he [has] not [got the right to] eat figs.
C. But [he does have the right to] refrain [from eating] until he gets to the best produce and then [to exercise his right to] eat.
D. And in all instances they have said [that he may eat from the produce on which he is laboring] only in the time of work.
E. But on grounds of restoring lost property to the owner, they have said [in addition]:
F. Workers [have the right to] eat as they go from furrow to furrow [even though they do not then work],
G. and when they are coming back from the press [so saving time for the employer];
H. and in the case of an ass [nibbling on straw in its load], when it is being unloaded.

7:5 A. A worker [has the right to] eat cucumbers, even to a denar's worth,
B. or dates, even to a denar's worth.
C. R. Eleazar Hisma says, "A worker should not eat more than the value of his wages."
D. But sages permit.
E. But they instruct the man not to be a glutton and thereby slam the door in his own face [to future employment].

7:6 A. A man makes a deal [with the householder not to exercise his right to eat produce on which he is working] in behalf of himself, his adult son, or daughter,
B. in behalf of his adult manservant or womanservant,
C. in behalf of his wife,
D. because [they can exercise] sound judgment [and keep the terms of the agreement].
E. But he may not make a deal in behalf of his minor son or daughter,
F. in behalf of his minor boy servant or girl servant,
G. or in behalf of his beast,
H. because [they can] not [exercise] sound judgment [and keep the terms of the agreement].

7:7 A. He who hires workers to work in his fourth-year plantings [the produce of which is to be eaten not at random but only in Jerusalem or to be redeemed for money to be brought up to Jerusalem (Lev. 19-24)] –

B. lo, these do not [have the right to] eat.
C. If [in advance] he did not inform them [of the character of the produce and the prohibitions affecting it], he [has to] redeem the produce and [permit them to] eat [of it].
D. [If] his fig cakes split up,
E. his jars [of wine] burst open [while yet untithed, and workers are hired to repress the figs and rebottle the wine],
F. lo, these do not [have the right to] eat [them].
G. If he did not inform them [that the produce on which they would be working was untithed and therefore not available for their random consumption],
H. he has to tithe [the produce] and [allow them to] eat [of it].

What we see is a very systematic and orderly exposition of the theme, with little initiative beyond the limits of the simple logic imposed by that theme. That is to say, first, we follow the established custom, M. 7:1. Second, we define precisely what one is permitted to eat while working, M. 7:2. Third, we explain how one is permitted to take produce, and the limits of what it means to work on produce, M. 7:3. M. 7:4 then proceeds to take up interstitial cases, for example, working on figs and eating grapes. M. 7:5, 6 ask about limits set to one's nibbling. M. 7:7 finally addresses special cases, for example, working on produce that no one may eat.

Anyone familiar with the way in which the authorship of the Mishnah analyzes any problem or addresses any theme will find a perfectly standard program of definition and exposition, consisting of a labor of extension and limitation of the rule. While this mode of thought in general may be deemed philosophical, it bears no abstract philosophical principle, for example, a doctrine applicable to a vast variety of cases, whether of a metaphysical or an ethical or a legal character. The mode of thought may be deemed philosophical in a rather general way, but it is not distinctive to philosophy in any limited sense by which we may define philosophy. That distinction between mode of thought and medium of thought will gain greater clarity in later parts of this study. At this point it suffices to note that the treatment of the topic at hand is simply how the Mishnah's authorship treats any topic of Scripture on which it has no particular perspective or in which it discerns no problematic external to the logic limits of the topic as Scripture sets it forth.

Second, let us consider what it means for a tractate to appear totally autonomous of Scripture, that is to say, in its entire repertoire of ideas and problems never to allude to Scripture. For that purpose I allude to a variety of tractates that take up issues that Scripture does not supply, topics Scripture does not treat, or problems Scripture does not imagine. My first candidate is Mishnah-tractate Kelim. This tractate is wholly devoted to the exposition of problems of classification, inclusive of connection and intentionality as issues of classification. Tractates on cleanness and uncleanness by definition form exercises of classification, since the ultimate taxa are unclean or susceptible to uncleanness and clean or insusceptible. But the exemplary power of detailed discourse to invoke fundamental principles of classification and to set forth the complexities of physics of connection is hardly exhausted by the generalizations, unclean or clean. Indeed, throughout, these form the mere result, but never the engaging problem of principled discourse. Mishnah-tractate Kelim deals with the status, as to cultic cleanness, of useful objects, tools or utensils. Its main point is that when an object has a distinctive character, form, use, or purpose, it is susceptible to uncleanness, so that, if it is in contact with a source of uncleanness, it is deemed cultically unclean. If it is formless, purposeless, or useless, it is insusceptible. Three criteria govern the determination of what is useful or purposeful. First come properties deemed common to all utensils, whatever the material. Second are qualities distinctive to different sorts of materials. Third is the consideration of the complex purposes for which an object is made or used, primary and subsidiary, and the intention of the user is determinative. These principles generate differing formulations of problems in the unfolding of a vast tractate. None of this comes from Scripture or addresses topics or problems known to Scripture.

Other tractates with no topical dependence whatsoever on Scripture include Mishnah-tractate Berakhot, where there is scarcely a single scriptural passage that plays a generative part in the formation of this tractate, even though some of the prayers that are recited make mention of verses of Scripture; Demai, in which not a single fact in this tractate derives from Scripture; Ketubot, in which, except for Chapter Three, the factual basis for this tractate is not scriptural; Moed Qatan, for which there are no pertinent verses of Scripture (Scripture knows restrictions on labor only for the opening and closing sessions of the festivals of Passover and Tabernacles, so Ex. 12:16, Lev. 23:7-8, 35-36, Num. 28:18, 25, 29:12-35); Qiddushin, for which, in the aggregate Scripture does not define the facts that form the expository center of this tractate; Tohorot, of the considerations and conceptions of which Scripture knows nothing; and so on and so forth. To make the point simple, I conclude with reference to Mishnah-tractate Middot. Its specification of the layout and measurements of the Temple bears no clear and systematic relationship to Scripture's treatment of the same subject. Scholarship generally holds that it follows the pattern of Solomon's Temple with some adaptations of

Ezekiel's, so F.J. Hollis, *The Archaeology of Herod's Temple. With a Commentary on the Tractate 'Middoth'* (London, 1934), p. 354: "The use made of Holy Scripture in the tractate is not such as to give the impression that somehow or other the words of Scripture are being followed...but rather that there was a fairly clear recollection of the Temple as it had been, with Holy Scripture appealed to illuminate the fact, not as authority to prove it."

The point is now clear that there are tractates that totally depend for the entirety of their program and analytical problematic upon Scripture, and there are tractates that to begin with address subjects or themes of which the Written Torah is simply ignorant. What about the middle range? Here we come to tractates that ask of a topic supplied by Scripture questions that Scripture in no way adumbrates. Let me give three examples of what I mean. Mishnah-tractate Makhshirin forms a well-crafted essay on the interplay of intentionality and classification. The prooftexts, Lev. 11:34, 37, establish the fact of the matter, but in no way permit us to predict the problematic of the Mishnah's treatment of that topic. The order of the tractate is so worked out that each point in the development of the study of that problem is in proper place. We start with the issue of the classification of liquid, with special attention to water capable of imparting susceptibility distinguished from water not capable of doing so: the wanted, the unwanted. This forthwith invites the issue of intentionality. Then, and only then, do we proceed to the consideration of the status of water used for one purpose and water used for a subsidiary purpose, and that leads directly into the question of whether what one is assumed to desire is taken into account at all, or whether we deem evidence of prior intentionality only post facto action. So there is no way of ordering matters to produce an intelligible sequence of problems other than in the way we now have them, and this tractate is philosophical not only in its topics but in its very structure.

A second example is Mishnah-tractate Nedarim, dealing with vows, on which Scripture sets forth rules. But nearly the entire tractate addresses a philosophical problem, specifically, the authorship provides lessons in showing how species relate in a common genus, or how the components of a common genus are speciated. That is so prominent a theme that were we to want to teach the method of classification through genus and species, this is the tractate that would provide rich and exquisitely executed examples of that method. The secondary interest, not surprisingly, is in the consideration of intentionality, on the one side, and the resolution of matters of doubt, on the other. These are subordinate to the main concern of this profoundly philosophical tractate.

A third example is Mishnah-tractate Negaim, addressing Lev. 13 and 14. This Mishnah tractate is a deeply philosophical treatment of a subject on which Scripture has supplied a rich corpus of information. As is common in tractates on uncleanness, the basic intellectual framework is defined by problems of classification of diverse data, yielding a single outcome: unclean, clean. The classification involves hierarchization, on the one side, and the resolution of doubts as to data (never as to the pertinent rule) on the other. That is the focus of interest of the bulk of the tractate, and we find ourselves in the same realm of inquiry as in Niddah, on the one side, and Miqvaot, on the other: classification and the resolution of doubt, mostly the former. This tractate provides a splendid and compelling exemplification of the power of classification to frame and solve problems. Specifically, classification makes possible hierarchical classification, which for its part renders plausible argument on shared premises yielding firm results. The power of hierarchical classification in framing issues is shown at M. Neg. 13:10: They said to R. Judah, "If, when his entire body is unclean, he has not rendered unclean that which is on him until he will remain for a time sufficient to eat a piece of bread, when his entire body is not unclean, is it not logical that he should not render what is on him unclean until he remains for a time sufficient to eat a piece of bread?" Tosefta's reply shows what is at stake: Said to them R. Judah, "The reason is that the power of that which is susceptible to uncleanness also is stronger to afford protection than the power of what is insusceptible to uncleanness is to afford protection. Israelites receive uncleanness and afford protection for clothing in the house afflicted with plague, and the gentile and beast do not receive uncleanness and so do not afford protection...." The same uses of hierarchical classification are shown at M. 13:11: "Whatever affords protection with a tightly sealed cover in the Tent of the corpse affords protection with a tightly sealed cover in the house which has a plague, and whatever affords protection merely by being covered over in the Tent of the corpse affords protection merely by being covered over in the house which has a plague," the words of R. Meir. R. Yosé says, "Whatever affords protection with a tightly sealed cover in the Tent of the corpse affords protection when merely covered over in the house which has a plague, and whatever affords protection when merely covered over in the Tent of the corpse even uncovered in the house which has the plague is clean." This argument and its numerous parallels are possible only within a system of classification, in which all thought is channeled into paths of comparison and contrast, inquiries into the genus and the species and the comparison of the species of a common genus, then the hierarchization of the results, one way or another.

Enough has been said to show how readily we differentiate among the relationships between various tractates of the Mishnah and Scripture. We can now not only describe those relationships, we may also analyze and interpret them. The analysis may be appropriately brief, since much that has already been said has suggested the analytical program I have devised. It is clear that where tractates are "scriptural," they merely repeat in the Mishnah's rhetoric and within the Mishnah's logic of cogent discourse what Scripture says in its rhetoric and within its logic of cogent discourse. Where tractates are not scriptural, as I have now indicated, they are philosophical. This is in two aspects. An interstitial tractate – one that is scriptural in topic but not scriptural in its treatment of its topic – will ask philosophical questions of classification of a subject that Scripture has described within a different program of questions altogether. A good example of that type of interstitial tractate is Mishnah-tractate Negaim, which, as I said, wants to teach lessons of the rules of classification. Another is Mishnah-tractate Makhshirin, which proposes to investigate the relationship between one's action and the taxonomic power of one's intentionality. As to the third category, what differentiates an interstitial tractate from a completely non-scriptural tractate is simply the topic. A completely nonscriptural tractate commonly will pursue a philosophical reading of a given topic; what makes the tractate nonscriptural is the fact that Scripture does not know its topic.

In setting matters forth, I have now to indicate the proportions of the document that are scriptural, those that are (in the definition just now given) interstitial, and those that are utterly nonscriptural. Among the 61 tractates of the Mishnah, seven are neither scriptural nor philosophical (again: in terms now clear). Of the 54 others, 41 are philosophical (whether dealing with a scriptural topic or not dealing with a scriptural topic), and 13 are wholly scriptural, in the model of Yoma, for instance, or Pesahim. Of the 54 tractates that may be classified as either wholly scriptural or fundamentally philosophical, three-quarters are philosophical. Of all 61 tractates, two-thirds are philosophical. And that brings us back to the point at which we started, Rabbi Judah the Patriarch's presentation of the Mishnah as a single, seamless, internally harmonious, unitary document. To state matters simply, what Rabbi has accomplished in his formalization of the whole is the union of philosophy and revelation. I say this in a very concrete and not in an abstract sense. He has joined profound discourse on the nature of classification, the relationship of genus to species and the comparison and contrast of species, the role of intentionality in the taxonomic system, the disposition of interstitial cases in which a variety of taxic indicators come into play – Rabbi has joined a profound discourse on the nature of classification with a loving and detailed repetition of the facts of Scripture as these concern certain topics. The result is a document, the Mishnah, in which we are taught both philosophy and Scripture. Rabbi demonstrates through the Mishnah that revelation and reason, that is to say, Scripture and Mishnah's framing of philosophical principles of classification on which all knowledge rests, are shown to form a single, seamless skein of truth.

These results must strike as familiar but also dissonant those familiar with the great work of Moses Maimonides, the pinnacle of Jewish philosophy, who set out to do precisely what I claim Rabbi has already done in the Mishnah. For, we are all taught in our elementary lessons, Rambam wished to unite reason and revelation, Aristotle and the Torah. And, it is clear, I maintain that Rabbi has done that in the Mishnah. He has chosen an aesthetic medium for his achievement – presenting within a single rhetoric and logic the entirety of the (written) Torah, revelation, and the whole of the philosophical principles of knowledge (classification of data into intelligible patterns, discovery of the rules and logic of things) of (Aristotle's) philosophy. When we turn our attention to Maimonides, we see a different choice as to how to accomplish the same purpose, and it is a choice, we now realize, that he did not have to make. Maimonides represented revelation, the Torah, in the *Mishneh Torah*, and he further portrayed reason, philosophy, in the *Guide to the Perplexed*, each document appealing to its own aesthetic choices as to rhetoric and logic of cogent discourse. The one is modeled after the Mishnah, the other has no antecedent in the received canon of the Dual Torah to which Maimonides appealed. Accordingly, it would appear to this outsider to Maimonidean scholarship, Maimonides invented a medium for representing philosophy, preserving another medium for representing the law; it was through the overarching intellectual system that he created that the two writings were shown to be seamless and harmonious.

If that picture, drawn by an outsider, is accurate, then we may identify a fundamental misunderstanding, on the part of Maimonides, of the character of the Mishnah, that is to say, the oral part of the one whole Torah revealed by God to Moses at Mount Sinai, and therefore of the Torah itself, and, it must follow, my ultimate goal is to correct the historic error of Maimonides, who identified Aristotle and his philosophical method as the source of correct knowledge, science, in his day. But in his misreading of the requirements of theology and philosophy of Judaism, he supposed he could present philosophy outside of the framework of law, and law without sustained and specific engagement with philosophy. This came about because he did not realize the full extent to which the Mishnah, Maimonides's correct choice of the foundation document of Judaism after Scripture, stood squarely within the Aristotelian philosophical tradition. Specifically, when Maimonides systematized philosophy in his original *Guide to the Perplexed* and law in his imitative *Mishneh Torah,* he misunderstood the fact that the law, for the Judaism of the Dual Torah, constitutes the medium for theological and philosophical reflection and expression. And that is the fact, even though at numerous specific examples, he introduced into the explanation or elucidation of the law philosophical considerations. All of these preliminary impressions await sustained clarification, but they do serve to place this project into perspective.

In his separation of the presentation of law from philosophy, he tore apart what in the Mishnah had been inextricably joined in a lasting union, which was (and is) the law of that Judaism and both its theology and also its philosophy. Seeing the law in *Mishneh Torah* as a problem merely of organization and rationalization, Maimonides did not perceive that that same law contained within itself, and fully expressed, the very same principles of theology and philosophy that in the *Guide to the Perplexed* are invoked to define what we should call Judaism. Maimonides therefore did not grasp that the law in the very document that, in his (correct) judgment contained its classic formulation, that is, the Mishnah, also set forth precisely those principles of philosophy that, in Aristotle's system as Maimonides adapted it, would frame the proposed philosophy and theology of Judaism of the *Guide to the Perplexed.* Then, in the *Guide* Maimonides (mis)represented philosophy and theology by divorcing them from their legal media of articulation, as though these could come to expression entirely outside the framework of the legal sources of Judaism. So the greatest scholar of the Mishnah of all time and the greatest Aristotelian Judaism has ever known misperceived the profound intellectual structure of the Mishnah.

The reason for this error, in my view, is that Maimonides did not understand the deeply Aristotelian character of the Mishnah, which is the initial and definitive statement of the law of Judaism. And that is the error that I am in the process of correcting in this paper and in the companion studies and volumes of which it forms an offshoot and a byproduct. I am showing, point by point, that the economics, politics, and philosophy, that is, the social order set forth by the Judaism of the Mishnah, finds its intellectual home in Aristotle's philosophy, method, and (in the main) results as well. The modes of thought and the basic categorical structures correspond to those of Aristotle. This has already been accomplished in my *Economics of Judaism* and *Politics of Judaism.* Now when we realize that the Mishnah stands squarely within the Aristotelian philosophical tradition in its economics, politics, and philosophical principles (a proposition, as I said, I already have shown for the first two of the three main lines of social thought), then we can understand what happened to mislead Maimonides. And from Maimonides onward, the law has served only episodically and notionally, not systematically and totally, in the formation of the theology and philosophy of Judaism. The scholars of the law in the main knew no theology and could not understand philosophy; the scholars of theology and philosophy, whether or not they knew the law, did not understand in a systematic way that the law would provide the very principles of philosophy that they thought the classic sources of Judaism did not afford. Seeing the law of Judaism, from the Mishnah forward, as essentially distinct from the philosophical science of Aristotle, Maimonides and everyone since then, if they dealt with law at all, simply arranged the law and turned to the philosophy and theology.

What Maimonides should have done, which I therefore am in the course of doing, was in a systematic and rigorous manner show the philosophy within the law. That meant not merely that the law has or exhibits a philosophy. Everyone recognizes that simple and commonplace observation. At numerous points in his *Mishneh Torah* Maimonides articulates the principle at hand; and, as to theology, this is encompassed within the *Mishneh Torah Sefer Ahabah*. But the fundamental modes of thought and some of the principal problems of reflection of Aristotle guide the intellectual processes of the Mishnah, and that fact Maimonides did not grasp; if he had, he would have worked out the *Guide to the Perplexed*'s main points within the very framework of legal exposition. In this way the marriage of law and philosophy, which, as a systematic program, eluded Maimonides, could have been consummated, yielding for the history of Judaism a very different result from the one that followed their divorce. For understanding the philosophical modes of thought and also the philosophical problematic of the Mishnah – issues of mixtures, issues of the potential and the actual, for instance – should have meant that the law is part of, and expresses in its distinctive idiom of rules, the rules of a well-composed and clearly defined philosophical tradition.

Not only so, but the earliest intellectual critiques of the Mishnah recognized its fundamental Aristotelianism and rejected it, as I demonstrated in *Uniting the Dual Torah: Sifra and the Problem of the Mishnah*.[1] And, as I now am showing in its principal components, that philosophical tradition in which the Mishnah stands is the very tradition that so engaged Maimonides to begin with, which is the Aristotelian one. Had he understood that fact, he would have allowed Aristotle to teach him philosophy through the medium of law and its structure and

---

[1](Cambridge, 1990: University Press).

system. For that is precisely what Judah the Patriarch did in his presentation of the Mishnah. That is to say, through the law of the social order that the Judaism of the Dual Torah set forth Judah the Patriarch gave full and ample expression also, and at one and the same time, to philosophy and its principles and rules. What Maimonides wanted to do, Judah the Patriarch actually had accomplished a thousand years earlier – and Maimonides did not know it. That explains his mistake. When, therefore, we ask the deceptively simple question, how does the Mishnah relate to Scripture, we find ourselves addressing the most profound structural questions of the relationship of reason to revelation in the Judaism of the Dual Torah we know as normative, classical, and orthodox.

## The Classification of Mishnah Tractates
### [1] As to Philosophy
### [2] As to Relationships to Scripture

Let me now give a complete survey of the entire matter. The indicated ratios are of philosophical to nonphilosophical pericopes; they are of course merely rough estimates, achieved by counting up the total number of pericopes in a tractate and identifying the ones that clearly present philosophical principles in legal formulation.

## 1.   Mainly or Exclusively Philosophical

### Abodah Zarah:

(88 percent/13 percent) The body of diverse passages present what seem to me reconsiderations of philosophical issues. But, on the other hand, I do not see that the tractate as a whole in its basic structure has been so organized as to express, through work of detail, the main philosophical principles under discussion. The principles play an important role in specific cases, but the cases are not so organized and expressed as to highlight the principles. Still, if we follow the theorems set forth from Chapter Four onward, what do we find? [1] Intentionality (inclusive of potentiality assessed by appeal to intentionality): M. 4:1, 2, 3, 4, 5, 6, 7, 8, 9 (resolving doubt by appeal to intentionality); [2] mixtures: M. 5:1, 2 (the way in which the character of an entire mixture is dictated by the dominant trait of the mixture), 5:8-12; [3] resolution of doubt: M. 5:3, 4; [4] classification of things: M. 5:5, 6, 7. Since the philosophical principles lie right on the surface, the characterization of the tractate as a whole as essentially philosophical, if not systematically philosophical, seems to me well founded.

**Berakhot:**

(56 percent/44 percent) The reason that, despite the statistics, I judge this tractate to be fundamentally philosophical is that two of the three great areas of philosophical reflection inquiry, classification and intentionality, define the boundaries of discussion of a variety of concrete liturgical issues. Not only so, but the basic positions that are worked out here are encompassing and address the range of possibilities that the system as a whole recognizes.

**Bikkurim:**

(60 percent/40 percent) This tractate's philosophical strength lies in its sustained exposition of the rules of hierarchical classification through polythetic taxonomy. Where this tractate is philosophical, it is ascriptural, and where it is scriptural, it is aphilosophical.

**Demai:**

(81 percent/19 percent) This tractate is devoted entirely to the exposition of two philosphical problems, connection and classification, on the one side, disposition of doubt, on the other. The main interest is in keeping separate what is distinct, not mixing what should not be mixed. The principles of the resolution of doubt are entirely subject to generalization.

**Erubin:**

(100 percent/0 percent) This tractate forms a profound exegesis on the problem of the commingling of distinct classifications or categories: the interstitial realm of the excluded middle.

**Hallah:**

(84 percent/16 percent) Mishnah-tractate Hallah presents a sustained and brilliantly articulated essay on the nature of classification and connection, pure and simple. Of the 38 pericopes, no more than 6 prove not pertinent to a philosophical principle, 16 percent of the whole, and the essential cogency of the rest is not fully represented by that overstatement of matters.

**Horayot:**

(100 percent/0 percent) This tractate – 100 percent philosophical – is a sustained essay on the interplay of intentionality and responsibility, a nearly wholly cogent and systematic exercise in stating a single principle in a variety of ways and for diverse, hierarchically organized cases. I cannot imagine a more elegantly executed tractate of philosophy stated through recondite rules, or a better case of the Mishnah's reworking Scripture into philosophy, a pure and perfect union of revelation and reason, where even the principle introduced by Scripture, that is, the concern for intentionality (witting or inadvertent sin) is transformed into

a philosophical conception involving public or political standing, responsibility, hierarchical classification, and the like.

### Hullin:

(100 percent/0 percent) This tractate is a sustained and somewhat systematic study of the issues of classification, mixture, and the rules of defining a genus and of the comparison and contrast of the species of a genus. The tractate forms a complex study of the problems of classification, inclusive of issues of mixture and connection. It is one-sidedly philosophical, and wherever it addresses a matter of interest to Scripture, it introduces its own range of issues, which is fairly well composed so as to permit repetition, for example, Chapters Five through Seven, Ten through Twelve.

### Kelim:

(100 percent/0 percent) This tractate is wholly devoted to the exposition of problems of classification, inclusive of connection and intentionality as issues of classification. Tractates on cleanness and uncleanness by definition form exercises of classification, since the ultimate taxa are unclean or susceptible to uncleanness and clean or insusceptible. But the exemplary power of detailed discourse to invoke fundamental principles of classification and to set forth the complexities of physics of connection is hardly exhausted by the generalizations, unclean or clean. Indeed, throughout, these form the mere result, but never the engaging problem of principled discourse. Mishnah-tractate Kelim deals with the status, as to cultic cleanness, of useful objects, tools or utensils. Its main point is that when an object has a distinctive character, form, use, or purpose, it is susceptible to uncleanness, so that, if it is in contact with a source of uncleanness, it is deemed cultically unclean. If it is formless, purposeless, or useless, it is insusceptible. Three criteria govern the determination of what is useful or purposeful. First come properties deemed common to all utensils, whatever the material. Second are qualities distinctive to different sorts of materials. Third is the consideration of the complex purposes for which an object is made or used, primary and subsidiary, and the intention of the user is determinative. These principles generate differing formulations of problems in the unfolding of a vast tractate.

### Keritot:

(100 percent/0 percent) The tractate takes up three philosophical issues: classification of many things in a single category; the role of intentionality in changing the classification of something, when the initial intention proves incorrect; the disposition of cases of doubt. The sole

point at which we appeal to Scripture is for facts to commence the philosophical inquiry.

### Kilayim:

(100 percent/0 percent) The entire tractate concerns the problem of mixture (commingling) of plants, animals, and garments. The consideration of human attitude or intentionality enters in. There is no pericope that ignores one or another of these matters. While resting on biblical foundations as to fact, therefore, the entire tractate devotes itself to exploring, through detail, the principles of classification and the rules of intentionality in respect to classification.

### Maaser Sheni:

(78 percent/22 percent) Scripture establishes the topic of this tractate, which is produce that has been designated as Second Tithe and has to be brought to Jerusalem and consumed there, Deut. 14:22-27. The principal concern of the tractate is to preserve in the classification of sanctification produce, or money that has been substituted for produce for the journey to Jerusalem. The money must not lose its value. If the produce is sold, then in exchange, the full value must be transferred to coin. So the problem of the tractate is the classification, on the one side, and preservation of true value, on the other, and that brings us not only to subsidiary issues of mixture and connection but to a principal concern of preserving in a given classification something that may be shifted from one classification to another, that is, maintaining the sanctification of what has been sanctified.

### Maaserot:

(100 percent/0 percent) Mishnah-tractate Maaserot is a sustained essay on the interplay of classification and intentionality. The main point is that the removal of offerings from produce is to take place when the owner deems the produce ready for use. So the attitude of the owner is determinative of the classification of the produce as to tithing.

### Makhshirin:

(100 percent/0 percent) Mishnah-tractate Makhshirin forms a well-crafted essay on the interplay of intentionality and classification. The prooftexts, Lev. 11:34, 37, establish the fact of the matter, but in no way permit us to predict the problematic of the Mishnah's treatment of that topic. The order of the tractate is so worked out that each point in the development of the study of that problem is in proper place. We start with the issue of the classification of liquid, with special attention to water capable of imparting susceptibility distinguished from water not capable of doing so: the wanted, the unwanted. This forthwith invites the issue of intentionality. Then, and only then, do we proceed to the

consideration of the status of water used for one purpose and water used for a subsidiary purpose, and that leads directly into the question of whether what one is assumed to desire is taken into account at all, or whether we deem evidence of prior intentionality only post facto action. So there is no way of ordering matters to produce an intelligible sequence of problems other than in the way we now have them, and this tractate is philosophical not only in its topics but in its very structure.

### Meilah:

What I find striking is not the disproportion of philosophical over non-philosophical paragraphs (76 percent/24 percent) but the stunningly logical order of the unfolding of problems and their principles. When I took up this tractate, I had in mind a tractate that would exhibit no philosophical character overall; that would allow me to point to evidence of a sort that would contradict my main thesis. This test of falsification itself fails in the face of the sustained unfolding of simple rules of classification – things that are unlike follow opposed rules, there are interstitial cases, then there are mixtures. No other order is possible, and the order before us is dictated by the logic of the principle to be expounded. Hence the character of the tractate as a whole, not merely of the larger part of its contents, seems to me to point to a deeply philosophical mind and a compelling philosophical problem and purpose. There can be no doubt that this is a profoundly philosophical tractate, not because most of the pericopes deal with philosophical issues, but because, without the considerations of a philosophical order, there can have been no Meilah at all – at least, not the tractate as we know it.

### Menahot:

The treatment of intentionality is philosophical; the rest of the tractate not. See below.

### Miqvaot:

(100 percent/0 percent) The tractate is a sustained and powerful essay on the principles of classification, with special attention to the traits of materials (liquids) and how they intermingle to form a body of liquid in a single classification. Nearly every important initiative refines and clarifies the conception of mixture and intermingling, and all of the secondary problems, for example, intermingling, derive from that main concern. There is no more philosophical tractate in the entire Mishnah than this one.

### Moed Qatan:

The whole (100 percent/0 percent) of Moed Qatan works out the application of well-crafted principles of differentiation to diverse actions, as these may or may not be carried out on the intermediate days of festivals. Within the grid established on these intersecting lines we work out how one may perform those acts of labor that, on intermediate days of festivals, are permitted at all. May these be done normally or only in an unusual way? The problem of dual classification is what generates the main exercises of the tractate, which concern farming, commerce, and special problems in connection with burying the dead. This is a standard problem of classification.

### Nazir:

A negligible number of pericopes (82 percent/18 percent) merely repeat and clarify facts supplied by Scripture. The tractate is devoted, in unequal parts, to problems of classification, for example, when are many things one thing, and when is one thing many things, and the resolution of doubt. Where Scripture is vague, the Mishnah tractate's authorship fills gaps. Where it is detailed and explicit, we nonetheless find here an essentially autonomous program. Scripture alludes to the vow but has little to say about it and identifies no interesting problems in connection with it. Even where Scripture is rich, philosophy imposes its own program, and it is a very specific one at that.

### Nedarim:

This is a decidedly philosophical tractate, both in proportions and in practical characteristics: 78 percent/22 percent. Nearly the entire tractate in its philosophical components – Chapters One through Nine – provides lessons in showing how species relate in a common genus, or how the components of a common genus are speciated. That is so prominent a theme that with some excisions, were we to want to teach the method of classification through genus and species, this is the tractate that would provide rich and exquisitely executed examples of that method. The secondary interest, not surprisingly, is in the consideration of intentionality, on the one side, and the resolution of matters of doubt, on the other. These are subordinate to the main concern of this profoundly philosophical tractate.

### Negaim:

Mishnah-tractate Negaim is a deeply philosophical treatment of a subject on which Scripture has supplied a rich corpus of information, 88 percent/12 percent, and that figure overstates the nonphilosophical quotient of the whole. The essentially nonphilosophical entries are mainly in the exposition of the purification rite, as by now we have come to expect. As is common in tractates on uncleanness, the basic intellectual framework is defined by problems of classification of diverse data, yielding a single outcome: unclean, clean. The classification involves hierarchization, on the one side, and the resolution of doubts as to data (never as to the pertinent rule) on the other. That is the focus of interest of the bulk of the tractate, and we find ourselves in the same realm of inquiry as in Niddah, on the one side, and Miqvaot, on the other: classification and the resolution of doubt, mostly the former. This tractate provides a splendid and compelling exemplification of the power of classification to frame and solve problems. Specifically, classification makes possible hierarchical classification, which for its part renders plausible argument on shared premises yielding firm results. The power of hierarchical classification in framing issues is shown at M. Neg. 13:10: They said to R. Judah, "If, when his entire body is unclean, he has not rendered unclean that which is on him until he will remain for a time sufficient to eat a piece of bread, when his entire body is not unclean, is it not logical that he should not render what is on him unclean until he remains for a time sufficient to eat a piece of bread?" Tosefta's reply shows what is at stake: Said to them R. Judah, "The reason is that the power of that which is susceptible to uncleanness also is stronger to afford protection than the power of what is insusceptible to uncleanness is to afford protection. Israelites receive uncleanness and afford protection for clothing in the house afflicted with plague, and the gentile and beast do not receive uncleanness and so do not afford protection...." The same uses of hierarchical classification are shown at M. 13:11: "Whatever affords protection with a tightly sealed cover in the Tent of the corpse affords protection with a tightly sealed cover in the house which has a plague, and whatever affords protection merely by being covered over in the Tent of the corpse affords protection merely by being covered over in the house which has a plague," the words of R. Meir. R. Yosé says, "Whatever affords protection with a tightly sealed cover in the Tent of the corpse affords protection when merely covered over in the house which has a plague, and whatever affords protection when merely covered over in the Tent of the corpse even uncovered in the house which has the plague is clean." This argument and its numerous parallels are possible only within a system of classification, in which all thought is channeled into paths of comparison and contrast, inquiries into the genus and the species and the comparison of the species of a common genus, then the hierarchization of the results, one way or another.

Niddah:
(100 percent/0 percent) The proportion of philosophical to non-philosophical pericopes accurately reflects the deeply philosophical character of the whole. The tractate works on the interplay of two methodological issues of a philosophical character, first, the rules of taxonomy through speciation and hierarchical classification, and, second,

the resolution of doubt, with the taxic facts providing the data for the discovery of the correct rules for dealing with not interstitial cases but cases in which the facts are simply not known. I cannot think of a finer example of how to resolve doubt by appeal to established facts and the limits established by them.

### Ohalot:

The entire tractate is philosophical, 100 percent/0 percent, and the range of philosophical issues is remarkably circumscribed. Essentially, we work on the single issue of commingling: space, corpse matter, and the effects of various objects and forms and materials on what is beneath them or on top of them. The classification is very specific. Throughout we want to know what is joined together or kept apart, and what kinds of materials or structures serve to commingle space or delineate and differentiate it. The principles are carefully spelled out and then conveyed through careful instruction by means of pertinent problems. Here then is another tractate in Purities that is a labor of classification, with special attention (in this instance) to the problem of mixtures. When that work is done, we turn briefly to consider the resolution of doubt, and, again, the issue is, doubt concerning mixtures (for example, dirt and corpse matter).

### Orlah:

The authorship of Mishnah-tractate Orlah has focused upon the issue of mixtures, with secondary attention to the problem of resolving cases of doubt. Other philosophical principles come into play but not so systematically.

### Parah:

All of the pericopes of the tractate in one way or another work out, or link to, philosophical issues (100 percent/0 percent). The principal focus of Mishnah-tractate Parah is on problems of classification, with much productive work done on hierarchization and how this is worked out. An important body of opinion in our tractate demands a degree of cleanness higher than that required for the Temple cult itself. Further, the whole matter of drawing water, protecting it, and mixing it with the ash is virtually ignored by the priestly author, while it occupies much of our tractate and, even more than in quantity, the quality and theoretical sophistication of the laws on that topic form the apex of our tractate. Accordingly, the biblical writer on the rite of burning the red cow wishes to tell us that the rite takes place outside the camp, understood in Temple times as outside the Temple. The rite is conducted in an unclean place. And it follows that people who are going to participate in the rite, slaughtering the cow, collecting its ashes, and the like, are not clean. The

Mishnaic authorities stress exactly the opposite conception, that people who will participate in the rite must be clean, not unclean, as if they were in the Temple. And they add a further important point, that the water which is to be used for mixing with the ashes of the cow must be mixed with the ashes without an intervening act of labor, not connected with the rite. So the tractate pursues the issue of the comparison of rites, distinguished by their taxic indicators, and the hierarchical relationship that exists between them. It is an exercise in classification, pure and simple.

## Peah:

Since I count either 93 percent/7 percent or 82 percent/18 percent (69/5 or 69/13) as the proportion of philosophical to nonphilosophical pericopes, I classify the tractate as philosophical. The paramount issue is that of classification, and, while several distinct types of taxonomic problems are worked out in the exemplification of operative principles, the main ones concern the interplay of intentionality and action, on the one side, and of intentionality and forgetfulness, on the other, with emphasis on the second of the two contrasts. Chapters One through Three work out the interplay of conflicting principles of classification: human intentionality, confirmed by actual deed, as against objective facts. The concrete issue is the classification of a field out of an indeterminate piece of land, with the consequence that a corner of that field must be left for the poor. Is the criterion the farmer's deed or the physical traits of the territory? The upshot is whether or not intentionality confirmed by deed constitutes a taxonomic fact.

## Qiddushin:

(80 percent/20 percent) I find that for the matters of taxonomic hierarchization and the matter of intention at stake are philosophical issues, philosophically analyzed. The same claim is hardly so strong for the third rubric, potentiality and actuality. The rules for cases of doubt come perilously close to examples of mere common sense: we simply rely on such evidence as we have, and avoid resolving issues where there is no evidence. But by the criterion by which a rule becomes philosophical – availability for application elsewhere or "generalizability" – I think that we may stand on the philosophical side of the boundary, but not far from the line. If we count up the total of pericopes, then, we have in the four chapters 47 in all. Of these, 9 cannot be read as concretizations of philosophical principles, nearly 20 percent of the whole. I see 29 as assuredly philosophical – that is, the items catalogued in Nos. 1, 2, 3 above, or just over 60 percent of the whole. The other 20 percent are less certainly classified. In the balance, the tractate is more general and philosophical than legal, particular, and ad hoc. Just as

Orlah concerns classification and Besah classification and the interplay of potentiality and actuality, so Qiddushin may be deemed a tractate with a primary concern for classification: mixture and the sorting out of mixture. That judgment is assuredly justified by reference to Chapters One, Three, and Four.

### Qinnim:

(100 percent/0 percent) The tractate is wholly devoted to a single philosophical problem, which is how to establish rules for the resolution of doubt as to mixtures of different classes of the same thing.

### Sanhedrin:

The structure and composition of Mishnah-tractate Sanhedrin present so cogent a picture that a statistical statement is hardly necessary to state that this is a deeply philosophical tractate. The method and program derive wholly from a philosophical problem, one of the organization of knowledge – chaotic facts – into intelligible propositions. Still, if we were to project a figure of 97 percent/3 percent, it would not exaggerate matters. The structure of the tractate is orderly in its presentation of two matters: the courts, the penalties for various sins and crimes. Each topic is then subjected to a clear plan of classification, the aim of which is to show how many things are readily joined into one thing. The discovery of the unity of diverse (commonly, but not always, scriptural) facts within such classifications then points toward the harmony and simplicity of a multiplicity of data. The further philosophical interest is in the hierarchization of these simple and encompassing classifications, so that the subspecies are shown to be species, and the species, a few readily identified common genera, the whole ultimately forming a single genus. I cannot imagine a more philosophical way in which to sift and sort out chaotic data, and that is what is achieved in this tractate. The orderly plan of the whole, in two parts, the orderly list making of both parts – these in form point toward the underlying sense of composition and structure that makes of facts intelligible knowledge, and that turns knowledge into important propositions. I can think of no more philosophical program than that.

### Shabbat:

This tractate on the face of it is profoundly philosophical (95 percent/8 percent), and, in fact, most of it is devoted to the clarification of a few fundamental principles of speciation, two being primary: the subspeciation of species, for example, generative acts of labor and their subdivisions, and the interplay of intentionality with classification, for example, the volume of a substance someone may deem valuable, the intentionality that governs the commission of a given action. Within those two basic problems of thought, worked over time and again, we find a place for most of the concrete analytical exercises in the tractate. Not only so, but we notice a considerable difference between the philosophical program of Mishnah-tractate Sanhedrin and the one of Mishnah-tractate Shabbat. While both tractates work on problems of classification, the former is interested in showing that many things fall into one category, while the later, to the contrary, wants to demonstrate how one thing is subdivided into many things. If I wanted to show the dynamics of speciation, a mode of thought that makes facts into intelligible propositions, I should do well to set forth both processes, indicating how the many are one, and the one, many. That is precisely what is demonstrated, in vast detail, in the two tractates just now considered.

**Shabuot:**
The entire tractate is a tight and cogent philosophical exercise, 100 percent/0 percent, in the principles of speciation and subspeciation. A uniform and consistent program demonstrates how we appeal to congruent taxic traits in differentiating within a genus and identifying the species. Concrete consequences of speciation and subspeciation (liability under two or more counts for a single statement or action, for example) then underline the abstract philosophical lessons of method and do so in a practical way. The speciation and subspeciation of oaths occupies the tractate. What is at stake is the number of counts for which one is liable, which is to say, the division of a given action or statement into its components and the identification of each completed action or statement, which is to say, the number of counts of liability. We have the speciation of oaths into four types, then the demonstration of the subspeciation of a given type by appeal to the language that is used. The tractate is unitary and cogent, works its way through large formal constructions, and repeatedly makes the same points, all of them of a taxonomic character, from beginning to end. The interests of Scripture and the problematic of the Mishnah's treatment of the subject scarcely intersect. The framers of the Mishnah classify oaths, something to which Scripture is not devoted. Scripture has supplied the topic, but the framers of the Mishnah have analyzed that topic in terms of their program in particular.

**Shebiit:**
Mishnah-tractate Shebiit falls into the class of philosophical tractates (89 percent/11 percent), because its generative problem through nearly the whole of the tractate is how to classify things. Specifically, the power of the tractate is to demonstrate how to apply a variety of distinct taxic indicators to a single category of thing, here, growing things. One set of

indicators derives from the time of the year, that is, Sixth Year, Seventh Year, Eighth Year; a second derives from the place, that is, Land of Israel, neighboring areas partially sanctified by Israelite occupation; a third derives from the natural traits of the crop. These and parallel, distinct taxic indicators are constructed into a single cogent composition, and the student of the problems of classification learns how to hold together and to apply in tandem a variety of classificatory systems, a very complex demonstration of a very complex problem. All of this, indeed, could be restated in mathematical symbols. Not only so, but the consideration of attitude or intentionality enters in. Newman's judgment of the tractate as a whole shows how important is that consideration, expressed as perception: "The cornerstone of Mishnah's theory of the Sabbatical Year is that ordinary Israelites, through their actions and perceptions, play a role in determining how the agricultural restrictions of the Sabbatical Year apply....Israelite farmers...have the power within specified limits to decide when, how, and where the laws...take effect."[2]

**Tebul Yom:**
The entire tractate (100 percent/0 percent) is devoted to the issue of connection. We begin with the principle of connection in the case of the Tebul Yom. There are items deemed connected in the case of the Tebul Yom but not in the case of any other source (or status) of uncleanness. We proceed to liquids and connection, then solids and connection, both in the case of the Tebul Yom, thus covering Chapters One through Three. Only Chapter Four is devoted to defining the question of the status as to uncleanness of the Tebul Yom, and this matter then centers on whether the Tebul Yom is essentially unclean but clean in a minor aspect, or essentially clean but unclean in a minor way. The unfolding of the theory of connection is systematic and orderly. We establish a complex grid of principles, for example, the interstitial status of the Tebul Yom, then the interstitial case of the status of what is subsidiary to a mixture and what is primary. The whole then provides problems of an increasingly complex character for solution by appeal to the appropriate theorems.

**Terumot:**
Mishnah-tractate Terumot (100 percent/0 percent) is one of the great philosophical treatises of the Mishnah. It works through every area of philosophical interest we have identified: classification of things into taxa, then the disposition of mixtures of distinct classes of things; the problem of the confusion of things that fall into different classifications;

---

[2]Louis Newman, *The Sanctity of the Seventh Year* (Atlanta, 1985: Scholars Press for Brown Judaic Studies), p. 17.

the recognition of what is potential as against what is actual; the role of intentionality in the classificatory process; the rules governing the disposition of doubt. Not only so, but the arrangement of the tractate is such as to move from the presentation of the simple governing principles to the formation and presentation of complicated cases in which several distinct principles of taxonomy are brought to bear. I cannot imagine a more profoundly philosophical reading of a topic that, in itself, bears no philosophical interest whatsoever. Avery-Peck generalizes as follows (pp. 2-3): "Mishnah's true interest must be expressed in terms of two separate, but related, issues. The first is the process of sanctification. This is to say that the tractate asks how a certain quantity of produce grown on the Land of Israel comes to be deemed holy. The second issue is the effect which this produce, the heave-offering, has upon common food with which it is mixed." That is to say, in two aspects we have a sustained essay on the problems of classification and mixture: classification of produce, mixture of produce of two distinct classes. But, as we see, that massively understates the profoundly philosophical traits of mind that come to full expression in this tractate.

### Tohorot:

A profoundly philosophical tractate (100 percent/0 percent), Mishnah-tractate Tohorot deals with problems of mixtures and issues of connection, as these effect uncleanness of food and liquid, and then with resolving matters of doubt in regard to mixtures and connection of food and liquid, that is to say, precisely the program of Mishnah-tratate Terumot. A further area of doubt has to do with the relationship of the *am haares* and the *haber,* which is a subset of the larger question of how to resolve cases in which the facts are unclear, and that draws the tractate into line with Mishnah-tractate Demai. So, overall, the tractate concerns those issues of classification and connection and of resolving doubt in connection with taxonomic problems that predominate elsewhere. The basic rules of the tractate thus involve classification as to uncleanness, with special attention to forming the requisite bulk, which is to say, connection or combination, and then differentiating between the case that applies before and after connection. In the formation of these and related issues of classification, we have a treatise on mixtures and their taxonomy.

### Uqsin:

Mishnah-tractate Uqsin contains 26 pericopes (counting M. 3:10-11 as a single), all of them (100 percent/0 percent) covering the philosophical issues of connection. Uqsin spells out the three relationships of substances to one another: wholly distinct, C, wholly mixed and united, B, and partly joined, partly autonomous, A. This is, of course, a theory of mixtures. The tractate further asks whether something can be deemed food for one purpose but not food for some other purpose. At issue is whether or not the same traits that classify an object in one respect classify it in all other respects; and the same decision as to classification for one purpose must apply for all purposes. These are the two philosophical issues that account for the detailed program of the tractate.

### Yadayim:

While an odd tractate, Mishnah-tractate Yadayim is indeed deeply philosophical (100 percent/0 percent), when we realize that the modes of thought with special reference to classification are fully exposed. Indeed, the exposition is in proper order. First we have the presentation of a simple taxonomic grid, then we have a second such grid, and the two are placed into relationship with one another, which is the point at which our authorship is aiming; that is accomplished in Chapters One and Two, and Chapter Two then adds the expected discourse on problems of doubt in the working out of the bifurcated grid that has been constructed. By definition, philosophical modes of thought appeal to rules of correct classification of things, by the presence or absence of taxic indicators. As noted, Mishnah-tractate Yadayim, in its legal passages, is philosophical in its modes of thought and in its repertoire of issues, because its mode of thought is analogical contrastive, spinning out its rules by appeal to the comparable ones of the rite of burning the red cow and mixing the ashes with water as described by Misnah-tractate Parah. So this is very much a philosophical tractate, because it is a tractate framed through analogical contrastive thinking on the foundations of Mishnah-tractate Parah. That is to say, this tractate spins out its laws through comparisons and contrasts with the rules governing the preparation of purification water for the rite of purification from corpse uncleanness described at Num. 19:1ff. That a utensil must be used is one such detail borrowed from the rite of the red cow; that water that has been used in connection with some act of labor may not be used for washing hands is another. Parallel to the rules on who may sprinkle purification water is the issue of who may pour out water on the hands, but here it is a matter of contrast: it may be anyone, even an ape. Uncleanness of hands is removed by water, preparation of the water is to accord with rules pertinent to the purification water of Mishnah-tractate Parah – when the matter is comparable, and to contrast with those rules when not. So here we have philosophical method in the mode of analogical contrastive thinking.

### Yebamot:

Nearly the whole of the tractate (95 percent/5 percent) works out principles of classification and problems of doubt, that is, interstitial cases, generated by those principles. The philosophical work of classification is carried on in two ways. First, and more commonly, we establish grids established by taxic indicators, and then we superimpose one grid with its indicators on another grid with its indicators. Then the problem of classification is solved by identifying the paramount indicator and applying it throughout in a consistent way. This problem of analytical thought predominates. A second mode of philosophical classification is accomplished by appealing to the principle that what is like follows the same rule, and what is unlike follows the opposite rule, that is to say, analogical contrastive reasoning. Here we accomplish classification through analogical thinking, and a number of important chapters are devoted to that matter. So the whole of the tractate is devoted to a sustained labor of philosophical classification. Principles for the resolution of doubt are set forth, and these turn out, upon closer inspection, to constitute little more than restatements of taxonomic conceptions, concerns, and methods.

### Zabim:

With its brilliant evocation of analogical contrastive reasoning in a process of sustained classification, this is one of the totally philosophical tractates, 100 percent/0 percent, as the extended exposition has already indicated. The conception that there is a hierarchy of conditions of uncleanness, that is to say, a hierarchical taxonomy thereof, based upon the difference between being in touch with a source of uncleanness and the uncleanness left after one no longer is in touch with such a source, forms the philosophical center of this deeply philosophical tractate. The anticipated interest, alongside, of course is in questions of doubt, for example, interstitial cases and how these are sorted out. The elaboration of the scriptural conception that things on which a Zab sits are unclean generalizes and treats that conception in an abstract way. The notion that follows is that anything that is normally used for sitting or lying on which a Zab exerts pressure or any person on whom he exerts pressure is unclean. Pressure uncleanness represents a powerful abstraction of Scripture's concrete statement. The further statement of Scripture, Lev. 15:5-6, is that one who touches the bed on which a Zab has sat will bathe and also wash his clothing; this is understood to mean that the clothes are unclean because they have been made unclean by contact with the person who has born the pressure of the Zab. The Zab further imparts uncleanness in a variety of ways, by contact, carrying, shifting objects without bearing their weight, and that, too, treats what is concrete in an abstract manner. Whether or not these constitute essentially philosophical conceptions precipitated by reflection on scriptural facts, or merely elaborations of scriptural facts, is clear. The work is deeply philosophical in its basic mode of thought. As we noted earlier, the framers of the Mishnah treat as exemplary Scripture's statement that the Zab imparts uncleanness to objects on which he sits or lies. This then is generalized into a classification and therefore serves as a taxonomic amplifier: whatever is *like* sitting or lying falls into the same classification, here, the medium by which the Zab communicates uncleanness. Taxic indicator of lying or sitting is deemed to be imparting weight or pressure; treating the "lying" or "sitting" as analogical for classificatory purposes therefore is the result of a philosophical process of comparison and contrast. The Zab then transmits uncleanness in a way different from the familiar – for every analogy must have its contrast. Since the contrast to pressure is contact without pressure, the upshot is simple. The Zab imparts uncleanness through pressure without contact, that is, merely by applying the force of his weight to a person or object.

**Zebahim:**
Mishnah-tractate Zebahim is a sustained (97 percent/7 percent) exercise in classification, showing us how different taxic indicators do their work to classify offerings as valid or invalid, and how diverse rules that serve to differentiate one offering from another may be held together in a single encompassing grid. The first third of the tractate takes up the issue of intentionality as a taxic indicator; the next major section is devoted to the differentiation of various offerings – animals, fowl – and the various categories of sacrifice that encompass them; then we deal with the classification of diverse mixtures, for example, of animals that are designated for different purposes, of blood that has derived from offerings subject each to its own rules as to the use and disposition of the blood, and the like. We see that Chapters One through Four undertake the first exercise, Chapters Five through Seven set the stage for the second, and Chapters Eight through Twelve then accomplish the work of disposing of mixtures of animals or fowl, or the blood thereof, that have been prepared in the classifications defined in Chapters Five through Seven. I cannot imagine a more carefully organized and systematic representation of matters than we are given here. The tractate is deeply philosophical in its interest in classification, both by means of [1] intentionality and by means of [2] objective taxic indicators, then [3] mixture and the resolution of cases of doubt. The established philosophical repertoire of so many other tractates, covering these three matters, is fully exposed in this one as well.

## 2.   Somewhat Philosophical

**Baba Batra:**
(53 percent/47 percent)

Hagigah:

(48 percent/52 percent) The philosophical side to this tractate is focused upon the one interest of hierarchical classification of two sets of categories: sanctification and uncleanness. We have to look at M. Kelim Chapter One for as fine a composition of diverse information into a single intelligible pattern.

Menahot:

Mishnah-tractate Menahot contains a sizable portion of philosophical pericopes, 33 percent/66 percent, but it is not essentially philosophical in its treatment of its subject. What we have is a significant section on the impact of intentionality upon classification, but this discussion is confined to those chapters that go over issues paramount in Mishnah-tractate Zebahim and make exactly the same points in the same way. When we complete the discussion of the role of improper intention in the invalidation of meal-offerings, M. 1:1-4-5, we find ourselves in a sustained reprise of facts, most of them scriptural, in which there is no particular concern for philosophical analysis or exposition.

## 3. Not Philosophical At All

Arakhin:

(10 percent/90 percent) This tractate has no philosophical program of any substance.

Baba Mesia:

(14 percent/86 percent) This is a classically legal tractate, pure and simple; its broader implications concern ethics, but not abstract philosophical principles that cut across many areas of law or of ethics.

Baba Qamma:

(26 percent/74 percent) Here we have a sustained exposition of facts of Scripture, but there are several important philosophical treatments within the composition.

Bekhorot:

(33 percent/66 percent [18 percent/82 percent]) The bulk of the tractate either amplifies Scripture or supplies relevant information. There are few important philosophical episodes.

Gittin:

(30 percent/70 percent) The bulk of the tractate sets forth rules of the scribes concerning the correct preparation and delivery of writs of divorce and complications attendant upon that process. There is no sustained philosophical program, though the premise that intentionality is a key consideration does make its appearance.

**Ketubot:**

(17 percent/83 percent) This tractate sets forth scribal rules about the preparation and enforcement of the marriage contract, with further sustained interest in the way in which the contract is paid off in the event of death or divorce. There is no philosophical program to speak of.

**Makkot:**

Mishnah-tractate Makkot is profoundly scriptural in its program, 12 percent/88 percent, and the interest in philosophy is episodic. I find only one important example of philosophical thought, at M. 3:7-9, the inquiry into how many actions are deemed a single act, and how a single act may encompass many diverse counts of culpability.

**Megillah:**

(3 percent/97 percent) I see nothing of philosophical interest in Mishnah-tractate Megillah, which is devoted to the regulations of reading the Scroll of Esther on Purim and the laws of synagogue property and lections, in Chapters One through Two and Three through Four, respectively. Neither half of the tractate concerns itself, even episodically, with anything I can identify as philosophical. As we shall note, the tractate also is not scriptural in any meaningful sense.

**Middot:**

(0 percent/100 percent) This tractate is purely descriptive, with no analytical program whatsoever.

**Pesahim:**

The statistics tell the story: 19 percent/81 percent. But the statistics exaggerate the philosophical quotient of the whole. The tractate in no way is to be characterized as philosophical, even though here and there important discussions do illustrate issues interesting to philosophy, since issues of philosophical inquiry do not generate the principal program and discourse of the tractate.

**Rosh Hashshanah:**

In a ratio of 17 percent/83 percent Mishnah-tractate Rosh Hashshanah devotes its interests to other than philosophical matters. It is rich in narrative, pays much attention to history and its periods and changes that have marked one age in comparison to another. But I identify only a few discussions of philosophical interest, and these are episodic and random; only one of them is clearly important, and that concerns the interplay of intentionality and deed in carrying out one's obligations. This tractate is neither philosophical nor, as we shall see, scriptural. It is to be classified as narrative, with important narratives or quasi-narratives in Chapters One, Two, and Four and a retelling of a scriptural event in Chapter Three.

### Sheqalim:

Not even expository of the law but mainly narrative and only episodically philosophical, in a ratio of 32 percent/68 percent, Mishnah-tractate Sheqalim includes only a few important demonstrations of philosophical principles, and these are mostly concerned with taxonomy, presented in an ad hoc and not in a sustained manner.

### Sotah:

The ratio of philosophical to nonphilosophical passages, 21 percent/79 percent, seems to me a valid indicator of the classification of the tractate. If I am correct in seeing M. Sot. 7:1ff. as an example of the correct mode of classification, following the demonstration of M. Sot. 6:1-3+4 that hierarchical classification without appeal to scriptural definitions of categories is an invalid taxonomic method, then those two chapters form a sustained and impressive exercise in method. But the bulk of the tractate is made up of a narrative of the rite, for Chapters One through Five, and exegesis of verses, for Chapters Eight and most of Nine, with a catalogue lacking all *listenwissenschaftliche* traits for M. 9:9-15.

### Sukkah:

By a ratio of 3 percent/96 percent, this tractate is anything but philosophical. It contains in fact scarcely a trace of philosophical interest, and even the simple exercises in *Listenwissenschaft* are poorly executed.

### Taanit:

At a ratio of 0 percent/100 percent, no, there is nothing of philosophical interest nor even a trace of philosophical method in the entire tractate.

### Tamid:

At a ratio of 0 percent/100 percent, Tamid is not philosophical. It is also not scriptural. It presents a sustained and continuous narrative.

### Temurah:

The principal purpose of Mishnah-tractate Temurah (20 percent/80 percent) is the amplification of the rules of Scripture through provision of complex cases to show the application of a simple rule, which is the one stated explicitly at Lev. 27:10. The tractate shows how philosophers undertake the exegesis of Scripture, but it is not a philosophical tractate at all.

### Yoma:

The tractate not only is not philosophical (6 percent/94 percent), it is wholly, and solely, scriptural in its program, order, and structure. The order of the tractate follows the sequence of the narrative of Scripture. The only way to make sense of the tractate's narrative, as it turns this way and that, is to refer to Scripture's account of the same events. All that the Mishnah's authorship has added to Scripture is the opening unit, the preparation of the high priest for the rite and the daily whole-offering, and the closing materials on Torah reading, prayer, and atonement, of which the priestly code is oblivious. The real contribution of the Mishnah's framers then is their recognition that it is necessary to join the topic of the daily whole-offering to that of the rite of the Day of Atonement and the added homiletical-theological materials at the end. These fall entirely outside of the thematic and narrative framework of the tractate as a whole.

Let us now turn to the classification of tractates as to their relationship with Scripture. We follow the same tripartite program as just now worked out: mostly, mixed, little subjection to the scriptural program.

## 1.   Mainly Scriptural in Contents, Structure, and Problematic

### Arakhin:
The entire program of the tractate is dictated by Lev. 25, 27, and the purpose is to spell out and apply or amplify the rules of those passages.

### Baba Batra:
Most of this tractate takes up rules that Scripture does not provide or topics that Scripture does not treat. Where facts of Scripture do enter, to be sure, these form the agenda for analysis, without an independent perspective. On this basis we can classify the tractate as either essentially scriptural or ascriptural, that is, in column 1 or 3.

### Baba Mesia:
Where this tractate has a scriptural topic, all it does is spell out how that topic is made into rules. Some of its topics are not supplied by Scripture, so this tractate can fit into column 1 or 3.

### Baba Qamma:
There can be no doubt that this tractate is profoundly scriptural, since the bulk of its program as to facts simply replicates the relevant passages of Scripture. Nor is the framework in which these facts are treated distinct from that of Scripture; it is secondary to, and derivative of, Scripture.

### Bekhorot:
The entire program of Bekhorot is supplied by Scripture, Num. 18:16, the firstborn of man; the firstborn of a clean beast, the firstborn of an unclean

beast (Ex. 13:13), which is redeemed in exchange for a lamb. The conclusion focuses upon tithe of cattle, Lev. 27:32-33.

### Bikkurim:

Chapter Three sets forth an exposition of the requirements of Scripture's rules, and that also is the quite unphilosophical part of the tractate. Chapters One and Two, which work out principles of hierarchical classification through polythetic taxonomy, are completely ascriptural. That accounts for the dual entry for this tractate.

### Hagigah:

Where this tractate treats scriptural facts, in Chapter One and Two, it is not very philosophical, and where it treats nonscriptural categories, for example, levels of sanctification, layers of cultic uncleanness, it is very philosophical. The scriptural side concerns the pilgrim's festal-offering, and this is worked out pretty narrowly within the secondary and amplificatory frame of reference: who brings how much and the like.

### Maaser Sheni:

Chapter Five of this tractate simply expands upon Scripture's rules. But the rest is autonomous of Scripture.

### Makkot:

Scripture forms the dominant source of the tractate's facts, Ex. 20:16, Deut. 4:20, Deut. 19:15-21, serving Chapter One, Num. 35:9-28, Deut. 19:1-13, Chapter Two, Deut. 23:1-3, Chapter Three. Not only so, but I find in the tractate no layer of discourse beyond that connected with Scripture. Overall, we classify the facts of Scripture in accord with whatever taxonomic principles the framers located in Scripture. Philosophical problems are few and episodic.

### Megillah:

The laws of reading the Scroll of Esther, 1:1-2:6, do not derive from Scripture in any detailed way, but they supply merely a program of rules for carrying out the regulation of Scripture. The rules for reading the Scriptures in synagogue worship, 3:4-6, 4:1-5, simply allude to passages of Scripture in assigning synagogue lections. Only a few passages of the tractate as a whole are unconnected with Scripture, for example, M. 3:1-3, the disposition of synagogue property.

### Menahot:

Two-thirds of this tractate centers upon the collection and arrangement of rules, many of them deriving from Scripture, on the correct presentation of the meal-offering. The first third works out the impact of intentionality upon classification. Where this tractate is philosophical, it is not scriptural, and where it is scriptural, it is not philosophical.

**Pesahim:**
Scripture's elaborate discussion of the Passover-offering and celebration, Ex. 12:1-28, defines both the topic and the program of Mishnah-tractate Pesahim, which comprises little more than a secondary expansion of the scriptural rules. Scripture covers these topics: setting aside and killing a lamb for the Passover; unleavened bread and the taboo against leaven; the lamb. The tractate covers the two topics in reverse order: prohibition of leaven, then, the offering and how it is prepared. There is a final chapter on the Passover meal.

**Sheqalim:**
Ex. 30:11-16 supplies the theme and facts for Mishnah-tractate Sheqalim, requiring the collection of a half-shekel from males to support the daily whole-offering in the sanctuary. The tractate covers collecting the money, disposing of it for use of the altar, and the financial administration of the Temple. The tractate is filled with narrative and contains nothing of sustained philosophical interest. It exemplifies those tractates that are only scriptural and not philosophical. That is to say, knowing the facts of Scripture and the requirement to amplify them and supply details pertinent to them, we can predict most of the contents of the tractate overall.

**Sotah:**
The first two-thirds of Mishnah-tractate Sotah take up the wife accused of adultery, Num. 5:1-31, then the laws of the draft exemption in time of war, Deut. 20:1-9, and the neglected corpse, Deut. 21:19. These items are tacked on via a list of rites conducted only in the Hebrew language, Chapter Seven: the rite of the accused wife, the speech of the anointed for battle, and the declaration of the elders of the town. The rest of the tractate then performs routine exegetical operations on the passages on the exemptions and neglected corpse. This tractate is built upon Scripture, little more than that.

**Sukkah:**
Mishnah-tractate Sukkah supplies information about objects and rites defined by Scripture's account of the festival of Sukkot (Tabernacles) at Lev. 23:33-43, Num. 29:12-38, Deut. 16:13-15. Like Mishnah-tractate Yoma (as we shall presently see), Sukkah is incomprehensible outside of the frame of Scripture and constitutes little more than a law code of fundamental facts pertinent to Scripture. The whole is conceptually dependent and a complementary exegesis.

**Temurah:**
Lev. 27:10 defines the topic of Mishnah-tractate Temurah: If one consecrates an animal, then the animal is deemed holy and cannot be

trade or exchanged for some other so that the latter takes the place of, becomes holy instead of, the former. If, further, one does designate a secular beast to take the place of a consecrated one, then the secular beast is deemed to take on the status of the consecrated one, but the consecrated one retains its holy status. These facts, deriving from Lev. 27:10, require rules of clarification, extension, and application, and that is what the tractate provides.

#### Yoma:

The first seven chapters of this tractate simply provide a flowing narrative, heavy with interpolated materials, on the sacrificial rite of the Day of Atonement. There is no understanding the tractate without constant reference, not only for facts but for order and structure, to Lev. 16:1-34. The concluding chapter sets forth amplifications of Scripture's requirements but in no way analyzes them in a philosophical mode or manner. Yet the closest analogue to this tractate is Tamid, which bears no close ties whatsoever to Scripture.

### 2. Scriptural Facts Worked Out in an Entirely Autonomous Framework with No Direct Relationship between the Facts of Scripture and the Philosophical Program of the Tractate

#### Abodah Zarah:

This tractate takes up the scriptural theme of the prohibition of idolatry, but the issues of the tractate are not dictated by facts of Scripture. The concerns are principally philosophical, though the scriptural prohibition generates the basic composition, so it seems to me.

#### Erubin:

I cannot imagine a better example of a tractate that is fundamentally autonomous of Scripture, even while working out the implications of a fact supplied by Scripture. For the basic program and interest of the tractate in no way can be predicted on the basis of the scriptural fact that forms the given of the tractate.

#### Gittin:

The basic rule of Scripture is developed where appropriate, but the rules of writs of divorce do not derive from Deut. 24:1-5, which does not set forth a scribal program to begin with.

#### Hallah:

The basic theme of the tractate derives from Scripture, but the tractate works on the problem of connection and classification in spelling out the rules governing the topic at hand, a fine instance of a case in which Scripture's fact serves philosophy's ends.

### Horayot:

Here we have a remarkable case in which Scripture's ample provision of facts does not prevent the Mishnah's framers from thinking through a deeply philosophical problem, which predominates throughout.

### Hullin:

The program of this tractate is supplied by facts of Scripture as these define the regulations for preparing food for the home.  A variety of scriptural rules are worked out.   The pattern that governs their exposition, however, is essentially philosophical.  Here is a case in which the scriptural program is rich, but the philosophical treatment of it commanding.

### Keritot:

Scripture supplies some basic facts on how various felons are punished, but the problematic of the tractate derives from an interest in classification, specifically, when many things are one thing, or one thing is many.

### Kilayim:

The facts come from Scripture's explicit rules, but the focus upon classification and the impact of attitude upon classification is entirely the Mishnah's.

### Maaser Sheni:

Scripture establishes the topic of this tractate, which is produce that has been designated as Second Tithe and has to be brought to Jerusalem and consumed there, Deut. 14:22-27.  But the principal concern of the tractate is to preserve in the classification of sanctification produce or money that has been substituted for produce for the journey to Jerusalem.  That abstract consideration is hardly Scripture's contribution.  But for Chapter Five, see the first catalogue.

### Maaserot:

This tractate rests on no determinate scriptural foundations so far as these considerations are addressed; Scripture contributes only some basic facts.

### Makhshirin:

Lev. 11:34, 37 provide the basic facts of this tractate, but the generative problematic is unknown to Scripture.   It is that the attitude or intentionality of the farmer in seeing water affect his produce dictates whether or not the produce has been rendered susceptible to uncleanness.

**Meilah:**

Lev. 5:15-16 provide the facts of this tractate concerning sacrilege. The tractate attends to the applicability of the laws of sacrilege to sacrifices and to Temple property. But the philosophical development of those laws is the primary power of the tractate, and as noted above, that program of philosophy in no way depends upon Scripture for more than the facts that are subjected to philosophical analysis.

**Menahot:**

See the entry given above.

**Miqvaot:**

Various references to the use of spring water for purification of unclean persons, for example, Lev. 15:13 for the Zab, 14:5-6 for the leper, bear no relationship to the immersion pool under discussion here, which is still water. The references of Scripture to something's being put into water, for example, Lev. 11:31-32, or washed in water, Lev. 15:16, are understood to refer to the immersion pool under discussion here. But apart from the fact that Scripture knows of the use of water for purification, this tractate derives no important information from Scripture, and its problems, the traits and characteristics of immersion pools, the varieties of water used for them, and the ways in which they serve for diverse purification processes, are those of its framers, not of Scripture.

**Nazir:**

The facts of Scripture – Num. 6:1ff. – are reworked by the framers of this tractate into an essay on problems of classification, for example, the application of taxic indicators, the issue of when many things are one thing and one many, and the resolution of doubt. Overall, the tractate works out Scripture's facts in a manner entirely autonomous of Scripture's elaborate treatment of those same facts.

**Nedarim:**

While Scripture sets forth elaborate rules as to the disposition of the vows taken by a woman, Num. 30:1-16, the passage on men's vows is simple: one must keep the vows he makes. Chapters Ten and Eleven of the tractate carefully expound the scriptural materials, inventing interstitial cases, addressing possibilities generated by scriptural rules, and clarifying all manner of details. But where we have no Scripture on the theme, there the framers invent a completely philosophical inquiry, centered on the distinction of genus and species and other problems of classification.

**Negaim:**

Mishnah-tractate Negaim takes up the issues of Lev. 13 and 14, the uncleanness and purification of those affected by *saraat,* often translated "leprosy." The foundations of the tractate therefore are broad. But, signaled by the tractate's use of a different word from *saraat,* namely, *nega,* pl., *negaim,* the focus of the tractate is entirely its own. Consequently, by the test of whether or not we should solely on the basis of Scripture have been able to predict the issues of the authorship behind Negaim, we find that we should not have been able to do so. The reason is not that the subject changes. It is that, quite systematically, our authorship has devised its own questions in the analysis of the shared subject.

**Niddah:**

Mishnah-tractate Niddah addresses the issues of three important scriptural rules, Lev. 18:19 and 20:18, a woman is unclean during her menstrual period and at that time imparts uncleanness to whatever she lies or sits on; Lev. 15:25-30, a woman who produces a flow outside of her menstrual period is unclean in the category of a Zabah, with the same result, and Lev. 12:1-8, a woman after childbirth is unclean for seven days in the classification of a menstruant. But while the facts of Scripture everywhere predominate, the program of the tractate is not to be predicted solely on the basis of the subject matter. In fact, the whole is profoundly philosophical. The treatment of these subjects attends to two principal problems, rather than the subjects themselves the classification of body fluids and the identification of unclean body fluids and the resolution of doubt in connection with them.

**Ohalot:**

The laws about tents at Num. 19:11-22 hold that if a corpse is located in a tent, whatever else is found underneath that same tent, even not touching the corpse, is contaminated by uncleanness produced by the corpse, which lasts for seven days and requires a purification rite. On the basis of that fact, there is no predicting what our tractate will cover. Scarcely a single pericope is shaped by the simple fact provided by Scripture.

**Orlah:**

The broad topic of this tractate is the biblical prohibition against the consumption and the use of the fruit of a tree in the first three years of the tree's growth. It is based on a single biblical verse: *When you come to the land and plant any kind of tree for food, you shall treat it as forbidden. For three years it will be forbidden, it will not be eaten* (Lev. 19:23). The fourth-year fruit, like Second Tithe, is to be brought to Jerusalem and eaten there. For this reason, the laws concerning the fourth-year fruit are located in M. Maaser Sheni. The authorship of Mishnah-tractate Orlah has focused upon the issue of mixtures, with secondary attention to the problem of resolving cases of doubt. The interest in classification is hardly provoked by Scripture's framing of the topic.

### Parah:

Treating the sacrifice of the red cow and preparation of purification water as described at Num. 19:1-10, the tractate devotes itself to issues not emphasized in Scripture and uses the discussion of those issues to make points of paramount philosophical interest. The predominant concerns of Mishnah-tractate Parah, deriving from the period before 70, are two: first, the degree of cleanness required of those who participate in the rite and how these people become unclean; second, how the water used for the rite is to be drawn and protected, with special attention directed to not working between the drawing of the water and the mixing of the ashes referred to in Num. 19:17. The theoretical concerns of Mishnah-tractate Parah thus focus upon two important matters of no interest whatever to the priestly author of Num. 19:1-10, because the priestly author assumes the rite produces uncleanness, is conducted outside of the realm of cleanness, and therefore does not involve the keeping of the Levitical rules of cleanness required for participation in the Temple cult. By contrast, Mishnah-tractate Parah is chiefly interested in that very matter.

### Peah:

Mishnah-tractate Peah deals with the provision of a share of the farmer's crop for the support of the poor, who form a privileged caste in this regard. The tractate takes up the offerings specified in Scripture, as follows: peah or corner of the field, Lev. 19:9, 23:22; gleanings, Lev. 19:9, 23:22; forgotten sheaves, Deut. 24:19; separated grapes, Lev. 19:10; defective clusters, Lev. 19:10, Deut. 24:21. The entire topical program of the tractate is scriptural. The poor are like the priests, in that for them is reserved food others may not eat. The food for both is set aside through designation without an identifiable cause. No one has acted so as to specify that produce within a crop that is to be set aside for the poor. Brooks puts matters in this way: "Whether it is the grain that happens to grow in the rear corner of the field or the stalks that by chance fall aside from the edge of the farmer's sickle, all this food apportioned seemingly by accident must be left for the poor.... God alone determines what produce falls into the category of poor offerings."[3] The issues brought to

---

[3]Roger Brooks, *Support for the Poor in the Mishnaic Law of Agriculture: Tractate Peah* (Chico, 1983: Scholars Press for Brown Judaic Studies), p. 18.

Scripture's facts derive from a variety of taxonomic problems, as specified above.

### Qinnim:

This tractate alludes to facts of Scripture but is in no way scriptural. It calls upon facts that one may vow an offering of a pair of sacrificial birds (*qinnim*), and that one may be required to offer a pair of birds on account of certain transgressions, as specified at Lev. 5:1-10, Lev. 15:14-15, Lev. 14:22, Lev. 12:8, Num. 6:10, Lev. 1:14. The issue of the tractate is how one deals with cases of doubt, specifically as to mixtures.

### Rosh Hashshanah:

The first half of Mishnah-tractate Rosh Hashshanah addresses the designation of the new month through the year, concerning which no scriptural verses contribute facts, and the second half, the sounding of the shofar, or ram's horn, on the New Year, which is indicated by Lev. 23:23-25 and Num. 29:1-6. The tractate is not particularly scriptural in its orientation, but it is also not philosophical in any material way.

### Sanhedrin:

Mishnah-tractate Sanhedrin rests on a thick foundation of scriptural facts. Organizing these received facts in two principal divisions, the organization of the Israelite government and court system and the catalogue of sanctions inflicted for various crimes, the tractate brings to these subjects no sustaining problematic. Its authorship asks no fructifying questions, and the data rarely provide evidence for analytical initiatives. All that happens is that facts are reorganized in a layout and order found by the framers to be more suitable than Scripture's. The factual substrate contributed by Scripture derives from the following, in order of appearance: Deut. 16:18-20, Deut. 17:8-13, Ex. 23:21, Num. 35:30, Deut. 17:6-7, Lev. 21:10-12, Deut. 17:14-20, Deut. 21:22-23, Deut. 21:18-21, Deut. 13:12-18. While Sanhedrin is profoundly scriptural in its factual substrate, what the framers do with the facts marks the tractate as philosophical at its deepest structure.

### Shabbat:

Mishnah-tractate Shabbat in a general way develops themes introduced by Scripture, specifically, Gen. 2:1-3, Ex. 16:22-26, 16:29-30, 20:8-11, 23:13, 31:12-17, 34:21, 35:23, Lev. 19:3, 19:30, 26:2, 23:3, Num. 15:32-36, Deut. 5:12-15, as well as various statements in prophetic literature and in the writings. There can be no doubt that the theme and numerous facts derive from Scripture.

### Shabuot:

The basic topical program of Mishnah-tractate Shabuot derives from Lev. 5 and 6: those who bring a guilt-offering. Lev. 5:1-6 concerns oaths, an oath of testimony, and one who touches something unclean in connection with the Temple cult, and finally, one who utters a rash oath. Lev. 6:1-7 turn to issues of bailment, involving a false oath. The program of the tractate then covers oaths of adjuration, uncleanness to the Temple and its holy things, taking a rash oath, and taking a false oath in connection with bailments. The framers of the tractate move the matter of imparting uncleanness to the cult forward and keep together the other discourses on oaths. But the treatment of these topics is profoundly philosophical, both in the disciplined form, and also in the repetitive demonstration of the same abstract rules of method. No tractate exceeds this one in its capacity to demonstrate the principles of classification.

### Shebiit:

Mishnah-tractate Shebiit, which deals with the Sabbatical Year, rests upon Lev. 25:1-7, which dictate that farmers may sow and prune for six years but must leave the land at rest in the seventh. The land is to be treated as ownerless in the Seventh Year. The land is enchanted, in a unique relationship to God and to the people, Israel. Sanctified through being given to the people as an exclusive possession, the land is to enjoy the same rest in the Seventh Year that the people do in the seventh day. Deut. 15:1-3 further dictates that in the Seventh Year debts are remitted. Louis Newman judges, "No topic raised by Scripture is ignored by Mishnah, and, conversely, no concern addressed by Mishnah's framers is foreign to the biblical sources.... The authorities who stand behind Mishnah Shebiit are content to develop the rules of Leviticus and Deuteronomy by clarifying ambiguities or by addressing issues that Scripture leaves open."[4] Chapters One through Six focus upon Lev. 25:22-25, Chapters Seven through Nine, Lev. 25:6-7, and Chapter Ten, Deut. 15:1-3. But the basic program of the tractate is to set forth how one classifies by reference to attitude or intentionality with respect to taxa defined by time, place, and genus of natural species. What concerns Scripture is not critical, except for Chapter Ten, where all I see is an amplification of facts important in the application of the Torah's law.

### Tebul Yom:

The status of Tebul Yom forms a stage in the movement from uncleanness to cleanness. Specifically, when a person or object has become unclean and then immersed in an immersion pool, that person or

---

[4]Louis Newman, *The Sanctity of the Seventh Year* (Atlanta, 1985: Scholars Press for Brown Judaic Studies), p. 16.

object remains unclean until sunset, but not so unclean as prior to immersion. Tebul Yom then is translated as *one who has immersed on that selfsame day and awaits sunset for the completion of the process of purification.* The intermediate status in which the Tebul Yom is situated then forms the fact on which this tractate is spun out. Scripture has provided the fact, at Lev. 11:31-32, "And it shall be put into water and it shall be unclean until evening, then it shall be clean." Further passages that convey the same fact are at Lev. 15:13, Lev. 11:32, 40, 14:8, 15:5, 15:16, and the like, as well as at Deut. 23:11-12. At stake in the tractate is how to sort out the interstitial issues: In what way is the Tebul Yom clean and in what way yet unclean? Is the Tebul Yom essentially clean, but unclean in some minor way, or essentially unclean, but in a lesser stage of uncleanness than prior to immersion? Scripture has not generated these issues, though its facts have assuredly made possible the identification of them.

### Terumot:
Mishnah-tractate Terumot refers to the designation ("separation") of a portion of the crop as heave-offering, that is, as rations for the priests. That produce is deemed sanctified, holy only for the priests' consumption and related purposes. Num. 18:8 refers to the gift of heave-offering to priests; 18:11-12, 25:32, Deut. 18:4 deal with the same theme. Outsiders to the priesthood are not to eat that food, so Lev. 22:10-14. While defining the requirement of designating a portion of the crop as priestly rations, Scripture in no way prepares the way for the treatment of the topic that defines the generative problematic of this tractate.

### Yebamot:
Scripture at Deut. 25:5-10 supplies the facts pertinent to Chapters One through Five, Twelve, on the levirate relationship and the rite of *halisah* or removing the shoe. Scripture at Lev. 22:2ff. provides the facts pertinent to Chapters Six through Nine, specifying that the wife of a priest may eat food in the status of heave-offering. I see no point at which Scripture contributes to the discussion of Chapters Ten through Eleven, marital ties subject to doubt, Thirteen, the rite of refusal accorded to a girl who has been betrothed prior to puberty, Fourteen, the infirm marital bond of the deaf-mute, Fifteen through Sixteen, severing the marital bond through the death of the husband, with special reference to cases of doubt by reason of either having to rely upon a woman's testimony (ordinarily not accepted in a court) or identifying a corpse. While for approximately half of the tractate, therefore, Scripture provides the facts, even there, the problematic that generates the analytical problems does not derive from the facts that Scripture has provided.

Zabim:

The condition of uncleanness considered here is defined at Lev. 15:1-15. The elaboration of the way in which the Zab's pressure imparts uncleanness derives from the scriptural conception at Lev. 15:4 that if a Zab sits on a bed, the bed is unclean; if he sits on anything used for lying or sitting, that becomes unclean. The further statement of Scripture, Lev. 15:5-6, is that one who touches the bed on which a Zab has sat will bathe and also wash his clothing. These fundamental principles are scriptural; what is done with them is not. A deeply philosophical mode of thought, consisting of a process of classification through comparison and contrast, takes over and develops its own problems and even its own generative principles *and categories.*

Zebahim:

While Mishnah-tractate Zebahim makes use of facts of Scripture as to the classification of sacrifices (meaning, procedures in killing and offering up animals on the altar fires, for example, sacrifices that are wholly burned up as against those that yield meat for the priest or for both the priest and the donor), in fact the framers make their own points about such questions as the role of intentionality in the cult, on the one side, and rules governing various altars used by Israel. Scripture knows of seven types of sacrifice, within the categories of Most Holy Things, the burnt-offering, beast or bird, the sin-offering, beast or bird, the guilt-offering; and Lesser Holy Things, peace-offerings, the firstling, the tithe of cattle, and the Passover. The first two are the focus of interest. There are four cultic acts: slaughtering the beast, collecting the blood, bringing the blood to the altar, and tossing drops of blood on the altar. These facts derive from Scripture. The conception, paramount in the opening part of the tractate, that the priest must form the correct intention in respect to these actions, for example, to carry out the rite for the purpose for which the beast is designated, for the service of the Lord, and the like, is framed essentially within the limits of the tractate itself. And the basic interest of the framers of the tractate is in problems of classification and mixture; these problems invoke the facts of Scripture, but the principles of hierarchical classification derive entirely from philosophical reading of scriptural themes and topics.

3.  **Not Scriptural At All ([1] Few or No Facts of Scripture Used or Even Mentioned; or [2] the Topical Program is Completely Independent of Any Subjects Dealt with in Scripture)**

Baba Batra:

See Baba Batra, in the first catalogue.

**Baba Mesia:**
See Baba Mesia, in the first catalogue.

**Berakhot:**
There is scarcely a single scriptural passage that plays a generative part in the formation of this tractate, even though some of the prayers that are recited make mention of verses of Scripture.

**Bikkurim:**
Chapters One and Two set forth essentially ascriptural problems. See catalogue one's entry.

**Demai:**
Not a single fact in this tractate derives from Scripture.

**Hagigah:**
See Hagigah, catalogue one.

**Kelim:**
I see no important ways in which this tractate relates to Scripture. There is some exegesis of the tractate that links specific laws to Scripture, but that is not an important trait of the whole or even of large parts of it The main problems are those of classification and the interplay of classification and intentionality.

**Ketubot:**
Except for Chapter Three, the factual basis for this tractate is not scriptural. This is an essentially nonscriptural tractate.

**Menahot:**
See this tractate in the first catalogue. The opening third of the tractate is essentially autonomous of Scripture. Compare Zebahim, below.

**Middot:**
The specification of the layout and measurements of the Temple bears no clear and systematic relationship to Scripture's treatment of the same subject. Scholarship generally holds that it follows the pattern of Solomon's Temple with some adaptations of Ezekiel's, so F.J. Hollis, "The use made of Holy Scripture in the tractate is not such as to give the impression that somehow or other the words of Scripture are being followed...but rather that there was a fairly clear recollection of the Temple as it had been, with Holy Scripture appealed to illuminate the fact, not as authority to prove it."[5]

---

[5]F.J. Hollis, *The Archaeology of Herod's Temple. With a Commentary on the Tractate 'Middoth'* (London, 1934), p. 354.

**Moed Qatan:**

There are no pertinent verses of Scripture. Scripture knows restrictions on labor only for the opening and closing sessions of the festivals of Passover and Tabernacles, so Ex. 12:16, Lev. 23:7-8, 35-36, Num. 28:18, 25, 29:12-35. The conception that there are restrictions applying to the intermediate days is not scriptural.

**Qiddushin:**

In the aggregate Scripture does not define the facts that form the expository center of this tractate.

**Taanit:**

Mishnah-tractate Taanit deals with rites in connection with times of distress, particularly drought. If rains do not come in their season, the community must fast. Scripture has no rules on that subject and scarcely acknowledges the conception. The presentation is orderly and well-composed: when the community fasts and why it will be called upon to do so; the liturgy that is followed; rules about public fasts; the sounding of the shofar; the character of the delegation that serves as the Israelite caste's counterpart to the priestly caste serving in the Temple; the wood-offering; diverse events of a catastrophic character that took place at various times.

**Tamid:**

Mishnah-tractate Tamid addresses the topic of Num. 28:3-4, the daily whole-offering. The tractate's contents are not to be predicted on the basis of that topic. What we have is a sustained narrative of the rite, start to finish. This tractate is not scriptural, and it also is not philosophical. Three examples of the character of discourse exemplify the purely narrative and descriptive traits of the entire tractate.

**Tohorot:**

As above, there is no scriptural basis for the program of this tractate, with its interest in connection, classification, and the resolution of doubt.

**Uqsin:**

As above, there is no scriptural basis for the program of this tractate, with its interest in the theory of connection that is set forth.

**Yadayim:**

Washing hands before meals for hygienic purposes enjoys no scriptural support. The analogy between the domestic table and the Temple altar, for those who observed purity rules at home, probably explains the concern for an act of purification prior to eating an ordinary meal. Accordingly, Yadayim is an entirely nonscriptural tractate. It is built out of analogies borrowed from Mishnah-tractate Parah and forms a secondary tractate, see my *History of the Mishnaic Law of Purities* (Leiden, 1977: E.J. Brill), 19:103-105.

Let us now see whether there is a correlation between the high philosophical quotient of a tractate and the low utilization of scriptural propositions or even facts in that same tractate – and vice versa. What we see is that there is such a correlation. It is not perfect, but it is preponderant. The correlation between the philosophical focus and the absence of a scriptural foundation is indicated by the use of boldface type. The correlation between the nonphilosophical discourse characteristic of a tractate and elaborate representation of scriptural rules is indicated in italics. Scribal tractates, neither philosophical nor scriptural, are indicated in italicized boldface type.

| 1. Mainly Philosophical | 1. Not Scriptural At All |
|---|---|
| **Abodah Zarah** | Abodah Zarah |
| **Berakhot** | Erubin |
| **Bikkurim** | Gittin |
| **Demai** | Hallah |
| **Erubin** | Horayot |
| **Hallah** | Hullin |
| **Hagigah** | Keritot |
| **Horayot** | Kilayim |
| **Kelim** | Maaser Sheni |
| **Keritot** | Maaserot |
| **Kilayim** | Makhshirin |
| **Maaser Sheni** | Meilah |
| **Maaserot** | Miqvaot |
| **Makhshirin** | Nazir |
| **Meilah** | Nedarim |
| **Miqvaot** | Negaim |
| **Moed Qatan** | Niddah |
| **Nazir** | Ohalot |
| **Nedarim** | Orlah |
| **Negaim** | Parah |
| **Niddah** | Peah |
| **Ohalot** | Qinnim |
| **Orlah** | Rosh Hashshanah |
| **Parah** | Sanhedrin |
| **Peah** | Shabbat |
| **Qiddushin** | Shabuot |

| | |
|---|---|
| Qinnim | Shebiit |
| Sanhedrin | Tebul Yom |
| Shabbat | Terumot |
| Shabuot | Tohorot |
| Shebiit | Uqsin |
| Tebul Yom | Yadayim |
| Terumot | Yebamot |
| Tohorot | Zabim |
| Uqsin | |
| Yadayim | |
| Yebamot | |
| Zabim | |
| Zebahim | |

| 2. Philosophical Use of Scripture | 2. Scripture Supplies Facts, But Not the Tractate's Problematic or Program |
|---|---|
| Baba Batra | Baba Batra |
| Menahot | Baba Mesiah |
| | Berakhot |
| | Bikkurim |
| | Demai |
| | Hagigah |
| | Kelim |
| | Ketubot |
| | Menahot |
| | Maaser Sheni |
| | Middot |
| | Moed Qatan |
| | Qiddushin |
| | Taanit |
| | Tamid |

| 3. Not Philosophical At All | 3. Essentially Scriptural |
|---|---|
| *Arakhin* | Arakhin |
| *Baba Mesia* | Baba Batra |
| *Baba Qamma* | Baba Mesiah |
| *Bekhorot* | Baba Qamma |
| *Gittin* | Bekhorot |
| *Ketubot* | Bikkurim |

| | |
|---|---|
| *Makkot* | Hagigah |
| *Megillah* | Makkot |
| Middot | Megillah |
| *Pesahim* | Menahot |
| Rosh Hashshanah | Pesahim |
| Sheqalim | Sotah |
| *Sotah* | Sukkah |
| *Sukkah* | Temurah |
| *Temurah* | Yoma |
| *Yoma* | |

In the aggregate, it would appear that where there is a deeply philosophical treatment of a topic, Scripture supplies no facts that generate important problems. Scripture commonly supplies facts that are treated in a philosophical way. Some tractates rest wholly on scriptural facts and undertake no philosophical inquiry, for example, into problems of classification and interstitiality. A few tractates are neither scriptural nor philosophical; these are classed as either scribal or priestly, for example, Gittin, on the one side, Middot, on the other. But, in the main, we now see with great clarity, most tractates of the Mishnah pursue a philosophical program. I count 41 essentially philosophical tractates, 13 essentially scriptural ones, so that the proposed correlation covers 54 of the 61 tractates. Among the correlated tractates, 76 percent are fundamentally philosophical, 24 percent are essentially nonphilosophical, and among all of the 61 tractates (again omitting all reference to Abot and Eduyot), 89 percent fall into one classification or the other, and only 11 percent prove anomalous. These are rough figures, of course, but a review of my detailed account of the tractates will strengthen the argument that the Mishnah is to be described as philosophical, but not only philosophical, in its basic mode and structure of thought and discourse. I therefore am justified in claiming to undertake through the sustained picture set forth here an analysis of the philosophy of Judaism in its first principles.

# 5

## The Mishnah in the Judaism of Its Time

Rabbinic Judaism is that Judaic system – way of life, worldview, addressed to the Jewish people or nation – that uniquely affirms the revelation, by God to Moses at Mount Sinai, of the Dual Torah, one in writing, the other oral. The Dual Torah is handed on from generation to generation by sages, honored with the title of rabbi. Sages, through mastering the Torah teachings and serving and imitating the ways of their masters, become themselves authentic representatives of the Torah, that "one whole Torah of Moses, our rabbi," that God reveals. No other system of Judaism then or now speaks of the Dual Torah, appeals to the authority of the rabbi, and lays stress upon the holy way of life and worldview, encompassing both sanctification in the here and how and salvation at the end of time, that is defined by the faith of the Dual Torah.

The canon of Judaism of the sort under discussion begins, beyond Scripture itself, with the Mishnah, ca. A.D. 200, and concludes its formative age with the Talmud of Babylonia, ca. A.D. 600. In between the canonical literature in the formative age consists of two types of books, one that provides systematic expansion and exegesis of the Mishnah, the other that does the same for Scripture. In the former category fall the two Talmuds, the one of the Land of Israel, the other of Babylonia, and some related writings. In the latter category are several compilations of scriptural exegesis, in particular of pentateuchal books. Some of these lay stress on how the Mishnah, a document that does not systematically join to its several statements scriptural prooftexts, in fact rests upon Scripture. Others provide verse-by-verse explanations of various biblical books. Still others develop ideas or themes by whole bursts of prooftexts, selected without relationship to their position in various biblical compositions.

The earliest stage in the formation of Rabbinic Judaism, hence "early Rabbinic Judaism," is represented, in literary form, by the Mishnah. When, therefore, we wish to describe the foundations of the now dominant and normative kind of Judaism, we look to the Mishnah for its evidence about its own formation. While other compositions in the canon of Judaism probably contain sayings framed in the period before the closure of the Mishnah, and while no one can doubt that ideas that surface only later on could have been held in an earlier period, the Mishnah is the sole evidence that indubitably testifies to the state of ideas held in those circles that laid the foundations for Judaism as it would come to fruition in the literature ending with the Talmud of Babylonia. Hence when we seek to describe early Rabbinic Judaism, that is to say, that stage in the formation of Judaism in its rabbinic formulation prior to the turn of the third century, we best start with the Mishnah in particular. What we seek to discover is those layers of the Mishnah's ideas that attest to the state of belief and behavior prior to the closure of the Mishnah itself. To the degree that we can find out, within the Mishnah, about ideas held in the later first and through the second centuries, we have a picture of the important fundamental traits of Rabbinic Judaism, if, to be sure, not a complete picture of all of the traits characteristic of that earliest period.

The Mishnah takes shape in four distinct periods of development. These are marked off by groups of names, commonly found in juxtaposition with one another but not found in juxtaposition with any other names, for example, Rabbis A, B, C, D intersect very often with one another, but never with Rabbis W, X, Y, and Z, who, for their part, come together in completed units of tradition only with themselves. There are four such groups. Ideas held in sayings attributed to one such group may be shown, on the basis of fact or logic, to be presupposed in sayings attributed to another such group. On that basis, the first of the two groups may be regarded as prior in logic and possibly also in time to the second of the two groups. Stories told about the first of the four groups indeed place that group in the period before 70; these would be sayings that correspond to rabbinic traditions about the Pharisees, since the names are the same as those on the chain of tradition of M. Avot 1:1-18. Stories told about the second of the four groups place that group in the period after the destruction of the Temple. Stories told about the third of the four groups take for granted that authorities of that group survived the Bar Kokhba War, 132-135. Stories told about the fourth of the four put the members of that group in the period of the closure of the Mishnah itself, that is, toward c.a. A.D. 200. An account of the earliest phase in the formation of the ideas now fully exposed in the Mishnah, therefore, places us in the first century, in the period just before and just after the destruction of the Temple. To state matters simply, earliest Rabbinic Judaism is that system of Judaism, surviving and developing in later rabbinic writings, that got under way in the aftermath of the destruction of the Second Temple in A.D. 70.

The only extant documents originating in the decades immediately after the destruction of the Temple in A.D. 70 are 2 Baruch and 4 Ezra. If we ask how the character of the Mishnah's system, its "Judaism," differs from that of the writings of other Jewish thinkers of the same general period, the first and second centuries after the destruction of the Temple, we have only 2 Baruch and 4 Ezra for comparison. Those writings give some perspective on the work of the framers of Mishnah, even though they have absolutely nothing in common with Mishnah. Still, it is in precisely the same period and under essentially common conditions that the authors of Baruch and Ezra choose one set of topics, which they treat in a particular way, and the earliest framers of Mishnah choose another set of topics, to be treated in a quite different way. If we wish to know what Mishnah does not discuss, all we need to do is to list the issues and concerns we have seen in writings in the names of Baruch and Ezra – and vice versa.

The crisis precipitated by the destruction of the Second Temple affected both the nation and the individual, since, in the nature of things, what happened in the metropolis of the country inevitably touched affairs of home and family. What made that continuity natural was the long-established Israelite conviction that the fate of the individual and the destiny of the Jewish nation depended upon the moral character both of the one and of the other. Disaster came about because of the people's sin, so went the message of biblical history and prophecy. The sins of individuals and of nation alike ran against the revealed will of God, the Torah. So reflection upon the meaning of the recent catastrophe inexorably followed paths laid out long ago, trod from one generation to the next. But there were two factors which at just this time made reflection on the question of sin and history, atonement and salvation, particularly urgent.

First, with the deep conviction of having sinned and the profound sense of guilt affecting community and individual alike, the established mode of expiation and guilt and of atonement for sin proved not inadequate but simply unavailable. The sacrificial system, which the priestly Torah describes as the means by which the sinner attains forgiveness for sin, lay in ruins. So when sacrifice turned out to be acutely needed for the restoration of psychological stability in the community at large, sacrifice no longer was possible – a crisis indeed.

Second, in August, A.D. 70, minds naturally turned to August, 586 B.C. From the biblical histories and prophecies emerged the vivid expectation that, through the suffering of the day, sin would be atoned, expiation attained. So, people supposed, just as before, in three generations whatever guilt had weighed down the current generation and led to the catastrophe would be worked out through the sacrifice consisting of the anguish of a troubled time. It must follow that somewhere down the road lay renewal. The ruined Temple would yet be rebuilt, the lapsed cult restored, the silent Levites' song sung once more.

Now these several interrelated themes – suffering, sin, atonement, salvation – from of old had been paramount in the frame of the Israelite consciousness. A famous, widely known ancient literature of apocalyptic prophecy for a long time had explored them. The convictions that events carry preponderant weight, that Israelites could control what happened through their keeping, or not keeping, the Torah, that in the course of time matters will come to a resolution – these commonplaces were given concrete mythic reality in the apocalyptic literature. Over many centuries in that vast sweep of apocalyptic prophetic writings all of the changes had been rung for every possible variation on the theme of redemption in history. So it is hardly surprising that, in the aftermath of the burning of the Temple and cessation of the cult, people reflected in established modes of thought upon familiar themes. They had no choice, given the history of the country's consciousness and its scriptural frame of reference, but to think of the beginning, middle, and coming end of time as it was known.

The second stage in the formation of the earlier phases of Rabbinic Judaism coincided with the flowering, in the second century, of that rather general movement, both within Christianity and also outside of its framework, called Gnosticism. It is as important as the apocalyptic movement in establishing a base for comparison and interpretation of earlier Rabbinic Judaism. How so? One principal theme of the Mishnah, and of the Judaism beyond it, involved the affirmation of God's beneficence in creating the world and in revealing the Torah. A principal motif of diverse Gnostic systems was God's malevolence in creating the world, or the malicious character of the creator-god, and the rejection of the Torah. In these two critical aspects of the Judaism of the sages represented in the Mishnah and later writings, we see a direct confrontation on paramount issues of the day between Rabbinic Judaism and the family of systems we call, for convenience' sake, Gnosticism.

The second-century Church Fathers refer to Christian heretics called Gnostics, people who believed, among other things, that salvation came from insightful knowledge of a god beyond the creator-god, and of a fundamental flaw in creation revealed in the revealed Scriptures of Moses. Insight into the true condition of the believer derives not from revelation but from self-knowledge, which is knowledge of God. Now in introducing the viewpoint of second-century Gnostics and juxtaposing their principal emphases with those of the Mishnah, I must emphasize that we know no writings of Gnostics who were Jews. We cannot claim that the viewpoint of Gnostic thinkers on two questions of fundamental importance to the Mishnah – creation, revelation – derives from Israelites of the Land of Israel. The only certainty is that the Mishnah takes up a position both specifically and totally at variance with the position framed, on identical issues, by people writing in exactly the same period. No one can claim that Gnostic and Mishnaic thinkers addressed, or even knew about, one another. But they did confront precisely the same issues, and when placed into juxtaposition with one another, they present a striking and suggestive contrast. It is that contrast which we now shall briefly contemplate.

If the apocalyptic prophets focused upon historical events and their meaning, the Gnostic writers of the second century sought to escape from the framework of history altogether. For Israel, Jerusalem had become a forbidden city. The Temple had long stood as the pinnacle of creation and now was destroyed. The Gnostic thinkers deemed creation, celebrated in the cult, to be a cosmic error. The destruction of the Temple had evoked the prophetic explanations of the earlier destruction and turned attention in the search for meaning in the destruction to the revealed Torah of God to Moses at Mount Sinai. The Gnostic thinkers declared the Torah to be a deceit, handed down by an evil creator. It is as if the cosmic issues vital to the first-century apocalyptic prophets were taken up one by one and declared closed, and closed in a negative decision, by the second-century Gnostics.

The thinkers of the Mishnah for their part addressed two principal issues also important to Gnostic thought, the worth of creation and the value of the Torah. They took a quite opposite position on both matters. The Mishnah's profoundly priestly celebration of creation and its slavishly literal repetition of what clearly is said in Scripture gain significance specifically in that very context in which, to others, these are subjected to a different, deeply negative, valuation. True, we have no evidence that Gnostics were in the Land of Israel and formed part of the people of Israel in the period in which the Mishnah reaches full expression and final closure. So we speak of a synchronic debate at best. In fact what we know in Gnostic writings is a frame of mind and a style of thought characteristic of others than Israelites, living in lands other than the Land of Israel. What justifies our invoking two ubiquitous and fundamental facts about Gnostic doctrine in the description of the context in which the Mishnah took shape is the simple fact that, at the critical points in its structure, the Mishnaic system counters what are in fact two fundamental and generative assertions of all Gnostic systems. Whether or not there were Gnostics known to Mishnah's philosophers, who, specifically in response to the destruction and permanent prohibition of the Temple, declared to be lies and deceit the creation celebrated in the Temple and the Torah governing there, we do not know. But these would be appropriate conclusions to draw from the undisputed facts of the hour in any case. The Temple designed by the Torah for celebrating the center and heart of creation was no more. Would this not have meant that the creator of the known creation and revealer of the Torah, the allegedly one God behind both, is either weak or evil? And should the elect not aspire to escape from the realm of creation and the power of the demiurge? And who will pay heed to what is written in the revelation of creation, Temple, and Torah? These seem to me conclusions distinctively suitable to be drawn from the ultimate end of the thousand-year-old cult: the final and total discrediting of the long pursued, eternally fraudulent hope for messianic deliverance in this time, in this world, and in this life. So it would have been deemed wise for those who know to seek and celebrate a different salvation, coming from a god unknown in this world, unrevealed in this world's revelation, not responsible for the infelicitous condition of creation.

Insofar as Gnosticism incorporated a cosmic solution to the problem of evil, the Gnostic mode of thought had the power to confront the disaster of Israel's two wars against Rome and their metaphysical consequences. The Gnostic solution, if we may posit what someone might have been intelligent to conclude, is not difficult to discern. These events proved beyond doubt the flaw in creation, for the Temple had been the archetype of creation. The catastrophes demonstrated the evil character of the creator of this world. The catastrophes required the conclusion that there is another mode of being, another world beyond this one of creation and cult. So, whatever positive doctrines may or may not have found adherents among disappointed Israelites of the later first and second centuries, there are these two negative conclusions which anyone moving out of the framework of the cult, priesthood, and Temple, with its Torah, celebration of creation and the creator, and affirmation of this world and its creations, would have had to reach. First, the creator is not good. Second, the Torah, the record of creator and the will of the creator, is false.

In the same time as the Mishnah's formation and promulgation, Christian communities from France to Egypt encompassed groups which took a position sharply at variance with that of the Hebrew Scriptures affirmed in the Church in general on precisely the questions of creation and revelation and redemption confronting the Israelite world of the second century. Among the many and diverse positions taken up in the systems reported by Christian writers or now documented through Christian-Gnostic writings found at Nag Hammadi there are three which are remarkably pertinent. First, the creator-god is evil, because, second, creation is deeply flawed. Third, revelation as Torah is a lie. These conclusions yield, for one Gnostic-Christian thinker after another, the simple proposition that redemption is gained in escape; the world is to be abandoned, not constructed, affirmed, and faithfully tended in painstaking detail. It is in the context of this widespread negative judgment on the very matters on which, for their part, Mishnah's sages register a highly affirmative opinion, that the choices made by the framers of the Mishnah become fully accessible.

Characterizing the Mishnah's ultimate system as a whole, we may call it both locative and utopian, in that it focuses upon Temple but is serviceable anywhere. In comparison to the Gnostic systems, it is, similarly, profoundly scriptural; but it also is deeply indifferent to Scripture, drawing heavily upon the information supplied by Scripture for the construction and expression of its own systemic construction, which in form and language is wholly independent of any earlier Israelite document. It is, finally, a statement of affirmation of this world, of the realm of society, state, and commerce, and at the same time a vigorous denial that how things are is how things should be, or will be. For the Mishnaic system speaks of the building of a state, government, and civil and criminal system, of the conduct of transactions of property, commerce, trade, of forming the economic unit of a family through transfer of women and property and the ending of such a family economic unit, and similar matters, touching all manner of dull details of ordinary and everyday life.

So the Mishnah's framers deemed the conduct of ordinary life in this world to be the critical focus and central point of tension of all being. At the same time, their account of these matters drew more heavily upon Scripture than upon any more contemporary and practical source. The philosophers designed a government and a state utterly out of phase with the political realities of the day, speaking, as we shall see, of king and high priest, but never of sage, patriarch, and Roman official. They addressed a lost world of Temple cult as described by the Torah, of cleanness, support of priesthood, offerings on ordinary days and on appointed times in accord with Torah law, and so mapped out vast tracts of a territory whose only reality lay in people's imagination, shaped by Scripture. Mishnah's map is not territory.

Accordingly, for all its intense practicality and methodical application of the power of practical reason and logic to concrete and material things, the Mishnah presents a made-up system which, in its way, is no more practical or applicable in all ways to ordinary life than are the diverse systems of philosophy and myth, produced in its day in other parts of the world, which fall under the name Gnostic.

What the framers of Mishnah have in common with the framers of the diverse world constructions of the Gnostic sort thus is, first, a system building, and second, confrontation with two issues addressed in the diverse Gnostic systems of antiquity, the nature of creation and the creator and the character of the revelation of the creator-god. If I may state in a few simple words the position of the Mishnah on these two burning issues of the day, it is that creation is good and worthy of man's best consideration, and that the creator of the world is good and worthy of man's deepest devotion. So out of creation and revelation will come redemption. The Torah is not only not false but the principal source of truth. A system which intersects with the rules of the Torah therefore will patiently and carefully restate, and, so, blatantly reaffirm, precisely what Scripture has to say about those same points in common. A structure coming in the aftermath of the Temple's destruction which doggedly restated rules governing the Temple so reaffirmed, in the most obvious possible way, the cult and the created world celebrated therein. For as soon as we speak of sacrifice and Temple, we address the questions of creation and the value of the created world and of redemption. When, therefore, a document emerges rich in discourse on these matters and doggedly repetitive of precisely what Scripture says about exactly the same things, the meaning in context is clear.

From these comparative remarks on the context of the system, let us turn directly to the earliest phases of the Mishnaic system, that is, those ideas that appear to have circulated in the period before A.D. 70. Those strata of Mishnaic law which appear to go back to the period before the wars, prior to A.D. 70, deal specifically with the special laws of marriage (in Yebamot), distinctive rules on when sexual relations may and may not take place (in Niddah), and the laws covering the definition of sources of uncleanness and the attainment of cleanness, with specific reference to domestic meals (in certain parts of Chalot, Zabim, Kelim, and Miqvaot). For the conduct of the cult and the sacrificial system, about which the group may have had its own doctrines but over which it neither exercised control nor even aspired to exercise control, there appears to be no systemic content or development whatsoever.

How do we account for these points of interest? Once a group takes shape around some distinctive public issue or doctrine, as in odd taboos about eating, it also must take up the modes of social differentiation which will ensure the group's continued existence. For the group, once it comes into being, has to aspire to define and shape the ordinary lives of its adherents and to form a community expressive of its larger worldview. The foundations of an enduring community will then be laid down through rules governing what food may be eaten, under what circumstances, and with what sort of people; whom one may marry and what families may be joined in marriage; and how sexual relationships are timed. Indeed, to the measure that these rules not only differ from those observed by others but in some aspect or other render the people who keep them unacceptable to those who do not, as much as, to the sect, those who do not keep them are unacceptable to those who do, the lines of difference and distinctive structure will be all the more inviolable.

The Mishnah before the wars begins its life among a group of people who are joined together by a common conviction about the eating of food under ordinary circumstances in accord with cultic rules to begin with applicable, in the mind of the priestly lawyers of Leviticus and Numbers, to the Temple alone. This group of lay people pretending to be priests, moreover, had other rules which affected who might join and who might not. These laws formed a protective boundary, keeping in those who were in, keeping out those who were not. If we wish to identify the social group in which the Mishnah originated, it is at this point that discourse must come to a conclusion. The reason is that the Mishnah does not tell us the name of the group represented by the names of Shammai and Hillel and their Houses, Gamaliel, Simeon b. Gamaliel, his son, and others who appear in the Mishnah and who clearly form the earliest stratum of its named authorities. More important: The convictions of the named authorities deal with details. The vast territories of agreement have not been surveyed and marked out by them in particular. So, for all we know, the concrete matters subject to dispute represent the points at issue for no more than a tiny sector of a much larger group, which, in other ways, will have had still other points of discourse and contention. What I say elsewhere on the Pharisees will give body to this proposal.

We come now to the second stage in the formation of the earliest expression of Rabbinic Judaism, the period beyond the destruction in 70. The principal initiatives and propositions of the law after 70 and before 135 prove to be either predictable on the basis of what had just now happened or wholly continuous with what had gone before. The point of interest in the catastrophe of the first war against Rome, for the people whose ideas came down to the framers of the Mishnah, therefore lies in the stunning facts that, first, the Temple building had been destroyed, and, second, the cult had come to a halt. To them these points of total disorientation and socio-cultic disorganization formed the problematic of the age. At issue were not salavation, tragedy, and catastrophic history, but sanctification, the shaking of the foundations of orderly life extending out of the Temple and heaven that governed the cult. Needed was not poetry but order. To the founders of the Mishnah the aftermath of the first defeat brought to an end the orderly life of the villages and the Land, the reliable relationship of calendar and crop with cult, all joined at the movement of moon, sun, and fixed stars. The problematic of the age therefore was located in that middle range of life between the personal tragedy of individuals, who live and die, and the national catastrophe of the history of Israel. The pivot had wobbled; everything organized around it and in relationship to it had quaked. Left out were those two things at the extremes of this middle world: private suffering and national catastrophe in the context of history, the encompassing history of Israel and of the world alike. That is why, when we contemplate how others of the same time framed the issues of the day, we are struck by the contrast.

The obvious and accessible dilemmas of Israel's suffering at the hand of gentiles, the deeper meaning of the age in which the Temple had been ruined and Israel defeated, the resort for expressing public sorrow to evocative symbols of private suffering and its mystery, the discourse on the meaning of human history in the light of this awful outcome for Israel – none of these to us accessible and sympathetic themes and modes of thought comes to the surface in those themes and topics which the precursors of the Mishnaic system deem the appropriate focus of discourse. It is as if before us in the Mishnah are bystanders. These are people taken up with the result of the catastrophe and determined to make a quite distinctive statement about what was important in it. But the miserable world of the participants – the people who had fought, lost, and suffered – seems remote. It would stand to reason that before us is the framing of the issue of 70 by the priests, alongside people who, before the wars, had pretended to be priests and imitated their cultic routines. To such people as these, the paramount issues of 70 were issues of cult. The consequences demanding sustained attention therefore were the effects of the wobbling of the pivot for the continued life of the cult in those vast stretches of the Israelite Land which remained holy, among those sizable Israelite populations of the country which remained vital. Israel had originally become Israel and sustained its perpetual vocation through its living on the Holy Land and organizing all aspects of its holy life in relationship to the conduct of the holy Temple, eating like priests and farming in accord with the cultic taboos and obsessions with order and form, dividing up time between profane and holy in relationship to the cult's calendar and temporal division of its own rites. Now Israel remained Israel, loyal to its calling, through continuing to live in the mirror and under the aspect of that same cult. Let us now survey those laws which appear to have emerged in the age between the wars.

The sole fact to be adduced as definitive for the interpretation of materials attributed to authorities in the aftermath of the destruction of the Temple is that the Temple was destroyed. That fact by definition affected all else. But it also is general. There is no way to move from the self-evident facts that the Temple building was destroyed, the cult was no longer carried on, and the priesthood and Levites were now unemployed, to the specificities of the laws on these topics reliably assigned to the period under discussion. But there is no need to do so. For the main point of interest in an account of Judaism's unfolding is the expansion of the topics subject to discussion among precursors of the Mishnah's ultimate form, frame, and system. And the two new themes brought under systematic discourse directly relate to the destruction of the Temple, namely, laws affecting the taxes paid to the class of the poor and the caste of the priests, on the one side, and laws governing the conduct of the cult itself, on the other side. Since, moreover, the production of crops in accord with certain taboos was intimately related to the life of the cult, the sustained interest in the application of at least one significant taboo, that concerning mixed seeds, formed part of a larger statement about the way in which the country would respond to the loss of the Temple. Matters were to go forward as if the Temple still stood, because the Land retained its holiness, and God, his title to and ownership of the Land. Therefore the class of the poor, for its part, retained a right to a portion of crops prior to the completion of their harvest, and the priesthood, its claim to a part of them afterward. Sustained interest in the conduct of the cult, of course, represented a similar act of hope, an expression of the certainty that, just as God retained ownership of the Land, so, too, Israel remained responsible to maintain knowledge of the proper conduct of the sacrificial cult which returned to God part of what belonged to God out of the herds and crops of the Holy Land and which so secured Israel's right to the rest. So from from the viewpoint of the Mishnah's precursors, what required sustained reflection in the aftermath of the destruction was the disorientation of the country's cultic life, both in its conduct of the agricultural – that is, the economic – affairs, governed as they were by laws emanating from the cult and meant to place economic life into relationship with the cult, and in its performance of the cult itself. The profound disorientation of defeat and destruction, the disorder brought about by the collapse of basic institutions of government, culture, and faith – these form the crisis defined in this particular way by these people.

Alongside these two fresh points of interest, the established one in the conduct of a meal in conditions of cleanness enjoyed continued interest. In addition to a close continuation of thinking already evidenced prior to the war, moreover, a number of new topics came up.

First, systematic attention was paid to sources of uncleanness which, prior to the war, seem in legal thought to have been neglected. That is, sources of uncleanness on which no work had been done in organizing and amplifying laws now received sustained attention. Important here is significant and rigorous work on the unclean persons and objects (houses, clothing) discussed at Lev. 13 and 14. These now join the unclean persons and objects of Lev. 11, 12, and 15, to which ample attention already had been paid.

Second, there was a quite original essay attempted on the one rite of the cult which was performed outside of the Temple building itself, namely, burning the red cow and mixing its ashes with spring water to make purification water for persons affected by corpse uncleanness (Num. 19:1ff.). What is said in this essay, as it is worked out between the wars, is that a place of true cleanness can be formed outside of the Temple. (Whether or not the rite itself was carried on is not information provided by the Mishnah; in fact, we do not know.) What had to be done was situating the conduct of the rite outside the Temple in an appropriate relationship to the Temple itself. That is, determining whether or not the rite should be done precisely as rites were done in the Temple, or, in a mirror image, precisely the opposite of the way rites were done in the Temple, was the principal focus. This fundamental inquiry into the governing analogies generated ongoing exegesis. Through imposing on participants in the rite perfect attentiveness and perpetual concern for what they were doing while they were engaged in the rite, the law would make possible that state of cleanness appropriate to the conduct of a sacred rite in the otherwise unclean secular world. It would follow that a state of cleanness still higher than that of the Temple would be contemplated. The rules would demand remarkable attentiveness. Why all of this should come under discussion at just this time is obvious. For the underlying notion is continuous with that of the laws of Purities prior to 70, that is to say, cleanness outside of the Temple building is possible. A state of cleanness outside of the conduct of the Temple cult therefore may be required for certain purposes. What now is added thus is predictable, given what had been said before 70. Just as a meal can and should be eaten in a state of cultic cleanness by people not engaged in the eating of bread and meat originating as priestly gifts in the Temple, so it is possible even to conduct that one rite which Scripture itself deems legitimate when performed outside the "tent of meeting," the Temple. The laws remain valid; the relevant ones require study.

The destruction of the Temple thus is important, in the unfolding of the history of the Mishnah's laws and ideas, principally because of what it does not demarcate. It does not mark a significant turning in the history of the laws of Purities. These unfolded within the generative principles of their own logic. The inner tensions embedded from before 70 in the exercise of locating the unclean on a continuum with the holy and of situating ordinary food in place of that continuum account for what was said after 70. The loss of the Temple, enormous though it was, does not. The expectation that the rites governing agriculture and the disposition of the produce of the Land would remain valid accounts for the evidence we have surveyed, just as that same expectation, that people would eat in a state of cultic cleanness, clearly is in evidence in the character of the laws of Purities between the wars. True, the destruction of the Temple and the supposedly temporary cessation of the cult precipitated thought on laws governing the Temple altar and the priests in the act of sacrifice. That was a natural interest among people who, to begin with, thought that what happened in the Temple formed the center and focus of Israelite life. With the Temple gone, people will naturally have wondered whether some deep flaw in the conduct of its rites might explain the awful punishment Israel suffered in the destruction of the Temple and the holy city. So, in that same, essentially priestly, perspective of the world, it was entirely predictable that sustained thought on the right conduct of the cult should have gotten under way. The themes and detailed principles collected in the Divisions of Agriculture, Holy Things, and Purities, the first and the third continuing from before the war, the second beginning in its aftermath, testify to a continuity of vision, a perpetuation of focus.

The people whose ideas come to full expression and closure in the Mishnah, as we shall see later on, were diverse. But insofar as the definition of the group is concerned, who, before and between the wars, contributed to the ultimate corpus of ideas contained in what was framed after the wars, that definition remains unchanged. They were priests and lay people who aspired to act like priests. These are the ones whose fantasy lies before us in the stratum, A.D. 70-135, of the laws of the Mishnah just now surveyed. Yet fresh elements in their thought turn out to have laid the foundations for what, in the end, is truly Mishnaic about the Mishnah, I mean, the Mishnah's message at its deepest structure about the interplay between sanctification, on the one side, and the human will, on the other.

The period between the wars, that is, after 70 and before 135, marks a transition in the unfolding of the Mishnaic law and system. The law moved out of its narrow, sectarian framework. But it did not yet attain that full definition, serviceable for the governance of a whole society and the formation of a government for the nation as a whole, which would be realized in the aftermath of the wars. The marks of the former state remained. But those of the later character of the Mishnaic system began to make their appearance. Still, the systemic fulfillment of the law would be some time in coming. For the system as a whole in its ultimate shape would totally reframe the inherited vision. In the end the Mishnah's final framers would accomplish what was not done before or between the wars: make provision for the ordinary condition of Israelite men and women, living everyday lives under their own government. The laws suitable for a sect would remain, to be joined by others which, in the aggregate, would wholly revise the character of the whole.

The shift would be from a perspective formed upon the Temple mount, to a vision framed within the plane of Israel, from a cultic to a communal conception, and from a center at the locative pivot of the whole. To be sure, this still would be what the cult-centered vision had perceived: a holy nation in a Holy Land living out a holy life and deriving sustenance from the source of life, through sanctification set apart from death and uncleanness. But the shift is made. The orbit moved to a path other than what it was. Between the wars the shift is yet to be discerned. But if the orbit was the same as it had been for well over half a millennium, still, we see a wobble in the pivot.

When we take up the changes in this transitional period, we notice, first of all, continuity with the immediate past. What was taking place after 70 is encapsulated in the expansion, along predictable and familiar lines, of the laws of uncleanness, so to these we turn first. If the destruction of Jerusalem and the Temple in 70 marks a watershed in the history of Judaism, the development of the system of uncleanness does not indicate it. The destruction of the Temple in no way interrupted the unfolding of those laws, consideration of which is well attested when the Temple was standing and the cult maintained. Development is continuous in a second aspect as well. We find that, in addition to carrying forward antecedent themes and supplying secondary and even tertiary conceptions, the authorities between the wars develop new areas and motifs of legislation. These turn out to be both wholly consonant with the familiar ones, and, while fresh, generated by logical tensions in what had gone before. If, therefore, the destruction of the Temple raised in some minds the question of whether the system of cleanness at home would collapse along with the cult, the rules and system before us in no way suggest so. To be sure, the destruction of the Temple does mark a new phase in the growth of the law. What now happens is an evidently rapid extension of the range of legislation, on the one side, and provision of specific and concrete rules for what matters of purity were apt to have been taken for granted but not given definition before 70, on the other. So the crisis of 70 in the system of uncleanness gives new impetus to movement along lines laid forth long before.

What happened in the third period of the Mishnah's development, that is, the period beyond the decisive catastrophe of Bar Kokhba's War in 135 to 160 or 170? We begin by reminding ourselves that the destruction of the Temple in 70 left alive the hope for its restoration. After 135, with Jerusalem forbidden to Jews and the Temple mount ploughed over, few could hope for a near-term rebuilding of the Temple and restoration of its bloody cult. So the real work of framing a system in response to the final end of a thousand-year-old mode of social organization fell upon the survivors after 135.

Before the two wars (70, 135) the people whose ideas come to full expression in the Mishnah formed a small group, perhaps to be categorized as a sect. If so, it was a cultic sect, a holiness order, expressing the aspirations of lay people to live as if they belonged to the caste of priests, and of priests to live as if the whole country were the Temple. It is no surprise that those definitive topics of the Mishnah which gain attention early on were the ones having to do with food and sex: how food is raised, the petty obsessions governing its preparation and consumption, and who may marry whom in the constrained circle of those who worried those small, compulsive worries. After the two wars the entire framework of the Mishnah would undergo revision. The range of topics so expanded that laws came to full expression to govern not merely the collective life of a small group but the political and social affairs of a whole nation. What had come from the then distant past, from the preceding century, would be taken into caring hands and carefully nurtured, as if it mattered. But the fresh and the new challenge of an age of new beginnings would lead to daring choices: laws for real estate and commercial transactions, laws for the scribal profession and the documentation of changes in the status of people and property, laws, even, for the governance of the Temple, then in ruins, and the conduct of its rites throughout the cycle of appointed times and seasons, for the maintenance of the Temple and its caste of priests and Levites, and (of all things) for the design of the Temple when it would be rebuilt and for the conduct of its everyday offering. All of this would follow in that remarkable time of fulfillment and closure which came in the aftermath of the wars.

What was achieved between them? Small things, little steps – a bridge between that completed statement constituted by the sectarian fantasy framed before the wars, and that also completed statement about everything and everyone: the political vision, the social policy, the economic program, in full and glorious detail, which would be the closed and ample Mishnah itself. When we consider the beginnings of it all in a narrowly priestly fantasy, acted out by a tight little circle of specialists in uncommon and egregious laws involving the contact of a loaf of bread of a specified status with a deceased reptile, we must wonder what swept the world out of the old and into the new orbit.

For the priestly vision, with its emphasis on the Temple as the pivot and the world as the periphery, the Temple as guarantor of life, the world as the threatening realm of death, the Temple as the security and strength of Israel, the world as its enemy, and, above all, the unreliable and perpetually threatening character of persons and substances on the borders between Temple and world – when we contemplate that vision, we must wonder that anyone could share it and yet expand it. That is just what happened. For the priestly component of the ultimate structure of the Mishnah remains paramount. Yet the Mishnah is not a priestly document. It is much more than that. Had the Mishnah come to closure before the wars, it would have consisted of the system of uncleanness, fully exposed if lacking numerous details, a part of the system of agriculture, a system (quite its own) about food preparation, with emphasis upon doing so on special occasions (when the group presumably was able to come together), and, finally, a half-system on suitable marital candidates under special conditions, a set of laws calculated (if observed) to render members of the group unacceptable to nonmembers as marriage partners. New, that version of the Mishnah spun about the Temple, in a stable orbit around the altar.

And the other Mishnah, the one we now have, pursues its predictable path in quite another orbit. It makes peripheral the Temple and its concerns, as they come to expression in everyday imitation of the priesthood. It treats as central other things entirely: civil and criminal law and political institutions and their power, in the Fourth Division; the conduct of the cult itself, not merely of people wishing to place themselves into relationship with a cult by setting their feet on a single continuous path to the altar, in the Second and Fifth Divisions; the web of documents which encase and protect transfers of persons and property, both in life and afterward, in the Third and Fourth Divisions; the full articulation of the rules governing the disposition of crops in accord with the holiness inhering in them, and the arrangement of relationships (hitherto remarkably ignored) between virtuosi of the law and outsiders so that all, all together, might constitute a single Israel, this in the First Division and in the Sixth. Now these changes, ultimately realized in the full expression and closure of the Mishnah itself, are no issue of small detail. They cut to the heart of the matter. They shift completely and ultimately the very center of focus of the document itself. They represent a Mishnah wholly other than the Mishnah (if we may call it that) which would have taken shape before the wars, if anyone had thought to make one.

But, of course, so far as we know, no one did. So the truly stunning change effected after the wars was the formation of the book itself, the book which brought together the ideas and principles and laws in circulation before its time, and put them all together into something far more than the components, the paltry corpus of conceptions available to the framers of the document. Now we see with full clarity the ponderous movement from one orbit to the other, the shift of the previous culture of, if not a millennium, then at least nearly seven or eight hundred years (from the second century backward to the sixth). That old, reliable, priestly way of life and worldview from the Temple mountain came to be subsumed by, and transformed into, a social vision framed on the plane of Israel. What is stunning is the shift in perspective, not the change in what was to be seen. Merely seeing the Temple and its altar from a vantage point other than the Temple mount itself is a remarkable movement in perspective. Only framing a code of law framed in rules made of words in place of practice codified in gesture and studied act constitutes an astonishing shift in focus. From interests limited to the home and hearth the opening lens of social thought takes in a larger frame indeed: from home to court, from eating and drinking, beds and pots and pans, to exchanges of property and encounters of transactions in material power. What moved the world on its axis, the ball of earth in its majesty? The answer is self-evident: seventy years of wars and the tumult of wars. These shattered a hope which, to begin with, had had little to do with the Temple at all. There was then a moment of utter despair about things which, from the perspective of the philosophers of the Mishnah, might as well have taken place on yet another planet (but, alas, things wholly within their experience). The previous culture of somewhat less than a millennium spun into another orbit, not because of the gravity of yet a new civilization of impressive density, though.

Having briefly surveyed the main developments in the earliest and formative stages of Rabbinic Judaism, from before 70 to after 135, we turn to the social question. We ask, specifically, what groups in Israelite society of the second century find a voice in the Mishnah as we have it. That is to say, what groups speak through the system of earliest Rabbinic Judaism?

Insofar as the Mishnah is a document about the holiness of Israel in its land, it expresses that conception of sanctification and theory of its modes which will have been shaped among those to whom the Temple and its technology of joining heaven and Holy Land through the sacred place defined the core of being, I mean, the caste of the priests. Insofar as the Mishnah takes up the way in which transactions are conducted among ordinary folk and takes the position that it is through documents with a supernatural consequence that transactions are embodied and expressed (surely the position of the relevant tractates on both Women and Damages), the Mishnah expresses what is self-evident to scribes. Just as, to the priest, there is a correspondence between the table of the

Lord in the Temple and the locus of the divinity in the heavens, so, to the scribe, there is a correspondence between the documentary expression of the human will on earth, in writs of all sorts, in the orderly provision of courts for the predictable and just disposition of exchanges of persons and property, and heaven's judgment of these same matters. When a woman becomes sanctified to a particular man on earth, through the appropriate document governing the transfer of her person and property, in heaven as well, the woman is deemed truly sanctified to that man. A violation of the writ therefore is not merely a crime. It is a sin. That is why the Temple rite involving the wife accused of adultery is integral to the system of the Division of Women.

So there are these two social groups, not categorically symmetrical with one another, the priestly caste and the scribal profession, for whom the Mishnah makes self-evident statements. We know, moreover, that in time to come, the scribal profession would become a focus of sanctification, too. The scribe would be transformed into the rabbi, locus of the holy through what he knew, just as the priest had been, and would remain, locus of the holy through what he could claim for genealogy. The tractates of special interest to scribes-become-rabbis and to their governance of Israelite society, those of Women and Damages, together with certain others particularly relevant to utopian Israel beyond the system of the Land – those tractates would grow and grow. Others would remain essentially as they were with the closure of the Mishnah. So we must notice that the Mishnah, for its part, speaks for the program of topics important to the priests. It takes up the persona of the scribes, speaking through their voice and in their manner.

Now what we do not find, which becomes astonishing in the light of these observations, is sustained and serious attention to the matter of the caste of the priests and of the profession of the scribes. True, scattered through the tractates are exercises, occasionally sustained and important exercises, on the genealogy of the priestly caste, upon their marital obligations and duties, as well as on the things priests do and do not do in the cult, in collecting and eating their sanctified food, and in other topics of keen interest to priests. Indeed, it would be no exaggeration to say that the Mishnah's system seen whole is not a great deal more than a handbook of how the priestly caste wished to design its life in Israel and the world. And yet in the fundamental structure of the document, its organization into divisions and tractates, there is no place for a Division of the Priesthood, no room even for a complete tractate on the rules of the priesthood, except, as we have seen, for the pervasive way of life of the priestly caste, which is everywhere. This absence of sustained attention to the priesthood is striking, when we compare the way in which the priestly code at Lev. 1-15 spells out its concerns: the priesthood, the cult, the matter of cultic cleanness. Since we do have divisions for the cult (the fifth) and for cleanness (the sixth) at Holy Things and Purities, we are struck that we do not have this third division: the priesthood.

We must, moreover, be equally surprised that, for a document so rich in the importance lent to petty matters of how a writ is folded and where the witnesses sign, so obsessed with the making of long lists and the organization of all knowledge into neat piles of symmetrically arranged words, the scribes who know how to make lists and match words nowhere come to the fore. They speak through the document. But they stand behind the curtains. They write the script, arrange the sets, design the costumes, situate the players in their place on the stage, raise the curtain – and play no role at all. We have no division or tractate on such matters as how a person becomes a scribe, how a scribe conducts his work, who forms the center of the scribal profession and how authority is gained therein, the rights and place of the scribe in the system of governance through courts, the organization and conduct of schools or circles of masters and disciples through which the scribal arts are taught and perpetuated. This absence of even minimal information on the way in which the scribal profession takes shape and does its work is stunning when we realize that, within a brief generation, the Mishnah as a whole would fall into the hands of scribes, to be called rabbis, both in the Land of Israel and in Babylonia. These rabbis would make of the Mishnah exactly what they wished. Construed from the perspective of the makers of the Mishnah, the priests and the scribes who provide contents and form, substance and style, therefore, the Mishnah turns out to omit all reference to actors, when laying out the world which is their play.

The metaphor of the theater for the economy of Israel, the household of Holy Land and people, space and time, cult and home, leads to yet another perspective. When we look out upon the vast drama portrayed by the Mishnah, lacking as it does an account of the one who wrote the book, and the one about whom the book was written, we notice yet one more missing component. In the fundamental and generative structure of the Mishnah, that is, at the foundations of Judaism, we find no account of that other necessary constituent: the audience. To whom the document speaks is never specified. What group ("class") generates the Mishnah's problems is not at issue. True, it is taken for granted that the world of the Mishnah expresses the sanctified being of Israel in general. So the Mishnah speaks about the generality of Israel, the people. But to whom, within Israel, the Mishnah addresses itself, and what groups are expected to want to know what the Mishnah has to say, are matters which never come to full expression.

Yet there can be no doubt of the answer to the question. The building block of Mishnaic discourse, the circumstance addressed whenever the issues of concrete society and material transactions are taken up, is the householder and his context. The Mishnah knows about all sorts of economic activities. But for the Mishnah the center and focus of interest lie in the village. The village is made up of households, each a unit of production in farming. The households are constructed by, and around, the householder, father of an extended family, including his sons and their wives and children, his servants, his slaves (bondsmen), the craftsmen to whom he entrusts tasks he does not choose to do. The concerns of householders are in transactions in land. Their measurement of value is expressed in acreage of top, middle, and bottom grade. Through real estate critical transactions are worked out. The marriage settlement depends upon real property. Civil penalties are exacted through payment of real property. The principal transactions to be taken up are those of the householder who owns beasts which do damage or suffer it; who harvests his crops and must set aside and so by his own word and deed sanctify them for use by the castes scheduled from on high; who uses or sells his crops and feeds his family; and who, if he is fortunate, will acquire still more land. It is to householders that the Mishnah is addressed: the pivot of society and its bulwark, the units of which the village is composed, the corporate component of the society of Israel in the limits of the village and the Land. The householder is the building block of the house of Israel, of its economy in the classic sense of the word.

So, to revert to the metaphor which has served us well, the great proscenium constructed by the Mishnah now looms before us. Its arch is the canopy of heaven. Its stage is the whole Land of Israel. Its actors are the holy people of Israel. Its events are the drama of unfolding time and common transactions, appointed times and holy events. Yet in this grand design we look in vain for the three principal participants: the audience, the actors, and the playwright. So we must ask why.

The reason is not difficult to discover, when we recall that, after all, what the Mishnah really wants is for nothing to happen. The Mishnah presents a tableau, a wax museum, a diorama. It portrays a world fully perfected and so fully at rest. The one thing the Mishnah does not want to tell us is about change, how things come to be what they are. That is why there can be no sustained attention to the priesthood and its rules, the scribal profession and its constitution, the class of householders and its interests. The Mishnah's pretense is that all of these have come to rest. They compose a world in stasis, perfect and complete, made holy because it is complete and perfect. It is an economy – again in the classic sense of the word – awaiting the divine act of sanctification which, as at the creation of the world, would set the seal of holy rest upon an again complete creation, just as in the beginning. There is no place for the actors when what is besought is no action whatsoever, but only perfection, which is unchanging. There is room only for a description of how things are: the present tense, the sequence of completed statements and static problems. All the action lies within, in how these statements are made. Once they come to full expression, with nothing left to say, there also is nothing left to do, no need for actors, whether scribes, priests, or householders.

So the components of the system at the very basis of things are the social groups to whom the system refers. These groups obviously are not comparable to one another. They are not three species of the same social genus. One is a caste; the second, a profession; the third, a class. What they have in common is, first, that they do form groups; and, second, that the groups are social in foundation and collective in expression. That is not a sizable claim. The priesthood is a social group; it coalesces. Priests see one another as part of a single caste, with whom, for example, they will want to intermarry. The scribes are a social group, because they practice a single profession, following a uniform set of rules. They coalesce in the methods by which they do their work. The householders are a social group, the basic productive unit of society, around which other economic activity is perceived to function. In an essentially agricultural economy, it is quite reasonable to regard the householder, the head of a basic unit of production, as part of a single class.

It remains to state, in a few words, the principal point expressed by the coalition of scribe, priest, and householder, for whom the Mishnah speaks. The Mishnah's principal message, which makes the Judaism of this document and of its social components distinctive and cogent, is that man is at the center of creation, the head of all creatures upon earth, corresponding to God in heaven, in whose image man is made. The way in which the Mishnah makes this simple and fundamental statement is to impute power to man to inaugurate and initiate those corresponding processes, sanctification and uncleanness, which play so critical a role in the Mishnah's account of reality. The will of man, expressed through the deed of man, is the active power in the world. Will and deed constitute those actors of creation which work upon neutral realms, subject to either sanctification or uncleanness: the Temple and table, the field and family, the altar and hearth, woman, time, space, transactions in the material world and in the world above as well. An object, a substance, a transaction, even a phrase or a sentence is inert but may be made holy, when the interplay of the will and deed of man arouses or generates its potential to be sanctified. Each may be treated as ordinary or (where relevant) made unclean by the neglect of the will and inattentive act of man. Just as the entire system of uncleanness and holiness awaits the intervention of man, which imparts the capacity to become unclean upon what was formerly inert, or which removes the capacity to impart cleanness from what was formerly in its natural and puissant condition, so in the other ranges of reality, man is at the center on earth, just as is God in heaven. Man is counterpart and partner and creation, in that, like God he has power over the status and condition of creation, putting everything in its proper place, calling everything by its rightful name.

So, stated briefly, the question taken up by the Mishnah and answered by Judaism is, What can a man do? And the answer laid down by the Mishnah is, Man, through will and deed, is master of this world, the measure of all things. Since when the Mishnah thinks of man, it means the Israelite, who is the subject and actor of its system, the statement is clear. This man is Israel, who can do what he wills. In the aftermath of the two wars, the message of the Mishnah could not have proved more pertinent – or poignant and tragic.

# 6

## Accommodating the Mishnah to Scripture in Judaism:

## The Uneasy Union and Its Offspring

From the formation of ancient Israelite Scripture into a holy book in Judaism, to begin with in the aftermath of the return to Zion and the creation of the Torah book in Ezra's time (ca. 450 B.C.), the established canon of revelation (whatever its contents) presented a considerable problem to coming generations. As new writers came along, what they wrote had to be set into relationship with the established, authoritative Scripture. Otherwise, in the setting of Israelite culture, the new writings could find no ready hearing. Over the next six hundred years, from ca. 400 B.C. to ca. A.D. 200, four conventional ways to accommodate new writings – tradition – to the established canon of received Scripture came to the fore. First and simplest, a writer would sign a famous name to his book, attributing his ideas to Enoch, Adam, Jacob's sons, Jeremiah, Baruch, and any number of others, down to Ezra. Second, he might also imitate the style of biblical Hebrew and so try to creep into the canon by adopting the cloak of Scripture. Third, he would surely claim his work was inspired by God, a new revelation for an open canon. Fourth, at the very least, someone would link his opinions to biblical verses through the exegesis of the latter in line with the former so Scripture would validate his views.

The authors of the pseudepigraphic books of the Old Testament took the first route; the writers of the Dead Sea Psalms and other compositions, the second; some of the pseudepigraphs, the third; the school of Matthew, the fourth. From the time of Ezra to the second century A.D., we have not got a single book, clearly claiming religious sanction, standing as a holy book and authority over Israel, the Jewish nation, that fails to conform to one or more of these conventions. In these ways the new found its place in the framework of the old. Accordingly, we may describe how Israelite culture over the period of six hundred years dealt with the intimidating authority and presence of Scripture. We find essentially two modes of accommodation: imitation and augmentation. The newcomers would either imitate the old or they would link the new to the established.

To skip ahead in my story, from the third century to the eighteenth century, the normal mode of expressing creativity in Israelite culture – in all contexts of Judaism – remained precisely the same. Either people would imitate established conventions of literature, or they would link their compositions to existing ones in the guise of commentary and exegesis. In that long period of time in which the Hebrew Scripture reigned unchallenged as arbiter of Judaism in all its forms, from the formation of the Torah book by Ezra to the advent of modernization in the nineteenth century, there were only two important alternatives available within the circle of the faith and the framework of the community of Judaism. Imitate or augment – in either case, avoid the appearance of innovation. The Zohar, a mystical work composed in the thirteenth century, attributed its materials to second-century authorities. The composition of collections of biblical exegesis (midrashim) constituted an ongoing convention of Jewish writing. Above all, like contemporary Christians and Moslems, Jewish writers composed their ideas into commentaries on established works of classical Judaic antiquity. Accordingly, the profoundly conservative and traditional traits of the ongoing culture of the Jewish people masked the equally deep-set qualities of minds that were open and capable of imagination and innovation. Given the condition of Israel, a small group absorbing within its life the diverse cultures of Oriental Islam and European Christendom, rigid constraints on creativity hardly present a puzzle. You could say anything you wanted, so long as it did not look new – not much of a limitation.

When, therefore, we come across an exception to the rule established by the literary conventions by which ancient writers made their way into the canon of Judaism, we must find the case remarkable. There was one document in which all of the established modes of saying the new in the guise of the old and enduring proved useless. I speak, further, of a document that, for its part, rarely cites Scripture and furthermore admits to no antecedents except for Scripture itself. The work at hand claims no point of contact with a single book written by a Jew from its own day backward for nearly seven hundred years, to the time of Ezra (as we should say), or to the time of Moses (as its framers would allege).

Further, from the document at hand, for the next eighteen hundred years to the present day, all important expressions of Judaism flow forth. It followed no models but itself served as a model for many. So all roads lead back to this book, but the book at hand leaps back to Sinai alone. If we want to know the exception to the iron rule of how in Judaism people say fresh and new ideas, we have therefore to confront the one document that violated all the rules and therefore established, from its time to ours, a whole new set of rules.

I refer to the Mishnah, a collection of exquisitely composed philosophical essays on various legal problems. Framed in carefully formalized and patterned sentences, put together within a nearly uniform set of literary conventions and redactional patterns, the Mishnah was established, from its time onward, as the principal source of Jewish law and mediator of the law of Scripture. In form it is a construction in six divisions, themselves comprised of sixty-three tractates. All divisions take up the issue of the sanctification of Israel, the Jewish nation, through provision of the laws of holiness as they touch these six successive dimensions of the national life: the (agricultural) economy, the division of time and seasons, the conduct of the life of the family, with special attention to women and their rights, the construction of government and the conduct of civil law, the correct conduct of the service of God through the cult, and the protection of the life of the cult and the bed and table of the ordinary Israelite from the contagions of uncleanness and for the possibility of sanctification.

## I. The Mishnah as a Crisis

Let me now explain why the Mishnah presents us with so stunning a literary anomaly and then raise the question of how the document was received by its continuators and brought into relationship with Scripture. When these two questions have been worked out, we shall have a fair picture of how the Hebrew Bible was received and mediated into the religion of Judaism, as that religion came to full expression in the Mishnah, the first definitive and normative document of Judaism, and the works that flowed from it. For when we recall that Judaism is the religion not of the Old Testament alone, any more than is the case with Christianity, but of the Old Testament as mediated by a second and central document, the issue at hand takes on considerable weight. Judaism is the religious tradition framed by the Hebrew Scriptures (called "the Written Torah") and the documents beginning with the Mishnah itself (later on called, all together, "the Oral Torah") which comprise (after the Mishnah) "the one whole Torah of Moses, our rabbi." So at issue is the birth of Judaism as we know it, in the age of the formation of the first document of Judaism after the Hebrew Bible itself. Judaism is the offspring of the uneasy but enduring union between Scripture and the Mishnah.

What the framers of the Mishnah did not do was what everyone else had done for well over a millennium. That is to say, the authorities in the Mishnah did not sign biblical names. Sayings in the Mishnah bear mainly the names of sages of the late first and second century A.D. Accordingly, we find not the slightest pretense of claiming antiquity for the documents' allegations. The Hebrew of the Mishnah is totally different from the Hebrew of the Hebrew Scriptures. Its verb, for instance, makes provision for more than completed and continuing action, but also for past and future times, subjunctive and indicative voices, and much else. The syntax is Indo-European, in that we can translate the word order of the Mishnah into any Indo-European language and come up with perfect sense. None of that crabbed imitation of biblical Hebrew, that makes the Dead Sea Scrolls an embarrassment to read, characterizes the Hebrew of the Mishnah. Mishnaic style is elegant, subtle, exquisite in its sensitivity to word order and repetition, balance, pattern.

The Mishnah moreover contains no allegation that any of its statements derives from God. Nor are the authors of the document alleged to have received revelation. To be sure, a rather odd and singular tractate, Abot, different from all other tractates of the Mishnah, begins with the allegation that Moses received Torah at Sinai. The implication may be that part of the Torah – the Mishnah – was handed on orally, not in writing alone. But even here there is no explicit claim that the Mishnah, in particular, is that Oral Torah of Moses at Sinai to which reference is made. Perhaps that is what is meant. Many suppose so. But it is not said in the way in which, for example, writers of Old Testament pseudepigrapha say God spoke to them. Finally and most striking, unlike the splendid exegetical composition of the school of Matthew, the Mishnah contains remarkably little exegesis of the antecedent biblical writings. We discern no systematic effort to link laws and statements in the Mishnah with biblical verses.

The absence of such explicit links to Scripture as well as failure to provide some sort of myth of the origin of the law of the document, together present a truly astonishing fact. The standing and authority of the Mishnah, the sanctions attending enforcement of the law, the reasons people ought to keep it and listen to the sages who enforced it – these are questions denied all attention. Perhaps the framers of the document, rather subtle philosophical lawyers, never imagined they should have to explain why people should obey the laws they made up, because they never imagined people would do so. Perhaps to begin with the founders conceived their book as a kind of theoretical and speculative collection. Every paragraph of the Mishnah bears its share of contradictory opinions, framed as disputes about a common point, and that may mean the framers had not the slightest expectation that their book would serve as a law code. Arranging contradictory possibilities – *sic et non*, so to speak – may have served to turn abstract thought into concrete problems for future reflection. Accordingly, why invoke the authority and inspiration of heaven for discourse on philosophical possibilities? But if that was the plan, it was never grasped by the successors and continuators of the document. For almost as soon as the work of framing the Mishnah was completed, it found its way into the service of the Jewish government of the Land of Israel of the day. The Mishnah enjoyed the political sponsorship of the head of that government, Judah, patriarch of the Jewish nation in its land and recognized by the Roman government as ethnarch of the Jews of the Holy Land. It became the constitution and bylaws of the Jewish nation.

Accordingly whatever the original, theoretical character intended by the authors (if that is an accurate guess of what they had in mind), the Mishnah almost immediately demanded what its framers denied it: a place within the canon of Judaism. In the nature of things, there were only two possibilities. Since no one now could credibly claim to sign the name of Ezra or Adam to a book of this kind, and since biblical Hebrew had provided no apologetic aesthetics whatever, the only options lay elsewhere. The two were, first, provide a myth of the origin of the contents of the Mishnah, and, second, link each allegation of the Mishnah, through processes of biblical (not Mishnaic) exegesis, to verses of the Scriptures. These two procedures, together, would establish for the Mishnah that standing that the uses to which the document was to be put demanded for it: a place in the canon of Israel, a legitimate relationship to the Torah of Moses.

There were several ways in which the work went forward. These are represented by diverse documents that succeeded and dealt with the Mishnah. Let me now state the three principal possibilities. (1) The Mishnah required no systematic support through exegesis of Scripture in light of Mishnaic laws. (2) The Mishnah by itself provided no reliable information and all of its propositions demanded linkage to Scripture, to which the Mishnah must be shown to be subordinate and secondary. (3) The Mishnah is an autonomous document, but closely correlated with Scripture. The first extreme is represented by the Tosefta, a corpus of supplementary information about the Mishnah, a small part of it deriving, indeed, from the same period as the Mishnah's own composition. The second extreme is taken by the Sifra, a post-Mishnaic compilation of exegeses on Leviticus. The Sifra systematically challenges reason (= the Mishnah), unaided by revelation (that is, exegesis of Scripture), to sustain positions taken by the Mishnah, which is cited verbatim, and everywhere proves that it cannot be done. The third, mediating view is that of the Talmud of the Land of Israel, among the various documents produced by the Jewish sages of the Land of Israel between the end of the second century and the sixth. The Talmud of the Land of Israel (a.k.a. "Palestinian Talmud," "Yerushalmi"), like the one made up at the same period, in the third and fourth centuries, in Babylonia, was organized around the Mishnah. It provided a line-by-line or paragraph-by-paragraph exegesis and amplification of the Mishnah. Produced in schools in Tiberias, Sepphoris, Lud (Lydda), and Caesarea, the Talmud of the Land of Israel developed a well-crafted theory of the Mishnah and its relationship to Scripture.

The Talmud of the Land of Israel forms the focus of the exposition to follow, on how the sages received the Mishnah and naturalized it into the framework of Scripture. The reason is that it is the most important holy book produced in the Land of Israel from the closure of the Mishnah to the beginning of the composition of collections of exegesis formed not around the Mishnah but around Scripture itself. These later collections, beginning in the fifth century with Genesis Rabbah, at the outset carried out with reference to Scripture precisely those procedures of exegesis and amplification established with regard to the Mishnah in the pages of the Talmud of the Land of Israel. They constitute therefore a literary echo of the controversies of the third and fourth century, debates precipitated by the peculiar character of the Mishnah, on the one side, and necessitated by its powerful political status and capital historical importance, on the other.

## II. The Talmud of the Land of Israel's Theory of the Mishnah

The proper interpretation of the Mishnah in relationship to Scripture served as the ultimate guarantee of certainty. We therefore should anticipate a splendid myth of the origin and authority of the Mishnah, on which, for sages, all else rests. Yet, so far as I can see, the Talmud presents no explicit theory of the Mishnah as part of The Torah, the revelation of Sinai. Implicitly, however, the Talmud's judgment of the Mishnah is self-evident, hardly demanding specification. After Scripture, the Mishnah is the authoritative law code of Israelite life, the center, the focus, the source. From it all else flows. Beyond the Mishnah, looking backward to Sinai, sages see only Scripture. At the same time, the very implicit character of the expression of this fundamental judgment is puzzling. While nearly every unit of discourse of the Talmud – 90 percent of the whole – pays its tribute to the importance of interpreting a cited law of the Mishnah, seldom does a passage of the Talmud speak about the Mishnah as a whole, let alone its origin and authority. It is rare to find an allusion to a complete tractate or even to a chapter as such. Accordingly, if we want to know how the sages of the Talmud explained to themselves the status and standing of the Mishnah as Torah, we are at a loss to find out. All is implicit, with views of the whole rarely expressed.

To be sure, in other documents contemporary to the Talmud at hand, the Mishnah is described as "Oral Torah," Torah revealed by God to Moses at Mount Sinai and formulated and transmitted through a process of oral formulation and memorization. The myth of the two Torahs, one in writing, the other transmitted orally but now contained in the Mishnah and its continuations in the Talmuds, plays no substantial role in the Yerushalmi's treatment of the Mishnah. That myth does find expression in the Babylonian Talmud. To be sure, it is easier to say what is, than what is not, in either one of the Talmuds. But it suffices at this stage to observe that the myth of the two Torahs is not invoked to account for the striking and paramount trait of the Yerushalmi: its consistent interest in the exposition and amplification of the Mishnah's laws. Nowhere are we explicitly told why that exercise is necessary.

Admittedly, the Yerushalmi knows full well the theory that there is a tradition separate from, and in addition to, the Written Torah. But this tradition it knows as "the teachings of scribes." The Mishnah is not identified as the collection of those teachings. An ample instantiation of the Yerushalmi's recognition of this other, separate tradition is contained in the following unit of discourse. What is interesting is that, if these discussions take for granted the availability to Israel of authoritative teachings in addition to those of Scripture, they do not then claim those teachings are contained, uniquely or even partially, in the Mishnah in particular. Indeed, the discussion is remarkable in its supposition that extrascriptural teachings are associated with the views of "scribes," perhaps legitimately called sages, but not in a book to be venerated or memorized as a deed of ritual learning.

### Y. Abodah Zarah 2:7:

III.   A.    Associates in the name of R. Yohanan: "The words of scribes are more beloved than the words of Torah and more cherished than words of Torah: 'Your palate is like the best wine' (Song 7:9)."

      B.    Simeon bar Ba in the name of R. Yohanan: "The words of scribes are more beloved than the words of Torah and more cherished than words of Torah: 'For your love is better than wine' (Song 1:2)."...

      D.    R. Ishmael repeated the following: "The words of Torah are subject to prohibition, and they are subject to remission; they are subject to lenient rulings, and they are subject to strict rulings. But words of scribes all are subject only to strict interpretation, for we have learned there: He who rules, 'There is no requirement to wear phylacteries,' in order to transgress the teachings of the Torah, is exempt. But if he said, 'There are five partitions in the phylactery, instead of four,' in order to add to what the scribes have taught, he is liable [M. San. 11:3]."

E.  R. Haninah in the name of R. Idi in the name of R. Tanhum b. R. Hiyya: "More stringent are the words of the elders than the words of the prophets. For it is written, 'Do not preach – thus they preach – one should not preach of such things' (Micah 2:6). And it is written, '[If a man should go about and utter wind and lies, saying,] "I will preach to you of wine and strong drink," he would be the preacher for this people!' (Micah 2:11).

F.  "A prophet and an elder – to what are they comparable? To a king who sent two senators of his to a certain province. Concerning one of them he wrote, 'If he does not show you my seal and signet, do not believe him.' But concerning the other one he wrote, 'Even though he does not show you my seal and signet, believe him.' So in the case of the prophet, he has had to write, 'If a prophet arises among you... and gives you a sign or a wonder...' (Deut. 13:1). But here [with regard to an elder:] '... according to the instructions which they give you...' (Deut. 17:11) [without a sign or a wonder]."

What is important in the foregoing anthology is the distinction between teachings contained in the Torah and teachings in the name or authority of "scribes." These latter teachings are associated with quite specific details of the law and are indicated in the Mishnah's rule itself. Further, at E we have "elders" as against prophets. What conclusion is to be drawn from this mixture of word choices referring to a law or tradition in addition to that of Scripture? The commonplace view, maintained in diverse forms of ancient Judaism, that Israel had access to a tradition beyond Scripture, clearly was well known to the framers of the Yerushalmi. The question of how, in that context, these framers viewed the Mishnah, however, is not to be settled by that fact. I cannot point to a single passage in which explicit judgment upon the character and status of the Mishnah as a complete document is laid down. Nor is the Mishnah treated as a symbol or called "the Oral Torah." But there is ample evidence, once again implicit in what happens to the Mishnah in the Talmud, to allow a reliable description of how the Talmud's founders view the Mishnah.

That view may be stated very simply. The Mishnah rarely cites verses of Scripture in support of its propositions. The Talmud routinely adduces scriptural bases for the Mishnah's laws. The Mishnah seldom undertakes the exegesis of verses of Scripture for any purpose. The Talmud consistently investigates the meaning of verses of Scripture, and does so for a variety of purposes. Accordingly, the Talmud, subordinate as it is to the Mishnah, regards the Mishnah as subordinate to, and contingent upon, Scripture. That is why, in the Talmud's view, the Mishnah requires the support of prooftexts of Scripture. That fact can mean only that, by itself, the Mishnah exercises no autonomous authority and enjoys no independent standing or norm-setting status. The task of the framers of the Talmud is not only to explain Mishnah law but to prove from Scripture the facticity of rules of the Mishnah. Accordingly, so far as the Talmud has a theory about the Mishnah as such, as distinct from a theory about the work to be done in the exposition and amplification and application to the court system of various laws in the Mishnah, it is quite clear. To state matters negatively (and the absence of articulate statements makes this the wiser choice), the Mishnah does not enjoy autonomous and uncontingent authority as part of the one whole Torah of Moses revealed by God at Sinai. That conclusion is made ineluctable by the simple fact that one principal task facing sages is to adduce prooftexts for the Mishnah's laws. It follows that, without such texts, those laws stand on infirm foundations. We now turn to the ways in which the Yerushalmi does this work of founding upon the secure basis of the Written Torah the fundamental propositions of the Mishnah's laws, taken up one by one.

### III. Scripture behind the Mishnah in the Yerushalmi

Most units of discourse in the Yerushalmi take up the exegesis and amplification of the Mishnah. Exegesis for the Talmudic sages means many things, from the close reading of a line and explanation of its word choices to large-scale, wide-ranging, and encompassing speculation on legal principles expressed in, among other places, the passage at hand. Yet two attitudes of mind appear everywhere.

First, the sages rarely, if ever, set out to twist the meaning of a Mishnah passage out of its original shape. Whatever problems they wish to solve, they do not resort to deliberately fanciful or capricious readings of what is at hand in the statement of the Mishnah's rule. Now that is an entirely subjective judgment, since one generation's plain sense is another age's fancy. What it means is (merely) that our sense and their sense of straightforward reading of a passage are the same. By our standards, they were honest men, because they thought then the way we do now. That fact is so ubiquitous and blatant as not to require further specification. Since a common heritage of intellectual procedures, a single view of the correct hermeneutics for a sacred text, read with philosophical clarity and honesty, joins us to them, we may reasonably express puzzlement with another paramount aspect of the Talmud's exegetical program.

The Talmud's sages, second, constantly cite verses of Scripture when reading statements of the Mishnah. These they read in their own way and framework. Let me spell this out. References to specific verses of Scripture are as uncommon in the Mishnah as they are routine in the Talmud. For the framers of the Talmud, certainty for the Mishnah's rules depended upon adducing scriptural prooftexts. The entire system – the laws, courts, power of lawyer philosophers themselves – thus is seen to rest upon the written revelation of God to Moses at Sinai, that alone. What this means for the sages' view of the Mishnah is that the details of the document depended for validity upon details contained within Mosaic revelation, in the Written Torah. While, as we saw, some traditions, deemed entirely valid, were attributed to scribes of olden times, these enjoyed a quite separate, and explicitly subordinated, status from the statements of the Written Torah.

The Mishnah to begin with was treated only as a collection of rules, each to be faithfully read by itself as a detail. That is why scriptural prooftexts were cited to support one rule after another, without any large-scale thesis about the status of the document containing those discrete rules. Just as the sages of the Talmud read the Mishnah bit by bit, so they adduced evidence from Scripture for its rules, bit by bit. There could then have been no consideration whatsoever of the proposition that the Mishnah stood alongside of, and next to, the Written Torah, as the oral part of "the one whole Torah of Moses, our rabbi." If that version of the Torah myth found its way into the Yerushalmi at all, it played no considerable role in the approach of the Yerushalmi to the question of the authority and certainty of the principal document, the Mishnah itself. The Talmud's fragmented vision of the Mishnah accounts for the character of the Yerushalmi's approach, through passages of the Mishnah, to verses of Scripture.

Let us now proceed to review the types of ways in which the Talmud presents prooftexts for allegations of passages of the Mishnah, a sizable repertoire. We begin with the simplest example, an instance in which a passage of the Mishnah is cited, then linked directly to a verse of Scripture, deemed to constitute self-evident proof for what has been said. The Mishnah's rule is given in italics.

### Y. Abodah Zarah 4:4:

III.   A.   *[citing M. A.Z. 4:4:] An idol belonging to a gentile is prohibited forthwith,* in line with the following verse of Scripture: "You shall surely destroy [all places where the nations whom you shall dispossess served their gods]" (Deut. 12:2) – forthwith.

      B.   *And one belonging to an Israelite is prohibited only after it will have been worshipped,* in line with the following verse of Scripture: "Cursed be the man who makes a graven or molten image, an abomination to the Lord, a thing made by the hands of a craftsman, and set it up in secret" (Deut. 27:15) – when he will set it up.

C.   There are those who reverse the matter:

D.   An idol belonging to an Israelite is prohibited forthwith, as it is written, "Cursed be the man who makes a graven or molten image."

E.   And one belonging to a gentile is prohibited only after it will have been worshipped, as it is written, "You shall surely destroy all the places where the nations whom you shall dispossess served their gods."

F.   R. Isaac bar Nahman in the name of Samuel derived that same view [that an idol belonging to a gentile is prohibited only after it will have been worshipped] from the following: If one has inherited [the idol] when it [already] is deemed a god, "in fire will you burn it," and if not: "whom the nations whom you shall dispossess... their gods." ["You shall tear down their altars and dash in pieces their pillars and burn their Asherim with fire..."] (Deut. 12:2-3).

The instance shows the convention. A statement of the Mishnah is given, followed by a verse of Scripture regarded as proof of the antecedent conception. All we have are sentences from the one document, the Mishnah, juxtaposed to sentences from the other, the Scripture.

Along the lines of the foregoing, but somewhat more complex, is the case in which the language of the Mishnah rule is not cited verbatim, but the underlying proposition is stated, then provided with a prooftext. Here is one example of this phenomenon.

### Y. Baba Mesia 2:1:

A.   What lost items are [the finder's], and which ones is he liable to proclaim [in the lost-and-found]?

B.   These lost items are his [the finder's]:

C.   "[If] he found pieces of fruit scattered about, coins scattered about, small sheaves in the public domain, cakes of figs, baker's loaves, strings of fish, pieces of meat, wool-shearings [as they come] from the country [of origin], stalks of flax, or tongues of purple – lo, these are his," [the words of R. Meir].

I.   A.   [Since the operative criterion in M. B.M. 2:1 is that, with undistinguished items such as these, the owner takes for granted he will not recover them and so despairs of them, thus giving up his rights of ownership to them, we now ask:] Whence do we know from the Torah the law of the owner's despair [of recovering his property constitutes relinquishing rights of ownership and declaring the property to be ownerless, hence available to whoever finds it]?

B.   R. Yohanan in the name of R. Simeon b. Yehosedeq: "'And so you shall do with his ass; so you shall do with his garment; so you shall do with any lost thing of your brother's, which he loses and you find; you may not withhold your help' (Deut. 22:3) –

C.   "That which is [perceived as] lost by him and found by you, you are liable to proclaim [as having been found], and that which is not [perceived as] lost by him [because he has given up hope of recovering it anyhow] and found by you, you are not liable to proclaim.

D.   "This then excludes that for which the owner has despaired, which is lost to him and to any one."

What is striking in the preceding instance is the presence of a secondary layer of reasoning about the allegations of a verse of Scripture. The process of reasoning then derives from the verse a principle not made explicit therein, and that principle turns out to be precisely what the Mishnah's rule maintains. Accordingly, the Mishnah's law is shown to be merely a reversal of the Scripture's, that is, the obverse side of the coin. Or the Scripture's rule is shown to deal only with the case pertinent to the Mishnah's law, rather than to what, on the surface, that biblical law seems to contain.

We proceed to an instance in which a disputed point of the Mishnah is linked to a dispute on the interpretation of the pertinent verses of Scripture. What is important now is that the dispute in the Mishnah is made to depend upon not principles of law, but readings of the same pertinent verses of Scripture. Once again the net effect is to turn the Mishnah into a set of generalizations of what already is explicit in Scripture, a kind of restating in other language of what is quite familiar – therefore well founded.

### Y. Makkot 2:2:

A.   [If] the iron flew from the heft and killed someone,
B.   Rabbi says, "He does not go into exile."
C.   And sages say, "He goes into exile."
D.   [If] it flew from the wood which is being split,
E.   Rabbi says, "He goes into exile."
F.   And sages say, "He does not go into exile."

I.   A.   What is the scriptural basis for the position of Rabbi [at M. 2:2D-E]?
     B.   Here it is stated, "...[and the head] slips [from the handle and strikes his neighbor so that he dies...]" (Deut. 19:5).
     C.   And later on, the same verb root is used: "[... for your olives] shall drop off..." (Deut. 28:40).
     D.   Just as the verb root used later means, "dropping off," so here it means, "dropping off."
     E.   What is the scriptural basis for the position of the rabbis [at M. 2:2F]?
     F.   Here the verb root "slipping" is used.
     G.   And later on elsewhere we have the following: "...and clears away many nations before you..." (Deut. 7:1).

H. Just as the verb root, "clearing away," refers to an [active] blow there, so here, too, it speaks of an [active] blow [by an object which strikes something, for example, the ax, not chips of wood].

We see that both parties to the Mishnah's dispute read the same verse. The difference then depends upon their prior disagreement about the meaning of the verse. The underlying supposition is that the Mishnah simply restates in general language the results of the exegesis of biblical law.

We consider, finally, an instance in which the discussion of the Talmud consists wholly in the analysis of the verses of Scripture deemed to prove the point of the Mishnah. The upshot is that we deal not with a mere formality but a protracted, sustained inquiry. That is to say, the discussion of the Talmud transcends the limits of the Mishnah and becomes a well-developed discourse upon not the Mishnah's rule but Scripture's sense. What is important in the next item is that the search for prooftexts in Scripture sustains not only propositions of the Mishnah, but also those of the Tosefta as well as those of the Talmud's own sages. This is a stunning fact. It indicates that the search of Scriptures is primary, the source of propositions or texts to be supported by those Scriptures, secondary. There is no limit, indeed, to the purposes for which scriptural texts will be found relevant.

### Y. Sanhedrin 10:4:

II. A. The party of Korach has no portion in the world to come and will not live in the world to come [M. San. 10:4].

B. What is the Scriptural basis for this view?

C. "[So they and all that belonged to them went down alive into Sheol;] and the earth closed over them, and they perished from the midst of the assembly" (Num. 16:33).

D. "The earth closed over them" – in this world.

E. "And they perished from the midst of the assembly" – in the world to come [M. San. 10:4D-F].

F. It was taught: R. Judah b. Batera says, "[The contrary view] is to be derived from the implication of the following verse:

G. "'I have gone astray like a lost sheep: seek thy servant [and do not forget thy commandments]' (Ps. 119:176).

H. "Just as the lost object which is mentioned later on in the end is going to be searched for, so the lost object which is stated herein is destined to be searched for" [T. San. 13:9].

I. Who will pray for them?

J. R. Samuel bar Nahman said, "Moses will pray for them:

K. "'Let Reuben live, and not die, [nor let his men be few]' (Deut. 33:6)."

L. R. Joshua b. Levi said, "Hannah will pray for them."

M. This is the view of R. Joshua b. Levi, for R. Joshua b. Levi said, "Thus did the party of Korach sink ever downward, until Hannah went and prayed for them and said, 'The Lord kills and brings to life; he brings down to Sheol and raises up' (1 Sam. 2:6)."

We have a striking sequence of prooftexts, serving, one by one, the cited statement of the Mishnah, A-C, then an opinion of a rabbi in the Tosefta, F-H, then the position of a Talmudic rabbi, J-K, L-M. The process of providing the prooftexts therefore is central, the differentiation among the passages requiring the prooftexts, a matter of indifference.

## IV. Conclusion

We began with the interest in showing how the Scripture is made to supply prooftexts for propositions of the Mishnah, with consequences for the Talmud's theory of the Mishnah requiring no repetition. But we see at the end that the search for appropriate verses of Scripture vastly transcended the purpose of study of the Mishnah, exegesis of its rules, and provision of adequate authority for the document and its laws. In fact, any proposition to be taken seriously will elicit interest in scriptural support, whether one in the Mishnah, in the Tosefta, or in the mouth of a Talmudic sage himself. So the main thing is that the Scripture is at the center and focus. A verse of Scripture settles all pertinent questions, wherever they are located, whatever their source. That is the Talmud's position. We know full well that it is not the Mishnah's position.

If the sages of the second century, who made the Mishnah as we know it, spoke in their own name and in the name of the logic of their own minds, those who followed, certainly the ones who flourished in the later fourth century, took a quite different view. Reverting to ancient authority like others of the age, they turned back to Scripture, deeming it the source of certainty about truth. Unlike their masters in the Mishnah, theirs was a quest for a higher authority than the logic of their own minds. The shift from age to age then is clear. The second-century masters took commonplaces of Scripture, well-known facts, and stated them wholly in their own language and context. Fourth-century masters phrased commonplaces of the Mishnah or banalities of worldly wisdom, so far as they could, in the language of Scripture and its context.

But, as we saw at the end, this quest in Scripture for certainty far transcended the interest in supplying the Mishnah's rules with ample prooftexts. On the contrary, the real issue turns out to have been not the Mishnah at all, not even its diverse sayings vindicated one by one. Once what a sage says, not merely a rule for the Mishnah, is made to refer to Scripture for proof, it must follow that, in the natural course of things, a rule of the Mishnah and of the Tosefta will likewise be asked to refer also to Scripture.

In other words, in phrasing matters as I have, I have turned matters on their head. The fact that the living sage validates what he says through Scripture explains why the sage also validates through verses of Scripture what the ancient sages of the Mishnah and Tosefta say. It is one, undivided phenomenon. The reception of the Mishnah constitutes merely one, though massive, testimony to a prevalent attitude of mind, important for the age of the Talmud, the third and fourth centuries, not solely for the Mishnah. The stated issue was the standing of the Mishnah. But the heart of the matter turns out to have been the authority of the sage himself, who identified with the authors of the Mishnah and claimed authoritatively to interpret the Mishnah and much else, specifically including Scripture. So the appeal to Scripture in behalf of the Mishnah represents simply one more expression of what proved critical in the formative age of Judaism: the person of the holy man himself, this new man, this incarnate Torah. When revelation – Torah – became flesh, Judaism was born.

Part Two

"DEFENDING" JUDAISM?

FOUR DEBATES WITH E.P. SANDERS

# 7

## Sanders's Misunderstanding of Purity: Uncleanness as an Ontological, Not a Moral-Eschatological Category (as He Imagines)

### Written with Bruce D. Chilton

### Systemic Analysis and Category Formation

Diverse Judaic systems, or Judaisms, interpret each in its own way the received categories of ancient Israelite religion as portrayed in the Old Testament.[1] Consequently, interpreting a given system's documentary representation of a category established in the Israelite writings of the sixth and fifth centuries B.C. requires considerable reflection. Opening the Old Testament and out of its resources declaring the meaning of an Old Testament category for a Judaism represented in much later writings is not merely anachronistic. It also distorts the later writers' systemic reading and adaptation of the received category.

For what a systemic construction makes of that category – not only the selection and definition, but the very classification and the importance accorded to one Old Testament category and not to another – all this finds realization in the systemic construction of all other categories, that is, in the composition, shape, and structure of the system itself. These simple and easily demonstrable principles of analysis that have emerged in the history of ideas, including theological ideas, over the past century or so do not always exercise the influence that they

---

[1]The first five parts of this article were written by Jacob Neusner and revised by Bruce D. Chilton. The sixth part was written by Bruce D. Chilton and revised by Jacob Neusner.

should. Consequently, even today we find harmonization where there should be differentiation, mere paraphrase where analysis ought to take place. Opening the Hebrew Scriptures as an encyclopaedia for first-century Judaism, people misinterpret the complexity of the Judaisms of that time by portraying as a single, unitary, harmonious, and linear development the chaos of Judaic systemic formation, reconstitution, and, even, dissolution.

These general remarks on the importance of differentiation and analysis, the centrality of context and nuance, will not elicit surprise and ought to be received as truisms. For who, in this day and age, imagines a single, unitary "Judaism," emerging in a linear unfolding straight out of the Old Testament, any more than a single, unitary "Christianity" is portrayed, as of its point of origin, by the New Testament? These conceptions, legitimate theological necessities, everyone understands, impede the description, analysis, and interpretation of the diverse Judaic, and Christian, systems that, leaving their detritus of holy books, holy doctrines, and holy rites, define the tasks of theology. A half-century or more of learning separates us from the age in which anyone fabricated a single "orthodox" Judaism, and we have gone beyond the, then fruitful, debates of Walter Bauer and H.E.W. Turner on the pattern of Christian truth.

Yet we still have accounts of the single, unitary, and internally harmonious "Judaism," described out of all sources deemed "normative," without regard to time and place of composition or auspices and circumstances of promulgation, that formed the background and setting for "Christianity." Sanders has given us the most current, as we shall see in Chapter Nine, below. So the pretense of one Judaism and one Christianity is maintained, as though that single, unitary, harmonious Judaism, spun in a linear path out of the Old Testament, were any longer accessible of description. And, more to the point, people still open the Old Testament as the handbook for that "Judaism" that "Christianity," even in the person of Jesus himself, addressed.

A single author, and a single point in question, will show the intellectual tasks that have yet to be accomplished, those of learning how to reframe our questions in light of our own knowledge of diversity and complexity. If we concede that there was a diversity of Judaic, and also Christian, systems, and that that diversity characterized not only (for Christianity) the second and third centuries but (even) the first, and even *ab origine*,[2] then we can no longer address matters under the title "Jesus and Judaism." The Gospels research of our day surely encourages us to speak, rather, of "Jesuses," as much as, virtually all scholarship knows, we describe "Judaisms." Then, of course, which Jesus and which Judaism become the centerpiece of inquiry, and category formation begins at what, at present, we perceive to be the very commencement of thought.

By way of illustrating the outcome of recognizing the diversity of Judaisms, inclusive of the Judaisms presented to us by the Old Testament, we turn to a simple problem of category formation. It concerns the classification or categorization of uncleanness, an important consideration in the Gospels' accounts of Jesus' relationship with persons and institutions in his time, and, also, a central category in Judaisms from the formation of the Old Testament Pentateuch in ca. 450 B.C. through the framing of the Mishnah in ca. A.D. 200. Specifically, uncleanness, here important, there not interesting at all, serves diverse systems in diverse ways, and any conception that there was a single reading of the matter is untenable. Not only so, but in one Judaism, the Essene Judaism of Qumran, uncleanness served as a metaphor for sin, while in another Judaism, the Judaic system first set forth in the Mishnah, ca. A.D. 200, on the foundations of materials originating over the prior two hundred years, some of them from Pharisees,[3] the conception of uncleanness functioned in an entirely different framework, so that associating uncleanness with sin bore no meaning and made no sense at all. Uncleanness addressed an issue quite distinct from a moral one, which can be proven very simply. To identify the category of a conception, address to an authorship the challenge: state the opposite. The antonym tells us the category that guides thought. In the Essene Judaism of Qumran, uncleanness served as a metaphor of evil, and the opposite of unclean was virtuous, for example, one who disobeyed the rule was punished by being declared unclean for a given spell. In the Judaic system of the Mishnah, by contrast, the antonym of uncleanness is holiness (just as in the case, in general, in the book of Leviticus, as we shall see presently). And virtue and holiness constitute distinct classifications, the one having to do with morality, the other with ontology. Indeed, as we shall now try to show, phenomenologically and also historically, in one important Judaism, with roots in the first century,

---

[2]Indeed, the theory of a single, unitary beginning itself contitutes a powerful polemic and apologetic, as Burton Mack demonstrates in his forthcoming book on Mark's Gospel.

[3]See Jacob Neusner, *Judaism: The Evidence of the Mishnah. Second printing, augmented* (Atlanta, 1988: Scholars Press for Brown Judaic Studies).

uncleanness formed an ontological category, not a moral one at all. To explain how uncleanness is an ontological, not a moral-eschatological, category, is very simple and may be presented with heavy emphasis: *To be able to become unclean formed a measure of the capacity to become holy, so that, the more susceptible to uncleanness, and the more differentiated the uncleanness to which susceptibility pertained, the more capable of becoming holy, and the more differentiated the layers and levels of holiness that entered consideration.*

That statement clearly bears no implications whatever for whether or not an unclean person was a sinner, or a clean person not a sinner. For in the classification of uncleanness at hand, the opposite of unclean is holy, precisely as, throughout the priestly code, for example, the book of Leviticus, the antonym of unclean is holy, far more than it is merely clean (*tamé/qaddosh* appears far more regularly than *tamé/tahor*). As we shall presently see, in the Mishnah, the more susceptible to uncleanness a person or an object (for example, food) is, the more layers or levels of sanctification that person or edible may attain. We think that to be "holier than thou" means to be more virtuous than the other. But in the context of the Mishnah's laws, we shall demonstrate at some length, to be "holier than thou," one has also to be more capable of becoming more unclean than thou, for example, to be more susceptible to uncleanness in more ways or at greater degrees of sensitivity to uncleanness, than whatever "thou" is at hand.

Throughout the Mishnah and much of its successor literature, "Israel," that is, the social entity of a Judaic system, is consistently represented as more susceptible to varieties and differentiated types of uncleanness than gentiles, and that forms, in a systemic context, an ontological judgment as to the ultimate being of that "Israel," and not a moral judgment as to the conduct and ethical character of Israelites or of "Israel," in general. That is why, as we shall see, representing uncleanness as sin and a sign of wickedness represents a systemic reading of uncleanness, not a broadly held conception generated by "the Old Testament," and, it must follow, representing uncleanness as part of a hierarchical classification of social entities likewise constitutes a systemic reading of the matter. In both cases we deal with how systems form their categories, and the way they do so is by making a systemic statement upon, and through discourse concerning, each of the systemic categories. What a system says anywhere, it says everywhere.

In the case at hand, whether or not uncleanness formed a moral or an ontological category or classification, it must follow, the representation of uncleanness as a mark of sin or wickedness which requires eschatological purification through baptism constitutes a Christianity's reading of uncleanness, not a generally accepted datum upon which Jesus in particular laid down a judgment or to which he responded. The Christianity that deemed eschatological immersion for sin to relate to the category, uncleanness, made its statement of an eschatological system through that detail, as through other details, and the representation of uncleanness as a matter of sin formed a systemic statement of that Christianity, not a response to or a use of a fact of "Judaism." There were no facts, there was no Judaism, so far as our sources tell us, for their accounts portray their respective systems. Any other reading of matters, in particular, the one that sees a unitary Judaism emerging in a linear and single development from the Old Testament, itself an essentially cogent and harmonious statement, yields only confusion. Evidence of that fact derives from the rather odd and contradictory representation of uncleanness in a recent work, as not a matter of morality on one page, then as a matter of sin and hence wickedness on the next page. Analysis will show what happens when a single Judaism, against which a single Christianity, in the person of its founder, Jesus, is to be represented, forms the generative analogy and the formative metaphor in the mind of scholarship.

The case at hand derives from E.P. Sanders, *Jesus and Judaism.* His confusion of categories yields a manifest contradiction in his account of uncleanness as at once merely functional to entry into the Temple (a trivialization that vastly understates matters) but also a symbolism of evil (a correct reading in one context but not in another context). So Sanders provides our occasion for the demonstration of the conceptual urgency, for purposes of clear thought, of the simple propositions with which we commenced.

## II. Uncleanness as a Moral Category in Current New Testament Theology

In portraying the laws of uncleanness, E.P. Sanders stresses that uncleanness in some instances in and of itself is a sin. Accordingly, he reads uncleanness as a moral category. Quite correctly, in describing the Old Testament account of uncleanness Sanders carefully stresses that "most impurities do not result from the transgression of a prohibition, although a few do."[4] He accurately emphasizes that an impure person is not a sinner; contact between an impure and a pure person is not ordinarily considered a sin. Once he has so represented biblical law, however, Sanders proceeds to allege the following:

> One should ask what was the situation of a person who disregarded the purity laws and did not use the immersion pool, but remained

---

[4]E.P. Sanders, *Jesus and Judaism* (Philadelphia, 1985: Fortress), p. 183.

perpetually impure. Here it would be reasonable to equate being impure with being a 'sinner' in the sense of 'wicked,' for such a person would have taken the position that the biblical laws need not be observed.[5]

That statement contradicts the judgments Sanders makes in his précis of the biblical representation of uncleanness, except for a single matter, which is sexual relations between husband and wife when the wife is menstruating. That is penalized by extirpation (Lev. 20:18), as Sanders says, and represents an exception, again explicitly specified by Sanders:

> But as a general rule, those who became impure...did not, as long as they lived their ordinary lives, sin. Normal human relations were not substantially affected.[6]

Now in order to harmonize the judgment made here with the position taken immediately following, Sanders gives an example, but, as we shall see, the example exemplifies only its own case:

> All the laws of purity and impurity are to be voluntarily observed. If, for example, a husband and wife agreed not to observe the prohibition of intercourse during menstruation, no one would ever know unless they announced the fact. If the woman never used the immersion pool, however, her neighbors would note that she was not observant....Not intending to be observant is precisely what makes one 'wicked', but the wickedness comes not from impurity as such, but from the attitude that the commandments of the Bible need not be heeded.
>
> Thus these biblical purity laws, which most people seem to have observed, did not lead to a fixed view that the common people were sinners.[7]

In fact, the case exhausts the category; the only Old Testament purity law that affects conduct outside of the cult is the one that serves Sanders's claim that being impure may be equated with being a sinner in the sense of wicked.

Sanders's categorization of impurity as (sometimes) an issue of morality leaves open the question of how (at other times) we should classify the matter. The answer to that question will prove diverse, as we move from one Judaism to another. No one need doubt, for example, that Sanders's reading of uncleanness as sin will have found, in the Essene Judaism of Qumran, a broader scope than merely menstrual uncleanness, and eschatological immersion from sin, so prominent a motif in the description of John the Baptist, assuredly conforms to Sanders's view. But were we to interrogate the Judaism represented, as

---

[5]Sanders, p. 184.

[6]Sanders, p. 183.

[7]Sanders, p. 184-85. Fathers According to Rabbi Nathan Chapter Two contains an explicit statement in accord with Sanders's example here, drawn from the privacy of marital relations.

to its initial statement, by the Mishnah, we should come up with a quite different view of matters.

## III. Uncleanness and the Ontology of the "Israel" of the Judaism of the Dual Torah

Let us start from the negative, which may be stated simply and categorically. *Not a single line in the entire Mishnah treats cultic uncleanness as in and of itself a representation of sin.* An unclean person is not a sinner, therefore not, in Sanders's language, wicked. An unclean person cannot do things that a clean person can do. We find at Mishnah-tractate Sotah 9:15 the following:

> Heedfulness leads to physical cleanliness, cleanliness to levitical purity, purity to separateness, separateness to holiness, holiness to humility, humility to the shunning of sin, shunning of sin to saintliness, saintliness to the Holy Spirit, the Holy Spirit to the resurrection of the dead.

Clearly, the unclean person is not on that account wicked, and a polythetical taxonomic scheme does not permit the contrast only of uncleanness with morality.

How, then, does the Mishnah's treatment of uncleanness identify the correct classification or categorization of the matter? The answer is that, for the authorship of the Mishnah, uncleanness and cleanness form ontological, rather than moral categories. The capacity to become clean, a stage on the route to holiness as we saw, finds a counterpart in the capacity to become unclean; the more "holy" something may become, the more susceptible it is to uncleanness. Then to be susceptible to varieties and differentiated forms of uncleanness is a mark of, not sinfulness but, holiness. That conception finds no place in Sanders's representation of matters. And yet, as we shall now show in a very specific case, it is fundamental to the concrete legislation of the Mishnah's authorship, a position so profound in its implications as to mark as simply beside the point the allegation that an unclean person was, or could be construed as, a sinner or wicked.

Let us consider two concrete cases that demonstrate the deep layers of thought on the hierarchization of uncleanness and holiness in the Mishnah's system. Both of these statements will show us two facts. First, that the opposite, for the authorship of the Mishnah, of unclean was not clean but holy. Second, that the synonym for unclean was not sinful or wicked but something of an ontological, that is, in context, hierarchical, ordering of matters. That forms the key to the identification as ontological of the matter at hand, the conception that through capacity to become unclean, on the down side, and holy, on the up side, we hierarchize the entities before us, for example, gentiles and "Israel," or common food and food that has been designated as tithe, priestly rations ("heave-offering") and even Most Holy Things of the Temple altar itself. The first case derives from the very matter in which we shall presently, in later writings of the same system, find a moral dimension, namely, "leprosy." What we find here is a simple statement that the more susceptible a person to uncleanness, the more capable that person is of warding off the effects of uncleanness. The second case, offered in the next section, then will give us a richer perception of what is at stake in the simple assertion of correspondences with which we now deal. The reader will want to see the entire matter as it is set forth in the Mishnah and successor writings, even though the operative language is presented only in italics at the end. The version of the matter at Mishnah-tractate Negaim 13:10 is as follows:

13:10  F.     If he [the leper] was standing inside and put his hand outside with his rings on this fingers, if he remained there a sufficient interval to eat a piece of bread, he is unclean.

G.     [If] he was standing outside and put his hand inside with his rings on his fingers –

H.     R. Judah declares [the ring] unclean forthwith.

I.     And sages say, "Until he will remain long enough to eat a piece of bread."

J.     They said to R. Judah, "Now if when his entire body is unclean, he has not made what is on him unclean until he remains a sufficient time to eat a piece of bread, when his entire body is not unclean, should he not render unclean that which is on him only after he remains a sufficient time to eat a piece of bread?" [M. Neg. 13:10].

To this point we have no account of Judah's thinking and therefore no reason to see the pertinence of the case to the principle we claim to locate here. To see what is at stake, we turn forthwith to the Tosefta's amplification of the matter. We present the operative language in italics:

K.     *Said to them R. Judah, "We find that the power of him who is unclean is stronger in affording protection than the power of him who is insusceptible to uncleanness.*

L.     *"Israelites receive uncleanness and afford protection for clothing in the diseased house. The gentile and the beast, who do not receive uncleanness, also do not afford protection in the diseased house" [T. Negaim 7:9].*

The Tosefta's authorship's amplification on Judah's reasoning provides the statement of correspondence and contrast, that is, of what is at stake, that we require. The reader will rightly ask why we maintain that the Tosefta's reading of the Mishnah's representation of Judah's view may be imputed to the Mishnah's authorship's conception, and the answer is, we can show that elsewhere, the Mishnah's authorship on its own presents precisely that view, only in a much more subtle and complex statement. So we beg the reader's indulgence.

To this point, we have offered only a statement of the single proposition that the opposite of unclean is holy, and the synonym of unclean is not sinful but outsider or gentile. The entire composition as it is represented by the authorship of Sifra, which cites the Mishnah and the Tosefta verbatim and then joins the whole to an exegetical framework, makes that point explicit, since it introduces the beast and the gentile as operative categories, and neither the beast nor (by systemic analogy) the gentile forms a moral category, but only an ontological one. We give the Mishnah in boldface type and the Tosefta in italicized boldface type, to make clear the sequence of unfolding and underline still-later work of the authorship of Sifra:[8]

7.   A.   Might one think that the beast and the gentile afford protection to garments in the diseased house?

     B.   Scripture says, "He will launder the garments" (Lev. 14:47) – as an inclusionary clause.

     C.   He whose clothing can be rendered unclean affords protection to clothing in the diseased house.

     D.   The beast and the gentile are excluded from the rule, for their clothing is not made unclean, and they do not afford protection for clothing in the diseased house.

     E.   In this connection sages have said:

     F.   **If he was standing inside and put his hand outside with his rings on this fingers, if he remained there a sufficient interval to eat a piece of bread, he is unclean.**

     G.   **[If] he was standing outside and put his hand inside with his rings on his fingers –**

     H.   **R. Judah declares [the ring] unclean forthwith.**

     I.   **And sages say, "Until he will remain long enough to eat a piece of bread."**

     J.   **They said to R. Judah, "Now if when his entire body is unclean, he has not made what is on him unclean until he remains a sufficient time to eat a piece of bread, when his entire body is not unclean, should he not render unclean that which is on him only after he remains a sufficient time to eat a piece of bread?" [M. Neg. 13:10].**

     K.   *Said to them R. Judah, "We find that the power of him who is unclean is stronger in affording protection than the power of him who is insusceptible to uncleanness.*

     L.   *"Israelites receive uncleanness and afford protection for clothing in the diseased house. The gentile and the beast, who do not receive*

---

[8]This sequence, Mishnah, which begat the Tosefta, which begat the Sifra and Sifrés, of course does not work everywhere in the later writings. But it does work here.

*uncleanness, also do not afford protection in the diseased house"*
*[T. 7.9].*

Now to review the main point: The most important language is Judah's assertion that a person who is more susceptible to uncleanness also affords greater protection from uncleanness than a person who is not. If Israelites are susceptible to uncleanness, they also can afford protection for clothing. Gentiles or beasts, insusceptible to the uncleanness of "leprosy," entering the afflicted house will forthwith produce contamination for garments or sandals which they may be wearing, even though they themselves are not susceptible to this form of uncleanness at all. What has all this to do with morality? Nothing whatsoever. The focus, the issue, these concern one's state or condition in an utterly abstract world of relationships that are intangible and unseen, yet, withal, critical. When Sanders correctly says that uncleanness has nothing to do with morality, he may point to a passage such as this one. Let us turn to what is at stake in what is clearly a set of ontological distinctions and points of differentiation.

### IV. Uncleanness and Holiness in the Mishnaic Stratum of the Judaism of the Dual Torah

Judah's position is personal, hence not normative. But the principle that he expressed in finding a hierarchical relationship between the capacity to receive uncleanness and the capacity to afford protection presents a very important and explicit statement of the matter at hand. In what follows we shall find a clear hierarchization of sanctification in terms of capacity to receive uncleanness, and the hierarchization is the premise of discourse, not the private opinion of one party, hence built into the normative structure of the legal theological system of the Mishnah. What we shall now see in a still less accessible case is that the greater one's susceptibility to uncleanness, the more exalted one's capacity for sanctification. To state the proposition in more abstract language, such as ontology demands: the greater the capacity for differentiation, the higher the potential of consecration. This fundamentally ontological principle of hierarchization is expressed in the detail of a legal case, and we shall have to work our way through the details of the case to see how profoundly imbedded in the law is the conception of a hierarchical, or rather, hierarchizing, ontology that is fundamental to the system at hand. This case then will leave no doubt whatsoever that uncleanness for the system at hand, that is, the systemic statement of the Mishnah in particular, forms in no way a moral, but only an ontological category. The system as a whole, which proposes a hierarchizing ontology expressed through sanctification, then makes its statement here, as it will, uniformly, at all other relevant points. And to that system, the conception of uncleanness as a metaphor for evil, is simply beside the point, monumentally irrelevant.

We see this in a discussion of the several removes from a source of uncleanness and how they affect food in several degrees of consecration or sanctification. Once more we turn first to the text, then to the exposition, of Mishnah-tractate Tohorot 2:2-7.

### Mishnah-Tractate Tohorot 2:2:

A.    R. Eliezer says, "(1) He who eats food unclean in the first remove is unclean in the second remove; (2) [he who eats] food unclean in the second remove is unclean in the second remove; (3) [he who eats] food unclean in the third remove is unclean in the third remove."

B.    R. Joshua says, "(1) He who eats food unclean in the first remove and food unclean in the second remove is unclean in the second remove. (2) [He who eats food] unclean in the third remove is unclean in the second remove so far as Holy Things are concerned, (3) and is not unclean in the second remove so far as heave-offering is concerned.

C.    "[We speak of] the case of unconsecrated food

D.    "which is prepared in conditions appropriate to heave-offering."

### Mishnah-Tractate Tohorot 2:3:

A.    *Unconsecrated food:* in the first remove is unclean and renders unclean;

B.    in the second remove is unfit, but does not convey uncleanness;

C.    and in the third remove is eaten in the pottage of heave-offering.

### Mishnah-Tractate Tohorot 2:4:

A.    *Heave-offering:* in the first and in the second remove is unclean and renders unclean;

B.    in the third remove is unfit and does not convey uncleanness;

C.    and in the fourth remove is eaten in a pottage of Holy Things.

### Mishnah-Tractate Tohorot 2:5:

A.    *Holy Things:* in the first and the second and the third removes are susceptible to uncleanness and render unclean;

B.    and in the fourth remove are unfit and do not convey uncleanness;

C.    and in the fifth remove are eaten in a pottage of Holy Things.

### Mishnah-Tractate Tohorot 2:6:

A.    *Unconsecrated food:* in the second remove renders unconsecrated liquid unclean and renders food of heave-offering unfit.

B.    *Heave-offering:* in the third remove renders unclean [the] liquid of Holy Things, and renders foods of Holy Things unfit,

C.    if it [the heave-offering] was prepared in the condition of cleanness pertaining to Holy Things.

D.     But if it was prepared in conditions pertaining to heave-offering, it
       renders unclean at two removes and renders unfit at one remove in
       reference to Holy Things.

### Mishnah-Tractate Tohorot 2:7:

A.     R. Eleazar says, "The three of them are equal:
B.     *"Holy Things and heave-offering, and unconsecrated food:* which are at
       the first remove of uncleanness render unclean at two removes and
       unfit at one [further] remove in respect to Holy Things; render
       unclean at one remove and spoil at one [further] remove in respect
       to heave-offering; and spoil unconsecrated food.
C.     "That which is unclean in the second remove in all of them renders
       unclean at one remove and unfit at one [further] remove in respect
       to Holy Things; and renders liquid of unconsecrated food unclean;
       and spoils foods of heave-offering.
D.     "The third remove of uncleanness in all of them renders liquids of
       Holy Things unclean, and spoils food of Holy Things."

Mishnah-Tractate Tohorot 2:2-7 presuppose knowledge of the Mishnaic
system of ritual purity. A review of some of its essential elements is
necessary for an understanding of the arguments and analyses that
follow. In the system, ritual impurity is acquired by contact with either a
primary or a secondary source of uncleanness, called a "father" or a
"child" (or "offspring") of uncleanness, respectively. In the first category
are contact with a corpse, a person suffering a flux, a leper, and the like.
Objects made of metal, wood, leather, bone, cloth, or sacking become
fathers of uncleanness if they touch a corpse. Foodstuffs and liquids are
susceptible to uncleanness, but will not render other foodstuffs unclean
in the same degree or remove of uncleanness that they themselves suffer.
Foodstuffs furthermore will not make vessels or utensils unclean. But
liquids made unclean by a Father of uncleanness will do so if they touch
the inner side of the vessel. That is, if they fall into the contained space of
an earthenware vessel, they make the whole vessel unclean.

Food or liquid that touches a father of uncleanness becomes unclean
in the *first* remove. If food touches a person or vessel made unclean by a
primary cause of uncleanness, it is unclean in the *second* remove. Food
that touches *second–remove* uncleanness incurs *third-remove* uncleanness,
and food that touches *third-remove* uncleanness incurs *fourth-remove*
uncleanness, and so on. But liquids touching either a primary source of
uncleanness (father) or something unclean in the first or second remove
(offspring) are regarded as unclean in the first remove. They are able to
make something else unclean. If, for example, the other side of a vessel is
made unclean by a liquid – thus unclean in the second remove – and
another liquid touches the outer side, the other liquid incurs not second-,
but first-degree uncleanness.

Heave-offering (food raised up for priestly use only) unclean in the third remove of uncleanness, and Holy Things (that is, things belonging to the cult) unclean in the fourth remove, do not make other things, whether liquids or foods, unclean. The difference among removes of uncleanness is important. First-degree uncleanness in common food will convey uncleanness. But, although food unclean in the second remove will be unacceptable, it will not convey uncleanness, that is, third-degree uncleanness. But it will render heave-offering *unfit*. Further considerations apply to heave-offering and Holy Things. Heave-offering can be made unfit and unclean by a first, and unfit by a second, degree of uncleanness. If it touches something unclean in the third remove, it is made unfit, but itself will not impart fourth-degree uncleanness. A Holy Thing that suffers uncleanness in the first, second, or third remove is unclean and conveys uncleanness. If it is unclean in the fourth remove, it is invalid for the cult but does not convey uncleanness. It is much more susceptible than are noncultic things. Thus, common food that suffers second-degree uncleanness will render heave-offering invalid. We already know that it makes liquid unclean in the first remove. Likewise, heave-offering unclean in the third remove will make Holy Things invalid and put them into a fourth remove of uncleanness. With these data firmly in hand, let us turn to a general discussion of M. Mishnah-tractate Tohorot 2:2-7.

Mishnah-tractate Tohorot 2:2 introduces the removes of uncleanness. Our interest is in the contaminating effect, upon a person, of eating unclean food. Does the food make the person unclean in the same remove of uncleanness as is borne by the food itself? Thus if one eats food unclean in the first remove, is he unclean in that same remove? This is the view of Eliezer. Joshua says he is unclean in the second remove. The dispute, Mishnah-tractate Tohorot 2:2A-B, at Mishnah-tractate Tohorot 2:2C-D is significantly glossed. The further consideration is introduced as to the sort of food under discussion. Joshua is made to say that there is a difference between the contaminating effects upon the one who eats heave-offering, on the one side, and unconsecrated food prepared in conditions of heave-offering, on the other. This matter, the status of unconsecrated food prepared as if it were heave-offering, or as if it were Holy Things, and heave-offering prepared as if it were Holy Things, forms a substratum of our chapter, added to several primary items and complicating the exegesis. Tosefta-tractate Tohorot 2:1 confirms, however, that primary to the dispute between Eliezer and Joshua is simply the matter of the effects of food unclean in the first remove upon the person who eats such food. The gloss, Mishnah-tractate Tohorot 2:2C-D, forms a redactional thematic link between Joshua's opinion and the large construction of Mishnah-tractate Tohorot 2:3-7.

Mishnah-tractate Tohorot 2:3-5, expanded and glossed by Mishnah-tractate Tohorot 2:6, follow a single and rather tight form. The sequence differentiates unconsecrated food, heave-offering, and Holy Things each at the several removes from the original source of uncleanness.

Eleazar, Mishnah-tractate Tohorot 2:7, insists that, at a given remove, all three are subject to the *same* rule. The contrary view, Mishnah-tractate Tohorot 2:3-6, is that unconsecrated food in the first remove makes heave-offering unclean and at the second remove spoils heave-offering; it does not enter a third remove and therefore has no effect upon Holy Things. Heave-offering at the first two removes may produce contaminating effects, and at the third remove spoils Holy Things, but is of no effect at the fourth. Holy Things in the first three removes produce uncleanness, and at the fourth impart unfitness to other Holy Things. Mishnah-tractate Tohorot 2:6 then goes over the ground of unconsecrated food at the second remove, and heave-offering at the third. The explanation of Mishnah-tractate Tohorot 2:6C is various; the simplest view is that the clause glosses Mishnah-tractate Tohorot 2:6B by insisting that the heave-offering to which we refer is prepared as if it were Holy Things, on which account, at the third remove, it can spoil Holy Things. At Mishnah-tractate Tohorot 2:7 Eleazar restates matters, treating all three – Holy Things, heave-offering, and unconsecrated food – as equivalent to one another at the first, second, and third removes, with the necessary qualification for unconsecrated food that it is like the other, consecrated foods in producing effects at the second and even the third removes. Commentators read *Eliezer.* They set the pericope up against Joshua's view at Mishnah-tractate Tohorot 2:2, assigning to Joshua Mishnah-tractate Tohorot 2:3ff. as well. To state the upshot simply: *So far as Eleazar is concerned, what is important is not the source of contamination – the unclean foods – but that which is contaminated, the unconsecrated food, heave-offering, and Holy Things.*

He could not state matters more clearly than he does when he says that the three of them are exactly equivalent. And they are, because the differentiations will emerge in the food affected, or contaminated, by the three. So at the root of the dispute is whether we gauge the contamination in accord with the source – unconsecrated food, or unconsecrated food prepared as if it were heave-offering, and so on – or whether the criterion is the food which is contaminated. Mishnah-tractate Tohorot 2:3-5 are all wrong, Eleazar states explicitly at Mishnah-tractate Tohorot 2:7A, because they differentiate among uncleanness imparted by unclean unconsecrated food, unclean heave-offering, and unclean Holy Things, and do not differentiate among the three sorts of food *to which* contamination is imparted. It is surely a logical position, for the three sorts of food do exhibit differentiated capacities to receive uncleanness; one sort *is* more contaminable than another.

And so, too, is the contrary view logical: *what is more sensitive to uncleanness also will have a greater capacity to impart uncleanness.* The subtle debate before us clearly is unknown to Eliezer and Joshua at Mishnah-tractate Tohorot 2:2. To them the operative categories are something unclean in first, second, or third *removes*, without distinction as to the relative sensitivities of the several types of food which may be unclean. The unfolding of the issue may be set forth very briefly by way of conclusion: the sequence thus begins with Eliezer and Joshua, who ask about the contaminating power of that which is unclean in the first and second removes, without regard to whether it is unconsecrated food, heave-offering, or Holy things. To them, the distinction between the capacity to impart contamination, or to receive contamination, of the several sorts of food is unknown. Once, however, their question is raised – in such general terms – it will become natural to ask the next logical question, one which makes distinctions not only among the several removes of uncleanness, but also among the several sorts of food involved in the processes of contamination.

This protracted and somewhat arcane discussion, akin to a kind of physics in its abstraction, shows us with great power how uncleanness looks when it forms an ontological category within a hierarchizing system. Readers should not, however, imagine that the view of uncleanness as an ontological category exhausts matters within the unfolding of the Judaism of the Dual Torah. The Mishnah formed only the initial statement. Other, successor documents made their own statements, sometimes in addressing Scripture, the Written Torah, sometimes in dealing with the Mishnah, the Oral Torah. A full picture of matters therefore requires us to show how uncleanness looks when, in the system of Judaism at hand, it serves as a moral, not an ontological, classification.

### V. Uncleanness as a Moral (Not Eschatological) Category in Later Canonical Writings of the Judaism of the Dual Torah

Now that we have a clear picture of how uncleanness serves within the system of the Mishnah, namely, as an ontological category, an indicator of holiness, we turn to the disposition of that same category in later stages of the same Judaic system. For, as time rendered still more remote the reality of the cult and as the focus of thought within the unfolding system shifted to the governance, by sages, of that holy community that persisted beyond the end of the holy Temple, the ongoing system, as represented in successive writings, exhibited categorical reconstructions in diverse ways. And one of these ways, we think symptomatic of systemic changes in other categories also, represented uncleanness as not an ontological but a moral category.

The representation of levitical or cultic uncleanness as a matter of sin emerges, in the unfolding of the writings of the Judaism originally set forth in the Mishnah (a Judaism we call "the Judaism of the Dual Torah"), only in much later stages, in documents brought to closure long after the destruction of the Temple. Then uncleanness does serve as a metaphor for evil. A very rapid survey of the representations of uncleanness in successive documents, beyond the Mishnah, shows us that a contrast between uncleanness and morality was drawn by the authorship of the Tosefta, which condemned the view that "the uncleanness of the knife is more disturbing to Israel than the shedding of blood."[9]

Explicit statements that uncleanness forms an indicator of wickedness emerge in documents that first reached closure not before A.D. 300, and possibly considerably after that time. Here is an explicit statement:

> R. Yosé the Galilean[10] says, "Come and see how strong is the power
> of sin, for before they put forth their hands in transgression, there were

---

[9]Tosefta Kippurim 1:12.

[10]It should be clear that the temporal assignment of sayings rests solely on the time of closure of the documents that contain those sayings, not on the attributions, which cannot be shown to go back to the time and person to whom the sayings are assigned. Since the same saying can be given by diverse authorships and their documents to various authorities, and since no attribution can be shown to derive from first-hand evidence, e.g., a book written by a named authority and preserved by his disciples in a chain of transmission we can trace as we can, for example, books by Philo, Josephus, Paul, Irenaeus, Justin, and other first- and second- (and later) century figures, there is no alternative for critical scholarship. We therefore trace the canonical history of ideas, that is, the point, in the unfolding of the writings, at which a saying first occurs or an idea first makes its presence known. The sequence of writings, first this, then that, is beyond serious doubt, since writings posterior to the Mishnah, such as the Tosefta, Sifra, and the two Sifrés, cite the Mishnah verbatim entirely outside the structure of their own discourse and comment on Mishnah passages. The received conception of these writings as deriving from the first and second centuries, that is, the same time as the period of the formation of the Mishnah, and not from the third or fourth or still later times, rests upon the occurrence of the same names in both the Mishnah and the Tosefta or Sifra or the two Sifrés. That same theory assigns to the first or second centuries all sayings in the two Talmuds that appear bearing attributions of authorities who lived in those early times. But absent the demonstration that that was so, we can no more assume that if the Tosefta or the Talmud of the Land of Israel or the Talmud of Babylonia assigns a saying to Yosé the Galilean, he really made that saying, than we can

not found among [the Israelites] people unclean through having a discharge and lepers, but after they put forth their hands in transgression, there were among them people unclean through having a discharge and lepers...."[11]

True, no rabbi ever declared a sinner to be cultically unclean on that account, while in the Essene Judaism of Qumran, being impure is a sin, just as committing certain sins automatically imposed a period of uncleanness.[12] Still, we cannot doubt that, for the authorship that has included the saying attributed to Yosé, uncleanness marked a moral category.

A still more explicit statement of the same viewpoint, quite specific to a single, identified sin, maintains that the skin ailment described at Leviticus 13 (wrongly translated "leprosy") is caused by a specific sin, namely, gossip. This view appears in Tosefta Negaim 6:7, Sifré to Deuteronomy 175, and Sifra Mesora Parashah 5:9, and is as follows:

8. A. "Saying" (Lev. 14:35) –
   B. the priest will say to him words of reproach: "My son, plagues come only because of gossip [T. 6:7], as it is said, 'Take heed of the plague of leprosy to keep very much and to do, remember what the Lord God did to Miriam' (Deut. 24:8).
   C. "And what has one thing to do with the other?
   D. "But this teaches that she was punished only because of gossip.
   E. "And is it not an argument a fortiori?
   F. "If Miriam, who did not speak before Moses' presence, suffered so, one who speaks ill of his fellow in his very presence, how much the more so?"
   G. R. Simeon b. Eleazar says, "Also because of arrogance do plagues come, for so do we find concerning Uzziah,
   H. "as it is said, 'And he rebelled against the Lord his God and he came to the Temple of the Lord to offer on the altar incense and Azzariah the Priest came after him and with him priests of the Lord, eighty strong men, and they stood against Uzziah and said to him, It is not for you to do, Uzziah, to offer to the Lord, for only the priests the sons of Aaron who are sanctified do so. So forth from the sanctuary. And Uzziah was angry,' etc. (2 Chr. 26:16)" [T. Neg. 6:7H].

The same inquiry into the moral foundations of cultic uncleanness leads the authorship of Babylonian Talmud Niddah at 31b to attribute to Simeon b. Yohai the following explanation for the requirement that a woman after childbirth bring a sacrifice:

---

take for granted that Moses really said everything that the pentateuchal authorships say he said.
[11]Sifré to Numbers Naso 2.
[12]See Neusner, *Idea of Purity in Ancient Judaism* (Leiden, 1973: E.J. Brill), p. 81.

> When she kneels in bearing, she swears impetuously that she will
> have no intercourse with her husband. The Torah...ordained that she
> should bring a sacrifice.

But this does not encompass levitical uncleanness in particular. To
summarize: The view that impurity is a sign of sin does not occur in the
Mishnah. It does occur in the Tosefta in the specific allegation that
leprosy is a sign that a person is guilty of having gossiped or is a sign of
arrogance. Even in these passages, however, no concrete sanction or
penalty of a moral order is invoked, as an explicit violation of the law
would precipitate a concrete sanction. Sages do not leave a record of
having imposed a penalty of uncleanness upon a gossip.

## VI. Confusion in Category Formation:
### Uncleanness and Sanders's *Jesus and Judaism*

As the discussion above demonstrates, the antithesis of cleanness
and holiness is centrally important to that system of Judaism which
animates the Mishnah. Indeed, that antithesis is irreducible or systemic:
there is no future in attempting to decipher the two conditions, of being
clean and being holy, as metaphors of moral station or of accessibility to
redemption. The issue naturally emerges, however, whether that
Judaism evinced by Mishnah is the milieu in which the movement that
resulted in the New Testament unfolded. Methodological skepticism is
warranted, but an undifferentiated exclusion of the evidence of Mishnah
would be most unwise. Early, pre-Mishnaic Judaism is not substantially
recoverable from sectarian, Hellenistic, and apocalyptic writings alone.
They are no more "normative" than Rabbinica was once taken to be. The
rabbis and their predecessors contributed to the mix of early Judaism,
although their dominance brought about a distinctive phase, a Judaism
in which purity was a matter of fidelity to halakhah, as defined by the
Dual Torah, and no longer a matter of what actually could occur in
association with worship in the Temple. But the issue of purity is
inherent within the Gospels, that is to say, within that development of
Judaism shaped by Jesus and his followers – which produced the
Gospels.

If we may limit our attention, for the moment, to one thematic
example from the Synoptic Gospels, the matter of purifying leprosy
proves to be of systemic importance. Jesus cleanses a leper, and orders
him to see a priest and bring an offering (Matthew 8:1-4/Mark   1:40-
44/Luke 5:12-14). Sometimes by the presentation of comparable material
(cf. Matthew 11:5/Luke 7:22), sometimes by employing differing
rhetorical tactics and materials altogether (cf. Matthew 10:8; Luke 17:14-

19), Matthew and Luke contrive to present cleansing from leprosy as a characteristic and paradigmatic feature of Jesus' ministry.

When Sanders deals with the question of sayings of Jesus in which practices of purity are commended or condemned, he makes short shrift of them, as being inauthentic in their present form.[13] He is not loath, in principle, to dismiss entire pericopae, such as the story concerning what happened when Jesus' disciples plucked grain on the Sabbath, as "creation(s) of the church."[14] It is possible that the pericope of the cleansing of the leper might be dealt with in that way (although that has not been the trend in recent scholarship), but Sanders's index gives no trace of such a treatment. It is interesting, in this context, that the eight "almost indisputable facts" about Jesus, upon which Sanders sets out to base his work, contain no reference at all to any of Jesus' disputes concerning purity and holiness.[15]

His closest approach to that nexus of issues is in his discussion of Jesus' occupation of the Temple. In that discussion, however, Sanders consciously dispenses with an approach based upon a sensitivity to purity,[16] and instead argues that "Jesus' action is to be regarded as a symbolic demonstration,"[17] in respect of the destruction of the Temple. The idea is that Jesus predicted the end of the extant Temple, and the establishment of a new one, as a prophet of restoration, after the pattern of Essene and apocalyptic literature.[18] Instead of serving as a focus of sanctity, in Sanders's judgment the Temple is purely where Jesus chooses to engage in a symbolic act. The category of cleanness is simply left to one side.

There appear to be two reasons for which Sanders proceeds in the manner he does. First, he genuinely believes that matters of purity, in the Judaisms of the first century, were expendable. He conceives of the Pharisees, for example, as a party devoted to the oral law and its explication, rather than as a movement concerned systemically with issues of purity.[19] "Ritual" and "trivia" are to Sanders's mind a natural

---

[13]*Jesus and Judaism* (Philadelphia, 1985: Fortress), pp. 260, 261, 276, 277 (on Matthew 23:25, 26, and p. 266 (on Mark 7:19). Luke 11:39 is not cited in the index.

[14]*Jesus and Judaism*, p. 266, on the same page on which Mark 7:19 is discussed.

[15]*Jesus and Judaism*, p. 11.

[16]*Jesus and Judaism*, pp. 67, 68.

[17]*Jesus and Judaism*, pp. 69-71.

[18]*Jesus and Judaism*, pp. 77-90.

[19]*Jesus and Judaism*, pp. 188, 388, 389. Sanders leaves out of consideration Neusner's *Judaism. The Evidence of Mishnah* (Chicago, 1981: University of Chicago Press), in which a systemic concern for sanctification is established. Two recent works, by scholars of the New Testament, accept the Pharisaic focus upon purity, cf. M.J. Borg, *Conflict, Holiness, and Politics in the Teaching of Jesus*, Studies in the

association,[20] so that a concern with such matters would not, on his assessment, characterize a group as important as the Pharisees undoubtedly were. Second, Sanders has a consistent interest in portraying Jesus as a teacher who accepted, not merely the impure, but the wicked into his fellowship. Indeed, the latter concern amounts to a driving force within *Jesus and Judaism*, and requires detailed explanation in respect of the present question.

In his longest consideration of the place of purity in Judaism,[21] Sanders accepts without demur that cleanness was fundamentally related to the suitability of persons or objects to approach the Temple. Once the issue is placed in that context, of course, the pericopae in which Jesus is said to engage in disputes concerning purity are naturally associated with those in which Jesus pronounces on cultic matters. His cultic teaching in Matthew includes reference to the taking of oaths (23:16-22), instructions for the offering of sacrifice (5:23, 24), and an elaborate story which relates to the payment of the half-shekel (17:24-27, cf. 23:23; Luke 11:42). All of those passages are uniquely Matthean, and yet are widely accepted as relating to the substance of Jesus' attitude toward the Temple. Multiple attested traditions – Jesus' teaching in respect of a widow's offering (Mark 12:41-44; Luke 21:1-4), his occupation of the holy precincts (Matthew 21:12, 13; Mark 11:15-17; Luke 19:45, 46), his discourse concerning the destruction of the Temple (Matthew 26:61; Mark 14:58) – consistently reinforce the impression that the Temple was no mere symbol, but a focus of active, practical concern within Jesus' movement. But Sanders ignores the natural association of purity with the Temple, and deconstructs purity, in terms of moral wickedness.

The collapse of purity, from a cultic category of integral meaning, into a subset of moral stature, is accomplished by means of dubious exegesis. Proceeding from a reading of Leviticus 7:22-27 (the prohibition

---

Bible and Early Christianity 5 (New York, 1984: Mellen) and R.P. Booth, *Jesus and the Laws of Purity. Tradition and Legal History in Mark 7*, Journal for the Study of the New Testament, Supplement Series 13 (Sheffield, 1986: JSOT). Sanders appears not to have observed that the Pharisaic and rabbinic movements did not regard their traditions as ends in themselves, but as instrumental. What distinguished them from the convenanters of Qumran, Philo, and the teachers of Wisdom in the Diaspora was not a concern for traditions of the elders, but what they did with such traditions.

[20]The linking of the two words in several forms appears in *Jesus and Judaism*, pp. 180, 187, 210. Sanders first refers to "ritual and trivia" when he characterizes the tendency of scholarship to equate ritual and trivia as Pharisaic preoccupations. In his defense of the Pharisees, he seems thoughtlessly to consign the issue of purity to puritanical "minutiae" (p. 187).

[21]*Jesus and Judaism*, pp. 182-85.

against eating fats and blood), Sanders comes to the conclusion that "a few purity transgressions, such as eating blood, are in and of themselves sins; that is, they require atonement."[22] The sole justification for the finding is a) that the penalty for the act in Leviticus is that the transgressor "shall be cut off from his people," and b) that "in the later Rabbinic interpretation, cutting off' puts the transgression strictly between human (sic!) and God, and is atoned for by repentance."[23] The simple fact of the matter is, that the phrase only appears in Leviticus within the nexus of purity and sacrifice (7:20, 21, 24, 27; 17:4, 9, 14; 18:29; 19:8; 20:17, 18; 22:3; 23:29).[24] That Sanders should cite a few verses in isolation, blandly ignore their literary setting, impute a foreign meaning to them, and then transfer that meaning to the whole of "the later Rabbinic interpretation," is nothing short of astonishing. And if we wish to discover what that "later Rabbinic interpretation" is, we are directed to that well-known source of ancient exegesis, Paul and Palestinian Judaism.[25] The relevant pages of Sanders's earlier work, however, in no way address the issue to hand. The point Sanders established in his book on Paul is that repentance effected atonement (as was only natural in the period after the destruction of the Temple),[26] not that anything which required atonement was to be seen as wicked. (As a matter of fact, Sanders particularly stresses, in the pertinent section, that "sins against God were more easily forgiven than sins against one's fellowman." In other words, the tendency of the argument is diametrically opposed to what is being said in *Jesus and Judaism*.) The assertion in respect of "later Rabbinic interpretation" in *Jesus and Judaism*, then, is made without support.

The basis of Sanders's perspective is less any text or group of texts than a global view of Judaism: "Wickedness comes not from impurity as such, but from the attitude that the commandments of the Bible need not be heeded."[27] Sanders's intentionalist construal of Judaism is also apparent in his earlier work;[28] the grounds of his confident

---

[22]*Jesus and Judaism*, p. 183.

[23]Ibid.

[24]20:17 may appear to be an exception, in that the issue is sexual, but the context of the chapter, and particularly the material which follows, establishes the normative perspective of Leviticus.

[25]Cf. *Jesus and Judaism*, p. 387, n. 41.

[26]E.P. Sanders, *Paul and Palestinian Judaism. A Comparison of Patterns of Religion* (Philadelphia, 1977: Fortress) pp. 179, 180.

[27]*Jesus and Judaism*, p. 185.

[28]*Paul and Palestinian Judaism*, p. 147. Sanders here calls the intentionalism on which he bases his scheme "all-pervasive." Unfortunately, the "intention" to which he appeals as a rabbinic category is not defined or defended.

generalization are less so. It is nonetheless used as a hermeneutical category which links early Judaism and Rabbinic Judaism:

> After the destruction of the Temple, repentance was substituted for all the sacrifices prescribed in the law, although the Day of Atonement maintained a special place in Jewish life. Ultimately, what is required is that one intends to remain in the covenant, intends to be obedient.[29]

Sanders's conclusion therefore requires a faulty exegesis of Leviticus, an excessively unitary view of Judaism, and a hypothetically invoked myth of intentionalism. Only so can impurity be equated with wickedness.

The thematic importance of that equation pervades *Jesus and Judaism*. Sanders treats "the sinners" as a primary category through which Jesus' ministry is to be approached.[30] Within that treatment, the category of impurity dissolves into that of sin, and sin, in turn, becomes wickedness. Sanders relates the term "sinners," in the accusation that Jesus' fellowship included the unacceptable, to the work "wicked" in Hebrew (*resa'im*), which Sanders construes to be a technical term for those outside the pale of Judaism. No argumentation whatever is offered for the equation with *hamartoloi* ("sinners") in the Gospels, apart from a reference (once again) to *Paul and Palestinian Judaism*.[31] The discussion in that work also does not substantiate a reading of *hamartoloi* in terms of *resa'im*, although it does establish that "the wicked" are, on the whole, scheduled more for punishment than for repentance. The central, linguistic equation of Sanders's case, however, remains unexamined. From the point of view of ordinary, exegetical practice, that is the Achilles' heel of the thesis under consideration.

Within the Septuagint, *hamartolos* corresponds to five roots in the Masoretic text (*ht', hnp, hrs, r', rs'*), only one of which would support the equation proposed by Sanders.[32] When the probabilities of translation into Aramaic are also taken into account, that equation appears difficult to sustain. The root *rs'* does appear, for example, in the Isaiah Targum, both adjectivally and as an abstract noun. The roots *rs'* and *hnp* are represented by the Aramaic usage, but the other three equivalents of

---

[29]*Paul and Palestinian Judaism*, p. 177.

[30]*Jesus and Judaism*, pp. 174-211.

[31]*Jesus and Judaism*, p. 386, n. 16, citing *Paul and Palestinian Judaism*, pp. 142f., 203, 342-45, 351-55, 357f., 361, 399-404, 414.

[32]E. Hatch and H.A. Redpath, *A Concordance to the Septuagint* (Athens, 1977: Beneficial), pp. 64, 65. Sanders's review of the evidence of the Septuagint is so incomplete as to be misleading, cf. p. 342. The simple fact is that *hamartolos* is used too flexibly to be equated with a "technical term" of restricted meaning, as Sanders claims in *Jesus and Judaism*, p. 177.

*hamartolos* are not.[33] Clearly, the linguistic range of *rs`* in Aramaic is not as wide as that of *hamartolos* in Greek. By contrast, the roots *rs`, hnp, ht'*, and several others are presented by appropriate forms of the Aramaic term, *hwb'* (or its verbal counterpart, *hwb*): "debtor," or "sinner," is the functional equivalent of words covering a variety of defects in the Masoretic Text. When the semantic range of Targumic *hwb'* is considered, two features of the usage are immediately striking from the present point of view. First, because *rs`* can be included within a wider list of roots for representation by a form of *hwb'*, the argument that "the wicked" is a technical term appears strained. (There is, of course, no question but that "the wicked" is a harsh designation; only its technical meaning, as putting someone beyond the pale of the covenant, is at issue here.) Second, the Aramaic usage *hwb'*, which may or may not represent (or correspond to) *rs`* in Hebrew, is the natural counterpart of *hamartolos* in the Septuagint. As a simple matter of fact, "debtors" can be seen in the Targum of Isaiah as punished by the Messiah (11:4), destroyed by the Lord (14:4, 5), but also as capable of repentance (28:24, 25), or a species of wicked gentile (34:2), or another enemy of Jerusalem (54:17).[34] Such various usages make any appeal to a univocal or exclusive meaning of the Aramaic term incredible. Quite evidently, a contextual construal of living instances of the word will alone produce an accurate appraisal of its meaning.

Within the Gospels, a coherent language of "debt" is attributed to Jesus. When, in the Matthean version of the Lord's Prayer, Jesus instructs his followers to ask God, "Forgive us our debts, as we also forgive our debtors," there is no doubt but that the New Testament is preserving an Aramaic idiom (6:12). Luke only partially preserves the usage: "Forgive us our sins, as we also forgive everyone who is indebted to us" (11:4). Jesus' recourse to the Aramaic idiom is not a mere matter of convention: several of his parables turn on the metaphorical and literal senses of "debt," much as in the Targum of Isaiah 50:1, where the term refers in one breath to money owed, and in another breath to sins before God.[35]

---

[33]J.B. van Zijl, *A Concordance to the Targum of Isaiah* (Missoula, 1979: Scholars), pp. 182, 183.

[34]Cf. van Zijl (1979) pp. 57, 58; A. Sperber, *The Bible in Aramaic III: The Latter Prophets* (Leiden, 1962: E.J. Brill), and B.D. Chilton, *The Isaiah Targum. Introduction, Translation, and Notes: The Aramaic Targum* (Wilmington, 1987: Glazier).

[35]The passage reads as follows: Thus says the LORD, "Where is *the* bill of divorce which I *gave* your *congregation, that it is rejected*? Or who *had a debt against me*, to whom I have sold you? Behold, for your *sins* you were sold, and for your *apostasies* your *congregation* was *rejected*."
As in Chilton (1987), italicized words represent innovative departures of the Aramaic rendering from the Hebrew text which underlies it. The first usage of

Several instances of parabolic presentation of "debt" in this sense are especially striking. In Matthew 18:23-35, a debtor is said to owe the astronomical sum of ten thousand talents (18:24). When it is borne in mind that the annual imposition of tax upon the whole of Galilee and Peraea amounted to merely two hundred talents (cf. *Antiquities* 17.9.4), the hyperbole involved in the parable becomes readily apparent. The debtor is in no position to repay such a debt, nor is there any credible way in which he could have incurred it. He behaves astoundingly, after his debt is forgiven (v. 27), in a manner all but calculated to trivialize such forgiveness: he refuses to deal mercifully with a colleague who owed him one hundred denarii (vv. 28-30). The latter amount is by no means insignificant: a single denarius has been estimated as the going rate for a full day of labor.[36] But the contrast with the king's incalcuable generosity cannot be overlooked, and the close of the parable makes it unmistakably plain that God's forgiveness demands ours (vv. 31-35). To fail to forgive one's fellow, even when what needs to be forgiven is considerable, is to betray the very logic of forgiveness which alone gives us standing before God.

Two other parables portray, in an apparently paradoxical fashion, the inextricable link between divine forgiveness and our behavior. Within the story of Jesus at the house of a Pharisee named Simon (Luke 7:36-50), a parable explains why Jesus chose to forgive a sinful woman (vv. 40-43). Of two debtors, the one who has been released from the greater debt will obviously love his creditor more. The sinful woman's great love, therefore, in an outlandish display of affection and honor (vv. 37-38, 44-46), is proof that God had forgiven her (v. 47). Her love is proof of her capacity to be forgiven.[37] She had succeeded precisely where the unforgiving servant of Matthew 18 had failed: her actions displayed the value of forgiveness to her. The same logic, developed more strictly in respect of debt, is evident in the otherwise inexplicable parable of the crafty steward (Luke 16:1-9). The lord praised the steward for his

---

"debt" corresponds well to the underlying idea in the Masoretic Text, which refers to creditors. The second usage (here rendered "sins") represents "iniquities" in the Hebrew text, and is also a straightforward, formally correspondent rendering. The point is, however, that both usages together produce a uniquely Targumic juxtaposition of "debt" in its literal and metaphorical senses.

[36]J. Jeremias (tr. S.H. Hooke), *The Parables of Jesus* (London, 1976: SCM), pp. 136-39.

[37]Cf. C.F.D. Moule, "'...As we forgive...': A Note on the Distinction between Deserts and Capacity in the Understanding of Forgiveness," *Essays in New Testament Interpretation* (Cambridge, 1982: Cambridge University Press), pp. 278-86, 282-84.

cleverness (v. 8) in reducing the debts of those who owed commodities to the lord (vv. 5-7). The scheme was devised so that the lucky debtors would receive the steward (v. 4) after his lord had followed through on the threat of dismissing the steward for dishonesty (vv. 1, 2). On any ordinarily moral accounting, the steward had gone from bad to worse, and yet his lord praises him (v. 8). Because God is the lord, what would be bribery in the case of any ordinary master's property turns out to be purposeful generosity. The effect of the steward's panic is to fulfill the lord's desire,[38] because he is the same as the unforgiving servant's king, the God who forgave the sinful woman.

The usage of "debt" attributed to Jesus in the Gospels, therefore, is initially to be understood as an Aramaism. But he appears, on the evidence prima facie, to have exploited the metaphorical possibilities of the term in a way which is precedented in the Targum of Isaiah, but in a characteristically parabolic fashion. The general activity of telling parables, of course, is well attested among early rabbis;[39] at issue here is not absolute uniqueness, but the relative distinctiveness which distinguishes any significantly historical figure from his contemporaries. A well-established theologoumenon of early Judaism spoke not only of debts, but of credit in respect to God.[40] Jesus appears to have exploited the latter metaphor, as well as the former (cf. Matthew 6:19-21; 19:21; Mark 10:21; Luke 12:33, 34; 18:22). But it was in his adaptation of an idiom and theology of "debt" that Jesus developed a systemic aspect of his message as a whole.

Jesus' usage of the language of debt has provided an opportunity to test the adequacy of Sanders's thesis. It has elsewhere been doubted whether the aspect of repentance can be eliminated from the message of Jesus as easily as Sanders would have it,[41] but the focus here is upon his attempt to use "wickedness" as an overarching concept, inclusive of impurity and sin, and more powerful than either. Jesus, as portrayed by Sanders, "could truly be criticized for including the wicked in his 'kingdom.'"[42] That portrayal is only possible, as we have seen, by tendentiously reducing impurity and sin to an artificial definition of "wickedness," as an intention to put oneself outside the covenant.

---

[38]Cf. B.D. Chilton, *A Galilean Rabbi and His Bible. Jesus' Understanding of the Interpreted Scripture of His Time*, Good News Studies 6 (Wilmington, 1984: Glazier), pp. 117-23.

[39]Cf. B.D. Chilton and J.I.H. McDonald, *Jesus and the Ethics of the Kingdom*, Biblical Foundations in Theology (London, 1987: SPCK), pp. 31-43.

[40]Cf. F. Hauck, "*opheilo*...," *Theological Dictionary of the New Testament* 5, ed. G. Kittel, tr. G.W. Bromiley (Grand Rapids, 1978: Eerdmans), pp. 559-66.

[41]Cf. Chilton and McDonald (1987), pp. 40, 41.

[42]*Jesus and Judaism*, p. 323.

Sanders has provided us with a definition of Judaism as "covenantal nomism," in which the law is an instrument of remaining within a graciously bestowed covenant. But having offered that useful insight, Sanders persists in understanding Jesus and Paul as in polar opposition to a central tenet of Judaism: Jesus includes the wicked, and Paul includes anyone who accepts participation in Christ.[43]

Where earlier scholarship portrayed the polarity as between works and grace (utilizing the language of Paul), Sanders transposes it between the concepts of covenant and universal inclusiveness. Moreover, Sanders pairs Jesus and Paul in contrast to early Christianity generally, and so provides – in effect – a new account of the essence of Christianity in the manner of Adolf von Harnack: the radical, practically antinomian teaching of the founders is rejected by Judaism and subverted by Christianity. But such an ultimately simplistic account is only conceivable when Jesus is set in opposition to a "Palestinian" Judaism denatured of a concern for purity, and when Paul is placed in the context of the same Judaism, although his natural habitat was Hellentistic. If Judaism in the first century were a unitary, ideological movement, and were Jesus and Paul characterized by philosophical reflection, there would be some plausibility in Sanders's reconstruction. As matters stand, however, his Jesus and his Paul appear as refugees from another century, and from a historiography which was discarded long ago.

---

[43]The plainest exposition of Sanders's overall picture is avalilable in "Jesus, Paul, and Judaism," *Aufstieg und Niedergang der romischen Welt* vol. 25, part 1, ed. W. Haase (Berlin, 1982: de Gruyter), pp. 390-450. The similarity with the romanticism of Adolf von Harnack is striking; cf. W.G. Kummel, *The New Testament. The History of the Investigation of Its Problems*, tr. S.Mc.L. Gilmour and H.C. Keel (London, 1973: SCM), pp. 178-84.

# 8

## Sanders's *Paul and Palestinian Judaism*

E.P. Sanders, *Paul and Palestinian Judaism: A Comparison of Patterns of Religion* (London, 1977: SCM Press). Pp. xviii+627. A review originally published in *History of Religions* 1978, 18:177-91.

"Palestinian Judaism" is described through three bodies of evidence: Tannaitic literature, the Dead Sea Scrolls, and Apocrypha and Pseudepigrapha, in that order. I shall deal only with the first. To each set of sources, Sanders addresses questions of systematic theology: election and covenant, obedience and disobedience, reward and punishment and the world to come, salvation by membership in the covenant and atonement, proper religious behavior (so for Tannaitic sources); covenant and the covenant people, election and predestination, the commandments, fulfillment and transgression, atonement (Dead Sea Scrolls); election and covenant, the fate of the individual Israelite, atonement, commandments, the basis of salvation, the gentiles, repentance and atonement, the righteousness of God (Apocrypha and Pseudepigrapha, meaning, specifically: Ben Sira, I Enoch, Jubilees, Psalms of Solomon, IV Ezra). There follows a brief concluding chapter (pp. 419-28, summarizing pp. 1-418), and then the second part, on Paul, takes up about a fifth of the book. Sanders provides a very competent bibliography (pp. 557-82) and thorough indexes. So far as the book has a polemical charge, it is to demonstrate (pp. 420-21) that "the fundamental nature of the covenant conception...largely accounts for the relative scarcity of appearances of the term 'covenant' in Rabbinic literature. The covenant was presupposed, and the Rabbinic discussions were largely directed toward the question of how to fulfill the covenantal obligations." This proposition is then meant to disprove the conviction ("all but universally held") that Judaism is a degeneration of the Old Testament view: "The once noble idea of covenant as offered by God's grace and obedience as the consequence of that gracious gift degenerated into the idea of petty legalism, according to which one had to earn the mercy of God by minute observance of irrelevant ordinances."[1]

Sanders's search for patterns yields a common pattern in "covenantal nomism," which, in general, emerges as follows (p. 422): (1) God has chosen Israel and (2) given the law. The law implies both (3) God's promise to maintain the election and (4) the requirement to obey. (5) God rewards obedience and punishes transgression. (6) The law provides for means of atonement, and atonement results in (7) maintenance or re-establishment of the covenantal relationship. (8) All those who are maintained in the covenant by obedience, atonement, and God's mercy belong to the group which will be saved. An important interpretation of the first and last points is that election and ultimately salvation are considered to be by God's mercy rather than human achievement. Anyone familiar with Jewish liturgy will be at home in that statement. Even though the evidence on the character of Palestinian Judaism derives from diverse groups and reaches us through various means, Sanders argues that covenantal nomism was "the basic type of religion known by Jesus and presumably by Paul...." And again, "covenantal nomism must have been the general type of religion prevalent in Palestine before the destruction of the Temple."[2]

The stated purposes require attention. Sanders states at the outset (p. xii) that he has six aims: (1) to consider methodologically how to compare two (or more) related but different religions; (2) to destroy the view of Rabbinic Judaism which is still prevalent in much, perhaps most, New Testament scholarship; (3) to establish a different view of Rabbinic Judaism; (4) to argue a case concerning Palestinian Judaism (that is, Judaism as reflected in material of Palestinian provenance) as a whole; (5) to argue for a certain understanding of Paul; and (6) to carry out a comparison of Paul and Palestinian Judaism. Numbers (4) and (6), he immediately adds, "constitute the general aim of the book, while I hope

---

[1]The polemic against New Testament scholarship on Judaism is a powerful theme which runs through the book and takes many forms. It is difficult to locate a major unit of thought which is not in some way affected by Sanders's apologetic interest. This example should not be thought to exhaust the matter, but shows how, at the very center of the book, issues are defined in contemporary theological terms. As we shall see in a moment, the very work of description itself becomes flawed on this account.

[2]So far as I can see, Sanders is reticent about the meaning of "religion" in this context, and other "types of religion" which are not to be found in Palestine before A.D. 70, but which might have been present there, also are not defined or discussed. I find a general lack of precision in terminology. But Sanders's purpose is not to contribute to the theoretical literature of religious studies.

to accomplish the others along the way." Since more than a third of the work is devoted to Rabbinic Judaism, Sanders certainly cannot be accused of treating his second goal casually.

Having described the overall shape of the work, let me make explicit the point at which I think historians of religion should join the discussion, since, it is self-evident, the long agendum of this book touches only occasionally upon issues of history, history of religions, and history of ideas. In fact, this is a work of historical theology: *wissenschaftliche Theologie*. But Sanders's very good intention deserves the attention of students of religions who are not theologians, because what he wanted to achieve is in my view worthwhile. This intention is the proper comparison of religions (or of diverse expressions of one larger religion): "I am of the view...that the history of the comparison of Paul and Judaism is a particularly clear instance of the general need for methodological improvement in the comparative study of religion. What is difficult is to focus on what is to be compared. We have already seen that most comparisons are of reduced essences...or of individual motifs...." This sort of comparison Sanders rejects. Here I wish to give Sanders's words, because I believe what he wants to do is precisely what he should have done but, as I shall explain, has not succeeded in doing: "What is clearly desirable, then, is to compare an entire religion, parts and all, with an entire religion, parts and all; to use the analogy of a building to compare two buildings, not leaving out of account their individual bricks. The problem is how to discover two wholes, both of which are considered and defined on their own merits and in their own terms, to be compared with each other."

Now let us ask ourselves whether or not Sanders has compared an entire religion, parts and all, with other such entire religions. On the basis of my description of the contents of the book, we must conclude that he has not. For the issues of election and covenant, obedience and disobedience, and the like, while demonstrably present and taken for granted in the diverse "Judaisms" of late antiquity, do not necessarily define the generative problematic of any of the Judaisms before us. To put matters in more general terms: Systemic description must begin with the system to be described. Comparative description follows. And to describe a system, we commence with the principal documents which can be shown to form the center of a system. Our task then is to uncover the exegetical processes, the dynamics of the system, through which those documents serve to shape a conception, and to make sense, of reality. We then must locate the critical tensions and inner problematic of the system thereby revealed: What is it about? What are its points of insistence? The comparison of systems begins in their exegesis and interpretation.

But Sanders does not come to Rabbinic Judaism (to focus upon what clearly is his principal polemical charge) to uncover the issues of Rabbinic Judaism. He brings to the rabbinic sources the issues of Pauline scholarship and Paul.[3] This blatant trait of his work, which begins, after all, with a long account of Christian anti-Judaism ("the persistence of the view of Rabbinic religion as one of legalistic works-righteousness" pp. 33-58), hardly requires amplification. In fact, Sanders does not really undertake the systemic description of earlier Rabbinic Judaism in terms of its critical tension. True, he isolates those documents he thinks may testify to the state of opinion in the late first and second centuries. But Sanders does not describe Rabbinic Judaism through the systemic categories yielded by its principal documents. His chief purpose is to demonstrate that Rabbinism constitutes a system of "covenantal nomism." While I think he is wholly correct in maintaining the importance of the conceptions of covenant and of grace, the polemic in behalf of rabbinic legalism as covenantal does not bring to the fore what rabbinic sources themselves wish to take as their principal theme and generative problem. For them, as he says, covenantal nomism is a datum. So far as Sanders proposes to demonstrate the importance to all the kinds of ancient Judaism of covenantal nomism, election, atonement, and the like, his work must be pronounced a success but trivial. So far as he claims to effect systemic description of Rabbinic Judaism ("a comparison of patterns of religion"), we have to evaluate that claim in its own terms.

Since in a moment I shall turn to the impact, upon Sanders's topic, of work completed since his book was written in 1973 or 1974, I wish to stress that my criticism at this point concerns how Sanders does what he has chosen to do: systemic comparison. His notion of comparing patterns of religion is, I believe, promising. But what he has done, instead, is to impose the pattern of one religious expression, Paul's, upon the description of another, that of the Tannaitic-rabbinical sources.[4] He therefore ignores the context of the sayings adduced in the service of comparison, paying little attention to the larger context in which those

---

[3]See above, n. 1.

[4]Try to imagine the scholarly agendum if Christianity were the minority religion, Judaism the majority one. Books on "the Christian background of Judaism" and "what Paul teaches us about the world of Mishnah" surely would distort the interpretation of Paul. After all, "Paul and the dietary laws" would not focus upon an issue at the center of Paul's thought, though it might be a principal point of interest to theological faculties. Proof that Jesus made important contributions to Judaism through his disciple, Hillel, or that Jesus was a Pharisee, would seem still more ridiculous, except that, the apologetic mind being what it is, they are written even here and now.

sayings find meaning. In this connection I point to the observation of Mary Boyce (*A History of Zoroastrianism* [Leiden, 1975: E.J. Brill], p. 246):

> Zoroaster's eschatological teachings, with the individual judgment, the resurrection of the body, the Last Judgment, and life everlasting, became profoundly familiar, through borrowings, to Jews, Christians, and Muslims, and have exerted enormous influence on the lives and thoughts of men in many lands. Yet it was in the framework of his own faith that they attained their fullest logical coherence....

What Boyce stresses is that, taken out of the Zoroastrian context, these familiar teachings lose their "fullest logical coherence." Sanders, for his part, has not asked what is important and central in the system of Tannaitic-rabbinic writings. All he wants to know is what, in those writings, addresses questions of interest to Paul. In my judgment, even in 1973 he would have been better served by paying close attention to his own statement of purpose.

But since 1973 the state of the art has shifted its focus, from the mass of writings in which authorities of the first and second centuries (Tannaim, hence Tannaitic literature) are cited, to the character of the documents, one by one, which contain and express Rabbinic Judaism. Future work of comparison, then, will have to take up the results of something less encompassing than "the Tannaitic view of...," all the more so, "the rabbinic idea of...." The work of description, first for its own purposes, then for systemic comparison, begins with Mishnah.

Mishnah certainly is the first document of Rabbinic Judaism. Formally, it stands at the center of the system, since the principal subsequent rabbinic documents, the Talmuds, lay themselves out as if they were exegeses of Mishnah (or, more accurately, of Mishnah-Tosefta).[5] It follows that an account of what Mishnah is about, of the system expressed by Mishnah and of the worldview created and sustained therein, should be required for systemic comparison such as Sanders proposes. Now if we come to Mishnah with questions of Pauline-Lutheran theology, important to Sanders and New Testament scholarship, we find ourselves on the peripheries of Mishnaic literature and its chief foci. True, Mishnah contains a very few relevant, accessible sayings, for example, on election and covenant. But on our hands is a

---

[5]In fact, all descriptions of the Talmuds tell us that the Talmud consists of the Mishnah and the Talmud (or Gemara, the terms are interchangeable), the latter being an exegesis of the Mishnah. I believed that view with perfect faith until I began work on Mishnah tractates for which we have Talmud and found that, after a certain limited point, the Talmud really is not much interested in Mishnah and does not pretend to be. Still, the Talmud is so put together as to constitute a kind of "commentary" to the Mishnah, and this formal trait, so predominant in the sight of literary theorists, has to be taken seriously.

huge document which does not wish to tell us much about election and covenant and which does wish to speak about other things.

Description of the Mishnaic system is not easy. It has taken me twenty-two volumes to deal with the sixth of Mishnah's six divisions,[6] and while I think I can describe the Mishnaic system of uncleanness, I still have no clear notion about the relationship between that Mishnaic subsystem and the other five divisions of Mishnah and their, as yet undescribed, subsystems.[7] We cannot therefore blame Sanders for not doing what has only just now been undertaken. But we have to wonder whether Sanders has asked of himself the generative and unifying questions of the core of Mishnah at all. Has he actually sat down and studied (not merely "read") one document, even one tractate, beginning to end, and analyzed its inner structure, heart, and center? By this question I do not mean to ask whether Sanders has mastered rabbinic writings. The evidence in his book is that he can look things up, presumably with Billerbeck's help. He knows Hebrew and is competent, if no expert (!). The question is, Does Sanders so grasp the problematic of a rabbinic compilation that he can accurately state what it is that said compilation wishes to express – its generative problematic? Or does he come to the rabbinic literature with a quite separate and distinct set of questions, issues in no way natural to, and originating in, the rabbinic writings themselves? Just now we noticed that Sanders's theological agendum accords quite felicitously with the issues of Pauline theology. To show that that agendum has not been shaped out of the issues of rabbinic theology, I shall now adduce negative evidence on whether Sanders with equal care analyzes the inner structure of a document of Rabbinic Judaism.

First, throughout his "constructive" discussions of rabbinic ideas about theology, Sanders quotes all documents equally with no effort at differentiation among them. He seems to have culled sayings from the diverse sources he has chosen and written them down on cards, which he proceeded to organize around his critical categories. Then he has constructed his paragraphs and sections by flipping through those cards and commenting on this and that. So there is no context in which a given

---

[6]*A History of the Mishnaic Law of Purities* (Leiden, 1974-77: E.J. Brill), vols. 1-22.

[7]Why a doctoral program, such as Brown's, calling itself "History of Religions: Judaism," should find its principal intellectual challenges to be those of exegesis, and how participants in that program conceive the purposes of history of religions to be served by their work, are not questions to be dealt with here, although the answers are suggested at the end of this paper. A general statement of our program is in William Scott Green, *Approaches to Ancient Judaism* (Missoula, 1978: Scholars Press for Brown Judaic Studies), with special reference to the papers by William Scott Green, Jonathan Z. Smith, and this writer.

saying is important in its own setting, in its own document. This is Billerbeck scholarship.

Of greater importance, the diverse documents of Rabbinism are accorded no attention on their own. Let me explain what I mean. Anyone who sits down and studies Sifra, in a large unit of its materials, for example, can hardly miss what the redactor of the document wants to say. The reason is that the polemic of that document is so powerfully stated and so interminably repeated as to be inescapable. What Sifra wishes to say is this: Mishnah requires an exegetical foundation. But Mishnah notoriously avoids scriptural prooftexts. To Sifra none of Mishnah's major propositions is acceptable solely upon the basis of reason or logic. All of them require proper grounding in exegesis – of a peculiarly formal sort – of Scripture. One stratum of the Talmuds, moreover, addresses the same devastating critique to Mishnah. For once a Mishnaic proposition will be cited at the head of a Talmudic pericope, a recurrent question is, What is the source of this statement? And the natural and right answer (from the perspective of the redactor of this sort of pericope) will be, As it is said..., followed by a citation of Scripture.

Now if it is so that Sifra and at least one stratum of Talmud so shape their materials as to make a powerful polemical point against Mishnah's autonomous authority ("logic"), indifferent as Mishnah is to scriptural authority for its laws, then we must ask how we can ignore or neglect that polemic. Surely we cannot cite isolated pericopae of these documents with no attention whatsoever to the intention of the documents which provide said pericopae. Even the most primitive New Testament scholars will concur that we must pay attention to the larger purposes of the several evangelists in citing sayings assigned to Jesus in the various Gospels. Everyone knows that if we ignore Matthew's theory of the law and simply extract Matthew's versions of Jesus' sayings about the law and set them up side by side with the sayings about the law given to Jesus by other of the evangelists and attitudes imputed to him by Paul, we create a mess of contradictions. Why then should the context of diverse rabbinic sayings, for example, on the law, be ignored? In this setting it is gratuitous to ask for an explanation of Sanders's constant reference to "the Rabbis," as though the century and a half which he claims to discuss produced no evidence of individuals and ideas having distinct histories. This is ignorant.

Still more telling evidence that Sanders does not succeed in his systemic description comes when he gives one concrete example (in the entire 238 pages of discussion of "Tannaitic" Judaism) of what a document wishes to tell us. I shall focus on the matter because Sanders raises it. He states (p. 71):

Rabbinic discussions are often at the third remove from central
questions of religious importance. Thus the tractate Mikwaoth,
"immersion pools," does not consider the religious value of immersion
or the general reason for purity, much less such a large topic as why the
law should be observed. It simply begins with the classification of the
grades among pools of water. This does not mean that there were no
religious principles behind the discussion; simply that they (a) were so
well understood that they did not need to be specified and (b) did not
fall into the realm of halakah.

Now on the basis of this statement we must conclude that Sanders has
looked at M. Miqvaot 1:1, perhaps even the entire first chapter of the
document. It is true that tractate Miqvaot does begin with classification
of the grades among pools of water. But a study of the tractate as a
whole reveals that it certainly has its own issues, its own critical
concerns, indeed, its own generative problematic.

In fact the shank of the tractate – M. Miq. 2:4-5:6 – asks about
collections of diverse sorts of water and how they effect purification. A
secondary development of the same theme follows: the union of pools to
form a valid collection of water, and yet a tertiary development, mixtures
of water with other liquids (wine, mud). Therefore the primary interest
of the tractate is in water for the immersion pool: What sort of water
purifies? Now anyone interested in the document must wonder, Why is
it that, of all the possible topics for a tractate on purification, the one
point of interest should be the definition of effective water? And the first
observation one might make is that Scripture, for its part, would be
surprised by the datum of Mishnah-tractate Miqvaot.[8] For, in the

---

[8]This is worked out in my *History of the Mishnaic Law of Purities*, vol. 13, Miqvaot.
Commentary, and vol. 14, Miqvaot. Literary and Historical Problems (Leiden,
1976: E.J. Brill). One of the most complex problems of Mishnah study is the
relationship of the diverse tractates of Mishnah to Scripture. I have dealt with
this problem in "From Scripture to Mishnah: The Origins of Mishnah-tractate
Niddah," *Journal of Jewish Studies*; "From Scripture to Mishnah: The Exegetical
Origins of Maddaf," *Festschrift for the Fiftieth Anniversary of the American Academy
for Jewish Research*; "From Scripture to Mishnah: The Case of Mishnah's Fifth
Division," *Journal of Biblical Literature* (March 1979); "The Meaning of Torah shebe
al peh, with Special Reference to Kelim and Ohalot," *AJS Review* I (1976): 151-70;
and in the various volumes of *Purities, Holy Things, and Women*. I do not
understand why Sanders does not begin his work of description with an account
of the Old Testament legacy available to all the groups under discussion as well
as with an account of how, in his view, each group receives and reshapes that
legacy. Everyone claimed, after all, to build upon the foundations of Mosaic
revelation ("covenantal nomism"), indeed, merely to restate what Moses or the
prophets had originally said. It seems to me natural to give the Old Testament a
central place in the description of any system resting upon an antecedent corpus
of such authority as the Mosaic revelation and the prophetic writings. Systemic
comparison on diverse relationsips to, and readings of, Scripture certainly is

opinion of the priestly authorities of Leviticus and Numbers, still water by itself – not spring water, not standing water mixed with blood or ashes, for example – does not effect purification. Water may remove uncleanness, but the process of purification further requires the setting of the sun. Water mixed with blood may purify the leper; water mixed with the ashes of a red cow may purify one made unclean by a corpse. But water by itself is inadequate to complete purification. At best, Scripture knows running water as a means of purification. But Mishnah-tractate Miqvaot stresses the purificatory properties of still water, and explicitly excludes spring water from the center of its discussion.[9]

My own conception of what it is that Mishnah wishes to say in this tractate is at best a guess,[10] but it is worth repeating so that the full character of Sanders's "defense" of this particular tractate may become clear:

> What is the fundamental achievement of our tractate? The Oral
> Torah [Mishnah] provides a mode of purification different from that

---

invited. In this context I must reject Sanders's critique of Vermes (pp. 25-29). His omission of reference to the Targumim because they are "generally late" is self-serving. The Targumim are diverse and hard to use; not all are in English. Sanders chokes on the gnat of the Targums and swallows the camel of the midrashim. Sanders says, "Even if generally late, the Targums may, to be sure, contain early traditions. But these must now be sought out one by one." True indeed. And the same is so for the whole of Tannaitic literature! By "Tannaitic literature," Sanders means literature containing sayings attributed to Tannaim, or authorities who are assumed to have flourished before A.D. 200. As I shall suggest in a moment, such "early traditions" as occur in the name of first- and second-century authorities in documents of the third and later centuries also must be sought out, one by one. Sanders's more honest reason follows: "In general, the present state of Targumic studies does not permit the Targums to be used for our purposes." That is, I suppose, they are hard to use as he wants to use them. My argument is that the same is self-evidently true of the earlier rabbinic documents. But Sanders successfully answers his own objection, with his stress on systemic – therefore diachronic – as against merely synchronic, comparison. Omission of the Targums is less damaging than failure to exploit the sizable legacy of the Old Testament, which surely is available, all parties concur, by the first century B.C. That omission is incomprehensible.

[9]That is the point of the redactor's beginning with the chapter of Miqvaot which Sanders does cite.

[10]It is a tribute to the kindness of the reviewers of my *Purities* that the theory now laid forth has been received with a certain patience. Louis Jacobs, writing in Bulletin of the School of Oriental and African Studies, vol. 40, no. 2 (1977), very correctly states, "Here, too, there is a fascinating theory about Pharisaic notions of purification, but one which does not necessarily follow from the acute analysis Neusner has given us of the Mishnaic sources." Jacobs then cites the passage before us. Jacobs is surely right that this theory does not necessarily follow from the sources. It is my guess at what the sources mean.

specified in the Written Torah for the Temple, but analogous to that suitable for the Temple. Still water serves for the table, living water [approved by Scripture] cleans the Zab, and, when mixed with blood or ashes, the leper and the person unclean by reason of touching a corpse. All those other things cleaned by the setting of the sun, the passage of time, in the Oral Torah [Mishnah-tractate Miqvaot] are cleaned in the still water [of the immersion pool, which, Mishnah makes clear, must be] gathered in the ground, in the rains which know no time, but only the eternal seasons.[11]

Now it may be that that is the whole story. What follows is my own obiter dictum on the matter, my conception of the world constructing meaning of the laws just now summarized:

In an age in which men and women immersed themselves in spring-fed lakes and rushing rivers, in moving water washing away their sins in preparation for the end of days, the Pharisees observed the passing of the seasons, which go onward through time, immersing in the still, collected water which falls from heaven. They bathe not in running water, in the anticipation of the end of days and for the sake of eschatological purity, but in still water, to attain the cleanness appropriate to the eternal Temple and the perpetual sacrifice [of the very real, physical Temple of Jerusalem]. They remove the uncleanness defined by the Written Torah for the holy altar, because of the conviction of the Oral Torah [Mishnah] that the hearth and home, table and bed, going onward through ages without end, also must be and can be cleaned, in particular, through the rain: the living water from heaven, falling in its perpetual seasons, trickling down the hills and naturally gathering in ponds, ditches, and caverns, for time immemorial. As sun sets, bringing purification for the Temple, so rain falls, bringing purification for the table.[12]

Now I cite this passage to juxtapose it to Sanders's judgment that Miqvaot "does not consider the religious value of immersion or the general reason for purity." I think it does exactly that – in its own way.

In my view, Sanders finds in Miqvaot no answers to questions of religious value because he has not asked how Miqvaot asks its questions to begin with. And that is because he has not allowed the tractate to speak for itself, out of its own deepest stratum of conceptions. He has brought to the tractate an alien set of questions and, finding nothing in the tractate to deal with those questions – that is, no sayings explicitly addressed to them – he has gone his way. It is true that the tractate does not consider "the religious value of immersion," and that is because it has quite separate, and, if I am right, more profound, issues in mind.[13]

---

[11]*Purities*, 14:204-5.

[12]Ibid., p. 205.

[13]I must concede that it is asking much of scholars to sit patiently to master the details of the Mishnaic (and other rabbinic) law and only then to raise the

To say "this does not mean that there were no religious principles behind the discussion" is not only patronizing, it also is ignorant. To claim that the "principles were so well understood that they did not need to be specified" is true but beside the point, if Sanders cannot accurately tell us what these principles were. Granted that we deal with a system of "convenantal nomism," what is it that that covenant was meant to express? And how did the ancient rabbis interpret that covenant and its requirements for their own trying times? Answering these questions requires Sanders to take Judaism seriously in its own terms. But this he does not do.

Now I must repeat that I do not propose to criticize Sanders on the basis of his not having read a book which appeared two or three years after his own work was completed (which I believe, on the basis of his discussion and bibliography, to have been in 1973 or 1974). It is to point out, on the basis of an example of his own selection and what he has to say about that example, that the promised systemic description simply does not take place. The claim, in this very context, that religious principles cannot be discussed in the Mishnah because of the character of Mishnah, would be more persuasive if there were substantial evidence that Mishnah to begin with has been studied in its own framework. Sanders says (p. 71):

> We should at least briefly refer to another characteristic of the literature which makes a small-scale analysis of basic religious principles impossible: they are not discussed as such. Rabbinic discussions are often at the third remove from central questions of religious importance.

There follows the treatment of Miqvaot cited above. I contend that it begs the question to say "basic religious principles" are not "discussed as such."[14]

---

questions of the deeper range of meanings of that law. But the work of interpretation begins in exegesis and only ends in the formation and history of ideas. If people find too arduous, or merely dull, the work of patient exegesis, then of the recombinant history of small ideas, let them write on some subject other than earlier Rabbinic Judaism. The legal materials are not easy to understand. They are still more difficult to interpret as statements of philosophical or metaphysical conceptions. My message is that only in the work of exegesis is that task of interpretation to be undertaken, and it is only through interpretation that the meaning of the law is to be attained. Nobody begged Sanders to come and defend the Jews.

[14]Anyhow, why should "the religious value" of immersion be spelled out by the second-century rabbis in terms immediately accessible to a twentieth-century theologian? Mishnah's audience is second-century rabbis. How can we expect people to explain to outsiders ("why the law should be kept" indeed!) answers to questions which do not trouble insiders to begin with. The whole statement of the question is topsy-turvy. I find deplorable Sanders's failure to object to the

The diverse rabbinic documents require study in their own terms. The systems of each – so far as there are systems – have to be uncovered and described. The way the several systems relate and the values common to all of them have to be spelled out. The notion that we may cite promiscuously everything in every document (within the defined canon of "permitted" documents) and then claim to have presented an account of "the Rabbis" and their opinions is not demonstrated and not even very well argued. We hardly need dwell on the still more telling fact that Sanders has not shown how systemic comparison is possible when, in point of fact, the issues of one document, or of one system of which a document is a part, are simply not the same as the issues of some other document or system. That is, he has succeeded in finding rabbinic sayings on topics of central importance to Paul (or Pauline theology). He has not even asked whether these sayings form the center and core of the rabbinic system or even of a given rabbinic document. To state matters simply, How do we know that "the Rabbis" and Paul are talking about the same thing, so that we may compare what they have to say? And if it should turn out that "the Rabbis" and Paul are not talking about the same thing, then what is it that we have to compare?

Even by 1973 it was clear that the issue of historical dependability of attributions of sayings to particular rabbis had to be faced, even though, admittedly, it had not been faced in most of the work on which Sanders was able to draw. I do not wish to dwell upon the problem of why we should believe that a given rabbi really said what is attributed to him, because I have already discussed that matter at some length.[15] Still, it seems to me that the issues of historical evidence should enter into the

---

notion of "central questions of religious importance" and "religious principles." Taken for granted is the conception that what are central questions to us are central questions to all "worthwhile" religious literature. It follows that if we cannot locate what to us are "religious principles," then we have either to condemn or to apologize for the documents which lack them. Stated in this way, the implicit position takes for granted "we all know" the meaning of "religion," "religious importance," "religious principles." In the case of the vast halakhic literature, we do not find readily accessible and immediately obvious "religious principles." When, moreover, we do find those conceptions, subject to generalization and analysis, which do address issues of common, even contemporary concern, we sometimes discover a range of topics under analysis more really philosophical than religious (in the contemporary sense of these words). An apology for Rabbinic Judaism bypassing the whole of the halakhic corpus which constitutes its earliest stratum is cosmically irrelevant to the interpretation of Rabbinic Judaism, therefore to the comparison of that system to others in its own culture. Is this a defense of Judaism at all? Who needs such friends!

[15]"The History of Earlier Rabbinic Judaism: Some New Approaches," *History of Religions* 16 (1977): 216-36.

notion of the comparison of systems. If it should turn out that "the Rabbis'" ideas about a given theological topic respond to a historical situation subject to fairly precise description, then the work of comparison becomes still more subtle and precarious. For if "the Rabbis" address their thought – for example, about the right motive for the right deed – to a world in which, in the aftermath of a terrible catastrophe, the issue of what it is that human beings still control is central, the comparison of their thought to that of Paul requires us to imagine what Paul might have said if confronted by the situation facing "the Rabbis."

A powerful motif in sayings assigned to authorities who lived after the Bar Kokhba war is the issue of attitude: the surpassing power of human intention in defining a situation and judging it. In many ways diverse tractates of Mishnah seem to want to say that there are yet important powers left in the hands of defeated, despairing Israelites. The message of much of Mishnaic halakhah is that there is an unseen world, a metaphysical world, subject to the will of Israel. Given the condition of defeat, the despair and helplessness of those who survived the end of time, we may hardly be surprised at the message of authorities who wish to specify important decisions yet to be made by people totally subjugated to the will of their conquerors. Now if we ignore that historical setting, the dissonances of theology and politics, in which the message concerning attitude and intention is given, how are we properly to interpret and compare "the Rabbis'" teachings on the effects of the human will with those of Paul, or those assigned to Jesus, for that matter? If they say the same thing, it may be for quite divergent reasons. If they say different things, it may be that they say different things because they speak of different problems to different people.

Now these observations seem to me to be obvious and banal.[16] But they are necessary to establish the urgency of facing those simple historical questions Sanders wishes to finesse (by quoting me, of all people!).[17] If we have a saying assigned to Aqiba how do we know it really was said by him, belonging to the late first and early second century? If we cannot show that it does go back to A.D. 100, then we are not justified in adducing such sayings as evidence of the state of mind of one late first-and early second-century authority, let alone of all the late first-and early second-century authorities – and let alone of "the Rabbis"

---

[16]Only people wholly ignorant of the way in which context, both literary and social, affects interpretation of ideas will even imagine that I here commit reductionism. I need hardly point out that I do not claim the context exhausts the meaning or even definitively establishes the parameters of meaning. That is why I insist these observations are obvious and banal.

[17]See pp. 63-64, 70.

of the later first and whole of the second centuries. I cannot concede that Sanders' notion of systemic description, even if it were wholly effected, has removed from the critical agendum these simple questions of historical study we have yet to answer.

Nor should we ignore the importance in the work, not only of comparison, but also of interpreting a given saying, of establishing the historical context in which the saying was said (or at least in which it was important to be quoted). Sanders many times cites the famous saying attributed to Yohanan b. Zakkai that the corpse does not contaminate, nor does purification water purify, but the whole thing is hocus-pocus. That saying first occurs in a later, probably fourth-century, midrashic compilation. Surely we might wonder whether, at the time of the making of that compilation, issues of magic were not central in rabbinic discourse.[18] The denial of efficacy, ex opere operato, of a scriptural purification rite, addressed to a world in which magic, including Torah magic, was deemed to work ex opere operato, may be interpreted as a powerful polemic against a strong current of the fourth-century Palestinian and Babylonian Jews' life, a time at which Rabbinical circles, among others, were deeply interested in the magical powers inherent in Torah. Now I do not mean to suggest that the proper interpretation of the saying is in accord with this hypothesis,[19] nor do I even propose the stated hypothesis for serious consideration here. I only offer it as an example of one context in which the saying is credibly to be interpreted and, more important, as evidence of the centrality of context in the interpretation of each and every saying. If we do not know where and when a saying was said, how are we to interpret the saying and explain its meaning?

In my view the meaning of a saying is defined, at the outset, by the context in which it is meaningful. To be sure, the saying may remain meaningful later on, so that, cited for other purposes, the saying takes on new meanings. No one denies that obvious proposition, which, after all, is illustrated best of all by the history of the interpretation, but, of greater systemic consequence, the deliberate misinterpretation, of the Old

---

[18]I assemble the evidence on rabbinical wonder-working (magic) in the period under discussion in my *History of the Jews in Babylonia*, vol. 3, *From Shapur I to Shapur II* (Leiden, 1968: E.J. Brill), pp. 102-30; vol. 4, *The Age of Shapur II* (Leiden, 1969: E.J. Brill), pp. 330-63; and vol. 5, *Later Sasanian Times* (Leiden, 1970: E.J. Brill), pp. 174-93. There is some indication that more wonder-working or magical stories are told about third- and fourth-century rabbis than about second-century ones, and this corresponds to a general rise in magical activity.

[19]That is, the story is meant as an antimagical polemic or an effort to claim that the Torah's ritual laws have magical power, a claim very widely advanced in rabbinical circles and also in regard to Jews or Jewish magicians.

Testament in Judaism and Christianity. If that is so, then we surely should not reduce to a fundamentalistic and childish hermeneutical framework the interpretation by sayings attributed to rabbis in rabbinic documents of diverse periods, put together, as I said earlier, for diverse purposes and therefore addressed, it seems to me self-evident, to historically diverse circumstances.

Since this is one of the most ambitious works in Pauline scholarship in twenty-five years and since, as I just said, it does adumbrate initiatives of considerable methodological promise, we must ask ourselves what has gone wrong with Sanders's immense project. I think the important faults are on the surface. First, his book should have been subjected to the reading of two kinds of editors, a good editor for style and a critical editor for the planning and revision of the book. As a whole, it simply does not hang together. Sanders writes in a self-indulgent way. Second, I think Sanders pays too much attention to the anti-Judaism of New Testament scholars. It is true, I suppose, that there is a built-in bias on the part of some of Christian scholarship on Rabbinic Judaism, leading to negative judgments based upon fake scholarship (Sanders's attack on Billerbeck is precise and elegant). But the motive for a major scholarly project must be constructive. One must love one's subject, that is, one's sources and scholarly setting. Third, if, as I believe, Sanders has given us a good proposal on "the holistic comparison of patterns of religion" (pp. 12-24), then he should have tried to allow his book to unfold as an exposition and instantiation of his program of systemic comparison. This he does not do. Fourth, his approach to the rabbinic literature covers too much or too little (I am not sure which). That is, he begins with a sizable description of methodological problems. But when he comes to the substantive exposition of the rabbinic theology important for his larger project, Sanders seems to me to have forgotten pretty much everything he said on method. There are acres and acres of paragraphs which in sum and substance could have been lifted straightaway from Schechter, Moore, or Urbach,[20] to name three other efforts at systematic dogmatics in early rabbinic religion. I found the systematic theology of the Dead Sea Scrolls equally tedious but know too little of the problems of working

---

[20]Solomon Schecter, *Some Aspects of Rabbinic Theology* (beginning in essays in *Jewish Quarterly Review,* 1894); George Foot Moore, *Judaism in the First Centuries of the Christian Era: The Age of the Tannaim* (Cambridge, 1927: Harvard University Press); and Ephraim E. Urbach, *The Sages: Their Concepts and Beliefs* (Jerusalem, 1975: Magnes Press). I cannot imagine how Urbach, fifty years after Moore, has advanced the discussion, except in some matters of detail. Indeed methodologically it is a giant step backward, excluding evidence Moore included and adding an explicit apologetic layer to the discussion left by Moore with a (merely subterranean) apologetic implication.

on those sources to suggest how things might have been done differently and better. But to produce Sanders's substantive results of the theological discussions, from election and covenant to the nature of religious life and experience (pp. 84-232), we simply do not need to be told about critical problems ("the use of Rabbinic material, the nature of Tannaitic literature") laid out earlier (pp. 59-83). In all, it seems to me a bit pretentious, measured against the result.

Still, in Sanders's behalf it must be repeated: He has defined the work to be done in terms which I think are valid and fructifying. He has done his scholarly homework with more than routine ambition. He has laid forth an apologetic for Rabbinic Judaism and a powerful critique of ignorant or malicious or out-and-out anti-Semitic reports of, and judgments on, Rabbinic Judaism (or simply "Judaism"). Even though that theological enterprise cannot be deemed consequential for the study of the history of the religious world of ancient Judaism, it surely is not irrelevant to the context in which that history is written. The book is more than a mere compendium of this and that. It is based upon a carefully thought-through program. Sanders's insistence that when Judaism is studied by Christian scholars, it must be considered without the endemic anti-Judaism characteristic of earlier work, is important for both social and academic reasons. The sort of people who believed that Judaism was depraved also maintained, like Kittel in 1933, that the best solution (if inexpedient) to the Jewish problem was to exterminate the Jews. In its apologetic aspect, Sanders's book addresses itself to a considerable social problem of our age. But, alas, it also is a service to scholarship in the history of religions to insist, as Sanders does, that religions, including Judaism, be studied *sine ire et studio*. So as it is a document of the times, Sanders's book is on the side of life and learning.

That is all the more reason to insist that, in regard to Rabbinic Judaism, Sanders's book also is so profoundly flawed as to be hopeless and, I regret to say it, useless in accomplishing its stated goals of systemic description and comparison. No, systems which have not been accurately described cannot be compared. And the work of description surely involves critical initiatives in selection and interpretation. But to take up the work of interpretation, to design a project of comparison and carry it through, to reckon with the complexities of diverse documents and systems – these are essentially the tasks of our own exegesis of these ancient texts and systems. To effect the comparison of patterns of ancient Judaism, what is needed is our self-conscious exegesis of their unself-conscious exegesis. For the history of religions is the exegesis of exegesis.

# 9

## Sanders's Pharisees and Mine: *Jewish Law from Jesus to the Mishnah*

Despite the risable misnomer of his book of miscellaneous essays, claiming to speak of "Jewish law to the Mishnah" while discussing mere anecdotes and episodes in Jewish law in the first century with special reference to the Gospels, Professor Edward P. Sanders's current account of his views should not be dismissed as the merely random thoughts of one who wanders aimlessly beyond the fence of his field of first-hand knowledge. Holding Sanders to his claim that he knows something about what he calls "Jewish law," let us take seriously his conception of the Pharisees of the first century. Since, intending to persuade colleagues that his picture of, and apologia for, the Pharisees, not mine, accurately portray how things really were in the first century, Sanders devotes two of his five chapters to that subject,[1] we turn forthwith to the contrasting results contained in his current book.

---

[1] I ignore Sanders's uninformed discussion of my *Judaism: The Evidence of the Mishnah*. This "critique" hardly commands attention, either among New Testament scholars, who have no pressing reason to want to know about that document and its place in Judaism; or among Mishnah scholars, to whose field Sanders has yet to make a serious and original contribution. Along these same lines, I find little of interest in the rather naive arguments of H. Maccoby, "Neusner and the Red Cow," *Journal for the Study of Judaism* 1990, 20:59ff. Maccoby states his basic objection to my treatment of that subject – and, by extension, of pretty much everything else – in the following statement:

His general thesis...is that the Mishnah expresses, through the details of ritual, a philosophy of holiness that is, in significant respects, different from that of the Bible, being a response to the historical circumstances of Jewish political helplessness after the destruction of the Temple. It may be objected, however, that this schema is flawed by considerable special pleading and innacuracy [sic!] on Neusner's part. Details of rabbinic law which Neusner wishes to attribute to innovative rabbinic philosophy turn out, time after time, to be mere responses to the biblical text. The 'myth' which Neusner wishes to extract from alleged rabbinic ritual innovations is constructed out of non-existent materials; while the myth to which the rabbis really subscribed is that of the Bible itself, with its major themes of Exodus, Revelation, Desert, and Promised Land – a myth powerful enough to induce submission to the text of scripture and faith in its ability to provide answers to all possible difficulties. Neusner's offered paradigm case of the Mishnah's treatment of the Red Cow rite may serve to illustrate the above criticisms.

There is no reason to quibble at great length with the vague, inaccurate, and misleading précis of my ideas that Maccoby seems to have fabricated for himself. The Mishnah took shape after the Bar Kokhba War, not "after the destruction of the Temple." It is represented by me as a response not to "Jewish political helplessness," which vastly understates Judah the Patriarch's power, but to the religious crisis represented by the failure of the scriptural paradigm, destruction, three generations, return and renewal. It is not the destruction of the Temple in 70 that precipitated a crisis, but the debacle of Bar Kokhba's effort to replicate the rebuilding in the time of the second Isaiah, that I think accounts for the distinctive emphasis of the Mishnah upon the enduring sanctification of the Land and of the people, Israel. Maccoby's inaccurate reading of both sources and scholarship is legendary, and he has yet to persuade a scholar in the area of his own concentration, which is the study of Jesus and Paul, that he has mastered either the sources or the secondary literature. His ignorance of the former and distortion of the latter as a matter of fact have denied him all hearing in reputable scholarship. That is why a protracted response to his "criticism" has not been found productive by any of the many scholars with whom he has tried to pick his fights. In the present context, a brief reply therefore is more than sufficient. On the face of it, this is a claim that the rabbinic system merely restated what the Written Torah (Maccoby's "Bible," but of course he cannot mean that the rabbis drew also upon the New Testament, which is one-half of the Bible) said. That hoary apologetic hardly serves the authentic Judaism of the Dual Torah, which alleges that the oral part of the Torah complements and completes the written part, but also is free-standing. Since numerous Mishnah tractates take up subjects of which the written Torah knows nothing, Maccoby's basic allegation is simply ignorant and inaccurate. But – despite his obvious program of theological apologetics for his particular Judaism to accord him a fair hearing – if I understand Maccoby, what he wishes to claim is that "details...turn out...to be mere responses to the biblical text." I gather that his argument is that since the framers of tractate Parah found support for some of their propositions in verses of Scripture, therefore any claim that they did more than state the plain meaning of Scripture must be rejected. If that is what he wishes to say, then his criticism is simply charming for its naiveté. Every writer from Ezra's closure of the Pentateuch in 450 found in Scripture whatever he wanted, whether Bar Kokhba, Philo, Jesus, or the Teacher of Righteousness, the School of Matthew, or the authorship of a tractate of the Mishnah. Mentioning those six who could well have claimed merely to say what the written Torah had said ("not to destroy but to fulfill") underlines that people could find not only what they wanted, but also the opposite of what they wanted. So at stake in explaining a piece of writing is not whether verses of Scripture could have been adduced in support of what an authorship wished to say, for they always can be and were found, ready at hand, when wanted. At issue, rather, is why someone went looking for proof, chose a

## I. What I Maintain We Know about the Pharisees and How in My View We Know It

Since the announced purpose of the pertinent chapters is to criticize my position and set forth a different one, to begin with let me rapidly summarize my views.[2] Viewed as a historical problem, identifying the

---

given subject to begin with. Maccoby begs the question, of course, unless he can explain why a particular verse of Scripture to begin with attracted attention. Maccoby does not seem to take seriously that the School of Matthew as much as the authorship of Mishnah-tractate Parah found ample support in Scripture for whatever they wished to say. Precisely what he says about the authorship of Mishnah-tractate Parah can and should be said about Mark, Luke, Matthew, and John (among many!). Then are we to dismiss the School of Matthew or can the authorship of Mishnah-tractate Parah therefore be dismissed as mere epigones of Scripture? Not very likely. To the contrary, when we wish to understand a document, the first question (in this context) must be, why this particular topic, as against a vast range of other scriptural topics that are neglected? If the Red Cow, then why not the flight to Egypt? I should be interested in Maccoby's evidence for his allegation that "the rabbis" (I assume in this context he means the authors of the tractate under discussion) have found in "Exodus, Revelation, Desert, and Promised Land" anything pertinent to their Red Cow. I should be curious to know just where, in the tractate under discussion, Maccoby finds his grand themes of "Exodus...," etc. While Sanders is a scholar (though in writing about the law of Judaism, he pretends to an expert knowledge that as we shall see he simply does not have), Maccoby persistently exhibits the deplorable tendency to make things up as he goes along. The widespread realization that his writings on Jesus and Paul are simply bigoted joins with the broad recognition that he is scarcely a master of the sources. Whenever I have had occasion to test an allegation on which Maccoby displays his marvelous certainty, I have found no evidence in support of that allegation, but rather, evidence of Maccoby's incomprehension of the sources and also of the considerations that have led scholars to the conclusions that they have reached. So if I ignore his treatment of the Mishnah, as much as Sanders's, it is because I find it ignorant, and as a matter of fact riddled with inaccuracy. Accordingly, there seems to me no reason to pay much attention to Maccoby any further, and, as I said, I have the impression that colleagues in New Testament scholarship have reached that conclusion as well. In any event the most decisive refutation of Maccoby is given in *Jewish Law* by Sanders himself: "The idea of human intention, greatly and correctly emphasized by Neusner, is original to the Pharisees so far as we know. Thus even when they are only defining or clarifying biblical law, they are operating with some post-biblical categories" (p. 187). What is said in this small context applies throughout, and with that we may dismiss Maccoby as not merely uninformed but, alas, simply uncomprehending. Sanders is a far more formidable figure and demands a sustained and serious hearing for all of his ideas.

[2] My principal results are in two major works, first, *The Rabbinic Traditions about the Pharisees before 70* (Leiden, 1971: E.J. Brill). I-III. I. *The Rabbinic Traditions about the Pharisees before 70. The Masters*. II. *The Rabbinic Traditions about the Pharisees before 70. The Houses*. III. *The Rabbinic Traditions about the Pharisees before 70. Conclusions*. And second, *Eliezer ben Hyrcanus. The Tradition and the Man* (Leiden, 1973: E.J. Brill). I. *Eliezer ben Hyrcanus. The Tradition and the Man. The*

Pharisees begins with attention to the sources that refer to them. No historical knowledge reaches us out of an a priori corpus of principles, and what we cannot show, we simply do not know. A principal problem in arguing with Sanders is his rich capacity to make up distinctions and definitions as he goes along,[3] then to impose these distinctions and definitions upon sources that, on the face of it, scarcely sustain them. Sanders proceeds to form out of a priori distinctions and definitions a deductive argument, which makes it exceedingly difficult to compose an argument with him. For how are those of us who appeal to evidence and the results of the analysis of evidence to compose an argument against fabricated definitions and distinctions, which to begin with derive not from evidence and analysis thereof? The fundamental difficulty in dealing with Sanders, therefore, begins with the basic problem of reading scholarship that is accessible only within its own framework of premises and even language.[4] Looking at the evidence in its own terms, by

---

*Tradition.* II. *Eliezer ben Hyrcanus. The Tradition and the Man. The Man.* I am not sure that Sanders has fully grasped the methodological issues that I have worked out in doing my analysis in this way, rather than in some other. I have given reprises of some of these results in the following: *Oral Tradition in Judaism: The Case of the Mishnah* (New York, 1987: Garland Publishing Co.). Albert Bates Lord Monograph Series of the journal, *Oral Tradition.*; *Das pharisäische und talmudische Judentum* (Tübingen, 1984: J.C.B. Mohr (Paul Siebeck)). Edited by Hermann Lichtenberger. Foreword by Martin Hengel, and *The Pharisees. Rabbinic Perspectives* (New York, 1985: Ktav Publishing House). On problems of method – how we claim to know what we know, on the basis of sources that exhibit the traits of those on which we work – my summary of matters is in *Reading and Believing: Ancient Judaism and Contemporary Gullibility* (Atlanta, 1986: Scholars Press for Brown Judaic Studies).

[3]One example: "Shall we call these 'oral law'? That is just the question. To get at it, I wish to make further distinctions: [1] between conscious and unconscious interpretation of the written law; [2] between interpretation and consciously formulated supplements, alterations or additions, which are known not to be in the law at all. These distinctions are easier to state than to demonstrate, since exegesis can be fanciful and produce results which are now thought to be remote from the text, and since we have no direct access to what was 'conscious' and 'unconscious.' Nevertheless, if we bear these distinctions in mind and consider some examples, we shall improve our understanding of the problem" (*Jewish Law*, pp. 102-103). The most powerful arguments against Sanders's distinctions are stated in his presentation of them: there is no evidence; we also do not know what was "conscious" and what was "unconscious." But these powerful considerations do not impede Sanders's progress. He simply dismisses them and moves ahead. That seems to me a fine instance of how he just makes things up as he goes along.

[4]As a matter of fact, Sanders's prose is so turgid and obscure, not to say deliberately obfuscatory, that reading him produces few of the ordinary pleasures of scholarship. Not only so, but his years in Oxford have left him isolated from the mainstream of learning, with the result that a certain self-

contrast, requires us to classify our documents and analyze them, only afterward turning to the issues of special concern to us.

The Pharisees formed a social entity, of indeterminate classification (sect? church? political party? philosophical order? cult?), in the Jewish nation in the Land of Israel in the century or so before A.D. 70. They are of special interest for two reasons. First, they are mentioned in the Synoptic Gospels as contemporaries of Jesus, represented sometimes as hostile, sometimes as neutral, and sometimes as friendly to the early Christians represented by Jesus. Second, they are commonly supposed to stand behind the authorities who, in the second century, made up the materials that come to us in the Mishnah, the first important document, after Scripture, of Judaism in its classical or normative form. Hence the Mishnah and some related writings are alleged to rest upon traditions going back to the Pharisees before A.D. 70. These views impute to the Pharisees greater importance than, in their own day, they are likely to have enjoyed. My description of the Pharisees, in order of closure: (1) the Gospels, (2) the writings of Josephus, and (3) the later rabbinic compositions, beginning with the Mishnah, hence, in time of closure, ca. A.D. 70-90, ca. A.D. 90-100, and ca. A.D. 200-600, respectively. No writings survive that were produced by them; all we do know is what later writers said about them.

The three separate bodies of information, first, the historical narratives of Josephus, a Jewish historian who, between 75 and ca. 100 A.D., wrote the history of the Jews from the beginnings to the destruction of Jerusalem, second, biographical traditions about, and sayings attributed to, Jesus, and third, the laws and sayings attributed to pre-70 Pharisees by their successors and heirs, the rabbis of late first- and second-century Palestine, are quite different in character. The first is a systematic, coherent historical narrative. The second is a well-edited collection of stories and sayings. The third consists chiefly of laws, arranged by legal categories in codes and commentaries on those codes. Moreover, the purposes of the authors or compilers of the respective collections differ from one another. Josephus was engaged in explaining to the Jewish world of his day that Rome was not at fault for the destruction of the Temple, and in telling the Roman world that the Jewish people had been misled, and therefore not to be held responsible for the terrible war. The interest of the Gospels is not in the history of the Jewish people, but in the life and teachings of Jesus, to which that history

---

indulgence, even solipsism, has taken over in his prose. Following Sanders's arguments requires us to examine evidence, the relevance of which to begin with is never entirely clear. A stream of consciousness seems to provide the momentum for much of his learning.

supplies   The rabbinical legislators show no keen interest in narrative, biographical, or historical problems, but take as their task the promulgation of laws for the government and administration of the Jewish community.

The several sources concerning pre-70 Pharisaic Judaism were generally shaped in the aftermath of the crisis of 70 A.D. With the Temple in ruins it was important to preserve and, especially, to interpret, the record of what had gone before. Josephus tells the story of the people and the great war. The Gospels record the climactic moment in Israel's supernatural life. The rabbis describe the party to which they traced their origin, and through which they claimed to reach back to the authority of Moses at Sinai. The issue in all three cases was: What is the meaning of the decisive history just passed? To Josephus the answer is that Israel's welfare depends upon obedience to the laws of the Torah as expounded by the Pharisees and upon peaceful relationships with Rome. The Gospels claim that, with the coming of the Messiah, the Temple had ceased to enjoy its former importance, and those who had had charge of Israel's life – chief among them the priests, scribes, and Pharisees – were shown through their disbelief to have ignored the hour of their salvation. Their unbelief is explained in part by the Pharisees' hypocrisy and self-seeking. The rabbis contend that the continuity of the Mosaic Torah is unbroken. Destruction of the Temple, while lamentable, does not mean Israel has lost all means of service to the Creator. The way of the Pharisees leads, without break, back to Sinai and forward to the rabbinical circle reforming at Yavneh. The Oral Torah revealed by Moses and handed on from prophet to scribe, sage, and rabbi remains in the hands of Israel. The legal record of pre-70 Pharisaism requires careful preservation because it remains wholly in effect.

The theological side to Pharisaic Judaism before A.D. 70, however, is not easily accessible, for the pre-70 beliefs, ideas, and values have been taken over and revised by the rabbinical masters after that time. We therefore cannot reliably claim that an idea first known to us in a later rabbinical document, from the third century and afterward, was originally both known and understood in the same way. For pre-70 Pharisaic Judaism, our sources of information tell little of theological interest. A number of books in the Apocrypha and Pseudepigrapha of the Old Testament are attributed to Pharisaic writers, but none of these documents positively identifies its author as a Pharisee. Secure attribution of a work can only be made when an absolutely peculiar characteristic of the possible author can be shown to be an essential element in the structure of the whole work. No reliance can be placed on elements which appear in only one or another episode, or which appear in several episodes but are secondary and detachable details. These may be accretions. Above all, motifs which are not certainly peculiar to one sect cannot prove that sect was the source. No available assignment of an apocryphal or pseudepigraphical book to a Pharisaic author can pass these tests. Most such attributions were made by scholars who thought that all pre-70 Palestinian Jews were either Sadducees, Pharisees, Essenes, members of the "Fourth Philosophy," or Zealots, and therefore felt obliged to attribute all supposedly pre-70 Palestinian Jewish works to one of these four groups. That supposition is untenable. That is why, in my account of the Pharisees, I omit all reference to apocryphal and pseudepigraphical.

The rabbinic traditions about the Pharisees before 70 are those pericopae in the Mishnah (ca. A.D. 200) and Tosefta (ca. A.D. 300), often subject to exegesis in later rabbinic writings, in which we find names of either pre-70 masters or the Houses of Shammai and Hillel. Pre-70 masters are the men named in the chains of authorities down to and including Simeon b. Gamaliel and masters referred to in pericopae of those same authorities. The reason these pericopae are held to refer to Pharisees and their authorities is that Gamaliel and Simeon b. Gamaliel are identified by Acts and Josephus, respectively, as Pharisees. They occur, in Mishnah-tractate Avot and other lists of authorities, and it is therefore generally assumed that all others on these same lists or chains of authorities also were Pharisees. Traditions of others who were evidently presumed by the Tannaitic tradents both to have lived before 70 and to have been Pharisees do not add up to much; the traditions are mostly concerned with the masters named in the Pharisaic chains. Few others are known. Authorities who began teaching before 70 but whose traditions derive chiefly from Yavneh, rather than pre-70 Jerusalem, are excluded. These figures in any event do not occur on the lists or chains of authorities, beginning at Sinai and ending with Gamaliel I and his son Simeon.

The rabbinic traditions about the Pharisees before 70 A.D. consists of approximately 371 separate items in the Mishnah – stories or sayings or allusions – which are spread over in approximately 655 different pericopae. Of these traditions, 75 percent – 280, in 456 pericopae – pertain to Menahem, Shammai, Hillel, and the Houses of Hillel and Shammai. A roughly even division of the materials would give twenty-three traditions in forty pericopae to each name or category, so the disparity is enormous. Exact figures cannot be given, for much depends upon how one counts the components of composite pericopae or reckons with other imponderables. As to subject matter covered by the rabbinic traditions that allude to persons or groups we assume to have been Pharisees, approximately 67 percent of all legal pericopae deal with dietary laws. These laws concern [1] ritual purity for meals and [2] agricultural rules governing the fitness of food for pharisaic consumption. Observance of Sabbaths and festivals is a distant third. The named masters normally have legal traditions of the same sort; only Gamaliel greatly diverges from the pattern, Simeon b. Shetah somewhat less so. Of the latter we can say nothing. The wider range of legal topics covered by Gamaliel's legal lemmas and stories goes to confirm the tradition that he had an important position in the civil government.

The rabbinic traditions about the Pharisees as a whole may be characterized as self-centered, the internal records of a party concerning its own life, its own laws, and its own partisan conflicts. The omission of records of what happened outside of the party is not only puzzling, but nearly inexplicable. Almost nothing in Josephus's picture of the Pharisees seems closely related to much, if anything, in the rabbis' portrait of the Pharisees, except the rather general allegation that the Pharisees had 'traditions from the fathers,' a point made also by the Synoptic storytellers. The rabbis' Pharisaic conflict stories moreover do not tell of Pharisees' opposing Essenes, Christians, or Sadducees, but of Hillelites' opposing Shammaites. Pharisaic laws deal not with the governance of the country but with the party's rules for table fellowship. The political issues are not whether one should pay taxes to Rome or how one should know the Messiah, but whether in the Temple the rule of Shammai or that of Hillel should be followed in a minor festal sacrifice. From the rabbinic traditions about the Pharisees we cannot reconstruct a single significant public event of the period before 70 – not the rise, success, and fall of the Hasmoneans, nor the Roman conquest of Palestine, nor the rule of Herod, nor the reign of the procurators, nor the growth of opposition to Rome, nor the proliferation of social violence and unrest in the last decades before 66 A.D., nor the outbreak of the war with Rome. We do not gain a picture of the Pharisees' philosophy of history or theology or politics. We should not even know how Palestine was governed, for the Pharisees' traditions according to the rabbis do not refer to how the Pharisees governed the country. The rabbis never claim the Pharisees did run pre-70 Palestine, at least not in stories told either about named masters or about the Houses, nor do they tell us how the Romans ran it. Furthermore, sectarian issues are barely mentioned, and other sects not at all. The rabbis' Pharisees are mostly figures of the late Herodian and Roman periods. In the rabbinic traditions, they were a non-political group, whose chief religious concerns were for the proper preservation of ritual purity in connection with eating secular (not Temple) food, and for the observance of the dietary laws of the day, especially those pertaining to the proper nurture and harvest of agricultural crops. Their secondary religious concern was with the proper governance of the party itself.

When we compare the rabbinic traditions about the Pharisees, upon which I have concentrated, with Josephus's and the Gospels' traditions, we find the sources not entirely symmetrical. Josephus's Pharisaic records pertain mostly to the years from the rise of the Hasmoneans to their fall. They were a political party which tried to get control of the government of Jewish Palestine, not a little sect drawn apart from the common society by observance of laws of table fellowship. Josephus's Pharisees are important in the reigns of John Hyrcanus and Alexander Jannaeus, but drop from the picture after Alexandra Salome. But the Synoptics' Pharisees appropriately are much like those of the rabbis; they belong to the Roman period, and their legal agenda are virtually identical: tithing, purity laws, Sabbath observance, vows, and the like.

The rabbinic tradition thus begins where Josephus's narrative leaves off, and the difference between them leads us to suspect that the change in the character of Pharisaism from a political party to a sect comes with Hillel. If Hillel was responsible for directing the party out of its political concerns and into more passive, quietistic paths, then we should understand why his figure dominates the subsequent rabbinic tradition. If Hillel was a contemporary of Herod, then we may commend his wisdom, for had the Pharisees persisted as a political force, they would have come into conflict with Alexander Jannaeus. The extreme rarity of materials of masters before Simeon b. Shetah, except those of Yohanan the High Priest = John Hyrcanus, suggests that few survived Jannaeus's massacres, and that those few did not perpetuate the policies, nor, therefore, the decisions of their predecessors. Hillel and his followers chose to remember Simeon b. Shetah, who was on good terms with Salome, but not his followers, who were almost certainly on bad terms with Aristobulus and his descendants, the leaders of the national resistance to Rome and to Antipater's family (see Josephus's story of Aristobulus's protection of the Pharisees' victims). As Herod's characteristics became clear, therefore, the Pharisees must have found themselves out of sympathy alike with the government and the opposition. And at this moment Hillel arose to change what had been a political party into a table fellowship sect, not unlike other, publicly harmless and politically neutral groups, whatever their private eschatological aspirations. All this is more than mere conjecture, but less than established fact. What is fact is that the vast majority of rabbinic traditions about the Pharisees relate to the circle of Hillel and certainly the best attested and most reliable corpus, the opinions of the Houses, reaches us from that circle's later adherents. The pre-Hillel Pharisees are not known to us primarily from the rabbinic traditions, and, when we begin to have a substantial rabbinic record, it is the record of a group very different from Josephus's pre-Hillelite, pre-Herodian party.

Clearcut and well-defined forms were used for the transmission of some of the rabbinic traditions about the Pharisees. This does not prove that these materials originally were orally formulated and orally transmitted. Part of the corpus seems to me to have been ritually shaped according to the myth of how Moses orally dictated, and Aaron memorized, lemmas, namely, those in the Aqiban Mishnah. But the allegation that the present rabbinic material about the pre-70 Pharisees consists of the written texts of traditions originally orally formulated and orally transmitted is groundless. The only allegation we find about pre-70 Pharisees is that they had traditions. Nothing is said about whether these traditions come from Moses, nor about whether they were in oral form. They generally are ascribed to the "fathers," and their form is not specified. No mention of an Oral Torah or a Dual Torah occurs in pre-70 pericopae, except for the Hillel and the convert story, certainly not weighty evidence. Moreover the Pharisaic laws contain no instructions on how materials are to be handed on, nor references to how this actually was done. Allegations that Moses dictated an Oral Torah to Aaron in much the same way as rabbis taught Mishnah first occur with Aqiba, who in fact undertook exactly that process in the formulation of his Mishnah. The myth of oral formulation and oral transmission is first attested by Judah b. Ilai, although a dispute between Eliezer and Aqiba presupposes oral formulation and transmission in Yavnean circles. The myth of the Oral Torah is first attested much later in the formation of the rabbinic literature and is never in a document prior to ca. A.D. 200 assigned to a Pharisaic authority (the attribution to Hillel of such a belief appears for the first time in the Talmud of Babylonia, ca. A.D. 600).

If, therefore, we ask, precisely what is known from the Mishnah about pre-70 Pharisaism, the answer is clear. The traditions pertain chiefly to the last half-century or so before the destruction of the Temple – at most, seventy or eighty years. Then the Pharisees were (whatever else they were) primarily a society for table fellowship, the high point of their life as a group. The laws of table fellowship predominate in the Houses disputes, as they ought to – three-fourths of all pericopae – and correspond to the legal agenda of the Pharisees according to the Synoptic stories. As we saw, some rather thin and inadequate traditions about masters before Shammai-Hillel persisted, but these do not amount to much and in several cases consist merely of the name of a master, plus whatever opinion is given to him in the chain in which he appears. The interest of the non-legal materials concentrates on the relationships of Shammai and Hillel, on the career of Hillel, and related matters. Materials on their successors at best are perfunctory, until we come to men who themselves survived to work at Yavneh, such as Hananiah Prefect of the Priests and, of course, Yohanan b. Zakkai. The chief interest of Hillel tradents, apart from the preservation of favorable stories of Hillel and the attribution of wise sayings to him, was Hillel's predominance in Pharisaism.

After the Houses disputes ceased to matter much, by the Bar Kokhba War, the growth of Hillel materials was undiminished. The rise to power stories then begin, very likely at Usha, and are rapidly glossed by patriarchal and antipatriarchal hands, so that by Judah the Patriarch's time everyone knows Hillel is the ancestor of the patriarchate in general, and of Judah in particular. The attribution of a Davidic ancestor to Hillel naturally means that the patriarch Judah also derives from the Messianic seed. The work of Yavneh consisted, therefore, in establishing viable forms for the organization and transmission primarily of the Houses materials. The Ushans continued to make use of these forms, and further produced a coherent account of the history of the Oral Torah from Moses onward. The Yavneans probably showed greater interest in the development of stories about the relationships between the Houses than did later masters, for whom the disputes were less interesting. The Ushans may have augmented the traditions of other early masters, besides Shammai-Hillel, and otherwise broadened the range of interests.

So, in all, we have from the rabbis a very sketchy account of the life of Pharisaism during less than the last century of its existence before 70, with at most random and episodic materials pertaining to the period before Hillel. We have this account, so far as it is early, primarily through the medium of forms and mnemonic patterns used at Yavneh and later on at Usha. What we know is what the rabbis of Yavneh and Usha regarded as the important and desirable account of the Pharisaic traditions: almost entirely the internal record of the life of the party and its laws, the party being no more than the two factions that predominated after 70, the laws being mainly rules of how and what people might eat with one another. The focus of interest of the rabbinic traditions about the Pharisees is the internal affairs of the Pharisaic party itself. The primary partisan issues center upon Shammai's and his House's relationship to Hillel and his House. The competing sects, by contrast, are ignored. Essenes and Christians make no appearance at all. The Sadducees are first mentioned by Yohanan b. Zakkai. The Romans never occur. The Hasmonean monarchy is reduced to a single name, Yannai the King, for Yohanan the High Priest, so far as the rabbinic traditions about the Pharisees are concerned, was a good Pharisee. In all, the traditions give the impression of intense concentration on the inner life of the party, or sect, whose intimate affairs take precedence, in the larger scheme of history, over the affairs of state, cult, and country. The state is a shadowy presence at best. The cult is of secondary importance. The country's life and the struggle with Rome as a whole are bypassed in silence. What we have, therefore, are the records of the party chiefly in regard to the life of the party itself.

There is a striking discontinuity among the three principal sources which speak of the Pharisees before 70, the Gospels, and the rabbinic writings of a later period, on the one side, and Josephus, on the other. What Josephus thinks characteristic of the Pharisees are matters which play little or no role in what Mark and Matthew regard as significant, and what the later rabbis think the Pharisees said scarcely intersects with the topics and themes important to Josephus. In this regard, the picture drawn by Matthew and Mark and that drawn by the later rabbis are essentially congruent, and together differ from the portrait left to us by Josephus. The traits of Pharisaism emphasized by Josephus, their principal beliefs and practices, nowhere occur in the rabbinic traditions of the Pharisees. When we compare what Josephus says about the Pharisees to what the later rabbinic traditions have to say, there is scarcely a point of contact, let alone intersection. Josephus says next to nothing about the predominant issues in the rabbinic traditions about the Pharisees. Shammai and Hillel are not explicitly mentioned, let alone their Houses. Above all, we find not the slightest allusion to laws of ritual purity, agricultural taboos, Sabbath and festivals, and the like, which predominate in the traditions of the Houses. In the detailed account of the reign of Alexander Jannaeus, Simeon b. Shetah does not occur. Apart from the banquet of John Hyrcanus, we could not, relying upon Josephus, recover a single significant detail of the rabbinic traditions about the Pharisees, let alone the main outlines of the whole.

As to the topical program of the Pharisees, Josephus's agenda of Pharisaic doctrine hardly coincide with those of the rabbis. For example, while Josephus seems to paraphrase Aqiba's saying, that all is in the hands of Heaven yet man has free choice, that saying is nowhere attributed to pre-70 Pharisees, certainly not to the Pharisees who would have flourished in the period in which Josephus places such beliefs. We find no references to the soul's imperishability, all the more so to the transmigration of souls. The Houses' debate on the intermediate group comes closest to Josephus's report. As to Josephus's allegation that the Pharisees are affectionate to one another, we may observe that is not how the Hillelites report matters. Josephus knows nothing of the Shammaites' slaughter of Hillelites, their mob action against Hillel in the Temple, and other stories that suggest a less than affectionate relationship within the Pharisaic group. So, for Josephus, the three chief issues of sectarian consequence are belief in fate, belief in traditions outside of the Laws of Moses, and influence over political life. The Pharisees believe in fate, have traditions from the fathers, and exercise significant influence in public affairs. The Sadducees do not believe in fate, do not accept other than Mosaic laws, and have no consequence in public life. For the rabbinic traditions about the Pharisees, the three chief issues of sectarian consequence are ritual purity, agricultural taboos, and Sabbath and festival behavior.

The relationship between the rabbinic traditions about the Pharisees and the Gospels' accounts of the Pharisees by contrast strikes me as entirely symmetrical. One topic on which these sources are apt to be essentially sound, namely, the themes of the laws they impute to the figures before 70 who we believe were Pharisees. The congruity in the themes of the laws attributed to the Pharisees by both the Gospels and the later rabbinic sources is striking. What it means is that, from speaking of traditions about the Pharisees, we are apt to address the historical Pharisees themselves in the decades before the destruction of the Temple in A.D. 70. The historical Pharisees in the decades before the destruction of Jerusalem are portrayed by legal traditions that seem to me fundamentally sound in topic, perhaps also in detailed substance, and attested by references of masters who may reasonably be supposed to have known what they were talking about. Which laws pertained primarily to Pharisaism, and which were part of the law common to all of Palestinian Jewry? Most of the laws before us, verified early or late, affect primarily the sectarian life of the party. The laws that made a sect sectarian were those which either were interpreted and obeyed by the group in a way different from other groups or from common society at large, on the one hand, or were to begin with observed only by the group, on the other. In the latter category are the purity laws, which take so large a place in the Pharisaic corpus. One primary mark of Pharisaic commitment was the observance of the laws of ritual purity outside of the Temple, where everyone kept them. Eating one's secular, that is, unconsecrated, food in a state of ritual purity as if one were a Temple priest in the cult was one of the two significations of party membership. The manifold circumstances of everyday life required the multiplication of concrete rules. Representative of the other category may be the laws of tithing and other agricultural taboos. Here we are less certain. Pharisees clearly regarded keeping the agricultural rules as a primary religious duty. But whether, to what degree, and how other Jews did so is not clear. And the agricultural laws, just like the purity rules, in the end affected table fellowship, namely, what one might eat.

The early Christian traditions on both points represent the Pharisees as reproaching Jesus because his followers did not keep these two kinds of laws at all. That is, why were they not Pharisees? The answer was that the primary concern was for ethics. Both the question and the answer are disingenuous. The questioners are represented as rebuking the Christians for not being Pharisees which begs the question, for everyone presumably knew Christians were not Pharisees. The answer takes advantage of the polemical opening: Pharisees are not concerned with ethics, a point repeatedly made in the anti-Pharisaic pericopae, depending upon a supposed conflict between rules of table fellowship, on the one side, and ethical behavior on the other. The obvious underlying claim is that Christian table fellowship does not depend upon the sorts of rules important in the table fellowship of other groups. As to the Sabbath laws, the issue was narrower. All Jews kept the Sabbath. It was part of the culture of their country. The same applies to the festivals. Here the Pharisaic materials are not so broad in interest as with regard to agricultural rules and ritual purity. They pertain primarily to gentiles' working on the Sabbath for Jews, on the one hand, and to the preparation of the *c*erub, on the other. Like the Levirate rule, the *c*erub laws must be regarded as solely of sectarian interest. The references to the unobservant Sadducee make this virtually certain. Since the tithes and offerings either went to the Levites and priests or had to be consumed in Jerusalem, and since the purity rules were to begin with Temple matters, we note that the Pharisees claimed laymen are better informed as to purity and Temple laws than the Temple priesthood.

The fact is, therefore, that the laws we have are the laws we should have: the rules of a sect concerning its own sectarian affairs, matters of importance primarily to its own members. That seems to me further evidence of the essential accuracy of the representation of the Houses in the rabbinic traditions. To be sure, not all laws before us portray with equal authenticity the life of pre-70 Pharisaism. But the themes of the laws, perhaps also their substance in detail, are precisely what they ought to have been according to our theory of sectarianism. When we review the substance of the laws, we find they pertain either immediately or ultimately to table fellowship, involve preparation of food, ritual purity, either purity rules directly relating to food, or purity rules indirectly important on account of the need to keep food ritually clean, and agricultural rules pertaining to the proper growing, tithing, and preparation of agricultural produce for table use. All agricultural laws concern producing or preparing food for consumption, assuring either that tithes and offerings have been set aside as the Law requires or that the conditions for the nurture of the crops have conformed to the biblical taboos. Ritual slaughter, appropriately, occurs in only one minor matter, likewise the taboo against milk with meat is applied to chicken and cheese. The laws of ritual cleanness apply in the main to the preservation of the ritual cleanness of food, of people involved in preparing it, and of objects used in its preparation. Secondary considerations include the ritual pool. These matters became practically important in the lives of Pharisees in regard to the daily preparation of food, in the lives of all

Jews only in connection with visiting the Temple, and of the priests in the cult itself. Laws regarding Sabbath and festivals furthermore pertain in large measure to the preparation and preservation of food on festivals and the Sabbath. The ritual of table fellowship also included blessings and rules of conduct at meals.

If the Pharisees were, as has often been taken for granted, primarily a group for Torah study (as the Qumranian writers describe themselves) then we should have looked for more rules about the school, perhaps also scribal matters, than we actually find. Indeed, we have only one, and that, while attested at early Yavneh, merely involves sneezing in the schoolhouse. Surely other, more fundamental problems presented themselves. Nor do we find much interest in defining the master disciple relationship, the duties of the master and the responsibilities and rights of the disciple, the way in which the disciple should learn his lessons, and similar matters of importance in later times. That is not to suggest that the historical Pharisees were only or principally a table fellowship commune. It is only to say that, whatever else they were, they surely identified themselves as Pharisees by the dietary rules, involving cultic cleanness, and certain other sectarian practices as to marital relationships, that they observed. More than this we do not know on the basis of the rabbinic evidence, as correlated with the Gospels' accounts. Josephus's picture of the group is asymmetrical to this picture, and a simple hypothesis is to assign his account to the period of which he speaks when he mentions the Pharisees as a political party, which is the second and first centuries B.C., and the rabbis' and Gospels' account to the period of which they speak, which is the first century A.D. But the matter remains open for continued inquiry, and no picture of the Pharisees has gained complete acceptance in twentieth-century scholarship. That is my picture of the matter.[5]

Now to Sanders's critique and his concommitant reconstruction of the matter. He deals with two consequential matters, first, "did the Pharisees have oral law?" and second, "did the Pharisees eat ordinary food in purity?" To these questions I state my answer up front. So far as Sanders claims to argue with me in particular, I have not called into question the proposition that, in addition to Scriptures, Pharisees, like pretty much every other group, had some further law or tradition, and that that additional material could have been formulated and transmitted orally, in memory. But, as a matter of fact, no evidence pertaining in

---

[5]Most recently I have summarized my views as set forth in my *Theologische Realencyclopädie* (forthcoming). In that restatement, I have taken account of important criticism of some of my earlier ideas and removed from the picture elements that no longer seem to me to be viable.

particular to the Pharisees permits us to impute to them the fully exposed myth of the Dual Torah, part in writing, part oral, that comes to complete expression only in the later documents of the Judaism of the Dual Torah, in particular, in the Talmud of Babylonia. As to whether Pharisees ate ordinary food in a state of cultic cleanness, I of course do not know what they actually did. I claim to know only how the earlier strata of the Mishnah's law represents matters in sayings attributed to authorities before 70. And the answer is, the earlier strata of the law take for granted that the laws of cultic cleanness, applicable to priests' eating their Temple food, are assumed to apply outside of the Temple, and also to persons who were not members of the priestly caste.

## II. Did the Pharisees have Oral Law?

While announcing that he agrees with me, Sanders claims to find confusing my treatments of this matter. But the source of his confusion is that he imputes to me that same confusion between history and theology that characterizes his work. I am consistently explicit on that distinction, for example, *"viewed from the perspective of Judaic faith,* the teachings of the named sages of late antiquity...preserve principles...handed on by tradition from Sinai."[6] I am equally clear that, *described historically,* the conception that "Moses received the Torah at Sinai in two media" emerges at a given point, fairly late in the formative history of the Judaism of the Dual Torah. Obviously, a critical historical account presents information of one kind, a theological statement, information of another.[7] Sanders states:

> He continues to publish things whose [sic!] fundamentalism would embarrass the most conservative talmudists.[8]

What Sanders means by "fundamentalism" is not clear to me, since, in Judaism, we have no "fundamentalism" in the Protestant sense. I have

---

[6]Sanders, p. 111.

[7]Sanders's representation of the matter becomes contemptible when he says, "It is possible that one of these completely contradictory stances is Neusner's real position, and that the other is adopted simply for tactical purposes, perhaps to sell books to a different audience." I would not have thought that a scholarly debate would sink to such a level, but, as I said above, perhaps the ambience at Oxford has made its impact, so that Sanders has lost such capacity as he once might have had to conduct civil discourse. I am amazed that a publisher of the repute of Trinity Press International and SCM Press would include such libelous statements in a book under their imprint. But suing for libel would be no fun; and anyhow, my books sell too well for me to require subterfuge; perhaps Sanders means to impute to me motives that in his mind would lead him to do what he says I have done?

[8]*Jewish Law,* p. 244.

never misrepresented myself. I am a believing and practicing Jew, without apology. I affirm with all my heart that God revealed the one whole Torah, oral and written, to Moses, our rabbi, on Mount Sinai. I have produced historical results that impart to that statement of faith and theology a set of meanings that are not historical at all. This I have shown in many passages (which as a Christian Sanders evidently finds offensive) of my writing, but especially in *Uniting the Dual Torah: Sifra and the Problem of the Mishnah.*[9] The closing lines of that book form a statement of what we can mean by "Moses received Torah at Sinai," when that is taken to refer to not historical but other matters altogether, matters of eternity, sanctification, and salvation, for example. I have not confused history with theology, nor have I followed the model of those biblical theologians whose historical work leads them to modify theological truth in light of facts of a different order altogether. In my view history contains no truth for theological consideration. A deeper understanding of Judaism as a living religion would have helped Sanders avoid the dreadful confusion that characterizes these remarks, which impede his appreciation of Judaism then as much as now.

In point of fact, however, Sanders concurs with everything that I have maintained on this topic. Explicitly concurring with my results, Sanders proceeds to give a survey of matters on Oral Torah that he finds in various rabbinic documents. Some of these passages attribute views to pre-70 authorities we assume were Pharisees; most do not, and therefore his account draws upon evidence not pertinent to the Pharisees in particular. Since Sanders himself admits that "we have come to a view proposed by Neusner on the basis of a partially different body of evidence," it hardly seems interesting to spell out all of the mistakes Sanders makes in selecting and interpreting the evidence he deems pertinent, nor is time devoted to pointing out the confusion of distinct bodies of evidence well spent.[10] In this chapter Sanders affirms precisely the results that I have set forth, and I congratulate him.

### III. Did the Pharisees Eat Ordinary Food in Purity?

Here again, Sanders's conclusion is "Neusner's standards for collective evidence mark a distinct advance." He concurs with much that I say, tinkering with nuance and emphasis, rather than with fact and substance.[11] But there can be an argument, since he also maintains, "He

---

[9](Cambridge and New York, 1990: Cambridge University Press).

[10]Sanders discusses so many groups that quite how evidence drawn from any one of them pertains to the principal group under discussion is not at all clear.

[11]Perhaps this fundamental agreement with my methods and results accounts for the captious and often deliberately insulting character of his treatment of not only

misinterpreted his own material. Use of his analytical work leads to other conclusions about the Pharisees than the ones which he drew."[12] On method Sanders and I differ in one fundamental way. He takes as generally reliable attributions of sayings to named authorities. Since in

---

my work but also my person. I cannot, for example, find in his writings a single point, beginning to end, at which he refers to me as a professor or by any other honorific title, only "Neusner." This is not merely a matter of form. Sanders takes up two conflicting positions – [1] respect for my methods and replication, with his own emphases, of most of my results, and [2] deep disrespect for me as a person and a scholar. These lead him to characterize in a thoroughly dishonest manner the reception of my books, e.g., in published book reviews. He says, "He has also produced a vast number of translations, to which there are only a few critical responses." Here he footnotes *one* book review alone, Saul Lieberman's in *Journal of the American Oriental Society* 1984, 104:315-19. There were other negative reviews, and also a great many more positive reviews, to which a footnote meant to be fair also would have alluded. Not that I have found much to learn, other than corrections of minor details, in even the most offensive reviews; my impression is that Sanders approves the intention of Lieberman and Zeitlin, among others, which always was merely to discredit, rather than to argue; but for his part, to his credit, he does argue. I take pride in the literature of discrediting that has been devoted to me; it has shown me the worst criticism a critic can fabricate, and that has proven lightweight and unpersuasive. Sanders, to his credit, has not gone along with the campaign of sustained *Todscheigen* – murder by silence, meaning, not reviewing, not citing, not arguing with my work – that Israeli and Yeshiva-scholarship (including university-based yeshivas) has practiced against me for thirty years. Indeed, lest anyone imagine that I would suppress the writings of these critics, I have included an entire volume of negative reviews of books of mine, by not only Lieberman, but also Zeitlin, S. J.D. Cohen, H. Maccoby, and others, in my edition of reprinted articles, *The Origins of Judaism. Religion, History, and Literature in Late Antiquity*. With William Scott Green (New York, 1991: Garland Press). Twenty volumes of reprinted scholarly essays, with introductions. He further states, "There are comments to be made at each point of his publishing enterprise." Here his footnote is as follows: "On Neusner's undergraduate textbooks, see my review of Judaism in the Beginning of Christianity, *Theology* 88, 1985, pp. 392ff. (He said the same thing about the same book in the same review in *Journal of Religion*.) A fair representation of positive reviews of my textbooks would have required pages of citations. The point is that he seems to find himself forced over and over again to affirm my methods and my results, revising only details, mainly of emphasis or evaluation, but that fact does not persuade him to treat with even minimal courtesy and respect someone from whom, by his own word, he has learned so much. I regret that it is necessary to call attention to this disagreeable fact about Sanders, but any reader of the book to which I am called upon to respond will have made the same observation, and it should be made explicit – and regretted. He could have disagreed with courtesy and even amiability – and above all, with honesty and objectivity. I do not believe that he has. And I do not think he has gained anything or made his position more plausible by expressing his disagreement, which turns out to be trivial and niggling, in such offensive language.

[12]*Jewish Law*, p. 131.

historical study what we cannot show, we do not know, I am inclined to a more reserved position, asking for evidence that permits us to assign to a period in which a named authority is assumed to have lived a saying attributed to that authority. Beyond that point, the evidence in hand does not permit us to go, since we do not have books written by specific, named authorities, or even collections of sayings formed prior to, and demonstrably utilized by, the compilers and editors of the late, anonymous documents that we do have. Sanders concedes that materials attributed to the Houses in fact were formulated after 70. But that does not prevent him from using those materials he chooses for evidence on the *topics* under discussion.[13] If however the attributions are not reliable, then how can we know for sure that people at that time talked about the topics?

Sanders accuses me of not noting "the importance of the distinctions which the Houses made between the priests' food and their own with regard to harvesting, handling, and processing it." The locus classicus for those distinctions between food prepared in conditions of cultic cleanness for use in the Temple by the priests, and food prepared in conditions of cultic cleanness for use other than in the Temple by the priests, must be Mishnah-tractate Hagigah 2:5-3:3. Because it is fundamental, let me place it into the hands of the reader, and only then specify why I think it is important.[14]

### 2:5

A.  They wash the hands for eating unconsecrated food, tithe, and heave-offering;

B.  and for eating food in the status of Holy Things they immerse;

C.  and as to [the preparation of] purification water through the burning of the red cow, if one's hands are made unclean, his entire body is deemed to be unclean as well.

### 2:6

A.  He who immerses for the eating of unconsecrated food and is thereby confirmed as suitable for eating unconsecrated food is prohibited from eating tithe.

B.  [If] he immersed for eating tithe and is thereby confirmed as suitable for eating tithe, he is prohibited from eating heave-offering.

---

[13]Ibid., p. 171.

[14]But there are equally probative examples to be adduced, e.g., from Mishnah-tractate Tohorot Chapter Two, which, like the passage at hand, place within a single continuum, so far as cultic cleanness of food in the Temple and not in the Temple is concerned, priests and nonpriests. That passage does not make explicit reference to the Pharisees, which is why I have given the present one as my single example, among countless candidates.

C.  [If] he immersed for eating heave-offering and is thereby confirmed as suitable for eating heave-offering, he is prohibited from eating food in the status of Holy Things.

D.  [If] he immersed for eating food in the status of Holy Things and is thereby confirmed as suitable for eating food in the status of Holy Things, he is prohibited from engaging in the preparation of purification water.

E.  [If, however,] one immersed for the matter requiring the more stringent rule, he is permitted to engage in the matter requiring the less stringent rule.

F.  [If] he immersed but was not confirmed, it is as though he did not immerse.

### 2:7

A.  The clothing of ordinary folk is in the status of midras uncleanness for abstainers [= Perushim, Pharisees].

B.  The clothing of abstainers is in the status of midras uncleanness for those who eat heave-offering [priests].

C.  The clothing of those who eat heave-offering is in the status of midras uncleanness for those who eat Holy Things [officiating priests].

D.  The clothing of those who eat Holy Things is in the status of midras uncleanness for those engaged in the preparation of purification water.

E.  Yosef b. Yoezer was the most pious man in the priesthood, but his handkerchief was in the status of midras uncleanness so far as eating Holy Things was concerned.

F.  For his whole life Yohanan b. Gudegedah ate his food in accord with the requirements of cleanness applying to Holy Things, but his handkerchief was in the status of midras uncleanness so far as those engaged in the preparation of purification water were concerned.

### 3:1

A.  A more stringent rule applies to Holy Things than applies to heave-offering,

I   B.  for: They immerse utensils inside of other utensils for purification for use with [food in the status of] heave-offering,

C.  but not for purification for use with [food in the status of Holy Things.

II  D.  [They make a distinction among] outer parts, inside, and holding place in the case of use for heave-offering,

E.  but not in the case of use for Holy Things.

III F.  He who carries something affected by midras uncleanness [may also] carry heave-offering,

G.  but [he may] not [also carry food in the status of] Holy Things.

IV  H.  The clothing of those who are so clean as to be able to eat heave-offering

I.  is deemed unclean in the status of midras uncleanness for the purposes of Holy Things.

J.  The rule for Holy Things is not like the rule for heave-offering.

| V | K. | For in the case of [immersion for use of] Holy Things one unties a knot and dries it off, immerses and afterwards ties it up again. |
|---|----|----|
|   | L. | And in the case of heave-offering one ties it and then one immerses. |

### 3:2

| VI | A. | Utensils which are completely processed in a state of insusceptibility to uncleanness [and so when completed are clean] require immersion for use in connection with Holy Things, |
|----|----|----|
|    | B. | but not for use in connection with heave-offering. |
| VII | C. | A utensil unites everything contained therein for the purposes of Holy Things, |
|    | D. | but not for the purposes of heave-offering. |
| VIII | E. | [That which is made unclean in] the fourth remove from the original source of uncleanness in the case of Holy Things is invalid, |
|    | F. | but only [that which is made unclean in] the third in the case of heave-offering. |
| IX | G. | And in the case of heave-offering, if one of one's hands is made unclean, the other is clean. |
|    | H. | But in the case of Holy Things one has to immerse both of them. |
| X | I. | For one hand imparts uncleanness to the other for the purposes of Holy Things, |
|    | J. | but not for the purposes of heave-offering. |

### 3:3

| XI | A. | With unclean hands they eat food which has not been wet down in the case of heave-offering, |
|----|----|----|
|    | B. | but not in the case of Holy Things. |
| XII | C. | He who [prior to interment of the deceased] mourns his next of kin [without having contracted corpse uncleanness] and one whose atonement rite is not complete [because an offering is yet required] require immersion for the purposes of Holy Things, |
|    | D. | but not for the purposes of heave-offering. |

The passage distinguishes between the cleanness required for eating unconsecrated food, food that has been designated as tithe or priestly rations ("heave-offering"), and food that is in the status of Holy Things. "Holy Things" are the share of the officiating (or other) priests in what has been offered on the altar, for example, the priests' share of the sin-offering. Priestly rations comprise the share of a crop that the farmer designates for transfer to the priesthood. Scripture certainly takes for granted that Holy Things will be eaten in the Temple, therefore in a state of cultic cleanness, and priestly rations are supposed likewise to be eaten in a condition of cultic cleanness; since the family of the priest likewise eats priestly rations, it is assumed that women and children not located in the Temple at the time of their meal likewise will be concerned about cultic cleanness when it comes to eating this food as well. The nub of the matter is the classification of food called "unconsecrated." Unconsecrated food is food that has no relationship to the cult or the

Temple. If one eats it with considerations of cultic cleanness in mind at all, then, there can be only one reason, and that is, that someone proposes to eat unconsecrated food in a state of cultic cleanness. That seems to me the simple fact of the matter, and Sanders's ingenious distinctions and definitions notwithstanding, that remains the plain sense of the numerous passages that distinguish among unconsecrated food, priestly rations, and Holy Things.

We see that there are diverse standards of cultic cleanness that pertain to food that is unconsecrated, priestly ration, and Holy Things, and these standards are of course hierarchical,[15] with the most stringent rules (the details of which we may bypass) required for Holy Things, less stringent ones for priestly rations, and least stringent for unconsecrated food. Now to my way of thinking, when at M. Hagigah 2:7A-C we are told that the clothing of ordinary folk is in the status of midras uncleanness for Pharisees, and that of Pharisees in the same state for those who eat heave-offering, in the present context it seems to me that a single conclusion must be drawn. Pharisees, 2:7A, are concerned with cultic cleanness; they are not the same as priests, who are dealt with at 2:7B, but are of a lesser standing in the hierarchy of cultic cleanness. Then priests eating priestly rations or heave-offering are hierarchically situated as well, now at a lesser status than priests who are going to eat Holy Things deriving from the altar. The context throughout is preparation for eating food, as the language that is used demonstrates. The explicit reference to Pharisees certainly yields the thesis that Pharisees are not classified as priest, that is, as persons who eat priestly rations or heave-offering. But they are persons who are placed within the hierarchy of cultic cleanness in eating food. The food that they eat is not food that is reserved for priests, so it can only be food that is not reserved for priests, which is to say, secular or unconsecrated food. That passage on the face of it therefore sustains the view that Pharisees are persons who eat unconsecrated food in a state of cultic cleanness, or, more accurately, within the hierarchy of states of cultic cleanness that the Mishnah's paragraph's framer proposes to spell out.

Now let us turn directly to Sanders's own thesis.[16] It is best to turn directly to the passage I have cited, since where and how Sanders's

---

[15]The hierarchical classification of all things define's the Mishnah's authorships' principal concern, as I have shown in my *Judaism as Philosophy. The Method and Message of the Mishnah* (Columbia, 1991: University of South Carolina Press).

[16]I cannot imagine that anyone is interested in my point by point refutation of either Sanders's critique of my work or Sanders's interpretation – or rather, systematic misinterpretation – of a vast number of passages. He constantly alludes to passages that he does not present and analyze, and he imputes to said passages positions and opinions that are not obvious to others who have read the

Pharisees differ from mine is best discerned on the common ground of shared evidence. He states the following:

> Hagigah 2.7 fits Pharisees into a hierarchy...it indicates that Pharisees were more scrupulous with regard to one (minor) form of impurity than were other laypeople.[17]
>
> How important were these rules to the Pharisees? Purity was certainly important to them, and protecting the priesthood and the temple from impurity was a very substantial concern. The purity of their own food seems to have been of less importance...[18]
>
> ...since Pharisees did not observe the purity laws of the priesthood with regard to their own food, why did they have so many rules about corpse impurity and midras impurity? I propose, To make minor gestures towards extra purity. I call them minor gestures in comparison with what they are thought to have done: expelled their wives, done all the domestic work one week in four, and so on. The word 'minor,' however, probably misleads us with regard to their own intention. It sounds as if they made the comparison which I have made, and found their own efforts trivial. This is most unlikely. We cannot assign precise motives, but I think we can safely assign a general one: to be pure, because purity is good.[19]

Apart from the rather subjective judgment at the end, which begs the question, I could not have said it better myself. That is precisely what my reading of this, and various other, passages tells me. When Sanders proceeds to announce that the Pharisees also did other things, for example, "they worked from dawn to dusk...and they had to study," he cannot imagine anyone is going to be surprised. But he proceeds, "The legal discussions attributed to Pharisees never take study as their topic, and thus mechanical counting failed to reveal to Neusner that it is a main theme. It is the basis of the entirety of the material, and every discussion rests on it." Here, alas, Sanders confuses an activity with the mythology attached to the activity. No one doubts people acquired information, that is, studied. What I have called into question is whether Torah study as the principal mode for the imitation of God, which the later rabbinic Torah myth set forth as a critical and central proposition, is attested in the rabbinic traditions about the Pharisees. I did not find it there, and Sanders's reminder that people learned things is, like much else that he says, monumentally irrelevant to the issue. In the successor system, first attested by writings that reached closure long after the first century,

---

same passages; we are left only with his claims. His catalogue of "rather a lot of things wrong with Neusner's work" (p. 183) serves to state merely that he disagrees with me about this and that, which I may stipulate as fact.

[17]*Jewish Law*, pp. 206-207.

[18]Ibid., p. 234.

[19]Ibid., p. 235.

knowledge more than merely informs, it saves. What happens to me in Torah study in the theory of the religious successor system that does not happen to me in Torah study in the theory of the Mishnah – itself no Pharisaic writing – is that I am changed in my very being. This transformation of the one who knows is not alone as to knowledge and understanding (let alone mere information), nor even as to virtue and taxic status, but as to what the knower *is*. The one who knows Torah is changed and saved by Torah knowledge, becomes something different from, better and more holy than, what he was before he knew, and whether the complement is "the mysteries" or "the Torah [as taught by sages]" makes no material difference.[20] When Sanders tells me that people learned things and so alleges that Torah study was a "main theme" of Pharisaism, he shows that he does not grasp the point of the myth of Torah study within the Judaism of the Dual Torah. Scarcely a single passage that is supposed to pertain to the pre-70 Pharisees imagines such a gnostic Torah. But of this Sanders grasps absolutely nothing.

## IV. Sectarianism, Exclusivism, and Sanders's Protestant Theological Apologetic for a Judaism in the Protestant Model

What is at stake? My reading of the evidence leads me to treat the Pharisees as ordinary people eating meals at home in conditions that are analogous to the conditions required of priests in the Temple or in their homes. Sanders treats Pharisees as people who were "more scrupulous with regard to one (minor) form of impurity than were other laypeople." I see here a distinction that yields no difference at all. Anyone who can tell me how this difference – scarcely in degree, but not at all in kind – has persuaded Sanders to spend so much time on details of the law of the Mishnah and Tosefta, which he time and again either reads out of context or simply does not understand at all, will win my thanks. Sanders minimizes purity laws, it would seem, because he wants to argue against the notion of Pharisaic "exclusivism."[21] Sanders wishes to deny that the category, "sect," applies to the Pharisees:

> ...we should reserve the word "sect" for a group which was to an appreciable degree *cut off* from mainline society. It should *reject* some important part of the rest of society, or it should *create* an alternative structure. Neusner frequently compared the Pharisees to the Dead Sea Sect, finding basic agreements and minor differences. But the

---

[20]I spell out this matter in my *The Transformation of Judaism. From Philosophy to Religion* (Champaign, 1991: University of Illinois Press).
[21]*Jewish Law*, pp. 236–42.

differences are large and clear, and they show that one was a sect and the other not.[22]

Of course a group that did not set up a commune off all by itself is different from a group that by all evidence remained within the common society, and if the former is a sect, then the latter is something else. We need not quibble; I think my definition, functions well: a group of people who interpreted and obeyed law "in a way different from other groups or from society at large."[23] But if he means that while the Essene Community was exclusivist but the Pharisees were not, then we really do differ in a fundamental way. In my judgment every Judaism, including the Pharisees' Judaic system, by definition is exclusivist, in that it identifies who is saved and who is not. That the authors of the Gospels saw the Pharisees as a distinct "group," whether the group be classified as a sect, a party, a club, or something else, seems to me to underline that the group was exclusivist, as indeed were the various Christianities and the other Judaisms of the same time and place – by nature, by definition. Why not?

Sanders responds to a long tradition of anti-Judaism and even anti-Semitism in New Testament scholarship. He denies that Judaism was what its academic and theological enemies maintain. His book in the context of contemporary Protestant theological debate makes a point important in its context:

> The Pharisees had a positive concern for purity; it was better to be pure than not. They were not alone. The same was true of a lot of Jews and of a lot of pagans.... "Ritual purity"...now has to many people an unfavorable connotation, and it is thought that what is wrong with the Pharisees is that they favored it. But this would only mean that what is wrong with them is that they lived in the ancient world – where most people favored it. Most Christian scholars...think that it was precisely "ritual" which Jesus and Paul attacked. Since the major point of the Jewish law which is treated negatively in both the synoptic gospels and Paul is the sabbath, the assumption that they attacked "ritual" implies that rest on the sabbath should be considered "ritual." It was instead commemorative (of God's rest) and ethical (not only men, but also women, servants, animals, and the land itself were allowed to rest). The Pharisees concern to be pure went beyond the requirements of the law – as did that of others.... People thought that purity was a good thing, and they tried to avoid impurity, even though it had no practical consequence. There were many who wanted to be able to "distinguish between the holy and the common...." The Pharisees fully participated in this spirit. They differed from others in many particulars, they

---

[22]Ibid., pp. 240-41.
[23]Ibid., p. 240; Sanders tends to attribute more language to me than I ordinarily use; he routinely uses ten words when one suffices. In the passage at hand, he adds words I do not require to say what I mean.

defined certain impurities very carefully, they probably extended corpse impurity more than did most, and they may have tried harder than did most to avoid the new sources of this impurity. The desire to be pure, however, they shared with the populace in general.[24]

I cite the passage at length, because it seems to me to point toward the benevolent intent of Sanders's scholarship. But the result is historically puzzling and theologically condescending.

It is puzzling because, first, there is no evidence that, in general, people wanted to be pure; the Mishnah and related sources take for granted ordinary folk wanted to be, and were, cultically clean when they observed the pilgrim festivals in Temple and in Jerusalem. I find in Sanders's book no evidence that *in other contexts* Jews of the first century other than Pharisees and Essenes may be described as desiring to be cultically pure (which is what is at stake in the debate). That absence of evidence probably accounts for the number of times he repeats his never substantiated assertion.[25] It is condescending because Sanders affirms that, if the Pharisees practiced "ritual," then they, and the Judaism that claims descent from them, would be subject to condemnation by Jesus and Paul. Throughout its history, Orthodox and Roman Catholic Christianities have not concurred, of course, and the conception of a religion without ritual of some kind – perhaps not this kind, but some other kind – scarcely matches the reality of Protestant Christianity as well.

As a believing Jew, I practice Judaism, and I do not appreciate – or require – a defense that dismisses as unimportant or inauthentic what in my faith is very important indeed: the observance of rituals of various kinds. They are mine because they are the Torah's. I do not propose to apologize for them, I do not wish to explain them away. I do not reduce them to their ethical significance. "Commemorative" and "ethical" indeed! The Sabbath is holy, and that is why I keep it, not because it may also be "commemorative" or "ethical." Judaism is not a culture that merely commemorates, nor is it a sociology that advances social policy. It is a religion that believes we serve God by what we say and do, and doing involves not only life with neighbor but also life with God: nourishing life in accord with God's revealed rules of sanctification.

Nor do I value a defense of my religion that implicitly throughout and explicitly at many points accepts at face value what another religion

---

[24]Ibid., pp. 245-46.

[25]Like the turgidity of his prose, the rambling and disorganized and run-on character of his exposition, so too, the utter vulgarity of Sanders's mind and intellectual processes has impressed more than a few readers of his books.

values and rejects what my religion deems authentic service to the living God. In the end Sanders wants to defend Judaism by his re-presentation of Pharisaism in a form that, in his view, Christianity could have affirmed then and should appreciate today – and now cease to denigrate. That approved Judaism turns out to be a Judaism in the model of Christianity (in Sanders's pattern). So if Sanders's Pharisees result from a mere tinkering with some details of mine, his "Judaism" is only a caricature and an offense. With friends like Sanders, Judaism hardly needs any enemies.

# 10

## Sanders's *Judaism. Practices and Beliefs. 63 B.C.E - 66 C.E.*

In his *Judaism. Practice and Belief. 63 B.C.E. - 66 C.E.* (London, 1992: SCM Press and Philadelphia, 1992: Trinity Press International), Sanders answers every question but the important one: If this was Judaism, then how come Christianity? That is to say, his defense of "Judaism" so trivializes "Judaism" that we have to ask why anyone would have found reason to criticize, and to reject, so unexceptionable a religion as did Jesus and Paul and all the others who, born Jews, became Christians.

That is not to suggest his is a potboiler dashed off for Judaeo-Christian friendship circles. He introduces his account of Judaism, as "the book I always wanted to write," and he certainly has done a far superior job to his predecessors; the work on the day of its publication replaces Jeremias's *Jerusalem in the Time of Jesus*, and in many ways excels other synthetic accounts known to me. That makes all the more regrettable the errors of method that ruin the book. These three important methods of his indeed mark the work as not so much idiosyncratic as bizarre. First, having paid his ritual obeisance to the critical problem, Sanders without ado cites whatever he wants to cite of the Mishnah for evidence of what he calls "Judaism" as far back as 63 B.C.E. So Sanders claims to know what is, and what is not, historical, not bothering to tell the rest of us how he knows. He never lets the rest of us in on the secret of how he knows the difference between what he can use and what he cannot. He accuses me of a lack of imagination. He certainly cannot be accused of the same flaw. Second, he claims to know sources about this Judaism that no one else knows, so that he can tell us what, if we found said sources, they would say. On that basis, moreover, he proceeds to blame me for not knowing what these sources say! This, too, scarcely permits reasoned argument and so has to be classified as (merely) bizarre. Third, and strangest of all, he is the first scholar ever to imagine that all sources produced by Jews, anywhere, any time, by any sort of person or group, equally tell us about one and the same Judaism. Schürer was far more critical nearly a century ago. The other major "Judaisms" – Bousset-Gressman's or Moore's, for instance – select a body of evidence and work on that, not assuming that everything everywhere tells us about one thing, somewhere: Judaism.

These strange methods of his call into question the reliability of his account of "Judaism as a functioning religion" with the "accent on the common people and their observances." That is not to suggest we must consign Sanders's book to the dust bin of academic curiosities. It is only to say that the work can be used only with enormous caution, until it is done all over again the right way. He has an enormous amount of information in the book. But because he fabricates out of it all a single, unitary Judaism, without ever telling us how he harmonizes all these conflicting sources, in the end his *Judaism* is unintelligible.

I.   **The Mishnah Tells Us about Judaism in the First Century B.C. and A.D. When Sanders Says It Does and Doesn't When He Decides It Doesn't**

In his methodological statement, Sanders explicitly tells us, "In this study, I shall sometimes cite second-century rabbinic passages in order to illustrate points; but when I wish to derive hard information about actual practice, I shall take a minimalist view of rabbinic evidence, making use only of material that can be confidently assigned to the early period" (p. 10). But whence this "confidence"? What Sanders does not tell us is the source of his confidence that he knows the difference. Let me give a single instance (p. 89) of how he uses a Mishnah paragraph to tell us what really happened long before the closure of the Mishnah:

> There is one interesting rabbinic passage that indicates that the sale of birds was subject to the law of supply and demand (and therefore was not monopolistic).
>
> > Once in Jerusalem a pair of doves cost a golden denar [= 25 silver *denars*]. Rabban Simeon b. Gamaliel said: By this Temple! I will not suffer the night to pass by before they cost but a [silver] *denar*. He went into the court and taught: If a woman suffered five miscarriages that were not in doubt or five issues that were not in doubt, she need bring but one offering, and she may then eat of the animal-offerings; and she is not bound to offer the other offerings. And the same

> day the price of a pair of doves stood at a
> quarter-denar each. *(Keritot* I.7)

The impurity under discussion is female 'discharge' - blood that was not menstruation, of which the most frequent cause was miscarriage. The impurity required a sin-offering (usually two birds). The anonymous mishnah (presupposed by the above discussion) states that for five cases that were in doubt, a woman need bring only one pair of birds, while for five cases that were not in doubt, she could bring one offering and then eat a share of sacrificial food, but she still owed the other four pair of birds, to be paid for later. Simeon b. Gamaliel wished to eliminate this future obligation. The result, we are told, is that the cost of birds fell to 1/100th of the previous value.

The details are at least exaggerated. Not many women, in any one year, had five 'discharges' or miscarriages; eliminating four future offerings, thus cutting such women's total expenditure by 4/5ths, could not have had such an effect on the overall price. Bird-sacrifices were required for many other purposes, and a fall of 80 percent in a minor category would not have been a catastrophe for dealers in pigeons. But apart from the details, the story is not unreasonable. People needed advice about what to sacrifice. They consulted experts, usually priests, but possibly non-priestly Pharisees. If their advisers told them that they need bring fewer sacrifices, they could do so with a clear conscience. The cost of sacrifices fluctuated with the market.

Now Sanders adduces this Mishnah paragraph in support of the proposition that the sale of birds was subject to the law of supply and demand and therefore was not monopolistic. It seems to me that his "therefore" scarcely follows from the story, which says that it was subject to the monopoly of the Temple, which was subject to rabbinical (Simeon b. Gamaliel's) authority. So the story does not prove what Sanders wants it to prove, but that is secondary (though common in his use of rabbinic literature). What he takes for granted is that Simeon b. Gamaliel could make such a rule and affect prices. But how does he know that fact? Does he then suppose that any reference to this Simeon b. Gamaliel tells us something that really happened: not only did he say it, but he could make it stick? Then why Simeon but not all the other rabbis? If only Simeon, then how have his practical and effective rulings survived, but no one else's? I do not know the answers to these questions, and I do not believe Sanders does either. It suffices then to repeat my mantra: If you cannot show it, you do not know it. If Sanders had evidence or even arguments to sustain his otherwise capricious selection of this paragraph as real history, his rejection of a thousand others as not real history, he can be relied upon to state them.

But when we look at how Sanders wishes to use the passage at hand, we see that he has botched the job. Let us proceed to examine the exact rationale he gives:

The details are at least exaggerated. Not many women, in any one year, had five 'discharges' or miscarriages; eliminating four future offerings, thus cutting such women's total expenditure by 4/5ths, could not have had such an effect on the overall price. Bird-sacrifices were required for many other purposes, and a fall of 80 percent in a minor category would not have been a catastrophe for dealers in pigeons. But apart from the details, the story is not unreasonable. People needed advice about what to sacrifice. They consulted experts, usually priests, but possibly non-priestly Pharisees. If their advisers told them that they need bring fewer sacrifices, they could do so with a clear conscience. The cost of sacrifices fluctuated with the market.

These are the facts that Sanders knows without showing proof. First, "not many women...." How does he know that? Do we have a gynecological survey? Whence does he know that the "flow" derived from a miscarriage at all? Our sages of blessed memory had a clear knowledge of the difference between miscarriages and other sources of nonmenstrual blood, as a study of tractate Niddah would have told Sanders.

But the very passage that he cites makes the distinction between miscarriages and other causes of vaginal flow:

|   |   |
|---|---|
| A. | The woman who is subject to a doubt concerning [the appearance of] five fluxes, |
| B. | or the one who is subject to a doubt concerning five miscarriages |
| C. | brings a single offering. |
| D. | And she [then is deemed clean so that she] eats animal sacrifices. |
| E. | And the remainder [of the offerings, A, B] are not an obligation for her. |
| F. | [If she is subject to] five confirmed miscarriages, |
| G. | or five confirmed fluxes, |
| H. | she brings a single offering. |
| I. | And she eats animal sacrifices. |
| J. | But the rest [of the offerings, the other four] remain as an obligation for her [to bring at some later time] – |

There follows the tale that Sanders cites. Now what is important is that we have a clear distinction between miscarriages and other "fluxes" (in my admittedly imperfect translation), and that distinction runs throughout. Sanders has in mind the demonstration of a critical attitude, so he announces as fact what, the sources makes clear, contradicts the premise of the discussion! So the conclusion Sanders draws ignores the distinction the text that he cites has made.

It is probably needless to ask him some more questions, for example, "They consulted expert...but possibly non-priestly Pharisees...." Now how does he know this, if not from his own supposititious imagination? Since Sanders maintains that the Pharisees were influential, he can add his "possibly...." But "possibly" substitutes for proof only if we want it to, and, I repeat, what we cannot show, we do not know. All of this is simply fabricated for the purposes of the apologetic that is in fact hidden in parentheses ("and therefore was not monopolistic"). Without that intent, the entire passage could have been omitted with no loss to Sanders's argument in context – whatever it might have been; the book is far too long because of pages and pages of wide-eyed reports of just this kind. Sanders seems to have in mind an audience of small-town Texans, though all the small-town Texans I know (and happily, I know many) are a whole lot smarter than he conceives them to be.

The same slight of hand occurs throughout the book, but let me give only a single example before moving on. Sanders's pan-Pharisaism persuades him that the slightest evidence, interpreted in the loosest and most self-indulgent way, proves what he wants it to prove, thus on p. 226:

> Since this rule about the use of an *'otsar* is found in rabbinic literature, and since archaeology shows that someone followed it before 70, we may attribute it to the Pharisees. The revolutionaries who defended Matsada after the destruction of the temple also accepted it; they built miqveh + 'otsar complexes, despite having Herod's capacious single miqva'ot to hand. The defenders of Matsada were Sicarii, and probably very few Pharisees were Sicarii. The inference is that the Pharisaic rule was accepted by at least some other pietists (though not the Qumranians). The distribution of miqveh + 'otsar complexes in Jerusalem is interesting from this point of view: one such complex has been found in the aristocratic Upper City, a good number in the poorer Lower City. There is also one in a Hasmonean palace at Jericho. At least some of the Hasmoneans had accepted the (apparently) Pharisaic theory, as did some of the die-hard revolutionaries and some of the people in the Lower City.

Bypassing the (somewhat infirm) details, let us focus on the "since" clause.

1.    The rule is found in rabbinic literature.
2.    Someone followed it before 70.
3.    We may attribute it to the Pharisees.

Lest this appear to be a lapse, Sanders repeats the same reasoning:

1.    The defenders of Matsada were Sicarii.
2.    Few Pharisees were Sicarii (he really means: few Sicarii were Pharisees).
3.    The inference is that the Pharisaic rule was accepted....

And of course, what is argued three sentences earlier becomes a fact very quickly, which is, after all, an occupational hazard for us professors (all of us): "At least some of the Hasmoneans had accepted the (apparently) Pharisaic theory." The "apparently" changes nothing. Let us start from the beginning. Somewhere in rabbinic literature we have a rule. We are not told the details, because they are not supposed to matter. Now, some time before 70, somebody did something that the rule, too, says should be done. There is no "therefore" here. But the omitted "therefore" is, "he did it because he knew the rule that later on was written down, and he did it in conformity to that rule and to the authority behind the rule." Sanders does not articulate these connections between Nos. 1 and 2, he just takes for granted "we all make them." That is not my conception of showing what we know, it is in fact know-nothingism. And, of course, he assumes, furthermore, that we all know that everything in rabbinic literature is Pharisaic in origin (except what is not), so "we may attribute it...." But of course, too, we may attribute it to anyone we wish. Do I claim he is wrong? Not at all. All I argue is: what we cannot show, we do not know. Pan-Pharisaism strikes again. Do I claim he is wrong? Not at all. I only pronounce: what we cannot show, we do not know.

For that reason I find in the following something akin to gibberish, as Sanders weaves this way and that, aiming at a destination only he knows for sure:

1. The socio-religious point is this: Herod and the Jerusalem aristocrats, many of whose houses have been excavated, had only single pools (with one exception). Some of the smaller houses of Jerusalem and Sepphoris also had single pools, but double ones are, with only the one exception, in smaller houses. The revolutionary defenders of Matsada also built double immersion pools. Thus I think it likely that *most people*, including the aristocrats, did not follow Pharisaic views about immersion pools, although other pietists (such as the defenders at Matsada) may have shared the Pharisees' definition of valid water.

2. That some people added 'drawn' water to their pools, and that the Pharisees and early rabbis objected, is proved by rabbinic passages. According to one, the Pharisees, down to the time of Shammai and Hillel, carried on a running dispute among themselves about how much drawn water could be added to a miqveh. They agreed that not much was allowed; proposals ranged from 0.9 to 10.8 litres in a pool that contained thousands of litres (*Eduyyot* I.3). Presumably non-Pharisees would allow more.

3. The second passage is even more interesting. According to *Shabbat* 13b, the House of Shammai (one of the main wings of the Pharisaic party, obviously after the time of Shammai and Hillel themselves) 'decreed' that people who immersed in drawn water, or who had drawn water poured on them, made heave-offering unfit to eat. This seems to be directed against the practice of the aristocratic priests, who did not use the Pharisaic second pool, but probably added

fresh 'drawn' water to the miqveh, and who bathed afterwards by sitting in a tub while a servant poured warm water over them. The Shammaites ruled that they rendered their own food (heave-offering) unfit and that they should not eat it. The aristocratic priests doubtless continued to do as they wished.

Whether or not I have correctly interpreted this passage, we see that, within general uniformity (miqva'ot in bedrock, seasonally filled with rain water) there were disagreements. Some people used water that other people considered invalid.

Now what Sanders seems to want to say is this: the Pharisees were influential, except where they weren't influential. Rich houses had one kind of immersion pool (assuming that the holes in the ground qualify as immersion pools for the purposes of the present context!). Poor houses had another. So most people didn't follow Pharisaic views about immersion pools. This "most people" should read, "we have X number of immersion pools, and of them, we have Y number of a given character or size." All the rest reads into archaeological data generalizations and rules and other considerations that the mute stones scarcely sustain or even announce.

I avoid discussions of matters of substance, dealing only with passages that seem to me to illustrate enormous methodological gaffes. But it is worth noting that when Sanders takes for granted everything in rabbinic literature derives from or represents the views of the Pharisees before 70 (except what Sanders knows does not stand for the Pharisees before 70), he solves a problem about which the rest of the people who work on that subject find full of difficulties and not yet settled. I worked on that problem in particular – it was the point of the project – in my *Eliezer ben Hyrcanus. The Tradition and the Man* (Leiden, 1972: E.J. Brill), I-II, and I published some of the results in separate articles afterward, for example, "'Pharisaic-Rabbinic' Judaism: A Clarification," in *History of Religions* 1973, 12:250-270 (reprinted in my *Early Rabbinic Judaism* [Leiden, 1975: E.J. Brill], pp. 50-73). That book does not appear in Sanders's bibliography, and he apparently has failed in any way to address its results.[1]

---

[1] It suffices to say that Sanders's certainties rest not only on how he reads ancient sources, but also on how he avoids considering contemporary scholarship that does not strike his fancy. The absence from the bibliography of his *Judaism* of any book of mine published after 1981 shows that he just does not feel like keeping up; but his anecdotal criticism of my *Judaism: The Evidence of the Mishnah* in his *Jewish Law from Jesus to the Mishnah* imputes to me ideas and positions contradicted in so many words in work done before, and in much work done after, 1981. Since he accuses me of arguments from silence, of a "lack of imagination," and of failure "to consider the accident of survival," I may say in my own defense that if he did his homework in my oeuvre instead of just quoting

Now back to the passage at hand: Here goes Sanders again, telling us which passages he decides are historical – but not explaining how he knows the difference between the historical ones and the others. His No. 2 has rabbinic passages "prove" his fact, since Sanders "knows" that Shammai and Hillel really said what is attributed to them in the Mishnah paragraph he cites. But then does Sanders know that they really said everything else attributed to them? If he does, then why does he cite so little? If he does not, then how can he cite so much? The "presumably" of course adds only an obvious inference, that if the fathers of the Houses took the positions they did, then outsiders took other positions, and presumably allowed more, rather than less. Why the second "presumably" follows I cannot say; Sanders tells us nothing about these "non-Pharisees," or how he knows their attitudes, rules, and principles. Sanders's "more interesting" passage of course raises the same difficulties. And yet, I hasten to add, what Sanders wants to prove, which is, "there were disagreements," stands to reason; my only problem is that he has not proved his surmise, he has only illustrated it by citing or paraphrasing stories and sayings that yield the same surmise. The problem of how these stories and sayings tell us precisely how things were in the first centuries B.C. and A.D. is not solved, it is simply finessed.

Now I hasten to add, in Sanders's defense, that wherever he wishes, Sanders will pronounce a rabbinic tale a tale (p. 258), so what bothers me is not what he selects or what he rejects but how he knows the difference – for what we cannot systematically show, we also never really know:

> The best-known instance of the epigrammatic epitome occurs in a story told of Hillel, the great Pharisee who was Jesus' older contemporary:
>
> > On another occasion it happened that a certain heathen came before Shammai and said to him, 'Make me a proselyte, on condition that you teach me the whole Torah while I stand on one foot'. Thereupon he repulsed him with the builder's cubit which was in his hand. When he went before Hillel, he said to him, 'What is hateful to you, do not to your neighbor: that is the whole Torah, while the rest is commentary thereof; go and learn it'. (*Shabbat* 3 I a)

---

– out of the context of a sustained and massive account of the sources and how they cohere – what he feels like quoting, he would find reason to rethink his conclusions about his subject and his judgments about my proposals.

Since this appears for the first time in a late source, and since other sources attribute epigrammatic sayings to Hillel, but not this one (for example *Avot 2.5-7)*, we cannot attribute it to him with confidence. Finally, we note that Paul twice summarized the law by quoting Lev. 19:18: Gal. 5. I 4; Rom. 13:8-10. In the second instance he also cited the commandments not to commit adultery, not to kill, not to steal and not to covet. Interestingly, he then explained that since 'love does no wrong to a neighbor' it 'is the fulfilling of the law' (Rom. 13:10). That is, Paul knew the negative form of the saying and found it useful.

But the story about Simeon b. Gamaliel, before 70, also appears in a late source, namely, the Mishnah of about 200. Why the Mishnah is a less "late source" than the Talmud I do not know. How appearances of Hillel's sayings in "other sources," for example, tractate Avot of A.D. 250 would have made them more authentic to the historical Hillel of the first century B.C. Sanders does not tell us.

But what is Sanders's real point here? As is often the case in his writing, it is not made explicit, but always prominent: he wants to introduce the Hillel saying to impress his wide-eyed readers: hey fellas, look at this! He's got Jesus, he's got Paul, and, right smack in the middle, he's got Rabbi Hillel. So, really, how weighty then is the qualification, "cannot attribute it to him with confidence"? In context, what he gives with both hands, he sets aside with his little finger. That is why I wonder what points he wants the readers to take away. If we cannot attribute this story to Hillel "with confidence," then why bother to cite it? And what is the purpose of juxtaposing something from the fifth or sixth century with something from Paul? We seem to have three positions. First, Sanders quotes what he thinks authentic to the first century. Second, he does not quote what he does not think authentic (or the relevance of which he does not grasp, as in the opening lines of the Mishnah paragraph that is the setting for the story about  Simeon b. Gamaliel!). Third, he quotes what he does not think authentic to the first century when it suits his polemical purpose.

The problem I find with Sanders's use of rabbinic evidence – he is capricious in believing as historical fact what he wills, ignoring as historical fiction (as to the first centuries B.C. and A.D.) what he wants – recurs throughout his book on *Judaism*. It would be tedious and unproductive to tote up every instance. I simply stipulate that there are many more examples of this bizarre insistence that we accept on faith Sanders's judgment. In the academy, there is no salvation by faith. Here, what we cannot show, we do not know.

## II. Neusner Doesn't Know the Sources Sanders Says Neusner Would Know, If We Ever Found Those Sources. So Now I'll Reject His Ideas Because He Doesn't Know the Sources We Don't (Yet?) Have

Sanders's principal criticism of my approach to the study of formative Judaism is that I have no imagination. In scholarship, salvation is never solely by faith, but invariably, and only, by evidence. In an unself-consciously hilarious instrusion of theology into history, Sanders accuses me of the sin of not believing enough. Specifically, the faith that he requires is in Sanders's knowledge of sources that do not now exist at all.[2] True to the theological animus that pervades the book, Sanders expresses outrage that I have not seen his particular vision of things. He accuses me of what he classes as a venal scholarly sin, absence of imagination. The first five times I read the relevant passage, I was persuaded that I was reading sloppily or stupidly, just as Sanders is always saying about me; he must have meant something else than what I was grasping. For what he seemed to be saying struck me as so stupid that I could not imagine he meant what the words before me seemed to communicate.

The sixth time, I laughed: it was right there. So, with genuine pleasure, I plead guilty to his indictment, first-degree failure of imagination – on hundreds of counts, surely! I hardly need to repeat the grounds for my plea, and, shifting from his role as prosecutor to the judge's bench, Sanders's verdict makes it unnecessary to do so. He declares the part of my work that he claims to know worthless. And, from his perspective, he is right.

Readers by this point must assume I exaggerate or misrepresent. So let us turn to the entire delicious passage – *ipsissima verba* – since this matter is so bizarre that anything other than Sanders's own words would prove insufficient evidence that he could have said something so silly. We shall now see that Sanders says precisely what I just now said he says (p. 414); I take the liberty of underlining the sentences that I find astounding:

> We have seen that, for details, we must have recourse to rabbinic literature, especially to the passages that we can attribute to the earliest layer. Early rabbinic literature, however, is largely legal; one can derive from it general theological beliefs, such as that charity is important, but nothing like the rich substance that the Dead Sea Scrolls provide for the Essenes. If all we had from Qumran were the *Community Rule*, without its concluding hymn, the evidence would be analogous to what the Mishnah tells us about the Pharisees: the Dead Sea sect would look like

---

[2]In Hyam Maccoby's critique of my *Judaism: The Evidence of the Mishnah*, and in his contribution to the symposium on the book that is reprinted below, he makes the same point.

a religion in which nothing mattered but rules. *Neusner, in fact, has proposed that this was true of the early rabbis. This shows a lack of imagination and a failure to consider the accident of survival. If we had a collection of private Pharisaic prayers, we would find them as deeply devotional as are the hymns from Qumran.* Since they did not survive, it will be important to reconsider the main themes of the Eighteen Benedictions, which probably show something of Pharisaic piety.

The accident of survival poses a further problem. If the earliest rabbinic literature tells us too little about Pharisaic theology and piety, it tells us too much about their legal interpretation; that is, too much to be adequately covered in the present chapter. The required stratification is, in the first place, very difficult to achieve. The earliest rabbinic document, the Mishnah, is usually dated c. 200-220 C.E. Much of the material is anonymous, while other passages are attributed to named sages. Of the attributed material, the bulk is second century rather than first (even assuming that all attributions are accurate). Separating the possibly first-century material from later passages in the Mishnah and other rabbinic sources is slow, difficult work, and categorizing it is almost equally hard. Neusner spent three volumes at the second task, but he mis-categorized the passages, and the entire job needs to be done again. I have attempted to do it for Purity (see n. 5), but the analysis of rabbinic legal debates is not really my métier, and I wanted to do just enough of it to see whether or not Neusner's passages support his conclusions. They do not.

Sanders knows that if we had a collection of private Pharisaic prayers, we would find them as deeply devotional as are the hymns from Qumran. I have no imagination, because, if I did, I would know that fact that Sanders knows. Not only so, but I also have no confidence in my capacity to make up evidence that does not exist, which accounts for my "failure to consider the accident of survival."

My plea to the charge? "Guilty, your honor. I certainly lack the imagination to make up sources we do not have. I indeed fail to consider the accident of survival. Wretched sinner that I am, in my unbelief I describe only the evidence we have.

"But, your honor, may I add, if I am guilty of first-degree absence of imagination, the prosecutor is guilty of inanity."

I do not know what that collection would say, and neither does Sanders, because at this time we have no such collection. So while what he says "stands to reason," or "is obvious," it is hardly very solid ground on which to base any conclusions whatsoever: what we cannot show, we do not know. Still, for not knowing what we cannot show, we should not accuse our academic adversaries of a "lack of imagination." I am proud to be accused of what I regard as a virtue: I do not make things up as I go along; Sanders does – proudly says so, and in so many words. He knows what has not survived, which is why "the accident of survival" is a consideration. I simply describe what we have and draw conclusions based on what we do know. I do not regard that characteristic of my scholarship as a vice but as a virtue. Scholarship in general regards certainty about what absent evidence says as bizarre, and conclusions based on imagination as fiction.

But we cannot leave the matter there. For the polemic concerns the legalism of Judaism. Nearly all New Testament scholarship before George Foot Moore, and most of it afterward, to our own day, and virtually the entirety of the preaching clergy in parishes and pulpits, describe the Judaism that Jesus reformed or rejected as legalistic. Sanders wishes to show that that is not so. In the paragraph just now cited, Sanders imputes to me the following view: because I do not know the evidence Sanders imagines, I describe Judaism as "a religion in which nothing mattered but rules." This is not by implication but stated in so many words: "Neusner, in fact, has proposed that this was true of the early rabbis." Surprised, I went to Sanders's evidence that that is my view. To that sentence, he appends this footnote, which, as we shall now see, is characteristic of someone who sees what he wants to see whether or not it actually is there – then accuses his adversary of blindness:

> For example, *Judaism: The Evidence of the Mishnah*, p. 86.

All I am left to work with in examining my record is a single example, but since Sanders regards that example as probative (finding it necessary to give no other), I determined to follow up and see how I could have given so egregious an account of my views – and so ignorant and wrong an account of the Judaism I was discussing in the Mishnah. And, the issue being critical, I have to ask readers to bear with me while I quote myself!

Since I have never said and obviously do not maintain that the Judaism of the rabbis of the Mishnah (or faithful Judaism today, in any of its systems) was (or is) one in which "only rules mattered," and since I have argued – quite to the contrary – that rules serve as a powerful medium of profound discourse, a way of making statements of principles about the social order and metaphysics alike, I looked up the reference. Where and how have I so badly composed sentences as to yield the stupid and wrong conclusion Sanders imputes to me? Or have I, unannounced and unknowing, changed my mind?

Here are the sentences of *Judaism: The Evidence of the Mishnah*, p. 86 (into p. 87) that may pertain (Sanders gives no hint as to which sentence or sentences he cites):

> [In the context of the wording of prayers:] Overall, the tendency appears to have been not to attempt to standardize more than the principal outlines of worship. Not much value was placed upon a fixed wording or even structure....

There also was some work at defining appropriate blessings for various natural benefits.... A fully articulated system of blessings after the meal is not attested for the present period. The rulings are episodic and not integrated.

Since it is not possible to suppose that there were no liturgies before the war [of 66], the probable reason for work on this topic at just this time has to be located in an intention not to create liturgy but to legislate about it. And even in the matter of legislation and thus standardization, it would appear that only the most basic issues came up, for instance, rules governing the saying of the Shema morning and night, for which, prior to the wars, we must assume there were established practices, as well as the saying of blessings for various gifts of nature. What is important in this part of the law is that matters were discussed which aforetimes people would have done in accord merely with local custom. But that same observation applies to the other matters – obeying the agricultural taboos, giving out the taxes to class and caste – which were subjected to substantial work of amplification and expansion at just this time.

My assumption here is that there were prayers that were long established; these were not written by the people under discussion ("rabbis," "Pharisees," whoever – not specified). After 70 some work was under way to standardize the outlines of worship (I refer here to *matbe'a shel tefilah,* the order of prayer). There was some further effort to make rules on liturgy, for example, when the *Shema* was to be recited. Overall, that would seem to me to have been part of a larger effort to order local custom into a generally prevailing pattern. Absent the notion that if you make a rule, you think that all that matters is the rule – a classic nonsequitur – I find no hint of a conception that "nothing mattered but rules." What I am saying is, *to these sages, rules did matter.* That is not the same thing as saying, to these sages, only rules matter. Sanders's capacity to imagine what is not there has led him to hear what I did not say and to pay no attention to what I did say.

So much for what I say in his "for example,...p. 86." Now onward to p. 87, where there may be better grounds for finding the view he imputes to me:

So what we see is that the method of the group which had taken shape before the war, which was to define itself through distinguishing [p. 87] and differentiating rules about eating and marrying, was carried forward. This same approach to confronting problems, namely, through making laws, now was taken over on a much larger scale, and for a broader range of purposes. Defining the way common practices were to be done then suggests that, in people's mind, was the intent to make even common practices into a mode of differentiation of an uncommon group. That at any rate is one possibility for interpreting both the continuation of an established mode of thought, namely, an obsession with rule making, and the expansion of the topics to which that mode of thought came to apply....

Now what I think I am saying, is, this:

[1]    Before 70, the group responsible for some ideas that are carried forward and set out in the Mishnah two hundred years later distinguished itself by making rules that that group kept and others did not.

[2]    These rules covered what food members of the group would eat or not eat (outsiders being assumed to eat anything) and also what genealogical rules would govern whom they would marry or not marry (for example, the laws of consanguineous taboos).

[3]    Defining themselves by setting forth rules that differentiated the group from outsiders (in Israel), the group after 70 carried forward its established mode of self-definition and self-differentiation.

Given the character of the Torah, with its chapters and chapters of rule, commencing with the Ten Commandments, I do not think this group, one marked by an obsession with rule making, vastly differed from the authors of JE, P, and D, and Sanders's "covenantal nomism" surely has already absolved the Torah of the charge of maintaining that "only rules matter." Even the priestly code in Leviticus joins right to rite, never imagining that all that matters is a slavish obedience to dumb rules.

How all this is to be reduced to "only laws matter" I cannot say. Sanders refers in context to the Essenes. They had rules of the same kind as the Pharisees. Sanders approves their piety. So why take offense at the notion that the group defined its boundaries by rules of food and marriage? In Chapter Eight, where I reprint my review of Sanders's first book, I elaborate on this tendency of Sanders to judge Judaism by the standards of liberal Protestant Christianity, which (in Sanders's imagination at any rate) has no rules; now, fifteen years later, Sanders carries forward his sustained effort to clean up Judaism by portraying it in a way liberal Protestant Christians might tolerate. And, since he has chosen me for his archadversary, he imputes to me the view that the Pharisees were robots, to whom the rules were everything, the reasoning nothing; then, Sanders imagines, salvation for them (in my perverted imagination) consisted of mindless obedience to laws, salvation by works without faith. It appears to me that Neusner's Pharisees as portrayed by Sanders are playing the role of Roman Catholics to Sanders's (really, truly) Lutheran Pharisees. *Your honor, I plead guilty as charged to lack of imagination.* Next case.

## III.  To Describe Judaism from 63 B.C. to A.D. 66, We Cite All Sources Equally to Tell Us about a Single, Unitary Judaism

Sanders really thinks that any and every source, whoever wrote it, without regard to its time or place or venue, tells us about one and the same Judaism. The only way to see everything all together and all at once, as Sanders wishes to do, is to rise high above the evidence, so high that we no longer see the lines of rivers, the height of mountains, the undulations of plains – any of the details of the earth's true configuration. This conflation of all sources yields his fabricated Judaism. The result of this Judaic equivalent of a "harmony of the Gospels" is more often than not a dreary progress through pointless information. I found myself wondering why Sanders thought the information he set forth important, how he imagined it mattered, what difference in the understanding of *Judaism. Practice and Belief,* one fact or another might make in his mind. If we know that his conflationary Judaism prevailed everywhere, then what else do we know about the Judaisms to which each source in turn attests (as well)? He elaborately tells us why he thinks various documents tell, or do not tell, what really happened; he never explains why he maintains these same documents and artifacts of archaeology, commonly so profoundly at variance with one another, all concur on a single Judaism or attest to a single Judaism.

Now that capricious conflation of all the sources Sanders thinks fit together and silent omission of all the sources he rejects is something Moore, Schechter, and even Urbach never did. Urbach cited Philo but not the Dead Sea Scrolls, having decided that the one was kosher, the other *treif.* Sanders has decided there are no intellectual counterparts to dietary laws at all: he swallows it all and chews it up and spits out a homogenized "Judaism" lacking all specific flavor. Nor can I point to any other scholar of ancient Judaism working today who cites everything from everywhere to tell us about one and the same Judaism. The contrast between the intellectually rigorous thinking of James Dunn on defining "Judaism" in his *Partings of the Ways* and the conceptually slovenly work of Sanders on the same problem – adding up all the sources and not so much finding as inventing through mushy prose what he conceives to be the common denominator – tells the story. Sanders's *Judaism* is a mulligan stew, a four-day-old, over cooked *tcholent* – for us plain Americans, Wonder Bread, full of air and not very tasty.

This fabrication of a single Judaism is supposed to tell us something that pertains equally to all: the Judaism that forms the basis for all the sources, the common denominator among them all. If we know a book or an artifact is "Jewish," then we are supposed automatically to know various other facts about said book or artifact. But the upshot is either too general to mean much (monotheism) or too abstract to form an intelligible statement. Let me be specific. How Philo would have understood the Dead Sea Scrolls, the authors of apocalyptic writings, those of the Mishnah passages Sanders admits to his account of Judaism from 63 B.C. to A.D. 66, we are never told. Each of these distinctive documents gets to speak whenever Sanders wants it to; none is ever brought into relationship – comparison and contrast – with any other. The homogenization of Philo, the Mishnah, the Dead Sea Scrolls, Ben Sira, apocryphal and pseudepigraphic writings, the results of archaeology, and on and on and on turns out to yield generalizations about a religion that none of those responsible for the evidence at hand would have recognized: lifeless, dull, hopelessly abstract, lacking all social relevance. After a while, readers come to realize, it hardly matters, the results reaching so stratospheric a level of generalization that all precise vision of real people practicing a vivid religion is lost.

To understand what goes into Sanders's picture of Judaism, let me now provide a reasonable sample (pp. 103-4), representative of the vacuity of the whole, the opening paragraphs of his discussion, Chapter Seven, entitled "Sacrifices":

> The Bible does not offer a single, clearly presented list of sacrifices. The legal books (Exodus, Leviticus, Numbers and Deuteronomy), we know now, incorporate various sources from different periods, and priestly practice evidently varied from time to time. There are three principal sources of information about sacrifices in the first century: Josephus, Philo and the Mishnah. On most points they agree among themselves and with Leviticus and Numbers; consequently the main outline of sacrifices is not in dispute. Josephus, in my judgment, is the best source. He knew what the common practice of the priesthood of his day was: he had learned it in school, as a boy he had watched and assisted, and as an adult he had worked in the temple. It is important for evaluating his evidence to note that his description of the sacrifices sometimes disagrees with Leviticus or goes beyond it. This is not an instance in which he is simply summarizing what is written in the Bible: he is almost certainly depending on what he had learned as a priest.
>
> Though the Mishnah is often right with regard to pre-70 temple practice, many of the discussions are from the second century: the rabbis continued to debate rules of sacrifice long after living memory of how it had been done had vanished. Consequently, in reading the Mishnah one is sometimes reading second-century theory. Occasionally this can be seen clearly. For example, there is a debate about whether or not the priest who sacrificed an animal could keep its hide if for any reason the animal was made invalid (for example by touching something impure) after it was sacrificed but before it was flayed. The Mishnah on this topic opens with an anonymous opinion, according to which the priest

did not get the hide. R. Hanina the Prefect of the Priests disagreed: 'Never have I seen a hide taken out to the place of burning'; that is, the priests always kept the hides. R. Akiba (early second century) accepted this and was of the view that the priests could keep the hides of invalid sacrifices. The Sages, however, ruled the other way (*Zevahim* 12.4). R. Hanina the Prefect of the Priests apparently worked in the temple before 70, but survived its destruction and became part of the rabbinic movement. Akiba died c. 135; 'the Sages' of this passage are probably his contemporaries or possibly the rabbis of the next generation. Here we see that second-century rabbis were quite willing to vote against actual practice in discussing the behavior of the priests and the rules they followed. The problem with using the Mishnah is that there is very seldom this sort of reference to pre-70 practice that allows us to make critical distinctions: not only are we often reading second-century discussions, we may be learning only second-century theory.

Philo had visited the temple, and some of his statements about it (for example the guards) seem to be based on personal knowledge. But his discussion of the sacrifices is 'bookish', and at some important points it reveals that he is passing on information derived from the Greek translation of the Hebrew Bible (the Septuagint), not from observation. The following description basically follows the Hebrew Bible and Josephus, but it sometimes incorporates details from other sources.

One may make the following distinctions among sacrifices:

> With regard to what was offered: meal, wine, birds (doves or pigeons) and quadrupeds (sheep, goats and cattle).

> With regard to who provided the sacrifice: the community or an individual.

> With regard to the purpose of the sacrifice: worship of and communion with God, glorification of him, thanksgiving, purification, atonement for sin, and feasting.

> With regard to the disposition of the sacrifice: it was either burned or eaten. The priests got most of the food that sacrifices provided, though one of the categories of sacrifice provided food for the person who brought it and his family and friends. The Passover lambs were also eaten by the worshippers.

Sacrifices were conceived as meals, or, better, banquets. The full and ideal sacrificial-offering consisted of meat, cereal, oil and wine (Num. 14:1-10, Ant. 3.233f.; the menu was sometimes reduced: see below).

Now let us ask ourselves, what, exactly, does Sanders wish to tell his readers about the sacrifices in this account of *Judaism. Practice and Belief*? He starts in the middle of things. He assumes we know what he means by "sacrifices," why they are important, what they meant, so all we require is details.  He will deal with Josephus, Philo, the Mishnah, and Leviticus and Numbers.  Does he then tell us the distinctive viewpoint of each?  Not at all.  All he wants us to know is the facts common to them all.  Hence his problem is not one of description, analysis, and interpretation of documents, but a conflation of the information contained in each that he deems usable.  Since that is his principal concern, he discusses "sacrifice" by telling us why the Mishnah's information is useless, except when it is usable.  But Sanders never suggests to his readers what the Mishnah's discussion of sacrifice wishes to find out, or how its ideas on the subject may prove religiously engaging.  It is just a rule book, so it has no ideas on the subject, so Sanders; that is not my view.  Philo is then set forth.  Here, too, we are told why he tells us nothing, but not what he tells us.  Then there follows the facts, the indented "with regard to" paragraphs.

Sanders did not have to tell us all about how Leviticus, Numbers, Philo and Josephus and the Mishnah concur, then about how we may ignore or must cite the several documents respectively, if his sole intent was to tell us the facts of the "with regard to..." paragraphs.  And how he knows that "sacrifices were conceived...," who conceived them in this way, and what sense the words made, "worship of and communion with God, glorification of him, thanksgiving, purification, atonement for sin, and feasting," and to whom they made sense, and how other Judaisms, besides the Judaism portrayed by Philo, Josephus, the Mishnah, and so on and so forth, viewed sacrifices, or the Temple as it was – none of this is set forth.  The conflation has its own purpose, which the following outline of the remainder of the chapter reveals: community sacrifices; individual sacrifices ("Neither Joseph, Philo, nor other first-century Jews thought that burnt-offerings provided God with food..."), a family at the Temple, an example; the daily Temple routine.  In this mass of information on a subject, one question is lost: what it all meant.  Sanders really does suppose that he is telling us how things were, what people did, and, in his stress on common-denominator Judaism, he finds it entirely reasonable to bypass all questions of analysis and interpretation and so forgets to tell us what it all meant.  His language, "worship of and communion with God, glorification of him, thanksgiving, purification, atonement for sin, and feasting" – that Protestant formulation begs every question and answers none.

But this common-denominator Judaism yields little that is more than simply banal, for "common theology," for example, "The history of Israel in general, and of our period in particular, shows that Jews believed that the one God of the universe had given them his law and that they were to obey it" (p. 240).  No one, obviously, can disagree, but what applies to everyone equally, in a nation so riven with division and rich in diversity, also cannot make much of a difference. That is to say, knowing that they all were monotheists or valued the Hebrew Scriptures (but which passages he does not identify, how he read them he does not say) does not tell us more than we knew about the religion of those diverse people than before. Sanders knows what people thought, because anything any Jew wrote tells us what "Jews" or most Jews or people in general thought. What makes Sanders's representation bizarre is that he proceeds to cite as evidence of what "Jews" thought opinions of Philo and Joseph, the Dead Sea Scrolls, rabbinic Literature, and so on and so forth. The generality of scholarship understands that the Dead Sea Scrolls represent their writers, Philo speaks for Philo, Josephus says what he thinks, and the Mishnah is whatever it is and is not whatever it is not. No one, to my knowledge, until Sanders has come to the facile judgment that anything any Jew thought has to have been in the mind of all the other Jews.

But it is only with that premise that we can understand the connections Sanders makes and the conclusions about large, general topics that he reaches. His juxtapositions are in fact beyond all understanding. Let me skim through his treatment of graven images, which captures the flavor of the whole:

> Comments by Philo and Josephus show how Jews could interpret other objects symbolically and thus make physical depictions acceptable, so that they were not seen as transgressions of one of the Ten Commandments, but as symbols of the glory of the God who gave them.

There follows a reference to War 5:214. Then Sanders proceeds:

> Josephus, as did Philo, found astral and other symbolism in many other things....

Some paragraphs later, in the same context, we have:

> The sun was personified and worshipped.... The most important instance was when Josiah...instituted a reform of worship...[now with reference to 2 Kings 23:4f]. This is usually regarded as having been a decisive rejection of other deities, but elements derived from sun worship continued. Subsequently Ezekiel attacked those who turned 'their backs to the Temple of the Lord...' (Ezek. 8:16). According to the Mishnah, at one point during the feast of Booths priests 'turned their faces to the west', recalling that their predecessors had faced east and worshipped the sun and proclaimed that 'our eyes are turned toward the Lord' (Sukkah 5:4). Despite this, the practice that Ezekiel condemned was continued by some. Josephs wrote that the Essenes 'are particularly reverent towards the divinity....'

This is continued with a citation of the Qumran Temple Scroll and then the Tosefta:

That the Essenes really offered prayer to the sun is made more probable by a passage in the Qumran Temple Scroll....

Above we noted the floor of the synagogue at Hammath that had as its main decoration the signs of the zodiac in a circle.... This synagogue floor, with its blatant pagan decoration, was built at the time when rabbinic Judaism was strong in Galilee – after the redaction and publication of the Mishnah, during the years when the material in the Tosefta and the Palestinian Talmud was being produced and edited. According to the Tosefta, Rabbi Judah, who flourished in the middle of the second century, said that 'If anyone says a blessing over the sun – this is a heterodox practice (T. Berakhot 6[7]). In the light of the floor, it seems he was opposing contemporary practice.

And so on and on he goes, introducing in the paragraph that follows references to Christian symbols (John 1:9, 15:1); the issue of whether "one God" meant there were no other supernatural beings (yielding a citation to Paul who was a Pharisee, with reference to Phil. 3:2-6). And so he runs on, for five hundred tedious pages. This is simply chaos.

Cui bono? Sanders aims at one conclusion. He sets himself up as judge of his data and issues a final ruling that surpasses, in condescension and self-absorption, any lines I have ever read, whether philo- or anti-Semitic in origin, about Judaism and the Pharisees:

> I rather like the Pharisees. They loved detail and precision. They wanted to get everything just right. I like that. They loved God, they thought he had blessed them, and they thought that he *wanted* them to get everything just right. I do not doubt that some of them were priggish. This is a common fault of the pious, one that is amply displayed in modern criticism of the Pharisees. The Pharisees, we know, intended to be humble before God, and they thought that intention mattered more than outward show. Those are worthy ideals. The other pietists strike me as being less attractive than the Pharisees. The surviving literature depicts them as not having much of a program for all Israel, and as being too ready to cultivate hatred of others: learn *our* secrets or God will destroy you. But probably they weren't all that bad, and we can give them credit for loving God and being honest.
>
> Mostly, I like the ordinary people. They worked at their jobs, they believed the Bible [sic! he means, the Old Testament, of course], they carried out the small routines and celebrations of the religion; they prayed every day, thanked God for his blessings, and on the sabbath went to the synagogue, asked teachers questions, and listened respectfully. What could be better? Every now and again they took their hard earned second tithe money to Jerusalem, devoutly performed their sacrifices, carried the meat out of the temple to share with their family and friends, brought some wine and maybe even some spirits, and feasted the night away. Then it was back to the regular grind. This may not sound like much, but in their view, they were living as God wished. The history of the time shows how firmly they believed in God, who gave them the law [he means, the Torah] and promised them deliverance.

In the world series of condescension toward the Jewish people and Judaism, Sanders here wins the gold medal. "I rather like the Pharisees" – indeed. Sanders comes from small-town Texas, and some think he talks like a hick. If coming to his defense, someone were to say, "But he's had speech lessons," he would understand why most Jews would rather not have supercilious friends of his kind.

Quite what is at stake here I cannot see; there is far less than meets the eye. Any objective person familiar with both this picture and also the Gospels is going to wonder what, in the Gospels, all the fuss is about. But that is beside the point in describing Judaism in the first century B.C. and A.D., since at issue is not history but theology. Asking what really happened and how things really were – the quest for the historical Jesus – forms a narrowly theological venture, in which what are called "historical facts" take the place of centuries of theological truths.

In the context of theology, not history, nothing I have said in criticism of Sanders bears consequence. For when we speak of theology, not history, then, with all my heart, I find in Sanders's words only goodness, and for that I honor him, as I did in 1978 with *Paul and Palestinian Judaism* and as I did in 1991 with *Jewish Law from Jesus to the Mishnah*. Christians like Sanders aim to shape a Christianity for the future different from the one we know in the past, a future Christianity in which "Silent Night" could never be sung by Christian racist murderers, as it was sung on Christmas after Christmas by the mass murderers, Poles, Germans, Lithuanians, and other good Catholics and Protestants and Orthodox Christians, at Auschwitz.

Never forget Sanders's vocation and its source: divinity students of Kittel and Jeremias served in the SS; priests and ministers worshipped Jesus Christ with, and for, the guards at Auschwitz. That fact defines the context in which Christian readers of Sanders's *Judaism. Practice and Belief 63 B.C.E. - 66 C.E.* are required to learn lessons of not history but theology. These are simple: [1] stop reviling Judaism – let it be, and [2] stop killing Jews.

# Appendix

## Another Harmony of All Judaisms

### *From Text to Tradition. A History of Second Temple and Rabbinic Judaism.*

By Lawrence H. Schiffman  (Hoboken, 1991: Ktav Publishing House, Inc.)


Sanders is not alone in representing a single Judaism, made up of all "Jewish" sources.  A variation on the same theme is worked out in a book that not only has a single Judaism, but also represents that Judaism as the increment of the ages: a tradition, which, amid change, persists essentially unimpaired.  One Judaism, the product of a single, unitary history, forms a yet more extreme harmony of the Judaisms.

Professor Lawrence H. Schiffman, New York University, here presents a textbook, not a work of scholarship but his conception of how the results of scholarship should be communicated to undergraduates. That that is his intention is not stated in so many words, the book lacking a preface; but since Schiffman provides no footnotes, no analysis of sources and defense of his reading and use of them, and no discussion of positions other than his own, we can only assume he means to speak to undergraduates, but not to people interesting in critical learning.

As a textbook, Schiffman's work exhibits several merits.  First, the writing is clear and careful, and the tone is pleasing; I cannot point to any other writing of Schiffman's that excels in presentation.  To be sure, the prose is lifeless, but it serves its purpose.  Second, the work follows a clear outline, beginning to end, and covers the topics that, within the framework of a topical, nondisciplinary work, one would expect.  That is to say, Schiffman works through an agenda of subjects, but he does not teach a discipline through the subject; so as a work for a generalist course in "Jewish studies," but not for a course in history, literature, history of religions, or texts, the book serves its purpose. He treats in no special order problems of history, literature, religion, and theology; presentations of particular books, for example, Apocrypha, Pseudepigrapha, and the Dead Sea Scrolls, which scarcely fall together as writing, as statements of Judaic systems, or as representative of a single circle or community, stand side by side with presentations of historical-religious problems (sectarianism in the second Commonwealth, Jewish-Christian schism, stand before and after the book chapter).

Anyone who wants to know what Schiffman thinks on most of the topics connected with the study of the Jews from biblical to medieval times, or of Judaism in that same period, will find it here. These are the chapters: the biblical heritage; Judaism in the Persian period; the Hellenistic age; Judaism in the Hellenistic diaspora; sectarianism in the second Commonwealth, Apocrypha, etc.; the Jewish-Christian schism; revolt and restoration; Mishnah; formative Judaism comes of age; the sea of the Talmud; the life of Torah; and the hegemony of the Babylonian Talmud. The book is illustrated throughout.

Has Schiffman achieved his goal? For those who are Modern Orthodox and who also think historical-critical research has to be coped with, the answer is yes. Schiffman posits a single Judaism, which is a continuous tradition. He acknowledges that the tradition unfolded or evolved, but it is one and singular: unitary, incremental, and harmonious. If you think so, use this book; if that position strikes you as naive and credulous, find something else.

He states, "This book provides an outline of the history of Judaism during...its post-biblical development, from the last years of the biblical period until the arrival of the consensus we know as Talmudic Judaism. By Judaism, we mean the collective religious, cultural, and legal tradition and civilization of the Jewish people as developed and passed down from biblical times until today. Judaism is not a monolithic phenomenon. Rather, it encompasses many different historical moments as well as many different approaches to the questions of god, man, and the world. All these 'Judaisms' are tied together by the common thread of the continuity of tradition and by the collective historical destiny of the Jewish People." Those who can show how a "common thread of the continuity of tradition" (assuming those words mean anything at all) link the authors of the Dead Sea Scrolls to Abbayye and Raba will also know how to make sense of this picture.

Schiffman claims his method is historical, but it is history tempered by a heavy dose of theology. He sees "the various approaches to Judaism as standing in a dynamic and interactive relationship to one another. In this case, each approach must be studied alongside those in the same period with which it competed and also in relation to those which preceded and followed it.... One observes the constantly reciprocal influences between approaches, but also recognizes what each period and approach bequeathed to that which came after." If this were a work of scholarship, Schiffman would find it necessary to explain what he means and to amass evidence and arguments in behalf of his position. In a textbook it suffices to say so. He also claims to conduct his work in a critical way, but he uses the rabbinic evidence as though we could simply lift sentences out of paragraphs, ignore all questions of literary history, and translate said sentences into historical facts. He thinks the Mishnah, Talmuds, and Midrash compilations are akin to encyclopaedias of facts about things that were really said or done. His introduction contains not a single word to suggest that there are other ways of seeing these sources besides his, and he offers not a hint to his students that his reading would receive a very puzzled hearing at any academic gathering outside of the Yeshiva and Jewish-Studies worlds.

Since most of the Yeshivas do not study history at all, this book can work well only at Yeshiva University, in the Orthodox world in this country, and possibly at Bar Ilan in the State of Israel. As to Jewish Studies departments, they do everything and its opposite, depending on the case, so there is no predicting what, if anything, they will make of this work; the secular programs will reject it because of its espousal of Modern Orthodox theology. University courses in departments of Religious Studies invest too much energy into problems of method – what we know, how we know it – to take seriously this wide-eyed report of the Judaic equivalent of UFOs: "common thread of continuity of tradition" indeed! If you believe it, you see it, if not, not; this is a book for believers. So, in all, I suspect the book will find for itself only a very tiny market. That is for three reasons. First of all, it is not an effective textbook, since students should be shown the character of evidence, how it is read, alternative views on it, and the reasons for taking a given position; otherwise, what you have is indoctrination, not education. Here the teaching process is doctrinaire and inert. Second, it is not a nuanced presentation of its subject, being altogether too descriptive and insufficiently illustrative; so the student is not invited into the sources. Once students have been taught this book, they can do little more than repeat the information in it; they have not been taught how to do the same thing with other subjects, or how to take up new problems within this subject. Third, it is not a reflective or profound book, covering much too much ground in a superficial manner, so teachers will not be aided by the book in presenting the subject. It is one dimensional; orthodoxy exacts costs, and Modern Orthodoxy imposes a heavy tariff of intellectual sloth.

That is a pity, since Schiffman is a fine scholar in a few of the many areas on which he passes his opinion in these pages, and he could have given us a work of intellectual vitality and topical interest.

# Index

Aaron, 221, 256

Abbayye, 298

Abihu, 33

Abodah Zarah, 40, 42, 129, 151, 162, 193, 196

abomination, 197

Abot, 16, 74, 107-108, 117, 164, 166, 190, 253, 283

Abraham, 66, 119

act of labor, 134, 137-138, 142

Adam, 187, 191

adultery, 102, 150, 182, 283

agglutination, 80

Akiba, 291

Alexander Jannaeus, 255, 258

Alexandra Salome, 255

Alexandria, 15

altar, 27-28, 31-33, 43-44, 55-56, 60, 64, 85, 100, 104, 150, 159, 161, 177, 180-181, 185, 197, 212, 221, 240, 267-268

Amen, 68

analogical-contrastive thinking, 142-143

analogy, 28, 33, 144, 161, 209, 213, 233, 240, 270, 284

angel, 14, 107

animal-offering, 276

animal sacrifice, 278

anoint, 59, 84, 150

anonymity, 69, 80, 107-108, 265, 277, 285, 290

anti-Semitism, 271

apocalyptic, 54, 61, 168-169, 222-223, 290

apocopation, 88-89, 92

Apocrypha, 231, 252-253, 290, 298

appendix, 40, 297

Aqiba, 25, 70, 109, 243, 256, 258

Arakhin, 44, 145, 148, 163

Aramaic, 14, 74, 226-227

argument a fortiori, 221

Aristobulus, 255

Aristotle, 126-128

ark, 44-45

Asia, 57

Assyrian, 18

atonement, 33, 75, 83, 148, 151, 167-168, 225-226, 231-232, 234, 267, 291-292

attributions of sayings, 242, 264

Augustine, 49

authorship, 65, 117-118, 121, 123, 134, 136, 142, 148, 154-156, 207, 211-213, 220-221, 248-249

Avery-Peck, Alan J., 29, 141

Baba Batra, 22, 40, 42, 111, 144, 148, 159, 163

Baba Mesia, 40, 42, 145, 148, 160, 163

Baba Qamma, 40, 42, 145, 148, 163

Babylonia, 16-17, 50-51, 165-166, 183, 192, 220, 244, 256, 262

Babylonian, 66, 82, 244

Babylonian Talmud, 81, 193, 221, 298

banishment, 41, 67

Baptist, 210

Bar Kokhba, 14, 35-36, 55, 57, 83, 248

Bar Kokhba War, 25, 31, 36, 166, 178, 243, 248, 257

Baruch, 51, 107, 167, 187

Bauer, Walter, 206

Baumgarten, Joseph M., 15

Bavli, 65

Bekhorot, 44, 145, 148, 163

Ben Sira, 231, 290

Berakhot, 36, 65, 69, 71, 88, 122, 130, 160, 162-163, 294

Besah, 22, 37, 111, 138

betrothal, 38, 158

Bible, 29, 43, 73, 80, 82, 106, 132, 136, 154, 157, 165, 167, 187-191, 198-199, 209-210, 223, 225, 227, 229, 238, 247-249, 260, 263, 290-291, 294, 298

Bikkurim, 36, 130, 149, 160, 162-163

blood, 28-29, 32, 144, 159, 220, 225, 239-240, 277-278

Bousset, 276

Boyce, Mary, 235

Brooks, Roger, 155

burnt-offering, 159, 292

canon, 50-51, 59-60, 78, 81, 106, 114, 126, 165-166, 187-188, 191, 219-220, 242

catalogue, 65, 70, 81, 137, 147, 152, 156, 159-160, 269

category formation, 205, 207, 222

childbirth, 45, 154, 221

Chilton, Bruce D., 74, 205, 227, 229

Chomsky, 95

Chr., 221

Christ, 56, 75, 77, 230, 295

Christianity, 18, 49, 52, 55, 60, 64, 77-78, 82, 168, 170-171, 188-189, 206, 208-209, 223, 230, 234-235, 245-246, 251, 254, 257, 259-260, 263-264, 271-273, 275, 288, 294-295, 298

Chronicles, 56

Church, 77, 168, 170, 223, 251

circumcision, 52

cleanness, 21-22, 27-28, 30-31, 45-47, 89, 96, 98, 100, 102-104, 111, 122, 124, 131, 134-137, 140, 148, 155, 157-158, 171-

172, 175-178, 183, 186, 208, 211, 215, 222-224, 240, 260-262, 265-268, 272, 278, 288

cogency, 17, 19-20, 41, 47, 53, 95, 101, 117-118, 125-126, 130, 138-140, 185, 209

Cohen, S.J.D., 264

commandment, 65, 72, 199, 210, 225, 231, 283, 288, 293

comparison, 18, 32, 37, 51, 53, 75, 124-125, 131, 135, 137, 144, 146, 159, 167-168, 171, 225, 231-235, 238, 241-246, 269, 290

compilation, 82, 165, 191, 236, 244, 299

composite, 16, 253

congruence, 47, 85, 93, 95, 98, 101

consecration, 27, 43, 81, 150-151, 214-215, 218

continuity, 31-32, 60, 167, 177-178, 252, 298-299

contrast, 16, 22, 32, 49-50, 84, 89-90, 107, 111, 124-125, 131, 135, 137, 142-144, 155, 159, 169, 174, 207, 211-212, 220, 227-228, 230, 247, 251, 257, 259, 289-290

convert, 256

corpse, 28-29, 32, 46, 98, 124, 135-136, 150, 154, 158, 216, 239-240, 244, 269, 272

corpse uncleanness, 32, 45, 56, 142, 176, 267

Creation, 36-37, 98, 168-172, 185-186

cult, 15, 21, 29-34, 37, 44, 54-55, 57, 63-64, 76, 82-83, 85, 103, 105, 111, 136, 155, 157, 159, 168-180, 182-183, 189, 210, 217, 219, 251, 257, 259, 261, 267

David, 68, 77

Davis, M., 53

Day of Atonement, 75, 83, 148, 151, 226

Dead Sea Psalms, 187

Dead Sea Scrolls, 13, 80, 190, 231, 245, 284, 289-290, 293, 298

deaf-mute, 158

death, 28-29, 38-39, 41-43, 57-58, 61, 102, 146, 158, 178, 180, 291

debt, 227-229

Demai, 22, 36, 111, 122, 130, 141, 160, 162-163

Deuteronomy, 58, 65-66, 119, 132, 149-152, 155-158, 194, 196-199, 221, 290

Diaspora, 16, 62, 101, 223, 298

disciple, 54-57, 73, 183, 220, 223, 234, 261

Divine Presence, 72

divorce, 18, 24, 38-39, 55, 94, 111, 128, 145-146, 151, 227

doctrine, 30, 49, 54, 57, 75, 107, 110, 121, 169-170, 172, 206, 258

domain, public, 197

dowry, 39

drink-offering, 27

Dual Torah, 126-129, 165, 211, 214, 219-220, 222, 248, 256, 262-263, 270

Dunn, James D.G., 52-53, 55, 62-63, 75, 289

economics, 127

Eduyyot, 87, 280

Egypt, 15, 69, 76, 170, 249

Eighteen Benedictions, 65, 69-70, 72, 285

Eleazar, 107, 216, 218

Eleazar Hisma, 120

Eliezer, 69-71, 215, 217-219, 249-250, 256, 281

Eliezer b. Hyrcanus, 249-250, 281

encompassing rule, 13

English, 65, 238

Enoch, 187, 231

Erubin, 22, 37, 111, 130, 151, 162

eschatology, 77, 205, 208-210, 219, 235, 240, 255

Essene, 15, 18, 50, 54-55, 62, 64, 73, 76, 104, 106, 207, 210, 221, 223, 253-254, 257, 271-272, 284, 288, 293-294

eternity, 56, 58-59, 68, 263

ethics, 145, 229, 259-260

ethos, 52, 91, 98

Europeans, 188, 190

evangelists, 237

Ex., 122, 149-150, 156, 161

execution, 41, 123, 130, 134, 147

exegesis, 15-17, 20, 23, 35, 90, 105, 108-110, 112, 114, 130, 147, 150, 160, 165, 176, 187-188, 190-192, 194-195, 199-200, 213, 217, 224-226, 233, 235-238, 240, 246, 250, 253

exile, 102, 198

Exodus, 70, 76, 107, 248-249, 290

expiation, 33, 42-43, 167-168

extirpation, 210

Ezek., 293

Ezekiel, 123, 160, 293

Ezra, 51, 65, 167, 187-188, 191, 231, 248

Father of Uncleanness, 216

Fathers according to Rabbi Nathan, 210

festal-offering, 149

festival, 29, 34, 37, 40, 46, 58, 75-76, 82, 100, 105, 122, 134, 150, 161, 254, 258-261, 272

fire, 27, 197

firstling, 159

flog, 41

flux, 21, 28, 45, 98, 110, 216

footnote, 264, 286, 297

forbidden, 13, 40, 42, 154, 169, 179

forgiveness, 67-68, 84, 167, 228

form-analysis, 69

France, 170

fraud, 39

fundamentalism, 262

Galilee, 62, 228, 294

Gamaliel, 65, 69, 71, 103, 253-254

Gemara, 235

Gen., 156

Genesis Rabbah, 192

gentile, 40, 57, 70-71, 78, 124, 135, 174, 196-197, 208, 212-214, 227, 231, 260

Gittin, 38-39, 111, 145, 151, 162-164

gloss, 217-218

Gnosticism, 168-172, 270

God, 15, 28, 36, 39, 46, 49, 51-52, 55-56, 59, 62-64, 66-68, 72, 74-77, 80-81, 84, 95, 98-100, 104, 106-107, 109-110, 113-114, 126, 155, 157, 165, 167-172, 175, 185-186, 187, 189-190, 193, 195-197, 221, 225, 227-229, 231-232, 263, 269, 271-273, 291-294, 298

Goodenough, Erwin R., 15

Gospels, 18, 50, 59, 103, 207, 222, 226-227, 229, 237, 247, 251-252, 255, 258-259, 261, 271, 289, 295

Greco-Roman, 53

Greece, 62, 74, 227, 291

Green, William Scott, 236, 264

Gressman, 276

guilt, 33, 44, 167-168, 222, 284-285, 289

guilt-offering, 41, 44, 157, 159

Hagigah, 37, 145, 149, 160, 162-164, 265, 268-269

halakhah, 13-15, 17, 19-20, 23, 25-26, 31, 36, 46-48, 222, 241, 243

halisah, 158

Hallah, 36, 130, 151, 162

Hananiah, Prefect of the Priests, 256

Hanina, 291

Hannah, 199

harmonization, 206, 210, 276

Hasmonean, 254-255, 257, 279-280

Hatch, E., 226

Hauck, F., 229

Havdalah, 70-71

heave-offering, 27, 32-33, 69, 104, 141, 158, 212, 215-219, 265-268, 280-281

Heaven, 28, 37-39, 43, 54, 58, 76-77, 102, 173, 181-182, 184-186, 191, 240, 258

Hebrew, 14, 18, 66, 75, 80, 82, 95, 150, 187-191, 226-227, 236, 291

Hebrew Scriptures, 58, 80, 106, 170, 189-190, 206, 293

Hebrews, 60

Heinemann, Joseph, 55, 65, 70-72

Hellenism, 53, 62, 222, 298

hermeneutics, 87, 195, 226, 245

Herod, 123, 254-255, 279-280

hierarchy, 124, 130-131, 134-138, 143, 145, 147, 149, 159, 208, 211, 214, 268-269

high priest, 41-42, 56, 148, 171, 255, 257

Hillel, 70, 104, 108, 173, 234, 253-258, 280, 282-283

Hillelites, 254-255, 258

historiography, 230

history, 14, 19, 23-26, 29-30, 34-35, 37, 54, 56-64, 76-78, 82, 86, 105-106, 112-114, 146, 162, 167-169, 173-174, 176, 205, 220, 223, 230, 231, 233, 235-236, 238, 240, 242, 244, 246, 251-252, 254, 257, 262-263,

272, 277, 281, 284, 292, 294-295, 297-299

history of Judaism, 11, 15, 17, 31, 128, 178, 298

Hollis, F.J., 123, 160

Holy Land, 16, 28, 36, 46, 76, 81, 86, 99, 102, 174-175, 178, 181, 183, 191

Holy of Holies, 44, 68

Holy Place, 64-65, 75

Holy Things, 15-16, 21, 29, 32-33, 35, 37, 43-44, 46-47, 98, 100, 104, 110, 157, 159, 177, 183, 212, 215-219, 238, 265-268

homiletics, 148

Horayot, 41-42, 83, 130, 152, 162

House of Shammai, 280

Houses (of Shammai and Hillel), 32, 70, 249, 253-258, 260, 265, 282

Hullin, 43-44, 131, 152, 162

husband, 18, 24, 34, 38-39, 82, 158, 210, 222

hypothesis, 71, 244, 261

Idi, 194

idiom, 128, 227, 229

idol, 40, 196-197

idolatry, 40, 151

incense, 221

intentionality, 122-123, 125, 129-134, 137-138, 140-141, 144-146, 149, 152, 157, 159-160

interpretation, 23, 52, 55-56, 60, 73, 105, 110, 113-114, 168, 175, 192, 194, 198, 206, 225, 228, 232-234, 240-241, 243-246, 250, 268, 285, 292

Isaac, 66, 119

Isaac bar Nahman, 197

Isaiah, 74, 226-227, 229, 248

Ishmael, 70, 109, 193

Islam, 188, 235

Israel, 15-17, 20, 28, 31, 35, 37-38, 43-44, 46-48, 49-68, 72-78, 80-84, 86, 93, 98-102, 106, 110, 112, 114, 140-141, 157, 159, 165, 169-170, 174-175, 177-178, 180-184, 186, 188-189, 191-194, 208, 211-212, 220, 232, 243, 248, 251-252, 288, 292, 294, 299

Israelites, 18, 20, 29, 31, 34, 36, 38, 40-44, 52, 55-58, 62-64, 66, 69, 74, 76-77, 80-85, 99, 102, 106, 108, 112, 124, 135, 140, 156, 161, 167-171, 174, 177-178, 181-182, 186, 187-189, 192, 196-197, 205, 208, 212-214, 221, 231, 243, 264

Jacob, 119, 187

Jacobs, Louis, 239

Jeremiah, 187

Jeremias, J., 228, 275, 295

Jericho, 279

Jerusalem, 14, 31, 42, 44, 55, 65, 68, 74-75, 82-83, 85, 104, 120-121, 132, 152, 154, 169, 178-179, 227, 240, 245, 251, 253, 259-260, 272, 275-276, 279-280, 294

Jesus, 18, 52, 54-55, 73-74, 77, 206-209, 222-230, 232, 234, 237, 243, 247-249, 251, 259, 271-272, 275, 281-283, 286, 295

Jew, 13-17, 34, 36, 49-50, 55-56, 58, 60-62, 65, 76, 78, 80-86, 99,

103-104, 113-114, 126, 165, 167, 169, 179, 188-189, 191-192, 226, 232, 235, 238, 240, 244-246, 247-253, 255, 259-264, 269-272, 275-276, 281, 290, 292-293, 295, 297-299

John Hyrcanus, 255, 258

John the Baptist, 210

Joseph, 292

Josephus, 51, 66, 103, 220, 251-255, 258, 261, 290-293

Joshua, 59, 69, 217-219

Joshua b. Levi, 199

Josiah, 293

Jubilees, 231

Judah, 107, 124, 135, 212-214, 294

Judah b. Batera, 199

Judah b. Ilai, 70-71, 256

Judah the Patriarch, 15, 82, 110, 117, 125, 129, 248, 257

Judaism, 11, 13-15, 17-18, 21, 29, 31, 49-56, 58-64, 66, 72, 75, 77-78, 81-82, 85-86, 98-99, 103, 105-106, 113-114, 126-129, 164, 165-168, 173, 175, 178, 181, 183, 185-186, 187-191, 194, 201, 203, 205-211, 214, 219-226, 229-230, 231-237, 240-242, 245-246, 247-252, 262-264, 268, 270-273, 275-276, 281, 283-284, 286, 288-292, 294-295, 297-299

Judea, 62

judgment, 34, 41-42, 53, 62, 67, 83-84, 86, 102, 118, 120, 127, 130, 138, 140, 157, 171, 182, 192, 194-195, 208-210, 223, 235, 240, 269, 271, 283-284, 288, 290, 293-294

Justin, 220

Kelim, 22, 30, 45, 56, 111, 122, 131, 145, 160, 162-163, 172, 238

Keritot, 43-44, 131, 152, 162, 277

Ketubot, 38-39, 111, 122, 146, 160, 163

Kilayim, 36, 132, 152, 162

king, 83-84

Kings, 59, 293

Kippurim, 220

Kittel, G., 229, 246, 295

knife, 220

Korach, 199

lamb, 149-150, 291

Land of Israel, 15-17, 44, 49-51, 53, 56, 62, 73, 82-83, 86, 140-141, 165, 169, 183-184, 191-192, 220, 251

law, 11, 13-21, 23-35, 39-44, 46-47, 52, 56, 60, 65, 69, 73, 76, 80, 82-83, 87, 91, 93-94, 96-97, 101, 104-106, 109-110, 112, 114, 126-129, 136, 140, 142, 145-147, 149-150, 153-155, 157, 160, 162, 171-181, 189-200, 208-210, 214, 222-223, 226, 230, 232, 234, 236-238, 240-241, 244, 247, 249-262, 264, 269-272, 276-277, 281, 283, 287-289, 292, 294-295

laws of sacrilege, 153

laws of uncleanness, 31, 178, 209

leavening, 150

leper, 153, 212, 216, 222-223, 239-240

Lev., 21, 28, 32, 41, 103, 121-124, 132, 143, 147-159, 161, 176, 182, 210, 213, 221, 283

Levine, Baruch A., 18

Levite, 36, 76, 168, 175, 179, 260

Leviticus, 27-28, 33, 41, 56, 58, 64, 83, 107, 109-110, 157, 173, 191, 207-208, 221, 224-226, 239, 288, 290, 292

liability, 98, 139

libation, 40

Lieberman, Saul, 264

list making, 138

Listenwissenschaft, 117, 147

literature, 59, 83, 156, 165-166, 168, 188, 208, 223, 231-232, 235-236, 238, 241, 245-246, 248, 256, 264, 277, 279-281, 284-285, 293-294, 298

loan, 34

logic, 18, 24, 33, 47, 87, 92, 94, 109, 117-118, 121, 125-126, 133, 166, 171, 177, 200, 228, 237

Lord, 65-68, 102, 104, 159, 182, 197, 200, 221, 227-229, 250, 293

Luke, 222-224, 227-229, 249

Lutheran, 235, 289

M. A.Z., 196

M. Abot, 74

M. B.M., 197

M. Ber., 69-71, 122

M. Git., 18

M. Hagigah, 103, 268

M. Kelim, 56, 122, 131, 145

M. Miq., 238

M. Neg., 124, 135, 212-213

M. San., 194, 199

M. Sotah, 103, 147, 150, 211

M. Tamid, 65

M. Toh., 33, 103

M. Yad., 103

M. Yebamot, 17

Maaser Sheni, 36, 132, 149, 152, 155, 162-163

Maaserot, 36, 132, 152, 162

Maccoby, Hiam, 247-249, 264, 284

Maimonides, 126-129

Makhshirin, 45, 123, 125, 132, 152, 162

Makkot, 41-42, 83, 146, 149, 164, 198

Mana, 33

Mark, 112, 207, 222-224, 229, 249, 258

marriage, 14, 24, 29-30, 38-39, 55, 58, 111, 128, 146, 172-173, 179-180, 184, 288

marriage contract, 14, 38-39, 146

Matthew, 112, 187, 190, 222-224, 228-229, 237, 248-249, 258

meal-offering, 27, 145, 149

meat, 27-29, 44, 76, 103-104, 159, 176, 197, 260, 291, 294

Megillah, 37, 146, 149, 164

Meilah, 43-44, 133, 153, 162

Meir, 107, 124, 135, 197

Menahem, 253

Menahot, 43-44, 72, 133, 145, 149, 153, 160, 163-164

menstruation, 32, 45, 98, 210, 277

Messiah, 55-57, 59-61, 63, 68, 75-78, 227, 252, 254

metaphor, 37, 183-184, 207, 209, 215, 220, 229

method, 18, 21, 25, 123, 126-127, 134, 138-139, 142, 147, 157, 245, 250, 264, 268, 275, 287, 298-299

Micah, 194

Middle East, 14

Middot, 44, 122, 146, 160, 163-164

midras uncleanness, 266, 268

Midrash, 188, 238, 244, 299

Midrash compilation, 244, 299

Millar, 66, 73

Miqvaot, 22, 30, 45, 111, 124, 133, 135, 153, 162, 172, 238-241

Miriam, 221

Mishnah, 13-23, 25-27, 29-32, 34-44, 46-48, 50, 53, 55, 59-60, 65-66, 69, 71, 79-99, 101-114, 117-119, 121-134, 136-142, 144-148, 150, 152, 154-159, 161-162, 164, 165-186, 187, 189-201, 207-208, 211-220, 222-223, 234-241, 243, 247-251, 253, 256, 262-263, 265, 268, 270, 272, 275-277, 281-286, 288, 290-295, 298-299

mixed seeds, 175

Moed Qatan, 37, 122, 133, 161-163

monotheism, 52, 55, 63, 290

Moore, George Foot, 245, 276, 286, 289

Moses, 15-16, 35, 65-66, 73-74, 77, 81, 106-110, 113, 126, 165, 168-169, 188-191, 193, 195-196, 199, 220-221, 238, 252, 256-258, 262-263

Most High, 66

Moule, C.F.D., 228

Mount Sinai, 15-16, 74, 106-107, 109-110, 126, 165, 169, 193, 263

Muffs, Y., 14-15, 18

murder, 57, 264, 295

Muslims, 235

Nadab, 33

Nag Hammadi, 171

Nazir, 38-39, 134, 153, 162

Nedarim, 38-39, 123, 134, 153, 162

Negaim, 21, 45, 110, 124-125, 134, 154, 162, 212, 221

Nehemiah, 65

Neusner, Jacob, 15, 18, 57, 205, 207, 221, 223, 239, 247-249, 262-264, 269-270, 284-286, 288

New Testament, 18, 77, 103, 206, 209, 222-223, 227-230, 232, 235, 237, 245, 247-249, 271, 286

New Year, 75, 156

Newman, Louis, 140, 157

Niddah, 21, 30, 45, 110, 124, 135, 154, 162, 172, 221, 238, 278

nonpriest, 265

Num., 65-66, 122, 142, 148-150, 153-156, 158, 161, 176, 199, 291

Numbers, 28, 173, 239, 290, 292

oath, 41, 157

Offspring of Uncleanness, 216

Ohalot, 22, 30, 45, 111, 136, 154, 162, 238

Old Testament, 53, 58, 64, 77, 106, 187, 189-190, 205-210, 231, 238, 244, 252, 294

ontology, 35, 98, 207, 211, 214

Oral Torah, 77, 189-190, 193-194, 219, 239-240, 252, 256-257, 263

ordinary folk, 34, 47, 51, 69, 94, 101-102, 181, 266, 268, 270, 272, 294

Orlah, 36, 136, 138, 154-155, 162

Orthodox Christianity, 272, 295

Orthodox Judaism, 51, 62, 129, 206, 298-299

paganism, 42, 51, 271, 294

Palestine, 14-15, 34, 40, 232, 251, 254-255

Palestinian, 53, 61-62, 75, 81-82, 192, 225-226, 230, 231-232, 244, 253, 259, 294-295

parables, 227-229

Parah, 22, 45, 111, 136, 142, 155, 161-162, 248-249

Passover, 75-76, 83, 122, 150, 159, 161, 291

Passover meal, 150

Passover-offering, 150

patriarchs, 86, 117, 171, 257

Paul, 75, 103, 220, 225-226, 230, 231-235, 237, 242-243, 248-249, 271-272, 275, 283, 294-295

peace-offering, 29, 159

Peah, 36, 137, 155, 162

Pentateuch, 73, 81, 106, 113, 165, 207, 220, 248

Pentecost, 75

pericope, 24, 69, 88, 94, 97, 108-109, 118, 129-130, 132-137, 141, 145, 154, 218, 223, 237

perjury, 41

Persia, 298

Pesahim, 37, 107, 125, 146, 150, 164

Pharisaic Judaism, 252

Pharisees, 18, 54, 56, 60, 62, 64, 76, 103-104, 166, 173, 207, 223-224, 228, 234, 240, 247, 249-266, 268-273, 277-282, 284, 287-289, 294-295

Philo, 15, 220, 223, 248, 289-293

philosophy, 18, 22, 42-43, 53, 62, 87, 105, 109, 112, 121, 123-147, 149-157, 159, 161-164, 170-172, 181, 189-191, 195-196, 230, 240-241, 247, 251, 253-254, 268, 270

phylactery, 70, 194

politics, 30, 35, 40-41, 47, 54, 56, 59, 64, 76, 83, 85-86, 101, 114, 127, 131, 171, 179-180, 191-192, 223, 243, 247-248, 251, 254-255, 258, 261

Porten, B., 14-15

prayer, 62-66, 68-74, 76, 122, 148, 160, 227, 285-287, 294

pressure uncleanness, 143

priest, 27-28, 33-34, 36, 41-42, 44, 54-58, 60-61, 63-66, 69, 76-78, 83-84, 98, 102-104, 148, 155, 158-159, 170-171, 173-175, 177, 179-185, 221-222, 252, 255-257, 259-262, 265-270, 277-278, 280-281, 290-291, 293, 295

priestly code, 27-28, 64, 112, 148, 182, 208, 288

prohibition, 13, 40, 43, 83, 121, 150-151, 154, 170, 193, 196-197, 209-210, 224, 265-266

prooftext, 108, 123, 132, 165, 195-197, 199-200, 237

prophet, 55, 58, 61-62, 73, 77, 80, 106, 112, 169, 194, 223, 227, 238, 252

proposition, 20, 103-104, 127, 138-139, 162, 171, 173, 191, 194-197, 199-200, 209, 213-214, 231, 237, 244, 248, 261, 269, 277

proselyte, 67, 282

Protestant, 262, 270-272, 288, 292, 295

Ps., 199

Psalms of Solomon, 231

pseudepigrapha, 50, 80, 108, 187, 190, 231, 252-253, 290, 298

purification, 22, 45, 47, 101, 111, 134, 142, 153-154, 158, 161, 208, 238-240, 244, 266, 291-292

purification water, 32, 142, 155, 176, 239, 244, 265-266

Q, 112

Qabbalah, 108

Qiddushin, 38-39, 122, 137-138, 161-163

Qinnim, 44, 138, 156, 162-163

Qumran, 15, 18, 50, 55, 104, 106, 207, 210, 221, 223, 261, 279, 284-285, 293-294

Raba, 298

Rabbah, 192

Rabbi, 55, 60, 77-78, 81, 102, 125-126, 165, 182, 189, 196, 198, 200, 210, 221, 229, 242, 252, 263, 283, 294

rabbinic, 51, 59-60, 113, 165-168, 173, 181, 223, 225-226, 231-238, 240-242, 244-246, 247-261, 263, 269, 276-277, 279-285, 291, 293-294, 297, 299

rabbis, 50, 57, 59-60, 78, 86, 102, 105, 166, 182-183, 198, 222, 229, 237, 241-245, 248-249, 251-252, 254-258, 261, 277, 280, 285-287, 290-291

red cow, 21-22, 111, 136, 142, 155, 176, 239, 247-249, 265

redaction, 23, 90, 96, 106-107, 109, 189, 217, 294

Redpath, H.A., 226

religion, 16, 43, 49, 51-55, 62, 64, 72, 75, 77-78, 81-82, 86, 97-99, 103, 106, 187, 189, 205, 225, 231-234, 236, 238, 240-242, 245-246, 248, 254, 259, 263-264, 270, 272-273, 275-276, 280-281, 285-286, 290, 292-294, 298-299

remarriage, 24

repentance, 67-68, 75, 225-227, 229, 231

resurrection, 70-71, 103, 211, 235

Reuben, 199

revelation, 16, 22, 62-64, 74, 77, 80-81, 106-110, 112-113, 117, 125-126, 129-130, 165, 169-172, 187, 190, 192, 196, 201, 238, 248-249

rhetoric, 91-97, 109, 117-118, 125-126, 222

rite of the red cow, 142

Roman Catholic, 272, 288

Roman Empire, 15

Rome, 25, 51, 53, 56, 83-84, 114, 170-171, 173, 191, 251-252, 254-255, 257, 272, 288

Rosh Hashshanah, 37, 146, 156, 162, 164

Sabbath, 13, 29, 34, 36-37, 52, 58, 70, 82, 103, 223, 254-255, 258-261, 271-272, 294

Sabbatical Year, 140, 157

sacrifice, 30, 33, 42-44, 55, 60, 64, 68-69, 77, 83, 105, 144, 151, 153, 155-156, 159, 167-168, 172, 175, 177, 221-222, 224-226, 240, 254, 277-278, 290-292, 294

sacrilege, 153

Sadducees, 62, 253-254, 257-258, 260

sage, 16-18, 23-25, 33, 35, 42, 49, 51, 55-61, 63, 69, 72, 75, 77-78, 82-87, 92-93, 103, 105, 113-114, 120, 165, 168, 171, 190, 192-193, 195-196, 198-201, 212-213, 219, 222, 245, 252, 262, 270, 278, 285, 287, 291

salvation, 60-61, 64, 66, 68, 74-76, 112, 165, 167-168, 170, 231-232, 252, 263, 283-284, 288

Sam., 200

Samuel, 197

Samuel bar Nahman, 199

sanctification, 15, 28, 32-33, 36-37, 39, 44, 46-47, 56, 61, 64, 72, 74, 76, 81, 83-84, 98-102, 112, 132, 140-141, 145, 149, 152, 156-158, 165, 173, 177-178, 181-185, 188-190, 208, 214-215, 221-223, 248, 263, 272

sanctuary, 43-44, 150, 221

Sanders, E.P., 75-76, 203, 205-206, 209-211, 214, 222-226, 229-230, 231-246, 247, 249-251, 261-265, 268-273, 275-295, 297

Sanhedrin, 41-42, 83, 138-139, 156, 162-163

Sarason, Richard S., 65

Schaefer, Peter, 55

Schechter, Solomon, 245, 289

Schiffman, Lawrence H., 13, 15, 297-300

Schuerer, 66, 73

Schürer, Emil, 276

scribe, 34, 54-56, 60-61, 63, 73, 76-77, 102-103, 145, 181-183, 185, 193-194, 196, 252

Scripture, 13-15, 17-23, 26-27, 32-33, 35-36, 38, 41, 51, 55, 58, 60, 64, 73-78, 80, 86, 99, 106-112, 114, 117-119, 121-127, 129-132, 134, 138-139, 143-164, 165, 168-172, 176, 187-201, 206, 213, 219, 229, 237-240, 244, 248-249, 251, 261, 267, 293

Scroll of Esther, 146, 149

sea, 13, 80, 187, 190, 231, 245, 270, 284, 289-290, 293, 298

sexual relations, 30, 172, 210

Shabbat, 37, 138-139, 156, 162-163, 280, 282

Shabuot, 75, 139, 157, 162-163

Shammai, 70, 108, 173, 253-254, 256-258, 280, 282

Shammaites, 254, 258, 281

Shebiit, 36, 139, 157, 163

Shebuot, 41-42, 83

Shema, 65-66, 69-71, 287

Sheqalim, 37, 147, 150, 164

shofar, 156, 161

Sifra, 109, 128, 191, 213, 220-221, 237, 263

Sifré to Deuteronomy, 221

Sifré to Numbers, 221

Sifrés, 213, 220

Simeon, 65, 107, 253, 277

Simeon b. Eleazar, 221

Simeon b. Gamaliel, 103, 119, 173, 253, 276-277, 283

Simeon b. Shetah, 254-255, 258

Simeon b. Yehosedeq, 197

Simeon b. Yohai, 221

Simeon Happaqoli, 65

Simon, 228

sin, 29, 33, 44, 102, 130, 167-168, 182, 207-211, 220-222, 226, 229, 284, 291-292

sin-offering, 29, 44, 159, 267, 277

Sinai, 16-17, 74, 77-78, 81, 107-108, 189-190, 192, 195-196, 252-253, 262-263

sinner, 167, 208-211, 221, 227, 285

skin ailment, 221

slaughter, 258, 260

slave, 66, 70, 184

Smith, Jonathan Z., 236

Smith, Morton, 53, 61-62

social entity, 14, 208, 251

sociology, 272

Song, 193

Sotah, 38-39, 147, 150, 164, 211

Sperber, A., 227

storyteller, 254

substitute, 77

successor system, 269-270

Sukkah, 37, 147, 150, 164, 293

Sukkot, 75, 150

syllogism, 19

synagogue, 62, 66, 73-74, 76, 83, 85-86, 146, 149, 294

Synoptics, 222, 251, 254-256, 271

T. Berakhot, 294

T. Neg., 221

T. San., 199

Taanit, 37, 147, 161, 163

Tabernacle, 75, 122, 150, 161

Talmud, 17, 60, 81-82, 94, 99, 108-109, 165, 192-196, 200, 220, 235, 283, 294, 298-299

Talmud of Babylonia, 16-17, 50-51, 165-166, 220, 256, 262

Talmud of the Land of Israel, 16-17, 192, 220

Talmudist, 262

Tamid, 22, 43-44, 65, 111, 147, 151, 161, 163

Tanakh, 58, 64, 106

Tanhum b. R. Hiyya, 194

Tanhuma, 45

Tannaite, 231, 234-235, 237-238, 246, 253

Tannaitic literature, 231, 235, 238, 246

tax, 175, 228, 254, 287

taxa, 77, 122, 131, 140, 157

taxonomy, 78, 113, 125, 130, 135, 137, 139, 141-144, 147, 149, 156, 211

Tebul Yom, 45, 140, 157-158, 163

tefillin, 70

Temple, 21-22, 27-29, 31-37, 42-44, 46-47, 52, 54-57, 60, 62, 64-66, 72, 75-77, 82-85, 100, 102-105, 107, 110-111, 122-123, 136-137, 150, 153, 155, 157, 160-161, 166-182, 185, 209, 212, 219-226, 232, 240, 247-248, 251-252, 254, 256, 258-262, 265, 267-270, 272, 276-277, 279, 290-294, 297

Temple Mount, 31, 178-179, 181

Temurah, 43-44, 147, 150, 164

Ten Commandments, 65, 288, 293

Tent of Meeting, 22, 111, 176

Terumot, 36, 140-141, 158, 163

theology, 11, 15-17, 20, 50, 62, 77, 87, 105, 115, 126-128, 148,
205-206, 209, 214, 229, 231-236, 241-243, 245-246, 248, 252, 254, 261-264, 270-272, 284-285, 292, 295, 298-299

tithe, 22, 33, 36, 103-104, 111, 121, 132, 149, 152, 154, 159, 212, 260, 265, 267, 294

tithe, second, 132, 152, 154, 294

Tohorot, 22, 33, 45, 111, 122, 141, 161, 163, 215-219, 265

topic, 17-20, 27, 33, 35-36, 42-43, 45, 47-48, 55, 79-80, 87-88, 92, 99, 101-103, 111, 114, 117-119, 121-123, 125-126, 132-133, 136, 138-139, 141, 148, 150-152, 154-155, 157-159, 161, 164, 167, 174-175, 179, 182, 234, 238, 241-243, 249, 254, 258-259, 263, 265, 269, 287-288, 290, 293, 297-298, 300

Torah, 15-17, 33, 35, 49, 52, 54-58, 60, 64, 66-68, 72-77, 81, 87, 106-108, 119-120, 123, 126-129, 148, 157, 165, 167-172, 187-197, 201, 211, 214, 219-220, 222, 238-240, 244, 248, 252, 256-257, 262-263, 269-270, 272, 282, 288, 294, 298

Torah study, 55, 261, 269-270

Tosefta, 16, 23, 90, 93-94, 124, 135, 191, 199-201, 212-213, 217, 220-222, 235, 253, 270, 293-294

Tractate Avot, 253, 283

traditions, 17, 19, 35, 53, 62, 65, 74, 94, 96, 166, 196, 223-224, 238, 249, 251, 253-260, 269

transgression, 67, 156, 194, 209, 220-221, 225, 231-232, 293 translation, 65, 74, 226-227, 264, 278, 291

Turner, H.E.W., 206

uncleanness, 21-22, 27-28, 30-33, 45-47, 56-57, 70, 89-90, 96, 98, 100-102, 110-111, 122, 124, 131, 134-137, 140-145, 148-149, 152-155, 157-159, 172, 176-178, 180, 185-186, 189, 205, 207-222, 236, 239-240, 265-268

unconsecration, 215-219, 259, 265, 267-268

unit of thought, 88-90, 109, 232

unleavened, 150

Uqsin, 22, 45, 88, 111, 141, 161, 163

Urbach, Ephraim E., 14, 245, 289

Usha, 257

Uzziah, 221

Valuation, 169

van Zijl, J.B., 227

Vermes, Geza, 66, 73, 238

violation, 40-41, 43, 102, 182, 189, 222

voice, 68, 79-80, 103, 181-182, 190

vow, 38-39, 123, 134, 153, 156, 255

West, 57, 62, 78, 105, 113, 293

whole-offering, 22, 44, 111, 148, 150, 161

widow, 39, 224

wife, 18, 24, 38, 102, 120, 150, 158, 182, 210

witness, 50, 59, 71, 183

woman, 15, 24, 28, 30-32, 34, 38-39, 45, 47, 55, 66, 70, 76, 82, 101-102, 104-105, 153-154, 158, 171, 178, 181-182, 185, 189, 210, 221, 228-229, 238, 240, 267, 271, 276-278

worldview, 15, 30, 47, 49, 51, 53, 61-64, 82, 86, 91, 97-99, 106, 113-114, 165, 173, 181, 235

wrath, 59

writ of divorce, 18, 24, 39

Written Torah, 17, 58, 64, 73, 77, 81, 123, 126, 189, 193, 195-196, 219, 240, 248

Y. Abodah Zarah, 193, 196

Y. Sanhedrin, 199

Y. Ta., 57

Yadayim, 45, 142, 161, 163

Yadin, Yigael, 55

Yannai the King, 257

Yaron, R., 14-15

Yavneh, 252-253, 256-257, 261

Yebamot, 30, 38-39, 142, 158, 163, 172

Yerushalmi, 192-196

yeshiva, 264, 299

Yohanan, 193

Yohanan b. Gudegedah, 266

Yohanan b. Matya, 119

Yohanan b. Zakkai, 57, 244, 256-257

Yohanan the High Priest, 255, 257

Yoma, 37, 107, 125, 147, 150-151, 164

Yosé, 107, 124, 135, 221

Yosé b. R. Judah, 120

Yosé the Galilean, 70, 220

Yosef b. Yoezer, 266

Zab, 28, 32, 45, 143-144, 153-154, 159, 240

Zabim, 21, 30, 32, 45, 110, 143, 159, 163, 172

Zealots, 60, 253

Zebahim, 43-44, 144-145, 159-160, 163

Zeitlin, Solomon, 264

Zion, 68, 187

zodiac, 294

Zohar, 188

Zoroaster, 235

# South Florida Studies in the History of Judaism

| 240001 | Lectures on Judaism in the Academy and in the Humanities | Neusner |
|---|---|---|
| 240002 | Lectures on Judaism in the History of Religion | Neusner |
| 240003 | Self-Fulfilling Prophecy: Exile and Return in the History of Judaism | Neusner |
| 240004 | The Canonical History of Ideas: The Place of the So-called Tannaite Midrashim, Mekhilta  Attributed to R. Ishmael, Sifra, Sifré to Numbers, and Sifré to Deuteronomy | Neusner |
| 240005 | Ancient Judaism: Debates and Disputes, Second Series | Neusner |
| 240006 | The Hasmoneans and Their Supporters: From Mattathias to the Death  of John Hyrcanus I | Sievers |
| 240007 | Approaches to Ancient Judaism: New Series, Volume One | Neusner |
| 240008 | Judaism in the Matrix of Christianity | Neusner |
| 240009 | Tradition as Selectivity: Scripture, Mishnah, Tosefta, and Midrash in  the Talmud of Babylonia | Neusner |
| 240010 | The Tosefta: Translated from the Hebrew: Sixth Division Tohorot | Neusner |
| 240011 | In the Margins of the Midrash: Sifre Ha'azinu Texts, Commentaries and Reflections | Basser |
| 240012 | Language as Taxonomy: The Rules for Using Hebrew and Aramaic in the Babylonia Talmud | Neusner |
| 240013 | The Rules of Composition of the Talmud of Babylonia: The Cogency of the Bavli's Composite | Neusner |
| 240014 | Understanding the Rabbinic Mind: Essays on the Hermeneutic of Max Kadushin | Ochs |
| 240015 | Essays in Jewish Historiography | Rapoport-Albert |
| 240016 | The Golden Calf and the Origins of the Jewish Controversy | Bori/Ward |
| 240017 | Approaches to Ancient Judaism: New Series, Volume Two | Neusner |
| 240018 | The Bavli That Might Have Been: The Tosefta's Theory of Mishnah  Commentary Compared With the Bavli's | Neusner |
| 240019 | The Formation of Judaism: In Retrospect and Prospect | Neusner |
| 240020 | Judaism in Society: The Evidence of the Yerushalmi,Toward the Natural History of a Religion | Neusner |
| 240021 | The Enchantments of Judaism: Rites of Transformation from Birth Through Death | Neusner |
| 240022 | The Rules of Composition of the Talmud of Babylonia | Neusner |
| 240023 | The City of God in Judaism and Other Comparative and Methodological Studies | Neusner |
| 240024 | The Bavli's One Voice: Types and Forms of Analytical Discourse and their Fixed Order of Appearance | Neusner |
| 240025 | The Dura-Europos Synagogue: A Re-evaluation  (1932-1992) | Gutmann |
| 240026 | Precedent and Judicial Discretion: The Case of Joseph ibn Lev | Morell |
| 240027 | Max Weinreich *Geschichte der jiddischen Sprachforschung* | Frakes |
| 240028 | Israel: Its Life and Culture, Volume I | Pedersen |
| 240029 | Israel: Its Life and Culture, Volume II | Pedersen |
| 240030 | The Bavli's One Statement: The Metapropositional Program of Babylonian Talmud Tractate Zebahim Chapters One and Five | Neusner |

| 240031 | The Oral Torah: The Sacred Books of Judaism: An Introduction: Second Printing | Neusner |
|---|---|---|
| 240032 | The Twentieth Century Construction of "Judaism:" Essays on the Religion of Torah in the History of Religion | Neusner |
| 240033 | How the Talmud Shaped Rabbinic Discourse | Neusner |
| 240034 | The Discourse of the Bavli: Language, Literature, and Symbolism: Five Recent Findings | Neusner |
| 240035 | The Law Behind the Laws: The Bavli's Essential Discourse | Neusner |
| 240036 | Sources and Traditions: Types of Compositions in the Talmud of Babylonia | Neusner |
| 240037 | How to Study the Bavli: The Languages, Literatures, and Lessons of the Talmud of Babylonia | Neusner |
| 240038 | The Bavli's Primary Discourse: Mishnah Commentary: Its Rhetorical Paradigms and their Theological Implications | Neusner |
| 240039 | Midrash Aleph Beth | Sawyer |
| 240040 | Jewish Thought in the 20th Century: An Introduction in the Talmud of Babylonia Tractate Moed Qatan | Schweid Neusner |
| 240041 | Diaspora Jews and Judaism: Essays in Honor of, and in Dialogue with, A. Thomas Kraabel | Overman/MacLennan |
| 240042 | The Bavli: An Introduction | Neusner |
| 240043 | The Bavli's Massive Miscellanies: The Problem of Agglutinative Discourse in the Talmud of Babylonia | Neusner |
| 240044 | The Foundations of the Theology of Judaism: An Anthology Part II: Torah | Neusner |
| 240045 | Form-Analytical Comparison in Rabbinic Judaism: Structure and Form in *The Fathers* and *The Fathers According to Rabbi Nathan* | Neusner |
| 240046 | Essays on Hebrew | Weinberg |
| 240047 | The Tosefta: An Introduction | Neusner |
| 240048 | The Foundations of the Theology of Judaism: An Anthology Part III: Israel | Neusner |
| 240049 | The Study of Ancient Judaism, Volume I: Mishnah, Midrash, Siddur | Neusner |
| 240050 | The Study of Ancient Judaism, Volume II: The Palestinian and Babylonian Talmuds | Neusner |
| 240051 | Take Judaism, for Example: Studies toward the Comparison of Religions | Neusner |
| 240052 | From Eden to Golgotha: Essays in Biblical Theology | Moberly |
| 240053 | The Principal Parts of the Bavli's Discourse: A Preliminary Taxonomy: Mishnah Commentary, Sources, Traditions and Agglutinative Miscellanies | Neusner |
| 240054 | Barabbas and Esther and Other Studies in the Judaic Illumination of Earliest Christianity | Aus |
| 240055 | Targum Studies, Volume I: Textual and Contextual Studies in the Pentateuchal Targums | Flesher |
| 240056 | Approaches to Ancient Judaism: New Series, Volume Three, Historical and Literary Studies | Neusner |
| 240057 | The Motherhood of God and Other Studies | Gruber |
| 240058 | The Analytic Movement in Rabbinic Jurisprudence | Solomon |
| 240059 | Recovering the Role of Women: Power and Authority in Rabbinic Jewish Society | Haas |

| 240060 | The Relation between Herodotus' *History* and Primary History | Mandell/Freedman |
| 240061 | The First Seven Days: A Philosophical Commentary on the Creation of Genesis | Samuelson |
| 240062 | The Bavli's Intellectual Character: The Generative Problematic: In Bavli Baba Qamma Chapter One And Bavli Shabbat Chapter One | Neusner |
| 240063 | The Incarnation of God: The Character of Divinity in Formative Judaism: Second Printing | Neusner |
| 240064 | Moses Kimhi: Commentary on the Book of Job | Basser/Walfish |
| 240065 | Judaism and Civil Religion | Breslauer |
| 240066 | Death and Birth of Judaism: Second Printing | Neusner |
| 240067 | Decoding the Talmud's Exegetical Program | Neusner |
| 240068 | Sources of the Transformation of Judaism | Neusner |
| 240069 | The Torah in the Talmud: A Taxonomy of the Uses of Scripture in the Talmud, Volume I | Neusner |
| 240070 | The Torah in the Talmud: A Taxonomy of the Uses of Scripture in the Talmud, Volume II | Neusner |
| 240071 | The Bavli's Unique Voice: A Systematic Comparison of the Talmud of Babylonia and the Talmud of the Land of Israel, Volume One | Neusner |
| 240072 | The Bavli's Unique Voice: A Systematic Comparison of the Talmud of Babylonia and the Talmud of the Land of Israel, Volume Two | Neusner |
| 240073 | The Bavli's Unique Voice: A Systematic Comparison of the Talmud of Babylonia and the Talmud of the Land of Israel, Volume Three | Neusner |
| 240074 | Bits of Honey: Essays for Samson H. Levey | Chyet/Ellenson |
| 240075 | The Mystical Study of Ruth: *Midrash HaNe'elam* of the Zohar to the Book of Ruth | Englander |
| 240076 | The Bavli's Unique Voice: A Systematic Comparison of the Talmud of Babylonia and the Talmud of the Land of Israel, Volume Four | Neusner |
| 240077 | The Bavli's Unique Voice: A Systematic Comparison of the Talmud of Babylonia and the Talmud of the Land of Israel, Volume Five | Neusner |
| 240078 | The Bavli's Unique Voice: A Systematic Comparison of the Talmud of Babylonia and the Talmud of the Land of Israel, Volume Six | Neusner |
| 240079 | The Bavli's Unique Voice: A Systematic Comparison of the Talmud of Babylonia and the Talmud of the Land of Israel, Volume Seven | Neusner |
| 240080 | Are There Really Tannaitic Parallels to the Gospels? | Neusner |
| 240081 | Approaches to Ancient Judaism: New Series, Volume Four, Religious and Theological Studies | Neusner |
| 240082 | Approaches to Ancient Judaism: New Series, Volume Five, Historical, Literary, and Religious Studies | Basser/Fishbane |
| 240083 | Ancient Judaism: Debates and Disputes, Third Series | Neusner |
| 240084 | Judaic Law from Jesus to the Mishnah | Neusner |